Judicial Law-Making in Post-Soviet Russia

GU00632191

The book explores the development of judge-made law in Russia since the demise of the Soviet Union. By using Russian case law it aims to show that the creation of law is intrinsic to the judicial function in contemporary legal systems, which appear to be shaped by both legislators and judges. The monograph has rich theoretical background in both Russian and Anglo-American jurisprudence and draws comparison between common law and Russian styles of adjudication.

The book concentrates on the principles applied by judges when interpreting legal acts. It also addresses the limits of judge-made law, and investigates the problem of 'hard legal cases' and the factors, which make them 'hard'. It gives detailed analysis of forms in which Russian courts make law; such as 'explanations' of supreme courts, various kinds of precedents, court rules and (usually unnoticed) judicial customs. Additionally, it contains case studies devoted to judicial law-making in Russian labour law and company law.

The author gives much attention to the rise of judicial review of legislation and the struggle between Russian supreme courts for superiority in this rapidly evolving domain. He estimates the degree of creativity of different branches of the Russian judiciary and explains the differences in their attitudes. In conclusion, he sets out certain proposals as to how the discrepancies in judicial practice can be avoided, thus making it more predictable and coherent.

Alexander Vereshchagin is Research Director of a Russian–Finnish law firm. He received a Candidate of Science degree from the Moscow State University and his PhD from the University of Essex, UK.

Judicial Law-Making in Post-Soviet Russia

Alexander Vereshchagin

To Lord Phillips of Sudbury from the author, with great respect and best wishes.

A. Вер

Routledge·Cavendish
Taylor & Francis Group

First published 2007
by Routledge-Cavendish
2 Park Square, Milton Park, Abingdon, Oxon OX14 4RN

Simultaneously published in the USA and Canada
by Routledge-Cavendish
270 Madison Ave, New York, NY 10016

*Routledge-Cavendish is an imprint of the Taylor & Francis Group,
an informa business*

© 2007 Alexander Vereshchagin

Typeset in Times New Roman by
Newgen Imaging Systems (P) Ltd, Chennai, India
Printed and bound in Great Britain by
Antony Rowe Ltd, Chippenham, Wiltshire

All rights reserved. No part of this book may be reprinted or
reproduced or utilised in any form or by any electronic,
mechanical, or other means, now known or hereafter
invented, including photocopying and recording, or in any
information storage or retrieval system, without permission in
writing from the publishers.

British Library Cataloguing in Publication Data
A catalogue record for this book is available
from the British Library

Library of Congress Cataloging in Publication Data
Vereshchagin, A. N. (Aleksandr Nikolaevich)
    Judicial law-making in post-Soviet Russia / Alexander
  Vereshchagin.
        p. cm.
    Simultaneously published in the USA and Canada.
    ISBN 978-1-84472-110-8 (hardback) –
  ISBN 978-1-84472-111-5 (pbk.) 1. Judge-made law–Russia
  (Federation) 2. Judicial process–Russia (Federation) I. Title.
    KLB1679.V45 2007
    347.47'05–dc22   2006039725

ISBN10: 1-84472-110-8 (hbk)
ISBN10: 1-84472-111-6 (pbk)
ISBN10: 0-203-94519-0 (ebk)

ISBN13: 978-1-84472-110-8 (hbk)
ISBN13: 978-1-84472-111-5 (pbk)
ISBN13: 978-0-203-94519-3 (ebk)

Contents

Table of abbreviations

BSC – Bulletin of the Supreme Court of the Russian Federation [Бюллетень Верховного Суда Российской Федерации]

CCRF – Civil Code of the Russian Federation, ed. and transl. W. E. Butler (2003)

FLJSS – Federal Law on Joint-Stock Societies (1995, as amended)

HCC – Herald of the Constitutional Court of the Russian Federation [Вестник Конституционного Суда Российской Федерации]

HSAC – Herald of the Supreme Arbitrazh Court of the Russian Federation [B*ecm*ник В*ыcшего* Арбитражного C*уда* Российской Ф*едерации*]

KZoT – Code of Laws of Labour of the Russian Soviet Federated Socialist Republic [Кодекс законов о труде Российской Советской Федеративной Социалистической Республики]

RCL – Russian Company Law, Comp. and ed. W. E. Butler and M. E. Gashi-Butler (2000)

RCCL – Russian Company and Commercial Legislation, ed. and transl. W. E. Butler (2003)

RF – Russian Federation

RLT – Russian Legal Texts, ed. W. E. Butler and J. E. Henderson (1998)

RSFSR – Russian Soviet Federated Socialist Republic

SAC – Supreme Arbitrazh Court of the Russian Federation

USSR – Union of the Soviet Socialist Republics

Law reports

AC – Appeal Cases. Appeal cases before the House of Lords and . . . the Privy Council, also peerage cases (London, 1876–)

All ER – All England Law Reports (1936–)

App Cas – The Law Reports, Appeal Cases, 1875–1890

Crim LR – Criminal Law Review (London, 1954–)

DLR (4th) – Dominion Law Reports (Toronto, 1912–)

FCR – Family Court Reporter

HLR – Housing Law Reports (Harlow, 1982–)

L Ed 2d – United States Supreme Court Reports (Lawyers' Edition, Rochester, NY: Lawyers Co-operative Pub. Co., 1969–)

OJC – Official Journal of the European Union: C. series (Communications and notices)

QB – Law Reports: Queen's Bench Division (London, 1876–)

US – Unites States Supreme Court Reports (Lawyers' Edition, Rochester, NY, 1926–)

WLR – Weekly Law Reports (London, 1959–)

Table of cases

Common law cases

European Court of Human Rights

Russian legal databases

Official court reports

Decisions of Russian courts

Constitutional Court of the Russian Federation

Plenum of the Supreme Court of the USSR

Supreme Court of the Russian Federation

Decrees of the Plenum

Surveys

Decisions of the Presidium

Cassation division

Civil division

Decisions of the Supreme Court as a court of first instance

Lower courts of general jurisdiction

Supreme Arbitrazh Court of the Russian Federation

Decrees of the Plenum

Letters, decrees and rulings of the Presidium

Lower arbitrazh courts

Decrees of federal arbitrazh courts

CENTRAL CIRCUIT

EASTERN SIBERIAN CIRCUIT

FAR EAST CIRCUIT

Table of Russian Laws and Regulations

Note: Locators with suffix 'n' refer to items in footnotes on relevant page.

Table of Foreign Laws and International Treaties

Acknowledgements

I am greatly indebted to several persons whose professional advice and disinterested help have enabled me to get through various stages of research and publication. My primary debt is to Professor W. E. Butler. His friendly encouragements and generosity in sharing his expertise were instrumental in both finishing my doctoral thesis and converting it subsequently into the present book. Peter Luther and Bob Watt from the University of Essex and Jane Henderson from Kings College, London did their best to improve the literary style and bring the initial messy draft closer to the received standards of English academic writing. They were attentive and insightful critics as well. Professor Veniamin Iakovlev, the Advisor to the President of the Russian Federation and formerly Chief Justice of the Supreme Arbitrazh Court, made me more confident in believing that this kind of scientific inquiry is indeed necessary for the Russian judiciary. All of them were very helpful, each in his or her own way. It goes without saying, however, that I alone should be blamed for any possible mistakes and deficiencies.

A special gratitude goes to my family which for a number of years had to tolerate my distraction with this work and created a comfortable environment for bringing it to completion.

Introduction

The aim of the book

For centuries the development of Russian law has been predominantly influenced by the civil law tradition, which prohibited judges from engaging in law-creation. It is no wonder, therefore, that judicial law-making has always been a controversial subject in Russian legal thought, and judicial decisions have never been explicitly granted the status of a source of law.

On the other hand, many scholars argued that it was merely a doctrinal fiction aimed to disguise the true role of the courts. Among lawyers, there have always been voices for recognition of judicial law-making as existing *de facto*. However, a significant number (perhaps, the majority) of Soviet legal theorists took the orthodox view. They contended that judicial law-making might result in judicial arbitrariness and threatened to undermine the supremacy of legislative bodies and the laws enacted by them.

Among the advocates and researchers of judge-made law are some Western and Russian lawyers. They argue that judge-made law has a venerable history in Russia, and in imperial era courts have definitely made an important contribution to the legal framework, particularly in the civil law. W. G. Wagner has shown that the Civil Cassation Department of the Ruling Senate (the court of last resort established by the judicial reform of 1864) was effective in making interpretations of the laws uniformly applied throughout the empire. In his conclusion, 'the rulings of the high court were widely known, especially among judicial personnel and legal practitioners. In short, in the wake of the judicial reform there emerged a juridical infrastructure that granted the courts...unprecedented influence over development of imperial law'.[1] As one pre-revolutionary author has demonstrated, many institutions of civil law only slightly touched upon by imperial legislation were built up by the Senate nearly from scratch.[2] Its explanations played the part of

---

1 W. G. Wagner, 'Civil Law in Late Imperial Russia', in P. H. Solomon (ed.), *Reforming Justice in Russia, 1864–1996: Power, Culture, and the Limits of Legal Order* (1997), p. 33. See also Wagner, *Marriage, Property and Law in Late Imperial Russia* (1994).
2 E. V. Vas'kovskii, Правотворческая деятельность новых судов в сфере процесса и права гражданого [The Law-Creating Activity of New Courts in the Sphere of the Civil Law and Procedure], in Судебные уставы за 50 лет [Court Statutes over 50 Years], Vol. II (1914).

subsidiary sources of law.[3] The Senate first made recourse to *analogia legis*; where this was impossible, it deduced general principles from the norms given (*analogia juris*). Where even this device did not help to solve a dispute, the Senate turned to the ideas of justice or expediency. In the areas of criminal law and procedure its law-making activity was, however, much weaker.[4] The prevalent view among Russian lawyers deemed analogy in criminal law inadmissible.

The 1864 judicial statutes have put an end to the dominant system of strict literalism. They prohibited judges from suspending proceedings 'under the pretext of incompleteness, vagueness, insufficiency, and contradiction of laws' (Art 10, Statute on Civil Procedure). Instead of being bound by the 'accurate and literal meaning' of statutes (Art 65, 1832 Basic Laws) the judiciary was instructed to be 'guided by the accurate sense of the law' and 'the general sense of the laws' (Art 9, Statute).

Legal doctrine was reflective of this profound change. The debate was opened by Sergei Muromtsev (1850–1910), a professor of Roman law at the Moscow Imperial University and later the chairman of the first Russian Parliament convened in 1906. Muromtsev stated that in normal life courts are creative just as legislators, but through different means, and contrasted the 'living' law (that is, the real legal order of society) as reflected in judicial decisions with the 'dead' legislation consisting of those written norms, which, although having force, fell into disuse and thus do not constitute part of that order.[5] His opponents, in particular Gabriel Shershenevich and Iosif Pokrovskii, pointed out the advantages of legislation compared with judge-made law and the dangers of judicial arbitrariness.[6] It should be noted that Muromtsev's writings were in the same current with the contemporaneous developments in the Western legal thought, such as the European free law school (E. Ehrlich, F. Geny, H. Kantorowicz), American pragmatic jurisprudence (O. W. Holmes), and even predated them.[7] His theory of judicial law-creation grew out of purely Russian needs; it aimed at

---

3 E. V. Vas'kovskii, Правотворческая деятельность новых судов в сфере процесса и права гражданого [The Law-Creating Activity of New Courts in the Sphere of the Civil Law and Procedure], in Судебные уставы за 50 лет [Court Statutes over 50 Years], Vol. II (1914), pp. 384–385.

4 Ibid., pp. 383, 387, 406–408.

5 S. A. Muromtsev, Определение и основное разделение права [The Definition and Basic Division of Law] (1879), p. 250. See also Muromtsev, Суд и закон в гражданском праве [The Court and the Law [*Lex*] in Civil Law], *Юридический вестник* [Legal Herald], no. 11 (1880).

6 G. F. Shershenevich, Общая теория права [The General Theory of Law] (1924), pp. 371, 754–756; I. A. Pokrovskii, Основные проблемы гражданского права [Main Problems of Civil Law] (1998; first published in 1916), pp. 98 ff.

7 The existent literature on free law movement in English is scanty. The best survey can be found in: J. E. Herget and S. Wallace, 'The German Free Law Movement as the Source of American Legal Realism', *Virginia Law Review*, Vol. 73 (March 1987) 399. The authors trace the roots of the movement back to some insights of Rudolf von Jhering (1818–1892) as of the 1860s, although it took definitive shape in Germany much later. It is hardly a mere coincidence that Muromtsev was a disciple of Jhering, with whom he was in correspondence (see A. N. Medushevskii, История русской социологии [History of Russian Sociology] (1993), p. 49).

'the evolutionary replacement of the absolutist regime with a liberal legal order'.[8] It did not allow, however, for the situation in which more 'progressive' norms and policies turned out to be 'dead', whereas judicial practice would preserve a 'living' but a more archaic legal order. But it was a real danger, given the traditional opposition among the Russian populace to any changes 'from above'. The liberal and enlightened judge who was a necessary precondition for his theory was an invented figure. And the reluctance of many liberal lawyers to accept the theory might be easily accounted for by their fear of judicial and administrative arbitrariness in a society with so weak a sense of legality.[9]

The great overturn of 1917 destroyed the imperial judicial system and terminated these discussions. In the view of Bolshevik leaders, law was nothing but a remnant of the previous stages of human development and had no future in a socialist society. Accordingly, the new 'proletarian' judges were supposed to rely in the first place on their 'revolutionary consciousness'. The laws of the *ancien regime* were applied unless they were incompatible with the new order of things. Revolutionary legislation, although binding, was too scanty to guide judges in every case.

The unlimited discretion initially given by Bolsheviks to their judicial officials (most of whom had no legal training) had little to do with judge-made law of any kind. There is no evidence of their attempts to consciously elaborate a uniform approach to like cases. On the whole, this policy proved to be short-lived and was mostly phased out by the time of the first Soviet codifications in early 1920s.

At the time of collapse of 'war communism' and transition to the New Economic Policy (1921) the Bolshevik leaders had to overcome their dislike of formal law.[10] The creation of socialist legal institutions began. The first Soviet codes adopted in 1920s had much in common with the pre-revolutionary tsarist legislation.[11] Simultaneously, a new system of courts was established. Courts of general jurisdiction, shaped by July 1923, included four levels, to start from the bottom: people's courts, regional courts, the supreme courts of the union republics and the Supreme Court of the USSR at the very top of the hierarchy. In 1931 beside general courts was built a special quasi-judicial system of State Arbitrazh that considered disputes between State enterprises in the light of economic expediency.[12]

The greatest potential for developing the law naturally rested in the USSR Supreme Court as a highest tribunal. Under 1924 USSR Constitution, its main

---

8 V. D. Zor'kin, Муромцев [Muromtsev] (1980), p. 5.

9 Cf. G. F. Shershenevich, О чувстве законности [On the Feeling of Legality] (1897), p. 26.

10 The best account of this evolution from primitiveness to formalism and sophistication can be found in J. N. Hazard, *Settling Disputes in Soviet Society. The Formative Years of Legal Institutions* (1960), esp. pp. 463–481.

11 For more details see G. M. Armstrong, *The Soviet Law of Property: The Right to Control Property and the Construction of Communism* (1983).

12 For an account of the history of Soviet judicial system see W. E. Butler, *Russian Law* (2nd edn., 2003), pp. 149–152.

responsibility was constitutional review: the Court was empowered to assess the laws of republics with respect to their (in)compatibility with all-Union legislation. But it could not vacate the laws. The Court was only entitled to prepare an expert opinion on their constitutionality. The actual vacating of normative acts was in the hands of the Presidium of the Central Executive Committee having both executive and legislative functions in the Soviet system which disregarded the 'bourgeois' doctrine of separation of powers. This right of the Court to interpret laws by way of constitutional review and to advise the authorities existed up to 1933.

The 1938 Law on court organisation passed in the wake of the 1936 USSR Constitution and the Great Terror expanded significantly the appellate powers of the Court and its role in the judicial system as a whole. It was in line with the highly centralised state-party system of mature Stalinism. Needless to say that the actual political role of the Court was by no means enhanced. However, with respect to civil law matters the situation was more complicated. Although the frontier between 'political' and 'non-political' was vague at that time, the Supreme Court had to take initiative in creating rules on a number of occasions. As Solomon wrote, 'in fact, during the last years of Stalin's rule (1946–53), legislative initiatives and clarifications came so rarely that the Supreme Court was forced to issue directives that not only interpreted laws but also created legal norms, thereby overstepping its legal competence'.[13]

A new turn occurred in 1957, when Khrushev's reforms directed at the decentralisation of government reduced the vast appellate responsibility of the Court. Thereafter it could review only cases from the supreme courts of republics, and only if their decisions might have contravened USSR legislation. However, the issuance of the so-called 'guiding explanations', that is, the shaping of judicial policy, remained as the most important function of the Court. Another novelty was that the right of legislative initiative was entrusted to the Plenum of the Supreme Court. This fact even gave rise to suggestions that this legislation abolished the law-creating activity of the Plenum.[14] But later, in 1979, a new law on the USSR Supreme Court strengthened the Supreme Court's position within the hierarchy by expressly obliging inferior courts to follow its 'explanations'. Moreover, their own interpretive decrees could be reversed by the USSR Supreme Court. It should be added that from 1950s onwards academic science became susceptible to an investigation into the real role of courts. Mainly, the debates among Soviet scholars hinged on the legal nature of guiding explanations (or decrees) of the supreme courts of the USSR and union republics.[15] The scope of argumentation was,

---

13 P. H. Solomon, 'USSR Supreme Court: History, Role, and Future Prospects', *The American Journal of Comparative Law*, Vol. 38 (1990), p. 131.

14 I. B. Novitskii, Источники советского гражданского права [The Sources of Soviet Civil Law] (1959), p. 151.

15 See S. N. Bratus (ed.), Судебная практика в советской правовой системе [Judicial Practice in the Soviet Legal System] (1975).

however, quite limited due to the official view of courts as purely law-enforcement agencies. Such were the position at the top of judicial hierarchy and the state of scholarship by the time when the Soviet system came to its end.

The demise of the Soviet Union (1991) and concomitant social changes have given a new role to courts. The judiciary became more independent, the jurisdiction of courts was expanded, the newly established Constitutional Court has become a powerful legal and (as some observers suggest) political actor. The system of State Arbitrazh was converted into a full-fledged branch of the Russian judiciary enabled to participate in shaping civil law institutions.

Although the foundations of the Russian judicial system were inherited from the Soviet State, the context in which the courts now operate has changed dramatically. The basic trend of these changes can be described as the revival of private law. Although not eliminated entirely during the Soviet era, it was, nonetheless, severely restricted and oppressed. The adoption from 1995 to 2001 of a new Civil Code (Parts 1, 2 and 3) modelled upon western codes rather than its Soviet predecessors is the chief landmark of this revival. Comprehensive and well-elaborated as it is, the Code, nevertheless, falls to be interpreted by judges. Conflicts between different pieces of legislation (old and new, federal and regional, secondary and primary) became quite common after the demise of the Soviet State with its coherent and centralised machinery of law-making and law-application. These conflicts are, in a sense, the price to pay for the democratisation of the legislative process – the price being especially heavy at the outset of this transition.

The stream of new laws, which was a remarkable feature of developments in this field during the last decade, still needs reshaping and filtering through judicial interpretation. It is far from being obvious that the courts in their present condition (which in many ways has not changed for the better since the Soviet era) are able to face this challenge. Their actual law-interpreting and law-creating role under socialism was rather limited, despite the fact that Soviet legislatures normally passed only a few legal acts per year. The newly gained independence of courts (if not necessarily the judges themselves) and the creation of constitutional tribunals charged with a duty to vacate or affirm the validity of legal norms has also complicated the situation in this area. The role of judges (especially judges of the superior courts) in adapting and fashioning the rules of a new civil law order now needs a fresh look.

Prior to addressing these matters, what the civil law is should be considered. It must be admitted outright that this matter remains controversial and the boundaries of civil law are still imprecise – a curious fact in light of the centuries of legal scholarship. It is a well-known fact that civil law was identified with the private law in some jurisdictions but distinguished from it in others. For the purposes of the present work, I shall adopt the definition proposed by Feldbrugge:

> Under 'civil law' I understand the law of obligations and the law of property as the undisputed nucleus, the law of persons, marriage, family and inheritance law, intellectual and industrial property, and also labour and

housing law. This definition is purely pragmatic, in the sense that it includes the most important components of what in most countries is considered covered by the label 'civil law'.[16]

Within contemporary Russian law, these branches are undergoing rapid changes. Apart from the Civil Code, other new legislation has been enacted (for example, the Labour Code, the amended version of the Federal Law 'On Joint-Stock Societies', etc). It is also noticeable that the rules of civil and arbitrazh procedure have been regularly updated during the 1990s and, eventually, in 2002 new codes were adopted. Even in the Soviet era, as has been convincingly demonstrated,[17] the number of instances where the supreme courts acted creatively was greater in civil law than in other areas of law. This fact, I believe, warrants the conclusion that civil law as defined above is the area where the traditions of judicial creativity are deeply rooted, and the possibilities for it emerge more frequently than elsewhere.

It is hardly possible to investigate the phenomenon of judge-made law in a particular country without having a clear notion of what it is in general. In developing a theoretical framework, this book draws upon the common law jurisprudence (H. L. A. Hart, R. Dworkin, J. Raz) and court cases underlying this reasoning. The present author is convinced that any general account of judicial law-making cannot ignore the richness of common law jurisprudence. For a variety of reasons, it is much more disposed towards reflection upon the nature of judicial power than is the continental tradition of legal thinking. In Romano-Germanic legal systems the judicial reasoning is less explicit (mainly due to the absence or rarity of open dissents in courts). Therefore, continental jurisprudence does not offer as sophisticated theories of the judicial function and interpretation as the ones developed within the common law world.

By and large, the position of judge-made law, although different from country to country, is somewhat ambiguous in continental Europe. The academic discourse is becoming more reflective of its role, but is still far from devoting to this matter as much attention as is the case in Anglo-American jurisprudence. The interrelated problems of judicial activism and discretion are much better explored in the common law countries. The judicial and academic thinking there is conscious of the creative role of judges and there is no deficit of discussion about its multifarious aspects.[18] The extensive opinions of judges interpreting

---

16 F. J. M. Feldbrugge, 'Epilogue: Reflections on a Civil Law for Russia', in G. Ginsburgs, D. D. Barry and W. B. Simons (eds.), *The Revival of Private Law in Central and Eastern Europe. Essays in Honour of F. J. M. Feldbrugge* (1996), p. 567.

17 D. D. Barry and C. Barner-Barry, 'The USSR Supreme Court and Guiding Explanations on Civil Law, 1962–1971', in D. D. Barry, W. E. Butler and G. Ginzburgs (eds.), *Contemporary Soviet Law* (1974), p. 83.

18 Cf. the remark of John H. Merryman: 'In the American system, the judge is the protagonist, the hero of our legal tradition' (Merryman, *The Loneliness of the Comparative Lawyer* (1999), pp. 69–70).

laws are published in law reports that provide an abundant resource for reflection, which has no parallel in civil law jurisdictions. In England case law and statutory interpretation were always the keystone of legal education and a central issue in jurisprudence.[19]

It should be acknowledged that many, perhaps the majority, of Russian academic lawyers are still reluctant to concede that common law concepts and techniques can be relevant for the Russian legal system. The old approaches still retain a hold over the minds of lawyers. Several decades ago it was noted that 'if one asks a Soviet jurist what place they (that is, judicial decisions) have in the USSR, he will reply, in all good faith, that it is an important one. If, on the other hand, the question is whether judicial decisions are a source of law, he will not hesitate to reply emphatically in the negative'.[20] At the same time, Western studies of Soviet law never took for granted that cases were not a source of law in Soviet legal system. Quite the opposite, the tradition of their study is at least half a century old.[21]

As for today's Russian scholarship, it leaves an ambivalent impression. On the one hand, there are plenty of books and articles on court practice in different branches of law. On the other hand, they are largely descriptive and lacking a deep theoretical and comparative perspective.[22] Comparative legal studies in Russia are just emerging, and an unduly cautious attitude towards judge-made law is deeply embedded in academic writings. There still exists a kind of 'iron curtain' between legal studies in the West and the East, which the demise of the Soviet system has failed to remove. It is typical of some Russian writers to reduce the problem to a simplistic syllogism: judge-made law is characteristic for common law countries; Russia is not a common law country; hence the common law experience is of no interest to Russian lawyers. For instance, the author of the most recent Russian book on judicial precedent confined herself to the assertion that 'Russian law belongs to the Romano-Germanic legal family, which is founded on Roman law.... Our country has its own history of development, its own way of emergence and development of legislation, a different legal thinking. Therefore it is necessary to avoid careless borrowing from the institutions of foreign legislation'.[23] It is difficult to understand what

---

19 See J. Raz, 'Why Interpret?', *Ratio Juris*, Vol. 9, no. 4 (1996), pp. 349 ff.

20 R. David and J. E. C. Brierley, *Major Legal Systems in the World Today: An Introduction to the Comparative Study of Law* (3rd edn., 1985), p. 244.

21 See J. H. Hazard, 'Understanding Soviet Law without the Cases', *Soviet Studies*, Vol. VII, no. 2 (1955), p. 121. See also later Hazard's works in bibliography, and W. E. Butler, 'Necessary Defence, Judge-Made Law, and Soviet Man', in W. E. Butler, P. B. Maggs and J. B. Quigley, Jr (eds.), *Law After Revolution* (1988), pp. 99–130.

22 This is true even of the most notable book written by senior judges and academics under the auspices of TACIS: Судебная практика как источник права [Judicial Practice as a Source of Law] (2000).

23 S. K. Zagainova, Судебный прецедент: проблемы правоприменения [Judicial Precedent: Problems of Law-Application] (2002), p. 158.

these warnings are driving at. As far as precedents are concerned they are not 'institutions of legislation' in common law countries. More importantly, this is not the right question for a comparative lawyer to ask. Comparative legal studies are not intended to prove the obvious, namely, that different systems have different ways of development. Neither do they purport to foster the borrowing of particular institutions from one legal system to another. More often they help to understand the processes already underway in the system which is native to the researcher. The right question would be whether there are certain features in a particular foreign system which would help us to better understand our own. If so, what are the lessons one can derive from this experience? On this basis, some practical solutions may be then proposed. Common law experience can be relevant and instructive for continental systems, and vice versa, and there is no reason why comparative lawyers and legal reformers should confine themselves to investigation of the legal systems which had been traditionally deemed closest to their own. On the contrary, it is the differences, and not similarities, that make such investigation a more fruitful and promising enterprise. Useful institutions and legal techniques must be carefully studied and to the necessary degree emulated wherever they are found.

Although some comparative lawyers think that Russia is still seeking its legal identity,[24] the links of the Russian legal system with the Roman law countries were historically the deepest. At the same time, one should not lose sight of the fact that the paradigmatic difference between continental and common law approaches to judge-made law is now thoroughly blurred. In one of the most recent works on this subject it is maintained that '*stare decisis* is in the ascendant in civil-law countries'.[25] Remarkably, this assertion draws upon the study of judge-made law in Germany and France, that is, the countries which have always served as the major source of ideas and concepts for Russian legal development. It seems that at present the rejection or acceptance of judge-made law can no longer be sufficient grounds for distinguishing between common law and civil law approaches to the subject for the purposes of comparative analysis. The present author believes that legal systems, albeit belonging to different legal families, have a lot to learn from each other, and it is no accident that in recent years it has become customary to consider legal institutions of continental and common law countries within the same context. Interestingly, on the tentative

---

24 M. N. Marchenko, Сравнительное правоведение. Общая часть [Comparative Law. General Part] (2001), pp. 542. A different view is expressed by A. Kh. Saidov in his Сравнительное правоведение [Comparative Law] (2000). He believes that Russian law belongs to Romano-Germanic family of legal systems (p. 274). The views of these authors on the prospects of judge-made law in Russia differ accordingly: Marchenko seems to be more optimistic than Saidov (cf. pp. 537–549 and 375–376, respectively).

25 H. W. Baade, 'Stare Decisis in Civil Law Countries: The Last Bastion', in P. Birks and A. Pretto (eds.), *Themes in Comparative Law. In Honour of Bernard Rudden* (2000), p. 19. See also J. H. Merryman, D. S. Clark and J. O. Haley (eds.), *The Civil Law Tradition: Europe, Latin America, and East Asia* (1994), esp. pp. 950–952.

scale of court activism found in a comparative study of judicial activism within 11 national legal systems (five common law countries plus five Romanist law regimes and the Soviet Union) the USSR found itself at the bottom, the United States, unsurprisingly, took the first place, whereas England, quite unexpectedly, occupied the ninth position and thus proved to be closest to the Soviet Union among all common law jurisdictions.[26] Quite recently one prominent American legal theorist and judge argued that the modern English legal system is, in fact, of the continental type, and the English career judiciary is much closer to that of the rest of Europe than to the United States.[27] Whether it is true or not is another matter, but there is little doubt that English jurisprudence can be of particular interest to everyone concerned with diverse aspects of the judicial function. Being a key common law jurisdiction and thus attaching great weight to role of judiciary, England, nevertheless, is not completely free from the familiar 'continental-type' ambiguity with respect to its creative role, which is not as easily recognised and accepted by English lawyers and judges as is the case with their American counterparts. This gives to England a unique position in the eyes of a comparative lawyer and makes it a sound basis for exploring both practical and theoretical implications of judicial law-making.

This study examines the development of judicial law-creation in Russian civil law. It is not a book on legal theory the special task of which is to analyse what judges should do and suggest where the right boundaries of their creativity must be drawn, although these issues will be touched upon wherever necessary, and the author shall point at the dangers posed by some controversial court decisions. Rather, its purpose is to explore what judges in a particular legal system actually do and why. In so doing, it impinges upon English and American case law which is used as a foil to the Russian style of adjudication and judicial interpretation. But it goes without saying that these tasks cannot be completely divorced from each other, and theoretical issues are pivotal for this inquiry. Therefore, I shall address, where appropriate, a number of jurisprudential theories of adjudication. In the end, my argument aims to show that contemporary legal systems are necessarily shaped by both legislators and judges, and the Russian legal system is not an exception to this rule. The making of law is integral to the activities of appellate courts in the Russian Federation, and the neglection or ignorance of this fact can no longer be sustained.

The book consists of six chapters. The first one concentrates on the principles applied by judges when interpreting legal acts and analyses a number of academic writings on this subject. The second addresses the boundaries of the realm of judge-made law. It also investigates the problem of 'hard cases' and the factors which make them 'hard'. The third chapter gives a taxonomy of forms in which Russian courts effectuate their law-creation functions. It shows that the recognition of judicial precedents is now underway in the Russian legal system. The fourth

26 K. M. Holland (ed.), *Judicial Activism in Comparative Perspective* (1991), p. 2.
27 R. A. Posner, *Law and Legal Theory in Europe and America* (1996), p. 36.

chapter is devoted to some controversial issues of judicial politics and the deficiencies of the institutional framework of the judicial system in Russia. The last two chapters are case studies devoted to judicial law-making in labour law and joint-stock society law, respectively. The choice of these areas of law is explained by their being within the jurisdictions of different branches of the judiciary – general and arbitrazh courts.

But before coming to the main contents of the book, its principal characters – Russian courts – need to be introduced to the reader.

The court structure at present

In fact, in 1991 the Russian Federation established the continental model of a court system. It means that unlike England or the United States or former Soviet Union it has no single court of last resort. At the federal level, the Russian judicial system is split into three autonomous parts: courts of general jurisdiction (or ordinary or common courts) headed by the Supreme Court of the Russian Federation, the system of arbitrazh courts with the Supreme Arbitrazh Court at the top of the pyramid, and the Constitutional Court of the Russian Federation which has no subordinate courts below. At the regional level there are justices of the peace and constitutional (or charter) courts of the subjects of the Federation. The establishing of the latter courts is still underway, and therefore they are beyond the scope of our inquiry.

In procedural terms, Russian courts can be classified as follows, starting from the bottom: there are trial courts (or courts of first instance), appellate courts, cassational courts and supervisory court instances. Appellate courts reconsider the decisions of trial courts both on merits and from the point of view of the correct application of the law; cassational courts are not allowed to review the merits of a case but only the legal correctness of the decision. They may reverse the decision if the court below has misapplied the law or has wrongly interpreted it.

Supervision (*nadzor*) as a stage of judicial process has been invented by Soviets in early 1920s. Since there were no justices of the peace in the Soviet Union the ordinary scale of judicial process included two steps only: the trial stage and cassation. The decision of a cassational instance was considered as final unless reversed by way of supervision upon the remonstrance (or 'protest') of a high judicial official or procurator. Bringing the protest was at the discretion of the official. He might bring it at his own initiative or upon receiving a complaint from a party aggrieved. So the supervision was an extraordinary stage at which lower courts' mistakes in law could be remedied. This procedure has been inherited by the post-Soviet judicial system, although it has undergone changes in 2002. The reform was driven, *inter alia*, by the desire to adapt supervision to the requirements of Art 35 of the European Convention on Human Rights regarding the 'exhaustion of domestic remedies' as a precondition for admissibility of a complaint to the European Court in Strasbourg. Since supervision was rightly assessed by the European Court as an 'exceptional' stage (because under it parties had no right for a court decision),[28] the domestic remedies were seen as exhausted by the decision of a cassational court, which is just the second court instance in a case. (In the arbitrazh system cassation it is the third stage, but very few arbitrazh cases give rise to applications to Strasbourg.) This fewness of 'regular' court instances caused the influx of applications from Russian citizens to the European Court of Human Rights in Strasbourg (Russia joined the European Convention on Human Rights in 1998). The reform of supervision by way of new procedural codes came as a response to this difficulty. First, it established a filtering mechanism for a preliminary consideration of supervisory complaints or procurator's representations (a new name for protests): henceforth it must be examined by a judge of the court of general jurisdiction (or a panel of three judges in the Supreme Arbitrazh Court) who decide whether the case deserves consideration by way of supervision. Second, it provided for certain terms within which complaints or representations can be submitted (the lack of any terms for instituting supervisory proceedings was one of the features which made supervision an extraordinary stage of judicial process). It is not occasional that the violation of universally recognised principles of international law is one of the grounds for reconsideration of a case by the Supreme Arbitrazh Court.[29] Yet this response was found unsatisfactory by the European Court, which is still of the opinion that supervision in civil and criminal procedure is an exceptional stage, regardless of the reform.[30] The reform was indeed a halved measure since the Chairman of the Supreme Court and his deputies are empowered to submit any civil case to the Presidium on the grounds of its violating the unity of judicial practice.[31] The exercise of this right has no limitations whatsoever. But, in spite of its inconsistency with Art 35 of the European Convention, the supervisory procedure is no doubt a very important element of judicial process, because the bulk of court decisions of norm-creating character are made at that stage.

Now let us turn to the structure and operation of the three federal branches of the Russian court system.

Courts of general jurisdiction. This system includes justices of the peace appointed in procedure provided for by regional laws (in fact, all justices are

28 See decisions of the European Court of Human Rights in *Tumilovich v Russia* (no. 47033/99, 22 June 1999), *Uralmash v Russia* (no. 13338/03, 4 September 2003) at [www.echr.coe.int/Eng/ Judgments.htm].

29 Article 304 of the Arbitrazh Procedure Code, as amended by the Federal Law of 31 March 2005, No. 25-ФЗ.

30 See judgments in *Denisov v Russia* (no. 33408/03, 6 May 2004) and *Berdzenishvili v Russia* (no. 31697/03, 29 January 2004). It is indicative that the reform had no impact upon the number of applications. In 2000 there were 2313 complaints against the Russian Federation, 4488 in 2001, 4716 in 2002, 6062 in 2003, and 6691 in 2004. This seems natural because the caseload of supervisory court instances has been simultaneously decreasing.

31 Article 389, 2002 Civil Procedure Code.

appointed by regional legislatures, not elected by people); district courts which are trial courts for some categories of cases and appellate courts for those considered by justices of the peace; intermediate courts (differently named), one in each subject of the Federation, mainly engaged in cassational work, although they have presidiums which exercise supervisory function, and at the same time may consider some cases as trial courts; and the Supreme Court of the Russian Federation whose dominant (but not only) function is supervision.

Our attention is to the Supreme Court, since its interpretations of laws are the most important. The Supreme Court has quite complex internal structure. It consists of the Plenum (a full bench of the Court), Presidium (13 senior justices) and divisions (collegia). Divisions are four: first of all, there are divisions for civil and criminal cases and a Military Division. They combine various functions: they serve as trial courts (for instance, when reviewing the legality of ministerial regulations), cassational courts with respect to decisions of intermediate courts as trial courts, and (last but not least) as supervisory court instances. There is also Cassational Division above those three. As its name indicates it works as a cassational court for the decisions made by other divisions of the Supreme Court in their capacity of trial courts. Each division has a chairman (who is *ex officio* a Deputy Chairman of the Supreme Court) and is divided into a few benches. Every bench has its own chairman.

A special role belongs to the Plenum and Presidium. The Plenum cannot consider concrete cases. But it issues the so-called 'explanations on the questions of judicial practice', which instruct judges how to apply certain statutes and thus constitute a very important source of judge-made law. They are approved by the majority vote of the members of the Supreme Court, sometimes after heated debate.

The Presidium consists of 13 senior judges, including the Chairman of the Court and his deputies. It exercises two main functions: first, it works as a final supervisory instance and, second, it issues reviews (summaries) of case law and gives answers to the queries of lower courts.

Thus the Supreme Court is rather an aggregate of different instances than a single court.

Arbitrazh courts. Despite being different from general courts in terms of competence, the arbitrazh courts apply the same law as the last.[32]

Arbitrazh courts are State commercial or economic courts, which consider cases involving entrepreneurial activity. They have grown from the system of State Arbitrazh, which existed between 1931 and 1991. Within the planned economy of socialism, State Arbitrazh had to settle disputes between enterprises. But it did so in the light of economic expediency, not civil law, and thus was not a judicial body. Arbitrazh courts have inherited the name from the State Arbitrazh system, but operate within predominantly market economy. Their proceedings

---

32 It is not accidental that the proposals for the amalgamation of these hitherto separate branches of judiciary became common during the last decade.

are regulated by a special procedure code. The structure of arbitrazh system is simpler than that of general courts. The district arbitrazh courts (one per each subject of the Federation) act as courts of first instance. The appellate arbitrazh courts (they are 20) reconsider their decisions upon the application of a party. Cassational work belongs to 10 circuit courts. Every circuit court has two appellate courts immediately below. The case law of these 10 circuit courts is of considerable importance and therefore is routinely monitored in legal periodicals. It is common understanding among practicing lawyers in Russia that the previous decisions of a relevant circuit court should be given careful consideration before engaging in a commercial dispute. But sometimes these courts diverge with respect to certain matters, and their practices appeal for unification. This need is satisfied through supervisory procedure exercised by the Supreme Arbitrazh Court. This Court also has the Plenum and the Presidium, which perform nearly the same functions as the equivalent institutions of the Supreme Court, namely, the Plenum issues instructions, whereas the Presidium decides concrete cases and issues minor instructions called 'information letters'. The application of a party seeking for reconsideration of a cassation decision must be first examined by a panel of three judges of the Court who may either dismiss the application or allow it to be considered by the Presidium, depending on whether they find grounds for reconsideration envisaged by the law. The final judgment is given by the Presidium. Thus within the arbitrazh system the four stages of judicial process basically match the levels of court structure.[33]

The Constitutional Court of the Russian Federation. The idea of constitutional control was not unfamiliar to Soviet legal doctrine and even the early Soviet law.[34] But this was put into effect not long before the collapse of the Soviet Union. The first law on the Russian Constitutional Court was adopted in 1991. It established a constitutional tribunal with quite significant competence. Under the 1991 law, the Court comprised of 15 judges elected by the Congress of People's Deputies – the major of the two legislative bodies of that time. They decided all cases in a plenary session.

The struggle for power between 'minor' Parliament – the Supreme Soviet – and President Yeltsin, in which the majority of judges sympathised with the Supreme Soviet, reached its peak in October 1993 and led to the dismissal of the Parliament and interruption of the Court's work. The new Constitution (1993) gave the Constitutional Court more attention than to other courts of last resort. The federal constitutional law adopted the following year gives further details of constitutional adjudication.

---

33 The only exception is the right of the Supreme Arbitrazh Court to review certain kinds of legal acts issued by the federal authorities and settle economic disputes between the Russian Federation and its subjects (Arts 34–35, Arbitrazh Procedure Code). In so doing, it works as a first-instance court. For more details on arbitrazh courts and procedure see Butler, *Russian Law* (2nd edn., 2003), pp. 166–172.

34 See M. A. Mitiukov, Судебный конституционный надзор 1924–1933 гг. [Judicial Constitutional Control in 1924–1933] (2005).

Now the Constitutional Court consists of 19 judges. Certain cases are to be decided in a plenary session, whereas other disputes are settled by one of the two chambers of the Court. Final judgments of the Court on the constitutionality of normative acts or the interpretation of the Constitution are called decrees (*postanovleniia*); other decisions are named rulings (*opredelenia*). There are circa 20 decrees and several hundred rulings per year, with the total number of applications about 15,000, most of which, however, fail to meet criteria of admissibility. The Court cannot revise the decisions of other tribunals but, if it finds a law to be contrary to the Constitution, then the decisions that gave rise to the constitutional dispute can be reversed.

The status of judiciary at large

Judges of all three courts of last resort are appointed by the Soviet of the Federation – one of the chambers of Russian Parliament – upon the recommendation of the President, whereas other judges are appointed by the President himself. At present the retirement age for all judges is 70. The Constitution and lesser laws provide general guarantees and immunities to ensure judges' independence and impartiality which are pretty universal for the judiciary in all countries of continental Europe. The question is, however, whether these guarantees work in practice. This question is frequently addressed in Russian political journalism and Western legal scholarship. As for the academic science in Russia, it is almost entirely unconcerned with that question and the socio-political role of the judiciary in general. It is perhaps characteristic that in the most recent inquiry into the Russian elite no attention has been given to the judges of the Constitutional Court, not to speak of others.[35] Probably, it is implied that they either do not participate in making decisions of national significance as long as the ability to do so is taken to be a distinctive feature of an elite,[36] or are not sufficiently independent in making them. At least with respect to the Constitutional Court this disregard contradicts widely known facts, such as its judgments in a number of politically sensitive cases (for example, Communist Party case, Chechen case or Yukos case) in which the Court split, with dissents being many and outspoken. Furthermore, it seems wrong to treat the issue of judicial independence in a yes-or-no manner. Rather, it should be considered as a matter of degree. It is observed that, even in the United States, due to the political nature of judicial appointments, the independence of judges 'is subtle and sometimes appears fragile'.[37]

I am tempted to dub the current state of affairs 'semi-independence', but this label is not devoid of a reference to an exact proportion (50–50) which is

---

35 O. Kryshtanovskaia, Анатомия российской элиты [An Anatomy of Russian Elite] (2005), p. 21.

36 Ibid., p. 17.

37 H. Jacob, 'Courts and Politics in the United States', in H. Jacob, E. Blankenburg, H. M. Kritzer and D. M. Provine (eds.), *Courts, Law, and Politics in Comparative Perspective* (1996), p. 79.

misleading and grossly inaccurate. In fact, the reality is much more complex, at least in commercial and company cases: it may vary between complete independence in the vast majority of disputes (which, of course, does not *per se* guarantee equitable and legally impeccable results) and clear dependence or, rather, bias in favour of powers-that-be in a much smaller but notable part of cases. President Putin and his associates are not responsible for this state of affairs, for it is mainly the Soviet legacy which those who ruled the country in 1990s were not eager to efface. Quite the contrary, they readily adopted it and turned it to their profit. Admittedly, bribing judges was common for Russian magnates (usually called 'oligarchs') during corporate wars, although no such suspicion could be definitely proved. Unlike Soviet judges who were formally elected for a certain term and thus could be easily ousted upon its expiry, Russian judges nowadays do have the necessary means for acting in an impartial fashion, and their supposed failure to do so in some politically sensitive cases is better accounted by the fact that many of them have informal links with the State institutions and their personnel, which can be traced back to the Soviet time and are a part of their personal background. In fact, judges (especially those of superior courts) are either the members of the Establishment (or elite) or associate themselves with it. The impression that they are merely servants of the State is a hangover of the subordinate role that courts did play under the Soviet rule. I hope it will be clear from this book that such evaluation is inconsiderate, and the role of courts in Russian legal and political life, however controversial some court decisions might seem, is important and deserves a careful examination.

* * *

The termination point for case law and legal developments discussed in the present book is 15 October 2006. All the web-pages referred to were last visited the same day. All Russian court decisions marked as 'unpublished' were taken from legal databases 'Garant' and 'ConsultantPlus' unless another source is clearly indicated.

Chapter 1

Interpretation and hard cases

It is customary for lawyers to connect adjudication with interpretation. Interpretation is an essential element in the process of understanding. 'To understand' and 'to interpret' often mean the same. Although many lawyers believe that *in claris non fit interpretatio*,[1] this opinion is not quite correct. Interpretation takes place even in the easiest cases, when the decision comes out obvious and unquestionable.

In the common law world a technical distinction is maintained between 'construction' and 'interpretation':

> 'Interpretation' is simply the process whereby a meaning is assigned to the words in a statute. The courts' primary task in interpretation is to ascertain and give effect to the meaning of the words used: the first inquiry of a court should be to ask: 'What do the words themselves mean?' 'Construction', on the other hand, is the process whereby uncertainties or ambiguities in a statute are resolved. It follows that every statute that comes before a court is interpreted, whereas only uncertain or ambiguous provisions require construction.[2]

In Russian legal terminology this distinction has no equivalent. Russian lawyers and judges commonly employ the term '*tolkovanie*' whose denotation is 'an explanation of a (true) meaning or sense'. Apparently, this word covers both 'interpretation' and 'construction', although in legal translations from Russian into English the term 'interpretation' is more frequent. Obviously, 'construction' can be regarded as an advanced form of interpretation, broadly understood.

Why judicial interpretation is so crucial for legal practice? Why so much attention has always been paid to it in legal scholarship? This phenomenon *per se* can be a subject of different explanations. One of them was offered by

---

1 What is clear does not require interpretation (Lat.). Cf. Andrei Marmor's remarks in his *Interpretation and Legal Theory* (1992), p. 154.
2 R. W. Ward, *Walker & Walker's English Legal System* (8th edn., 1998), p. 34.

Professor Joseph Raz.[3] He finds a distinguishing feature of legal norms among other kinds of norms in its unique claim to supremacy over the other normative systems, especially moral and religious ones, which also prescribe to people the right way of behaviour. Thus, law is premised upon the idea of authority. This fact accounts for the role of interpretation. The main reason which makes interpretation so important is the moral respect for the law and its sources. 'In legal interpretation we value – other things being equal – continuity. We also value authority, legal development and equity.' These are the four factors of legal interpretation.[4]

The legal development and the application of equity are a universally recognised task of courts, 'for it is impossible to have general rules the application of which may not on occasion lead to injustice if not mitigated by equity'.[5] But the key factors, in Raz's view, are continuity and authority because the considerations of equity and legal development can not explain the central role of interpretation: if these principles dominate the reasoning of judges, it would be no different from that of the legislators. Both key factors, however, are in a permanent conflict with the other two: continuity and authority work in favour of the conservative approach to the interpretation, whereas the principles of equity and legal development call for innovation. In this tension are the roots of many problems, including the following: what is law if there can be a plurality of valid interpretations? J. Raz does not provide a direct answer to this question. He just notes that in human societies law and adjudication must fulfil several functions, and therefore even an ideal law cannot fulfil them in an ideal fashion.[6]

This picture of an interplay between different factors can be complemented with an account of real driving forces that put in action the conflict between them. Why, indeed, so much of legal thinking is about 'hard' or 'borderline' cases of interpretation? Are not such cases too rare to deserve so disproportionate an attention? What makes lawyers reflect on them so much? Again, the answer to these queries flows from the main function of legal norms, that is, to guide people's conduct by laying down its limits. So the law creates a certain 'corridor' of admissible ways of behaviour in particular circumstances, within which individuals or groups are free to move. Since people naturally want to know the limits of their legitimate freedom and, if possible, to expand them, it seems inevitable that the interest of the legal community is focused on ascertaining the limits of this 'corridor' as accurately as possible. All persons pursuing their goals within the area demarcated by legal rules are interested in such inquiry, because it improves their chances to achieve desirable ends and avoid a conflict with the law. At the same time, the possibilities found in a close (sometimes dangerous) proximity to those borders are often the most promising in terms of their potential advantages. Among all conceivable ways of pursuing any of the

---

3 J. Raz, 'Why Interpret?', *Ratio Juris*, no. 4 (1996), p. 359.
4 Ibid., p. 359.
5 Ibid., p. 360.
6 Ibid., pp. 361–363.

human goals, the most valuable are usually those which remain unnoticed by other actors. In law, interpretation enables one to find out such hidden opportunities. But, if there are several feasible interpretations of a rule, the legal case is usually treated as a 'hard' one. For this reason, such 'borderline cases' represent cross-points of general jurisprudential problems. This fact makes cases in which courts may act 'creatively' a central preoccupation of legal scholarship despite their being just a drop in the stream of cases coming before courts.

Interpretation of law is an integral part of judicial work, whether law-applying or law-creating. Judicial creativity starts where law-application ends. But where exactly? This is not the only question to be addressed when speaking about 'law-creation', 'law-enforcement', 'interpretation' and the like. Although the ways courts deal with statutory law vary considerably in different legal systems, the problems of its interpretation are common for all of them. They relate to such issues as the nature of judicial interpretation, the rules and principles guiding it, and the ways to determine the legislator's will, to name only the most important.

There is a sheer paradox: in Russia the rules of interpretation are not legislatively established, but a wrong interpretation is a ground for the reversal of a judicial decision.[7] On the whole, Russian academic lawyers did not pay as much attention to judicial interpretation as it probably deserves, so that the topic seems to be relatively underdeveloped in Russian legal theory. That is not the case in Britain, where one finds a number of sophisticated theories of interpretation.

The rules of interpretation in the English legal system

Admittedly, there are three basic rules of interpretation in the English law. It seems appropriate to reiterate them here, as a starting point for further comparison with continental and Russian attitudes to interpretation. The first is the *literal rule* (or what is sometimes called 'strict constructionism') which was defined in 1892 by Lord Esher as follows:

> If the words of an Act are clear, you must follow them, even though they lead to a manifest absurdity. The Court has nothing to do with the question whether the legislature has committed an absurdity.[8]

---

7 As envisaged by Art 363 of the 2002 Civil Procedure Code and Art 288(2) of the 2002 Arbitrazh Procedure Code. The only exception is the interpretation of treaties which constitute a part of the Russian legal system by virtue of Art 15(4) of the Russian Constitution. It is governed by the rules of Vienna Convention on the Law of Treaties (1969). See also points 9–10, Decree of the Plenum of the Supreme Court of the Russian Federation of 10 October 2003, No. 5, on the implementation of international norms by courts, Бюлловноь Верховного Суда Российской Федерации [Bulletin of the Supreme Court of the Russian Federation; hereinafter: *BSC*], no. 12 (2003), p. 6.

8 *Regina v Judge of the City of London Court* [1892] 1 QB 273, at p. 290.

Under the literal rule, even if there is a strong suspicion that the language and the legislator's intentions do not coincide (which may be caused by a 'scrivener's error' or something like that), the judge should not be troubled by it. All responsibility for any unjust or absurd consequences of the application of the rule is placed upon the legislator.

But it has always been acknowledged in the legal doctrine that strict literalism should be mitigated to avoid absurd results. Such a need is frequently illustrated by a medieval statute of Bologna providing 'that whoever drew blood in the streets should be punished with the utmost severity', and also by an English statute of the time of Edward II, according to which a prisoner who breaks prison shall be guilty of felony. It was assumed that the first rule did not extend to the surgeon who opened the vein of a person that fell down in the street in a fit, whereas the second ought not to be applied to a prisoner who breaks out when the prison is on fire.[9] A reckless application of statutory words is thought to be threatening to other equally important values inherent to the legal system, such as its wholeness and coherence.[10]

Although the literal rule is no longer prevalent in English courts, it is premature to deem it to be fallen in disuse. American judges still employ it in some cases, as is exemplified by the US Supreme Court decision in *Smith v United States*,[11] in which the defendant was sentenced for selling a machine-gun in exchange of drugs on the ground of the law which provided for 30 years imprisonment for everyone who 'during and in relation to any crime of violence or drug trafficking crime...*uses*...a firearm' (emphasis added). In his dissent A. Scalia, J., noted that the meaning of a word should not be determined in isolation but should be drawn from the context in which it is used. So when someone asks, 'Do you use a cane?,' he is not inquiring whether you have your grandfather's silver-handled walking stick on display in the hall; he wants to know whether you *walk* with a cane. However, 'the Court does not appear to grasp the distinction between how a word *can be* used and how it *ordinarily is* used'.[12]

The next rule, the *golden* one, does not necessarily contradict literal interpretation. Rather, as was explained by Lord Blackburn in *River Wear Commissioners v Adamson* (1877), according to this rule:

> We are to take the whole statute together, giving the words their ordinary signification, unless so applied they produce an inconsistency, or an absurdity or inconvenience so great as to convince the Court that the intention could not have been to use them in their ordinary signification,

---

9 J. F. Manning, 'The Absurdity Doctrine', *Harvard Law Review*, 2003 (June), p. 2388.

10 V. M. Dougherty, 'Absurdity and the Limits of Literalism: Defining the Absurd Result Principle in Statutory Interpretation', *American University Law Review* (Fall, 1994), p. 134.

11 *Smith v United States* [1993] 508 US 223.

12 Ibid., at p. 242.

and to justify the Court in putting on them some other signification, which, though less proper, is one which the Court thinks the words will bear.[13]

The 'golden rule' is based on the belief that the legislator could not have desired to enact an absurdity. If, nevertheless, the absurd consequences seem to be inevitable under literal construction the judge should retrieve 'the true meaning' of the statute so as to avoid such consequences.

The mischief rule goes much further. It invites judges to actively promote the attainment of the legislative purpose. In so doing, they must clearly understand this purpose, along with the motives and incentives of the legislator. According to the classical formula in *Heydon's case* (1584), judges must consider:

'What remedy the Parliament hath resolved and appointed to cure the disease of the commonwealth', 'and then the office of all the judges is always to make such construction as shall suppress the mischief, and advance the remedy and to suppress subtle inventions and evasions for continuance of the mischief...and to add force and life to the cure and remedy, according to the true intent of the makers of the Act'.[14]

For instance, in the notorious American case *Church of the Holy Trinity v The United States* (which, interestingly, is contemporaneous to Lord Esher's definition of literal rule), the US Supreme Court unequivocally abandoned the plain language of the statute in favour of the desirable outcome of the case.[15] The Court held that 'it is a familiar rule, that a thing may be within the letter of the statute and yet not within the statute, because not within its spirit, nor within the intention of its makers'.[16] Since then, as Justice Antonin Scalia noted, 'the *Church of the Holy Trinity* is cited to us whenever counsel wants us to ignore the narrow, deadening text of the statute, and pay attention to the life-giving legislative intent. It is nothing but an invitation to judicial law-making'.[17] The principle of the *Church of the Holy Trinity* was followed, for instance, in the notable case *United Steelworkers of America v Weber* in which the majority of the US Supreme Court set aside the plain meaning of the Civil Rights Act.[18]

Strictly speaking, these three rules are not rules proper, since they can be applied to the same cases. Rather than being compulsory norms, they are more like competing attitudes, and it is up to the judge to choose which one to follow

13 *River Wear Commissioners v Adamson* [1877] 2 App Cas 743, at pp. 764–765.
14 *Heydon* case [1584] 3 Coke's Reports 7a.
15 *Church of the Holy Trinity v The United States* [1892] 143 US 457.
16 Ibid., at p. 459.
17 A. Scalia, *A Matter of Interpretation: Federal Courts and the Law* (1997), p. 21.
18 *United Steelworkers of America v Weber* [1979] 443 US 193. Contending views on that case may be found in R. Bork, *The Tempting of America: The Political Seduction of the Law* (1991), p. 106, and in R. Dworkin, *A Matter of Principle* (1985), pp. 316–333.

in a concrete case. The choice itself can be accounted for in a variety of ways, and this fact has in the past repeatedly cast doubt upon the fidelity of judges to the rule of law.

The real differences between the rules are also disputable. Only the literal rule seems to be sufficiently clear, but only to the extent that the very language of the statute is also plain and inescapable. As to the other two, the difference is not so evident. At what point should the golden rule be set aside and the mischief rule come into play? The genuine meaning of the rules is itself a subject of interpretation. The contention that under the 'golden rule' the decision should be found 'within the four corners of the statute' inevitably fails, for the mischief rule also does not bluntly deny it. Sometimes the golden rule was identified with the so-called 'purposive approach', which is concerned with the search for legislative purpose, or intent. A concise explanation of their nature can be found in the 1969 Law Commission Report. The Commission approved 'the purposive approach', but rejected 'the mischief rule' in the form the latter was cast in *Heydon's* case, because 'it tends to suggest that legislation is only designed to deal with an evil and not to further a positive social purpose'.[19] But, upon reflection, it does not finally clarify the matter. It merely substitutes one question with another: 'What is the difference between negative and positive social purposes? Can they be easily distinguished in practice?' And one more question: 'How many purposes can be assigned to a legislative norm?'

These issues may become less difficult if we assume that the difference between these two rules is a matter of degree. Neither the mischief rule nor the golden one can provide a clear guidance for a judge in every case. Rather, they are incentives of differing force for judges in their search for a decision that would better accord the statutory purpose. That is why we have to refuse the idea of compulsory rules which cannot be dismissed. Rather, they ought to be regarded as 'principles' in the sense Dworkin assigns to this word. Briefly, the logical distinction Dworkin draws between norms and principles comes to the following: whereas legal norms are mutually exclusive (that is, if a question is regulated by a norm, other norms do not contribute anything to its solution), principles have such dimension as 'weight'. Principle does not make a certain decision unavoidable but, rather, serves as an argument in its favour. Therefore, if one principle 'outweighs' another, the latter is not hereby excluded from legal system and may 'survive'.[20]

19 The Law Commission and the Scottish Law Commission. The Interpretation of Statutes (1969) (Law Com. No. 21; Scot. Law Com. No. 11), pp. 19–20.
20 For the distinction see R. Dworkin, *Taking Rights Seriously* (1978), pp. 22–28, 71–80. A criticism of this distinction by Raz, and Dworkin's reply to Raz can be found in M. Cohen (ed.), *Ronald Dworkin and Contemporary Jurisprudence* (1984), pp. 73–87. Raz thinks that principles may have a legal force of the same sort as norms. Just as norms they can be introduced by the constitution or statute, etc. Dworkin urges not to dwell on this distinction which was introduced just to show that there are legal standards different from those which we usually mean when speaking about 'norms'.

Perhaps, the difference between those three rules can be explained not in terms of a positive statement but in the form of questions which underlie them. It may be phrased as follows:

- The literal rule seeks to answer the question: 'What did the legislator say?'
- The golden rule is concerned with the question: 'Did he really want to say that?'
- The mischief rule asks: 'What did he want to say?'

So, each rule takes the words of the legislator as a point of departure in seeking an answer, but treats them in a distinct way. Therefore, even if the statutory text before a judge is the same, his solution can be different depending on which question he asks.

Rules of interpretation in the Russian legal system

As we already noted, Russian law lacks an Interpretation Act or another similar authoritative aid capable of guiding judges as to how laws should be interpreted or 'construed'. In the absence of immediate prescriptions, the appropriate rules can be obtained indirectly – for instance, through an analysis of the interpretation of *contracts* under Russian law. Both contracts and statutes are legal texts expressing the will (often compromised) of human beings – legislators or parties; therefore one may reasonably assume that interpretation of both should be governed by analogous principles.[21] The rules we are looking for are contained in Art 431 in the Russian Civil Code ('Interpretation of Contract'). It provides:

> In the event of the interpretation of the conditions of a contract by a court the literal meaning of the words and expressions contained therein shall be taken into account. The literal meaning of the condition of a contract in the event of its ambiguity shall be established by means of comparing with the other conditions and with the sense of the contract as a whole.
>
> If the rules contained in para 1 of the present Article do not enable the content of the contract to be determined, the true common will of the parties must be elicited by taking into account the purpose of the contract. In so doing, all the respective circumstances, including negotiations preceding the contract and correspondence, practice being established in the mutual relations of the parties, the customs of business turnover, and the subsequent conduct of the parties, shall be taken into account.[22]

---

21 There are also rules governing the interpretation of testaments of wills in Art 1132 of the Civil Code (see Butler, W. E. (ed. and transl.), *Civil Code of the Russian Federation* (2003), p. 415. Hereinafter: *CCRF*). But this clause admits only literal and systematic methods. It is a moot point of the Russian legal doctrine whether other methods are permissible here.

22 *CCRF*, p. 160.

It is clear that the article encompasses both 'interpretation' and 'construction'. It starts with 'literal interpretation' and ends up with the 'conduct of the parties'. But how should the concept of 'literal meaning' be understood? In the view of the present author, it is merely a metaphoric expression to stress the judges' obligation to focus primarily on the words of the statute. Surely, *litera* or a 'letter' is not capable of having a meaning of its own (unless it makes up a separate word). Therefore, the most elementary form of 'interpretation' possible is a *verbatim* one. It corresponds to 'grammatical interpretation' (*grammaticheskoe tolkovanie*) traditionally employed in Russian legal doctrine. If such interpretation does not help in understanding the meaning of a legal text, then one has to 'construe' it.

As follows from Art 431 of the Civil Code, the sequence of interpretation of contracts in Russia is the following:

Text-based interpretation:

1   ascertaining the 'literal meaning' of the words;
2   comparing a particular provision with other provisions;
3   comparing a particular provision with the sense of the contract as a whole.

Purposive interpretation, that is, revealing the true common will of the parties and the purpose of the contract. This should proceed as follows:

4   preceding circumstances should be taken into account;
5   practice of the parties and customs of business turnover;
6   subsequent conduct of the parties.

Under Ward's definition cited at the beginning of this chapter, only point 1 corresponds to 'interpretation', while the rest of the scheme should be subsumed under the notion of 'judicial construction'. It is not quite clear, however, whether methods of purposive interpretation (points 4, 5 and 6) should be invoked exactly in this sequence, or whether a judge is allowed to use all three devices at once in a more or less concurrent manner. If the first is true, then they also represent different *stages* of interpretation. All the same, there is little doubt that point 1 ('interpretation') should precede 2 and 3 (initial stages of 'construction') unless an ambiguity is revealed (no mention of possible 'absurdity' is made in Art 431). It is also clear that points 2 and 3 should precede 4, 5 and 6.

On this basis one may build, by way of analogy, a hypothetic scheme of statutory interpretation rules in Russia.

Text-centred interpretation:

1   'literal meaning' of the words;
2   comparison of the provision in question with other provisions of the statute;
3   comparison of the provision with the sense of the statute as a whole.

Purposive interpretation:

4   the analysis of preparatory (contextual) materials (drafts of the legislative act, speeches made in the chambers of Parliament, and so forth – in other words, the legislative history of the act in question);

5–6   among the rules of statutory interpretation, there is no direct equivalent for such concepts as 'the practice of the parties and customs of business turnover' or 'subsequent conduct of the parties'. The reason is that those who made statutes and those who apply them in practice are (at least, notionally) different subjects, whereas contracts are designed, in the first place, to coordinate the behaviour of the persons (juridical or natural) who concluded them. However, it can be suggested that 'customs' may correspond, however vaguely, to the 'usages of the law-application practice' (frequently referred to in Russian Constitutional Court decisions). As for the 'practice' and 'subsequent conduct' of the parties, it may be deemed analogous to the subsequent steps of the legislator, which may be of help in ascertaining the meaning of previously enacted legal acts.

Now let us compare it with the rules of statutory interpretation as they are normally singled out by Russian *legal doctrine*. It should be noted that these are common for the continental jurisprudence and go back to the works of the famous German lawyer F. K. von Savigny (1779–1861). There are four basic interpretive canons (or methods):

1   linguistic (or grammatical);
2   systematic (or contextual);
3   historico-political (or functional);
4   logical.

The linguistic method corresponds to the 'literal' interpretation; the systematic one matches points 2 and 3 of the hypothetic scheme above. The third canon appears to rely on sources as various as the legislative history (point 4 of the scheme) and the societal realities at the time of interpretation (their partial match can be a business or administrative customs and practices). Under logical interpretation (the fourth canon), the text of the legislative act is given either broad (liberal) or narrow (restrictive) meaning in the light of the rules of formal logic and common sense.[23] The most elementary example is given by a statutory text which mentions 'a citizen' who is subsequently referred to as 'he'. In the light of the logical analysis, it is clear that such a statute may extend to women as well as men unless its content clearly suggest the opposite. There is, however, no place for logical method in our hypothetical scheme.

A similar account of interpretative canons is given by the German legal scholar W. Brugger. There the fourth place is held by 'teleological analysis', in which

---

23   A. B. Vengerov, Теория государства и права [Theory of State and Law], Part 2 (1997), p. 81.

the other three elements 'are only deemed indicative, not determinative, of the contemporaneous purpose of the legal provision or document'.[24] What remains questionable in the continental theory of interpretation is the sequence in which different rules of interpretation should be invoked and which rule is to be preferred in case of competition between them. Moreover, it is unclear at which stage the result of interpretation is deemed to be 'sufficiently good' so as to stop interpreting. Brugger says that in Germany 'legal scholars support various methods of ranking, but the standard generally relied upon by both scholars and judges does not amount to much more than the following precept: When interpreting a provision, make use of all methods'.[25] Russian legal theorist Cherdantsev also thinks it impossible to formalise the rules of interpretation.[26] In American legal literature the expression 'an interpretive regime' has been coined for describing current preferences of courts which are perceived as a system of latent rules followed by courts when interpreting the law.[27] There are debates as to who should establish such a regime – either Congress or the Supreme Court.[28]

Some assistance can also be derived from the internationally recognised 'general rule of interpretation' as consolidated in Arts 31 and 32 of the Vienna Convention on the Law of Treaties. The interpretative procedure in the Convention (with parallel comparison to the hypothetical scheme based on Russian Civil Code) is the following:

1   A treaty shall be interpreted in good faith in accordance with the ordinary meaning to be given to the terms of the treaty in their context and in the light of its object and purpose. (Corresponds to points 1–3 of the scheme.) Besides, recourse may be had to:
2   any subsequent agreement between the parties regarding the interpretation of the treaty or the application of its provisions (similar to the so-called 'authentic' interpretation, which is issued by the rule-maker himself. No analogy in the scheme);
3   any subsequent practice in the application of the treaty which establishes the agreement of the parties regarding its interpretation (point 6 of the scheme);
4   any relevant rules of international law applicable in the relations between the parties (closest to point 5 on the scheme);

---

24   W. Brugger, 'Legal Interpretation, Schools of Jurisprudence, and Anthropology: Some Remarks from a German Point of View', *American Journal of Comparative Law*, Vol. 42 (1994), pp. 396–397.

25   Ibid., p. 400.

26   A. F. Cherdantsev, Толкование права и договора [Interpretation of Law and of a Contract] (2003), p. 216.

27   W. N. Eskridge and P. P. 'Frickey, "Law as Equilibrium,"' *Harvard Law Review*, Vol. 108 (November 1994), pp. 65–66.

28   N. Q. Rosenkranz, 'Federal Rules of Statutory Interpretation', *Harvard Law Review*, Vol. 115 (June 2002), p. 2085.

5   supplementary means of interpretation, including the preparatory work of the treaty and the circumstances of its conclusion, in order to confirm the meaning resulting from the application of the preceding rules, or to determine the meaning when the application of these rules leaves the meaning ambiguous or obscure or leads to a result which is manifestly absurd or unreasonable. (Analogous to point 4 on the scheme.)

It is seen that almost every link of one scheme finds a match in the other, and vice versa, but their rankings are different. This analysis also demonstrates that what is habitually called 'the rules of interpretation' is not a uniform concept. It relates to three distinct phenomena: (1) interpretative devices, (2) methods (or ways) of interpretation, and (3) approaches to interpretation. For example, the Russian Civil Code and Vienna Convention each give a scale of interpretative devices,[29] whereas the continental legal doctrine operates with methods, and the English legal system operates with approaches (or general attitudes) to interpretation. 'Device' can be defined as a technique used by a court to ascertain the meaning of a rule. Techniques or devices are instruments of interpretive methods, the latter being aggregates of similar techniques. Besides, methods and devices may be presented as individual stages and sub-stages of interpretation. 'Approaches' determine the sequence and priority of methods and corresponding devices. To be more specific, the 'literal rule' says that only grammatical method applies. The 'golden rule' prescribes that one should start with it, but permits one to proceed next through the logical and systematic methods (in a somewhat unclear sequence) so as to end up, to all appearance, with the historical one. The 'mischief rule' seems to approach the problem in exactly the opposite way.

The comparison of rules of interpretation in different legal systems and branches of law draws the present author to the conclusion that, although these rules do help to confine the discretion of judges, the latter still enjoy a freedom of choice as to which rule (or method or approach) to follow. Their choice can be influenced by a number of factors, including the prevailing judicial philosophy and the expectations of the general public, to name only two. But there seems to be no 'mathematical' test to prove in every single case that the judge has erred when he opted to follow one rule rather than the other.

Legislative intent

As we have seen, the historico-political method of construing the meaning of statutes is not completely alien to Russian legal doctrine. But at present it is rarely employed in actual practice. Few cases of its use are either an analysis of the development of legislation as regards a certain issue or mere references to social and political realities that existed at the time of the adoption of the

---

29 Except for the 'object and purpose' clause in Vienna Convention, which surely gives a method (logical), not a device, of interpretation.

legislative norm and the understanding of which, being a matter of 'common knowledge', does not presuppose careful inquiries. Very seldom judges make recourse to legislative materials and there are no cases in which they studied how the meaning of legislative words had changed. It is not surprising in itself, because the Russian legislation is relatively young so that the overwhelming majority of applicable laws has been adopted in the post-Soviet period. But it is not impossible that in the course of time there will be more interest on the part of the legal community to various aspects of the historical method of interpretation.

In the common law countries one does not find a strict distinction between historical and purposive (teleological) methods of interpretation, for in any case all the debates concerning the rules of interpretation turn on such notions as 'legislative intent' or 'legislative purpose'. There is, of course, a rationale behind it, because it is questionable whether the purposive analysis constitutes a separate method of interpretation – after all, the other ways of interpretation of legal norms are equally focused on discovering their purpose, although by using different techniques. Cherdantsev suggests to distinguish two methods of interpretation instead of a single historico-political one: first, a historical method which is based on comparisons between the new and old legislation, a study of draft laws and the reasons for making new rules; and, second, a 'functional' method whose focus is the social and ideological environment in which the norm existed, alongside with value concepts and their changeable content.[30] I do not think this distinction is crucial since both methods emphasise the temporal factor and both rely on such means of clarification of the rules' meaning which lie outside the legislation itself. This is their common feature as opposed to the textually oriented methods of interpretation, such as grammatical (linguistic) and systematic. Moreover, the 'functional' analysis cannot avoid a historical retrospection, because it aims to show that social conditions have changed indeed, and how exactly. At the same time, the court which uses the functional analysis will not necessarily prefer a more up-to-date meaning of the words used in the legal act.

Ronald Dworkin, the author of the most influential theory of interpretation in the modern legal thought, gives much attention to the concept of 'legislative intent'. Dworkin rejects the so-called 'the plain fact view' of the grounds of law as past decisions of legal institutions, like legislatures and courts, and insists that law is entirely interpretative so that there is always a 'right answer' to any question put before the judge. He believes that the word 'statute' bears two meanings: 'It can describe a physical entity of a certain type, a document with words printed on it', but also 'the law created by enacting that document, which may be a much more complex matter'. The problem is how to construe a 'real' statute from the text in the statute book. Considering several complex cases by way of example,

---

30 Cherdantsev, Толкование права и договора [Interpretation of Law and of a Contract], pp. 130, 187.

Dworkin analyses different approaches taken by judges. One of these attitudes is 'literal interpretation'. It means that the words of the statute at hand should be given their 'acontextual meaning', as if there could be no information about the surrounding context the words are in or the intentions of the legislator. The second version comes to this: the judges construing a statute must respect the legislature's intentions. It falls into two sub-versions. One is 'excessively weak': if the acontextual meaning of statutory words is clear, then the court must assign to them that meaning unless it is shown that the legislature actually wanted the opposite results. The stronger version says that the courts should accept an absurd result only if they find compelling evidence that *it* was intended.[31]

Even the 'literal' approach, in Dworkin's view, is not 'mechanical', but 'interpretative', because there are always some moral and legal considerations behind it.[32] As to both versions of the second approach, they are embedded in the concept of 'legislative intention'.

In his discussion, Dworkin sets out several questions against the so-called 'speaker's meaning theory of legislative intention': 'Which historical people count as the legislators? How are their intentions to be discovered? When these intentions somewhat differ from one to another, how are they to be combined in the overall, composite institutional intention?' These questions, Dworkin thinks, 'cannot be answered just by exploring the internal connections between intention and legislation conceived as a form of speech. They must be answered in political theory, by taking up particular views about controversial issues of political morality'. It is impossible to separate a judge's personal convictions from the way he reads a statute.[33]

Who count as legislators? All the members of a legislature or only those who voted for? What about the executive officials and assistants who prepared the initial draft? What about the various lobbies and action groups who played their role? Should their intentions be taken into account? What about later legislators, who did not repeal the statute and thereby allowed it to remain valid? Perhaps their decision reflects some understanding about the point and purpose of the statute? These are the interrelated questions Dworkin seeks to answer.

The idea of an integral and indivisible 'legislative intent' does give much difficulty to the analyst.[34] Dworkin shows that 'intention' frequently falls into clashing hopes and expectations which can dramatically contradict each other. A member of the legislature may hope that the statute enacted will be interpreted by judges in a certain way. But his more realistic expectations make him think that it would not.[35] A judge may rely on his convictions, that is, the beliefs about what justice or sound policy would require, which may be different from either his

---

31 R. Dworkin, *Law's Empire* (1986), pp. 17–23.
32 Ibid., p. 18.
33 Ibid., p. 316.
34 More on this in: Jeremy Waldron, 'Legislators' Intentions and Unintentional Legislation', in Andrei Marmor (ed.), *Law and Interpretation* (1995), pp. 329–356.
35 R. Dworkin, *Law's Empire* (1986), p. 323.

hopes or expectations. But not infrequently people have quite different views and beliefs, and the ideal judge (Hercules, as Dworkin calls him) has to treat some of them as more basic and fundamental than others, and some as depending on others, or supporting them, or both. In the end, the judge will inevitably reach the point in his argument when he must decide under which circumstances the legislator's various convictions should conflict and, if they do, which convictions should be preferred. In doing so he has to take up the 'interpretative' view.[36]

The Dworkinian list of unresolved difficulties could be easily expanded. Since the legislative chambers consist of people taking different views on legal and political problems, the legislative acts are ordinarily the result of compromises. If the legislature is divided into more than two factions, the statute passed may, as a whole, reflect the opinion of none of them. Therefore, such acts will embody the genuine intentions of any group of parliamentarians. Some provisions can be introduced by way of concession to the 'last drop groups' to induce them to support the whole statute and thereby to ensure the legitimate majority needed. Hence such provisions of necessity reflect the desires of a small minority. Moreover, some members of Parliament can vote for a bill even though it does not meet their true intentions. In so doing they can pursue career considerations or obey party discipline. Some members of the legislature could vote even though they did not read draft laws or were absent during the hearings. What can be called 'the intention of Parliament' in such a case?

But, perhaps, Dworkin has exaggerated the difficulties of discovering the legislative intention to the extent that some of his arguments look like sophisms. If subsequent legislators did not vacate a statute, it simply means that they respected the intentions of their predecessors, whatever they might be. The argument that 'some people are not in charge of their words'[37] does not sound persuasive as far as the legislators are concerned: of course, a hostage, telephoning at gun-point (Dworkin's analogy), may really hope not to be understood the way he expects to be. But a member of a legislature who voluntarily submitted to the rules of legislative procedure in no way is in such a position. These rules do not save his 'true intentions' from being distorted, and the message to citizens that he sent should not necessarily be the finest expression possible. Anyway, he might vote against the proposal he does not approve of or not vote at all. If he voted nevertheless, it follows that he found it to be a better alternative. He really had a choice.[38]

---

36 R. Dworkin, *Law's Empire* (1986), p. 333.
37 Ibid., p. 322.
38 J. Waldron thinks such conclusion is 'purely an artifact of our particular parliamentary procedures' (J. Waldron, 'Legislators' Intentions and Unintentional Legislation', p. 336). However, these procedures are real and pretty universal. It seems strange to find their results less coherent than the output of the hypothetical 'Wollheim's machine' producing a statute in a mechanical fashion on the basis of voting on its various aspects put into it by parliamentarians (Ibid., p. 337). Unlike a typical 'incoherent' draft, the output of such machine would hardly pass a final voting as a whole.

As for someone who signs a group letter (another Dworkin example) but cannot rewrite for the group, or the author of that letter who drafts it to attract the greatest number of signatures possible,[39] they are indeed in the position very close to that of a legislator. However, their 'true intentions' should not be counted, irrespective of whether they are intelligible or not. Only what such a person said to other people who put on their signatures is a matter of importance. Perhaps the author was going to mislead them by deliberately giving different explanations. But it is difficult to carry the analogy further, as long as in legislative bodies such comments and explanations on a draft law are usually given to all their members together, not separately. That is why the claim that the typical senator-backbencher 'treats the document, not himself or any other person, as the author of the message he agrees to send' is hardly correct.[40]

Although it is true that not every text is adequate to the intentions of its author, it is not yet a reason to call into question the link between the text and the author. Let us take an individual writer as an example. Suppose that a censor expurgated or somehow changed a few pages in his novel. Assume that was a price to pay for its publication, and the author had to accept it. Does it follow that he is no longer the real author of the novel? Of course, future commentators may successfully retrieve the original draft. But sometimes it is impossible, and we should accept the text as it is. The situation may be even harder if we assume that the author made some concessions to the tastes of general public or his editor. How can we discern these changes and determine their scope? In such a case we can speculate what he actually wrote or would have written, but, in the absence of reliable evidence about his intentions, the text remains the only authority for an interpreter.

It should be added that there are two things not to be confused – 'an intention' and 'an expressed will'. The difference between them has been a subject of controversy as early as in Roman jurisprudence in the contexts of the interpretation of wills in which there was a contradiction between the actual desire of a testator and the literal meaning of the words he used.[41] Likewise, in the case of legislators they do not necessarily coincide. For whatever reason, members of a legislature may vote for a statute as it was explained by its drafters and sponsors, even though it was not in accordance with their beliefs. Furthermore, the said explanations may, in their turn, differ from what has been finally enacted. But one may argue that by voting for they affirm the application of the statute in accordance with the ordinary meaning of the words used,

39 R. Dworkin, *Law's Empire* (1986) p. 322.

40 Ibid., p. 322.

41 The celebrated 'causa Curiana' ('a case of Curius') told by Cicero (*De Oratore*, I. 39, 56, 57, II. 6, 32, 54. *Brutus*, 39, 52, 53, 73, 88). The controversy continues to present day. As it is clear from the account of Russian rules of the interpretation of contracts, the form of expression has a priority over the actual desire of the party. The French attitude is exactly the opposite (Art 1156 of the French Civil Code). For further reading see K. Zweigert and H. Kotz, *Introduction to Comparative Law*, Vol. 2 (2nd rev. edn., 1992), pp. 268 ff.

and thus all their intentions and expectations are superceded by this meaning so long as it is clear and unambiguous. Unsurprisingly, Dworkin's opponents tend to dismiss his arguments by simply saying that only words count, not intentions. They adhere to the view that only statutory text should guide people's conduct and control judicial decisions. Judge Bork expressed it in the most straightforward manner:

> When lawmakers use words, the law that results is what those words ordinarily mean. If Congress enacted a statute outlawing the sale of automatic rifles and did so in the Senate by a vote of 51 to 49, no court would overturn a conviction because two senators in the majority testified that they really had intended only to prohibit the use of such rifles. They said 'sale' and 'sale' it is. [. . .] Law is a public act. Secret intentions count for nothing.[42]

This point, however healthy it might be in respect of many statutory provisions, has much lesser force in the context of constitutional adjudication. It can be exemplified by rich and exciting polemics between Justice Antonin Scalia and Ronald Dworkin. The latter maintained that textualists like Scalia defer only to one kind of intention – 'semantic' intention. They miss what he believes to be a crucial distinction 'between what some officials intended to say in enacting the language they used, and what they intended – or expected or hoped – would be the consequence of their saying it'.[43] For instance, 'the framers of the Eighth Amendment laid down a principle forbidding whatever punishments are cruel and unusual. They did not themselves expect or intend that that principle would abolish the death penalty, so they provided that death could be inflicted only after due process. But it does not follow that the abstract principle they stated does not, contrary to their own expectation, forbid capital punishment'.[44] In Dworkin's opinion, key constitutional provisions set out abstract principles rather than concrete or dated rules. Therefore, the death penalty can become unconstitutional, because in the course of time the contents of the principle forbidding cruel and unusual punishments change.[45]

Scalia responded by saying that the Eighth Amendment is indeed no mere 'concrete and dated rule' but rather an abstract principle. 'What it abstracts, however, is not a moral principle of "cruelty" that philosophers can play with in the future, but rather existing society's assessment of what is cruel. It means not

---

42 Bork, *The Tempting of America*, p. 145.

43 R. Dworkin, 'Comment', in Scalia, *A Matter of Interpretation*, pp. 116, 121.

44 Ibid., p. 121.

45 Similar view was advanced by Judge Boris Ebzeev who wrote about 'the gradual transformation of the Constitution under the influence of the social development' and its ability to change 'without changes in its text'. All the same, he warns against 'arbitrary treatment of the norm under interpretation on the ground that this norm does not always express the true intention of its creators' (see Ebzeev's dissent in the Decree of the Constitutional Court of 12 April 1995, No. 2-П, and his article in *HCC*, no. 2/3 (1995), pp. 27–28, 83).

(as Professor Dworkin would have it) "whatever may be considered cruel from one generation to the next," but "what we consider cruel today"; otherwise, it would be no protection against the moral perceptions of a future, more brutal, generation."[46] It makes a lot of sense to guarantee to a society that 'the freedom of speech you now enjoy (*whatever* that consists of) will never be diminished by the federal government'; it makes very little sense to guarantee that 'the federal government will respect the moral principle of freedom of speech, which may entitle you to more, or less, freedom of speech than you now legally enjoy'.[47]

In fact, the deference to the views of framers' (or other constitutional legislators') is quite compatible with developing such abstract provisions by pulling them in different directions, while preserving their original 'dated' content. First of all, legislators in cases such as Eighth Amendment ought not be specific: it would be quite unreasonable of them to enumerate all kinds of cruel and unusual punishments, simply because some completely new ones might be invented in the future.[48] But this does not *per se* permit us to discount their views as to which punishments among those already known were cruel and which were not. This only allows us to make our own judgment when there is no evidence that they had a particular punishment in mind and, if they did, what their opinion was. With respect to death penalty, the fact that it was mentioned in the Fifth Amendment seems to be a sufficient proof that they did not consider death penalty as a cruel punishment. At least, a continental lawyer has no need for Hercules in order to obtain such conclusion by means of habitual systematic interpretation which requires to avoid, as much as possible, any inconsistencies in the text being interpreted.[49] However, when applied to such abstract provisions, these interpretive techniques customary for continental lawyers may lead to quite surprising results. For example, within such interpretive framework it would be quite logical to assert that a punishment is expected to be *simultaneously* cruel and unusual in order to be outlawed. Then further argument shall deploy as follows: there can be very light but unusual punishments, which the framers could hardly intend to prohibit; moreover, both denotations ('cruel' and 'unusual') are treated within the constitutional clause as equally important (at least, nothing in its text indicates that one denotation is more significant than the other); this implies that, if the nature of a punishment is converse (that is, it is not unusual, although might be very cruel) it could not be held unconstitutional either!

---

46 A. Scalia, *A Matter of Interpretation*, p. 145.

47 Ibid., p. 148. Dworkin's reply to this point is buried in the footnote to his lecture in which he says that the most plausible alternative to Scalia's approach is the 'one which translates the Eighth Amendment to punishments that really are cruel' (R. Dworkin, 'The Arduous Virtue of Fidelity: Originalism, Scalia, Tribe, and Nerve', *Fordham Law Review*, Vol. 65 (1997) footnote 5, p. 1268). It is not clear to me what Dworkin means by 'cruel in fact' and how this alternative helps to refute those who would argue that, say, decapitation is not 'in fact' a cruel punishment.

48 The use of the word 'unusual' strongly suggests that the framers were indeed anticipating this.

49 Similar point was made by Bernard Schlink (B. Schlink, 'Hercules in Germany?', *International Journal of Constitutional Law*, Vol. 1 (October 2003), p. 613).

This conclusion, however, seems to be counterintuitive and therefore unacceptable. Such outcome highlights the peculiar character of interpretive conventions: they are workable with respect to their 'mother' legal systems (or even particular documents like constitutions) but not necessarily the others, due to constraints of legal culture. This example also shows that, in the face of such difficult issues, any interpretive approach is fraught with important dangers and is not invulnerable. Perhaps, Jeremy Waldron is right in stating that:

> The meaning of 'cruel'... is contestable, and for some jurists that is a flaw: if only the framers had specified whether capital punishment was permissible or not, then we would know where we stand. But knowing where we stand may not be the point of the provision. Instead, the point may be to ensure that certain debates take place in our society: this should not be a society which simply imposes punishments without regard to whether or not they are cruel. Maybe execution is cruel, maybe it is not. But a society which executes criminals without hesitation and without public debate on that question is arguably a poorer society, from the point of view of the ethical theory underlying the Eighth Amendment, than a society which makes it an issue.[50]

Let us now revert to legislative intent or purpose. In the final analysis, this concept is a sensible one, although it should not be understood in terms of an individual intention. However, it does not mean that the concept is incoherent, only that it is a distinctly different concept.[51] Joseph Raz puts the question 'How can institutions have intentions?' and answered it as follows:

> If they can act intentionally, after much deliberation (for example, 'after discussing the matter for 7 hours the House of Commons approved the Bill as amended in committee') they can have intentions. We find no problem in attributing intentions to corporations, groups and institutions in ordinary life, and the law assumes that corporations and some other legal subjects who are not human beings can act intentionally.[52]

It should be remarked that the terms 'purpose' and 'intention' are to some extent misleading. They imply a false analogy between the inner processes of human mind and those within a collective body of men. But they are entirely different. Furthermore, instead of a single purpose there may be a number of them in a legislative act, and they may even conflict. I think in many cases

---

50 J. Waldron, 'Vagueness in Law and Language', *California Law Review*, Vol. 82 (May 1994), p. 539.

51 B. Bix, 'Questions in Legal Interpretation', in A. Marmor (ed.), *Law and Interpretation: Essays in Legal Philosophy* (1995), p. 144.

52 Ibid., p. 142. Cf. the opinion of Sir R. Cross in his *Statutory Interpretation* (3rd edn., 1995), p. 28.

judges would agree that what they are looking for is not 'intention' in the sense applicable to an individual. But, with all the necessary reservations, the 'legislative intention' seems to be a useful concept. There are several arguments for it. First of all, any word or expression, however vague, has a limited range of meanings;[53] otherwise the very process of communication would fail. Though legislators may have different expectations, hopes or desires, their mental processes should meet at some point to produce a meaningful result, that is, a certain message to citizens and law-appliers; otherwise no written rule would be capable of guiding human behaviour. Thus, the legislative provision is not the product of a single mind, but, rather, a point to meet for a number of mental processes.[54] It was rightly noted that the terms 'intention(s) of Parliament (and similar phrasings)' are no more than 'merely a place-holder for all the (text-centred) rules of interpreting legislation', and 'there is no Platonic idea of "legislative intent" that we must discover and try to describe'.[55]

Legislative history

If the ordinary meaning of words is unclear or ambiguous, judges and advocates may resort to legislative history. In their search for legislative intent, American judges frequently have recourse to the legislative history of the act in question. It may comprise a wide variety of documents, like parliamentary reports, discussions on the floor, statements of the promoters and sponsors of the bill, and so forth. In Russia, as well as in the rest of Europe, the recourse to these aids was much less common. The rules concerning their admissibility vary from one legal system to another and may be described as a part of the 'rule of recognition' in the Hartian sense. For instance, in the United States preambles and committee reports are normally regarded as evidence of the legislator's intention. As for the speeches of congressmen on the floor, their use is more disputable, though they have been employed frequently in the decisions of the courts. But now the latter rely more on contextual harmonisation (other parts of the statute, and the like).

Previously, British courts did not systematically refer to legislative history in their judgments. Such references were only occasional. However, this approach was changed by the famous decision of the House of Lords in *Pepper v Hart*.[56] This case seems to be a turning point. The Law Lords permitted, to some extent, the use of legislative records (Hansard). The debate regarding the new rules

---

53 'Words do have a limited range of meaning, and no interpretation that goes beyond that range is permissible' (Scalia, *A Matter of Interpretation*, p. 24).

54 For a detailed discussion of this problem (in the context of Wittgensteinian idea of 'forms of life' as a common background which enables people to have shared concepts) see B. Bix, *Law, Language, and Legal Determinacy* (1993), pp. 62 ff., 177.

55 Bix, *Questions in Legal Interpretation*, pp. 144–145; cf. Bix, *Law, Language, and Legal Determinacy*, pp. 184–187.

56 *Pepper (Inspector of Taxes) v Hart* [1993] 1 All ER 42.

established by the House of Lords touches upon some crucial questions for the statutory interpretation in the United Kingdom.

The arguments in favour of the traditional rule have also been discussed in the House of Lords. They were four:

1   the traditional rule preserves the constitutional proprieties, leaving Parliament to legislate in words and the courts (not parliamentary speakers) to construe their meaning;
2   the expensiveness of researching parliamentary materials;
3   the need for the citizen to have access to a known defined text which regulates his legal rights; and
4   the improbability of finding helpful guidance from Hansard.

The first and the third of the opposing arguments were principled ones, the others were practical. However, the latter produced much more debate in the House than the former. In the end the House decided that considerations for relaxing the rule overweigh the arguments to the contrary.

It should be acknowledged at the very beginning that it is perhaps impossible to offer rules of admissibility which would leave no questions, and the rules imposed by the House in the instant case are definitely not such. The first rule is that Hansard may be consulted if the legislation is ambiguous or obscure or the literal meaning leads to an absurdity. As to the concept of 'absurdity', it is particularly imprecise. Some people see absurdity where others think everything is all right. The second rule is that the materials to rely on should consist of statements by a minister or other promoter of the bill which led to the enactment of the legislation, together if necessary with such 'other parliamentary material as is needed to understand such statements and their effect'.[57] The last addition can also be understood broadly. The third rule says that the statements should be clear. But it seems to contradict the previous rule: if the statements are clear, what is the use of other parliamentary materials? As a practical matter, the result of the decision may be that citizens and lawyers should no longer rely on the statutes only but also on their legislative background. It would complicate the contents of the laws and make the statutes themselves bad guidance for them.[58]

It can be said that the solution in *Pepper v Hart* changed the 'rule of recognition' in the English legal system. As Bix commented, 'the House of Lords, when acting in its legislative capacity, changed the conditions under which the expressions which indicate conclusions of law are warranted. Thus, there is a sense in which the House of Lords can change – and has changed – the meaning of terms like 'contract', 'recklessness' and 'consideration' for the purposes of English law'.[59]

---

57 *Pepper (Inspector of Taxes) v Hart* [1993] 1 All ER 42, at p. 43.
58 Cross, *Statutory Interpretation*, p. 153.
59 Bix, *Questions in Legal Interpretation*, p. 146.

Another aspect of the decision of the House of Lords, not considered enough, is that the recourse to legislative history may, in principle, shed a new light upon some provisions that previously seemed to be plain, and in that way make questionable what would be undisputed under the former rules of admissibility. To put it differently, ambiguity may be *a consequence*, not *the reason* of application of this method.

The words of the promoters of an act cannot be treated in every case as those of the legislature. The more legislative history is involved in judicial decisions, the more likely it would be that much time in the parliamentary debates will be devoted to attempts to direct future court decisions by giving certain interpretations to the statute's words. On the whole, the legislative history is not a very reliable source in each case. As Lord Hailsham said:

> What was said by a Minister or a private member at two o'clock in the morning in the course of a report stage on a hot June night is more likely to mislead than enlighten, and criticism of it by judges, which would not only be legitimate but necessary were it to be admissible, would be constitutionally undesirable.[60]

These objections are not intended to diminish the relevance of parliamentary materials, but to show a number of difficulties in their use. As for the decision in *Pepper v Hart*, there is some evidence that *Hansard* is referred to more often than the rule in that case would justify.[61] It should be noted that in the United States lawyers and judges avail themselves of legislative history more freely than in England. It gave birth to the joke that 'one should consult the text of the statute only when the legislative history is ambiguous'. Justice Scalia comments: 'Alas, that is no longer funny. Reality has overtaken parody.'[62]

This may be the reason that brought to life the opposite trend. In the case *Regina v Hinks*, considered in the House of Lords, Lord Steyn quoted the words of Lord Reid: 'We often say that we are looking for the intention of Parliament, but that is not quite accurate. We are seeking not what Parliament meant but the true meaning of what they said.'[63] These views are not those which underlie the decision in *Pepper v Hart*. However, he recognised that 'relevant publicly available contextual materials are readily admitted in aid of the construction of statutes. On the other hand, to delve into the intentions of individual members of the Committee, and their communications, would be to rely on material which cannot conceivably be relevant. If statutory interpretation is to be a rational and coherent process a line has to be drawn somewhere'. Then he proposed an alternative way of interpretation. His idea was to construe the meaning of the

---

60 Lord Q. H. Hailsham of St. Marylebone, *Hamlin Revisited: The British Legal System Today* (1983), p. 69.
61 Cross, *Statutory Interpretation*, p. 159.
62 Scalia, *A Matter of Interpretation*, p. 31.
63 *Regina v Hinks* [2000] 3 WLR 1590, at p. 1596.

relevant provisions without reference to the report which preceded them, but to rely instead on their interpretation by the House of Lords in previous decisions, such as *Lawrence* [1972] and *Gomez* [1993].[64]

The refusal of the Law Lords to resort to the legislative history of the Theft Act 1968 was not indisputable. Mrs Hinks was convicted for theft because she induced an old man of limited intelligence to make her gifts amounting to a total of £60,000. Under s 1(1) of the Theft Act 1968, 'a person is guilty of theft if he dishonestly appropriates property belonging to another with the intention of permanently depriving the other of it; and "thief" and "steal" shall be construed accordingly'. The question before the House of Lords was: 'Whether the acquisition of an indefeasible title to property is capable of amounting to an appropriation of property belonging to another for the purposes of section 1(1) of the Theft Act 1968?'[65]

There was trustworthy evidence that the drafters of the Act did not agree 'that a person appropriates for himself property of which another person is the owner every time he gratefully accepts a gift or buys an apple', because 'one really cannot have a definition of stealing which relies on the word 'dishonestly' to prevent it covering every acquisition of property'.[66] But the House of Lords did not take notice of it. As Sir John Smith wrote, the drafters of the bill 'had no doubt, that a person who obtained the ownership in property by deception did not "appropriate" it'.[67] According to the natural meaning of the words of the Act and in the light of drafters' intentions the appellant could be defined as 'dishonest', but not as a person who 'appropriates' someone's property and is liable to the conviction for theft. But in the Law Lords' opinion, this narrower (and more reasonable) construction 'could complicate fair and effective prosecution', and was therefore discarded.

Although in Russia neither doctrine nor legislation prohibits the so-called 'historical or political interpretation', including judges' resort to contextual aids, thus far Russian courts made very little use of it. On a number of occasions they did avail themselves of the historical method which, however, came to nothing but exploring the development of legislation regulating the appropriate issue, without invoking any background materials. The earliest example was a constitutional case in which Judge Oleinik said that the decision would be more persuasive had the Court indicated the modes of interpretation it used, including the 'politico-historical one'.[68] In his view, it would require the analysis of

---

64 *Regina v Hinks* [2000] 3 WLR 1590, at p. 1596.

65 Ibid., at p. 1591.

66 Ibid., at p. 1592.

67 J. C. Smith, 'The Sad Fate of the Theft Act 1968', in W. Swadling and G. Jones (eds.), *The Search for Principle: Essays in Honour of the Lord Goff of Chieveley* (1999), p. 111; see also the dissenting opinion of Lord Lowry in *Gomez* [1993] 1 All ER 1, esp. at p. 17.

68 Decree of the Constitutional Court of 23 March 1995, No. 1-П, concerning the interpretation of Art 105(4) and Art 106 of the Russian Constitution, Вестник Конституционного Суда Российской Федерации [*Herald of the Constitutional Court of the Russian Federation*; hereinafter: *HCC*], no. 2/3 (1995), pp. 3–16. The concurring opinion of Judge Oleinik was not published. It can be found in electronic databases.

historical conditions in which the 1993 Constitution was framed and of the socio-political aims the legislator pursued. He invited his Court to use verbatim records of the Constitutional Conference and the opinions of the drafters of relevant clauses. Remarkably, it was the first case considered by the Court after the lengthy break following the events of October 1993, and the first case under the new Constitution. Perhaps, it was a good time for innovation (if it was indeed a novelty!), but the Court failed to follow his invitation. More recent examples are only two: in one case Judge Ebzeev attempted to prove by means of the recorded opinions of the Constitutional Conference that the concept of 'the general number of the deputies of the State Duma' is not identical to the notion of the 'composition of the Duma',[69] and in another case Judge Ametistov relied upon the documents of the Commission when trying to show that the term 'an advocate (or defender)' used in Art 48(2) referred to a larger group of persons than only members of the bar.[70] It is utterly characteristic that in all these cases the resort to legislative materials failed to influence the decisions of the Court and was used by dissenting judges.

On the other hand, nothing prevents judges or advocates to refer to legislative history during the proceedings. But there is no reflection on these issues capable of emulating that of *Pepper v Hart*. The lack of reflections and settled practices makes the rule of recognition of the Russian legal system rather vague. Generally, the reluctance of Russian judges to make a more efficient use of this interpretive tool may be explained by the pressure of time (courts in Russia are tremendously overloaded), the lack of appropriate habits, techniques, and staff in the courts, as well as by the fear of everything unusual. At the same time, it is important to stress that at present there is no formal restrictions on the use of legislative history when substantiating a particular interpretation, whereas the records of parliamentary debates are published and readily available. Moreover, the body of applicable law mostly consists of recent enactments, and this fact, *ceteris paribus*, may enhance the relevance of legislative intent in interpreting statutes, for there is still a long way to the point where the views of legislators could be regarded as obsolete and therefore inappropriate in modern conditions.

The uncertainty of law and hard cases

There is no doubt that neither legislative history nor other aids to statutory construction such as dictionaries or presumptions (sometimes conflicting) are unable to provide a definite answer in every case. Perhaps the majority of judges, practitioners and academics would agree that some degree of uncertainty is intrinsic to statutory language. This means that 'hard cases',

---

69 Decree of the Constitutional Court of 12 April 1995, No. 2-П (Judge B. S. Ebzeev, dissenting), *HCC*, no. 2/3 (1995), pp. 27–28.

70 Decree of the Constitutional Court of 28 January 1997, No. 2-П, concerning Art 47(4) of the RSFSR Criminal Procedure Code, *HCC*, no. 2 (1997), p. 37.

in which there is no 'right answer', cannot be avoided. But statutory provisions are helpful in a negative sense, for they at least rule out the decisions that would not be correct.

Hart wrote that the rule of recognition itself, as well as particular rules of law identified by reference to it, may have some 'penumbra' of uncertainty, or 'open texture'. It is accounted for by the fact that the world in which we live is characterised by an infinite number of features, and we cannot know in advance all of them and the modes in which they can combine. Legislation, being a device for communication of standards of behaviour, uses general classifying terms concerning matters of fact. The uncertainty at the borderlines of the legal rules is the price to be paid for it. Hart uses the example of the prohibition, 'No vehicle may be taken into the park'.[71] Does it include roller-skates? He says that the law is just unspecific about them. So, in making his decision the judge creates a new rule for the future relating to roller-skates.[72]

The Hartian conception concerning 'hard cases' was called into question by Dworkin. To put it in a nutshell, the disagreement is this: in Hart's view, 'easy cases' (or 'clear', or 'ordinary') are pivotal for any legal system, and uncertainty is only a penumbra tolerable at the margins of it, whereas Dworkin claimed the distinction between easy and hard cases to be non-existent. If the law is no longer identifiable by clear rules, there is no law on the matter. But the judge is obliged to come to a decision. It means that he must make it on grounds other than legal ones. Positivists put such strong emphasis on certainty and view hard cases as penumbral ones because they want to preserve the idea of law as objectively determinable plain fact. But they are wrong, Dworkin insists. In his view, the assumption that a case is clear is the *result* of reasoning and not the start. 'Hard cases' are hard only because there are genuinely competing arguments as to what is the best understanding of the law. 'Easy cases' are simply those where there are no such doubts.[73] 'We will not call a statute unclear unless we think there are decent arguments for each of two competing interpretations of it'.[74] Against Hart's 'no-answer thesis' he sets out the idea that the right answer can always be found but aside from the legal sources, such as considerations of justice and fairness.

These points are largely unobjectionable. There are clear cases in the sense that the decisions in them have never been controversial (for example, the necessity to observe the speed limits). Dworkin believes, however, that there is no guarantee that they will never become a matter of controversy in the future, however unlikely such possibility might seem.[75]

---

71 H. L. A. Hart, *The Concept of Law* (2nd edn., 1994), p. 125.
72 Ibid., pp. 123–124. Hart's example could originate from *Corkery v Carpenter* [1951] 1 KB 102, where the question arose whether bicycle is a carriage.
73 Dworkin, *Law's Empire*, Ch. 9.
74 Ibid., p. 352.
75 Ibid., p. 354.

Perhaps it is a simplification to speak about 'hard' or 'easy cases' only. It is a common feature of human languages to use antinomies as rubrics for classifying objects and to draw sharp distinctions between them. But in reality we have to deal with a range or a scale of cases with varying degrees of difficulty, which from the upper end imperceptibly shade at the lower end into cases where no clear answer can be found. To put it another way, the level of difficulty in the so-called 'hard cases' may be very different. Nevertheless, classifications are necessary for the purposes of legal analysis. Perhaps, it would be better to assume that there are three, not two, types of cases:

1   Easy or clear cases which can be decided only in one way and not in another (for example, cases relating to the violation of speed limits).
2   Complex, or unclear, cases. In such cases the court may face difficulties in interpreting the law. However, a more detailed analysis may (and should) eventually demonstrate that only one of a few possible solutions is correct in law. The right answer may be found in other legal materials, such as legislative history of the act in question, preamble, the formal rules of interpretation, the normal usage of the words, etc. Although such situations are not an area of judicial creativity, sometimes they can be misrepresented as really hard.
3   Hard cases, or 'unregulated disputes' (in Razian terminology)[76] are those in which the law fails to provide a sole 'right answer'. There are several legitimate solutions open for a judge, each of which can be justified in the light of pre-existing legal rules or moral principles and values. The judge should rely on extralegal sources such as considerations of policy and morality. In these circumstances statutory interpretation brings a negative outcome which justifies the exercise of the rule-making function of the judge.

Although the decisions in unregulated disputes seem to have little bearing upon interpretation proper, Dworkin insists that judicial activism exists precisely in the form of interpretation. Furthermore, as long as all judicial decisions are interpretative, such activism is intrinsic to any decision. In his book *Taking Rights Seriously* he argues that the positivist's conception of judicial law-making at the borderlines of law is wrong because it implies that the creative function of courts is a violation of the principle of separation of powers, and, second, it has a retrospective character and disappoints the reasonable expectations of citizens.[77] The argument that all judicial decisions are interpretive and therefore activism is intrinsic to judicial work enables Dworkin to decline the objections of the conservatives who claim that American judges and in particular the US Supreme Court in a number of its consequential decisions broke the line between adjudication and legislation. Therefore Dworkin's defence of judicial activism is paradoxical, because its endeavour is exactly to show that there is no judicial

---

76 J. Raz, *The Authority of Law: Essays on Law and Morality* (1979), p. 183.
77 Dworkin, *Taking Rights Seriously*, pp. 84–85.

law-making in such cases – judges do not betray their duty to apply the existing norms, but interpret the law in its entirety which embraces both norms and principles.

The arguments put forward by the positivists are, of course, a result of a view of law which in main tenets is the opposite to Dworkin's. They try to rebut his thesis concerning the status of norms and principles and put forward a 'narrower' view of law as a system of norms.

The most distinguished theorist of modern positivism, Joseph Raz, is critical about a popular view on the creative role of courts which says that courts supposedly reveal the 'spirit' of the law or its inner logic or potential. He puts the question: how can the law provide the impetus for its own development? If the law itself points to a certain rule as the right legal rule, is not that rule a legal rule now? If it is, then recognising it and acting on it is merely acting on the basis of existing law. Raz believes that the solution of this puzzle is necessary in order the thesis concerning the internal dynamism of law would make any sense.

First of all, he observed that the development of the law by judges tends to be piecemeal and organic. Unlike Parliament, courts have little control over the cases coming before them, and therefore they cannot manage the opportunities available to them for changing the law.[78] But even when they do have such an opportunity, the latter is always very limited, because the rest of the law is beyond their reach. Therefore the changes judges make should necessarily be in harmony with the bulk of the law.[79] But the main problem is, how can the law be an autonomous reason for its own development?

In answering this question Raz draws an analogy with the delegated legislative powers. In many instances the grant of such powers (Raz calls them 'directed powers') is combined with the imposition of a duty to use them in a certain way, to promote certain ends.[80] As a rule, the use of such powers entails the exercise of moral judgment. This, for instance, may be a case where power is given to make rules for the protection of public safety and freedom. Since these goals and values may conflict with each other, they cannot be reconciled without resort to moral judgments. The cases in which such judgments are not necessary are quite rare.[81]

This analogy with the ordinary law-making powers helps to answer the puzzle. Raz takes for granted that two things are universal for all legal systems: (1) judicial decisions must be reasoned (that is, be based on general propositions of law applicable to a class of cases), and (2) they are the source of law (in those legal systems which do not have a doctrine of precedent, its role is assumed by judicial custom, that is, a line of consistent decisions). The fact that judicial decisions must be based on reasons and constitute a source of law does not by

---

78 J. Raz, *Ethics in the Public Domain: Essays in the Morality of Law and Politics* (1994), p. 224.
79 Ibid., pp. 223, 224.
80 Ibid., p. 226.
81 Ibid., pp. 227–228.

itself prove that they change the law. But when the courts correctly apply a legal doctrine (which can be expressed in legislation), two typical situations may emerge: the doctrine either provides a determinate solution to the case in hand or it may fail to do so. In the latter eventuality it is the decision of the court that makes determinate what had been uncertain before. This is a law-making decision, since the law has been thus changed or modified.[82]

But Joseph Raz goes further. He suggests that the law is developed even in the first instance. To substantiate this point he deploys the following arguments. When an attorney advises the client as to the case which comes to litigation for the first time he will indicate which outcome of the case is dictated by general rules. But he would also warn his client that this is a case of first impression, that there is no legal authority on the issue, and given that the law is yet unsettled much will depend on the political and moral convictions of the judges. For instance, there is a legal doctrine that prescribes that contracts which tend to corrupt public life are invalid. This doctrine yields the rule that a contract securing a contribution to an election fund in return for a promise how one would use one's power if elected is illegal.[83] But such a conclusion should be made on the basis of moral considerations, that is, that ideally one's wealth should not determine one's political influence and office-holders should not be bound by contractual obligations as to how they will use their powers. Since Raz, as a 'strict' positivist, draws a rigid line between law and morality, he consistently believes that there were no laws to that effect prior to the judicial decision which therefore is a law-making one.[84]

Courts use 'directed powers' in order to promote certain goals in very much the same way as the subordinate legislators use theirs. But even if the law indicates a certain rule as the only possible one, it does not entail that the latter becomes law until established as such by the courts. If, for instance, Art 119 of the Treaty of Rome obliged member states to enact laws guaranteeing women workers equal pay, this did not mean that women workers have had a right to equal pay until such laws were enacted. Under Art 119 they only had a right to demand from their governments the enactment of such laws and nothing more. But it was not made on time, and it is due to the decision of the European Court of Justice in 1976 that Art 119 was made directly applicable.[85]

In that way, according to Raz's opinion, the notion of 'directed powers' explains how law can provide impetus for its own development. He thinks such powers are pervasive. They exist in all cases in which judicial decisions are a source of law (either as precedent or as judicial custom) and in which courts are legally required to apply certain moral considerations.[86] The recognition of the

82 Ibid., p. 231.
83 Ibid.
84 Ibid.
85 Ibid., p. 234–235.
86 Ibid., p. 234.

law-shaping role of such judgments is one of the main points of debate between Raz and Dworkin.

Dworkin's solution to the problem of 'retrospective legislation' is a case in point. It lies within his conception of the 'society of principle'. If law includes moral principles, it may provide a 'right answer' to any problem. An argument of principle 'makes us look upon the defendant's claim, that it is unjust to take him by surprise, in a new light. If the plaintiff does indeed have a right to a judicial decision in his favour, then he is entitled to rely upon that right. If it is obvious and uncontroversial that he has the right, the defendant is in no position to claim unfair surprise just because the right arose in some way other than by publication in a statute'.[87]

But this is not a satisfactory solution. It appears to be just a fiction or pretence that the rights in question have already existed. Had the parties been aware of them, many actual disputes would have scarce chance to arise. It is precisely because people hold diverging opinions about their rights and duties they go to a court. Conceptually, the 'sole right answer' claim may well apply to any practical controversy which requires a sound judgment, be it a court dispute or an issue from legislative agenda or buying a car for someone's personal needs or whatever. In every such circumstance there is, notionally, a solution that would prove to be the best. But if this means that in such choices there is no room for sound judgment and discretion, such assertion simply does not hold.

In his later works Dworkin argued that the right answer thesis is correct for the simple reason that one possible answer to a particular problem is better than others, and this best answer can be identified with the right one.[88] He also relies on the distinction between uncertainty (as to which answer is really best or right) and the state of indeterminacy in which no right answer is presumed to exist. Legal cases, he argues, are at worst uncertain, not indeterminate.[89]

When delving into such metaphysical debate, it is easy to lose sight of its practical, mundane implications. Of course, 'judges disagree because they believe different decisions to be best, which means that one decision is the best'.[90] They do not recognise (perhaps, even to themselves) that no decision is the best. And they make honest efforts to achieve the best solution when a legal issue comes to them. But in spite of their aspirations, this best solution may escape their notice or be rejected. Or they find it, but many still remain unconvinced of its superiority, for the law (both judge-made and statutory) evolves by trial and error, unexpected findings and losses. This, again, is an intrinsic feature of any decision-making, not only in law. Let me give just one example taken from outside of law. When the king of Portugal refused to give support to Columbus

---

87 R. Dworkin, *Taking Rights Seriously*, p. 278.
88 See, for instance, R. Dworkin, 'Response to Overseas Commentators', *International Journal of Constitutional Law* (October 2003), p. 660.
89 See his article 'Indeterminacy and Law' in *Positivism Today* (1996), pp. 1–9.
90 R. Dworkin, 'Response to Overseas Commentators', p. 661.

who wanted to reach India by sailing westward, the king was guided by utterly sound considerations which seemed irrefutable at the moment: indeed, the Portuguese were already very close to achieving this goal, for they had just reached the Cape of Good Hope. So in those circumstances his refusal was perfectly 'right' or 'best' decision. But in a grand scheme of things (which, however, could not be seen by anybody) it was, perhaps, wrong.

In other words, it is not always possible to say beforehand that some rule is indeed the best at the moment of its making. Even a stronger claim could be made: a decision may become the best just *later*, given various contingencies and developments which at the moment of its making could not be rationally predicted and taken into account with full certainty. Sometimes only the (unpredictable) future may bring the quality of 'rightness' and confer it upon a judicial decision. This consideration seems to be underestimated by those who want judges to fall back upon some kinds of past or present legal practices or morality. Such judges would of necessity be inclined to issue decisions favouring *status quo*.[91]

In any event, if judges are wrong, that is, adopt a decision which is not the best, they nonetheless may develop the law by so doing, due to the binding force of their decisions. Actually, it does not matter for any practical purposes whether the judges *make* law in accordance with morality or, alternatively, are guided by their moral judgments as to what *existing* law is. This dilemma seems to be purely metaphysical and of little help to judges trying to resolve the difficulties they face in adjudicating disputes, as well as to scholars wanting to comprehend how such disputes differ among themselves – both in degree and in kind. It is noticeable that in recent works Dworkin seems to concede that there are important differences between constitutional and statutory interpretation: whereas the former is pervasively moral enterprise, the latter is indeed about borderline cases.[92]

Exploring the domain of hard cases

Judges legislate when they have to correct defects of the law in the process of settling disputes. A legal rule can be ambiguous; it may contain a gap; it may conflict with another rule; finally, it can be absurd or obsolete or lead to undesirable effects in spite of being clear and unambiguous. The idea of a 'gap' suggests that the legislator has not anticipated a particular situation, whereas ambiguity is premised upon the belief that it has been envisaged, but it is not clear how exactly. This distinction reflects the real occurrences, however difficult it might be to discern between a gap and ambiguity in real life. But, as a matter

---

91 On the essentially conservative nature of Dworkin's theory of adjudication see more in J. Raz, 'Dworkin: A New Link in the Chain', *California Law Review*, Vol. 74 (1986), p. 5.

92 R. Dworkin, 'The Judge's New Role: Should Judge's Personal Convictions Count?', *Journal of International Criminal Justice*, Vol. 1 (2003), p. 6.

of practice, an ambiguity can be treated as a partial gap which has arisen because the legislator, when enacting a rule, had overlooked its imperfectness. He thought it to be clear enough, but in fact it was not. Notionally, what ambiguity implies is not an insufficiency of prevision on the part of the law-maker, but an insufficiency of expression, which is a matter of form, not substance. Furthermore, the conflict of rules can also be regarded as a gap in or ambiguity of those operational (or background) rules that must resolve such a conflict. Therefore, the conception of a gap can be expanded so as to cover other defects as well. This notwithstanding, it is useful to distinguish between them and gaps proper, because different defects, although having much in common, call for different remedies: for instance, an ambiguity is remedied by means of recourse to legislative materials, but they would be inappropriate as an instrument of gap-filling. Keeping these considerations in mind, we can single out four general causes giving rise to hard cases or 'unregulated disputes':

1   An ambiguity, or a conflict of interpretations. A statutory provision or a precedent is ambiguous and can be interpreted in different ways. No single interpretation is capable of receiving support from a vast majority of experienced lawyers. Each interpretation can be buttressed by weighty legal arguments. As a result, there is strong disagreement between judges and academics as to which interpretation is more appropriate and ought to be applied.

2   A conflict of rules. The judges may find that there are a few inconsistent statutory provisions or precedents relating to the case at hand. Taken individually, they are clear enough, but they may be incompatible or create uncertainty when considered together. Each of them would be normally deemed to be binding on the court, but because they are several, their binding force is 'paralysed'. This situation is not difficult if the legal system contains rules providing how such cases should be approached. But if such rules, in their turn, are absent or contradictory, the court has to exercise its discretion in choosing which statutory provision or precedent is more relevant and should be followed.

3   Gaps in the law. It means that the judge finds himself in the position where there is no rule having binding force on him. In such a case he must somehow create a new rule. In so doing, he can resort to a variety of extralegal sources in order to justify his decision. Obviously, in the case of a gap in the law the rule-creating power of courts is the most direct and indisputable. However, not all legal systems avow their failure to provide solution to every legal problem. If so, courts have to disguise their law-creative role when dealing with gaps in the law. They are required to justify their decision by reference to pre-existing rules no matter how strained such references might seem.

4   If we look outside the law proper conceived as the sources of law, this classification can be supplemented with one more category of cases,

namely, those which are legally easy (as the solution required by law is plain) but morally hard due to practical implications of that solution. In the face of such a dilemma – whether to keep loyalty to the plain language of the law or obtain an enjoyable result – courts sometimes opt for the latter and, consequently, bend the law.

If we apply this taxonomy of hard cases to real disputes, we shall find that sometimes it is rather difficult to understand whether we deal with conflicting interpretations or a conflict of rules. An instructive example of this difficulty was provided by the decision of the House of Lords in *R v R (Marital exemption).*[93] This notorious case could be viewed from any of the four perspectives enumerated above. The question in that case was whether it is an offence for a husband to have sexual intercourse with his wife without her consent. There was only one common law authority making an explicit exemption for marital rape, namely, *Pleas of the Crown*, written by Sir Matthew Hale in the seventeenth century. He said:

> But the husband cannot be guilty of a rape committed by himself upon his lawful wife, for by their mutual matrimonial consent and contract the wife hath given herself up in this kind unto her husband, which she cannot retract.[94]

For three centuries this proposition was adopted as a general rule, although since *R v Clarence*[95] some 23 judges had tried to revise it.[96]

In 1976 Parliament produced the first definition of rape. Section 1(1) of the Sexual Offences (Amendment) Act 1976 provided:

> For the purpose of section 1 of the Sexual Offences Act...a man commits rape if – (a) he has unlawful sexual intercourse with a woman who at the time of the intercourse does not consent to it; and (b) at the time he knows that she does not consent to the intercourse or he is reckless as to whether she consents to it.

The common law rule laid down by Hale was not explicitly repealed by this Act. So, it was open to argue (as actually happened in *R v R*) that the word 'unlawful' in the statute means 'outside the bond of marriage' and hence preserves the marital exemption in the offence of rape. Although it is normally presumed that in the case of a conflict between a common law rule and a statutory provision the latter should prevail, it was a matter of statutory interpretation in

---

93 *R v R (Marital exemption)* [1992] AC 599.
94 M. Hale, *History of Pleas of the Crown*, Vol. 1 (1736), Ch. 58, p. 629.
95 *R v Clarence* [1888] 22 QBD.
96 For detailed account of this development see C. Manchester, D. Salter and P. Moodie, *Exploring the Law: The Dynamics of Precedent and Statutory Interpretation* (2nd edn., 2000), p. 391.

R v R what the true meaning of the word 'unlawful' was and, accordingly, whether such conflict had arisen or not.

The opponents of marital exemption in the offence of rape were inclined to take the word 'unlawful' as a 'mere surplusage'.[97] In their view, there could be no exemption or immunity for a husband under the Sexual Offences Act 1976. But even if there were, the court was nonetheless entitled to develop the common law in accordance with the new social conditions and public views recognising equality between spouses in the modern society. In Lord Lane's view, Hale's proposition was 'no longer acceptable. It can never have been other than a fiction, and fiction is a poor basis for the criminal law'. Therefore, 'this is not the creation of a new offence', but 'the removal of a common law fiction which has become anachronistic and offensive and we consider that it is our duty having reached that conclusion to act upon it'.[98]

Nevertheless, this interpretation could seem arguable to the defendants convicted of marital rape because they could think that the court created a new offence unknown to the law. It should be noted that the 1976 Statute ought to have been construed along with the 1956 Act, in which the expression 'unlawful sexual intercourse' was used a few times. It was argued for the defendant that the word 'unlawful' in s 19(1) of that Act meant just 'illicit' and implied either intercourse contrary to some positive enactment or intercourse in a brothel or something of that kind.[99] But the Law Lords refused to support that conclusion. They decided that this word was a 'mere surplusage'.

Smith and Hogan argue that this word in the 1956 Act had an important function and meant exactly 'outside the bond of marriage'. For instance, it was used in the latter sense in order to exclude the responsibility of a man, who, being validly married to a girl under 16 by the law of his domicile, would commit an offence when he had sexual intercourse with her in this country.[100]

On the one hand, the decision in *R v R* could be represented as a conflict of interpretations caused by an ambiguity of a key concept – a conflict in which the court yielded to the one that was more in line with new social conditions. On the other hand, one of the alternative interpretations assumed that there was a conflict between a common law rule and a later legislative norm. In either case the solution was not evident. It was uncertain whether the court ought to have preferred the legislative norm in any event or only if there were no doubt that the legislator truly intended to abolish the common law rule. In other words, absent a clear evidence to the contrary, it could be maintained that the legislator had missed some aspects of his decision, including its conflict with the common law rule, otherwise he might have opted for preserving it. That is to say, the problem could be perceived as a gap, too.

---

97 [1992] 1 AC, at pp. 609–611 (per Lord Lane C.J.).
98 Ibid., at pp. 610–611.
99 Ibid., at p. 622.
100 J. C. Smith and B. Hogan, *Criminal Law* (7th edn., 1992), p. 452.

But what was it really? Since the decision of the House of Lords was delivered shortly before *Pepper v Hart* (1993), the Lords could not have recourse to Hansard in order to ascertain the parliamentary intention in respect to this provision of 1976 Act. But if they had been allowed to do so, they would have discovered that 'in spite of strong support for making a husband liable for raping his wife, the intention was to leave in place the common law rule preserving the marital exemption'.[101] In the light of this discovery, the case might well be reassessed as an easy one. But perhaps it might not, provided that some judges could still think that the decision in favour of the accused would be grossly incompatible with the new social trends.

The decision in *R v R* was also subject to criticism for its failure to take into account the need for predictability in the application of rules. It was the basis of R's appeal to the European Commission on Human Rights, claiming that he was convicted of rape even though at the time of the incident his conduct did not constitute a criminal offence. Although his complaint was finally dismissed, this controversial case made the House of Lords warn the judges that they must be cautious when changing established rules of law and this power should be exercised carefully. The guiding principles were set out by Lord Lowry (one of the judges in *R v R*) in another case. He said:

> It is hard, when discussing the propriety of judicial law-making, to reason conclusively from one situation to another...I believe, however, that one can find in the authorities some aids to navigation across an uncertainly charted sea:
>
> 1   If the solution is doubtful, the judges should beware of imposing their own remedy.
> 2   Caution should prevail if Parliament has rejected opportunities of clearing up a known difficulty or has legislated, while leaving the difficulty untouched.
> 3   Disputed matters of social policy are less suitable areas for judicial intervention than purely legal problems.
> 4   Fundamental legal doctrines should not be lightly set aside.
> 5   Judges should not make a change unless they can achieve finality and certainty.[102]

The contradiction between these principles and the decision of the House of Lords in *R v R* is patent. If the House had followed these recommendations, the decision in *R v R* ought to have been different. However, it can be argued for the judges that it was the failure of Parliament to legislate that led them to take the initiative. At the same time, the decision in this particular case should

---

101 Manchester, Salter and Moodie, *Exploring the Law*, p. 409.
102 *C. (A Minor) v Director of Public Prosecutions* [1996] 1 AC, at p. 28.

be separated from a broader issue of judicial policy, namely, whether it was an appropriate exercise of judicial function or not. Could the House meet the growing need to adjust the law to new social conditions and abolish the marital exemption without being charged of convicting a person of a previously unknown criminal offence? The solution might be found in prospective overruling, when a new rule is not applied to the case in hand, but only to future cases. But in the United Kingdom, unlike the United States, the judiciary does not accept this method. Lord Reid expressed the prevailing view as follows:

> There is the importance of not upsetting existing proprietary or contractual rights. We cannot say that the law was one thing yesterday but is to be something different tomorrow. If we decide that the rule...is wrong we must decide that it always has been wrong.[103]

But in another case it was said that this method deserves closer consideration.[104] At the same time, if the precedent is overruled only prospectively and was not applied to the instant case it can be argued that such decision should be considered as mere *obiter dictum* and has no binding force.

This highly discreet approach to prospective overruling does not preclude the House of Lords from overruling its previous decisions by virtue of the *Practice Statement (Judicial Precedent)*.[105] Although this power is usually justified by the need to change the rules laid down in previous cases which later come to be considered as wrongly decided, it can create new hardships instead. In the *Practice Statement* special emphasis was put on the necessity to provide the certainty of law. For this reason, the House of Lords in *DPP v Knuller* refused to overrule its decision in the *Shaw* case because many sentences of imprisonment had been already passed on the basis of the latter. This approach 'appears to prefer consistency to justice'.[106] But in 1986 in *R v Shivpuri*[107] the House of Lords overruled its recent decision in *Anderton v Ryan* concerning the impossible attempt. The argument in favour of the overruling was that no one could yet have acted in reliance on that decision. However, it did not prevent the House of Lords in *Howe*[108] from overruling its long-standing decision in *Lynch*[109] that the defence of duress by threats was available to an accomplice to murder. So the considerations of justice, certainty and stability are in a very shifting and changeable interrelation in the eyes of the House of Lords. It is not easy to

---

103 *Birmingham City Corporation v West Midland Baptist (Trust) Association (Incorporated)* [1969] 3 All ER 172, at p. 180.
104 *Jones v Secretary of State for Social Services* [1972] 1 All ER 145, at p. 198 (per Lord Simon).
105 *Practice Statement (Judicial Precedent)* [1966] 3 All ER 77.
106 R. Card, R. Cross and Ph. A. Jones, *Criminal Law* (12th edn., 1992), p. 11.
107 *R v Shivpuri* [1987] 1 AC 1.
108 *R v Howe* [1987] 1 All ER 771.
109 *DPP v Lynch* [1975] 1 All ER 913.

foresee which principle will be put aside in order to give way to another, especially if the established rules are not clear enough.

Each legal system has its rules as to how conflicts of norms should be settled (or avoided). Besides, there are two doctrinal principles, which are universally recognised across contemporary legal systems. According to them, *lex posterior derogat priori* (more recent law takes priority over a prior one) and *lex specialis derogat generali* (specific law takes priority over a general one). But they may conflict as well, if a more recent law proves to be of a general nature. It is not settled in legal doctrine how such a collision is to be resolved. Although it is more frequently maintained that *lex posterior generalis non derogat legi priori (anteriori) speciali*, that is, a specific law should prevail in any event, this is not a unanimous view. Interestingly, Russian textbooks on legal theory as well as court decisions carefully evade this issue. The only exception is a 2004 decree of the Constitutional Court that gives priority to *lex specialis* as against *lex posterior*.[110] But this utterance was not a necessary step in Court's conclusions and therefore can be regarded as an *obiter dictum*. Therefore, the judicial practice remains unstable. When a more recent federal law provided a lighter fine for the violation of a tax norm than had been envisaged by an earlier law of a more specific nature,[111] the arbitrazh courts split: some opted for the latest norm, whereas others preferred the specific one.

The problem is aggravated by an uncertain position of codes within the Russian system of legislation. They usually contain provisions which make them superior with respect to other laws belonging to respective branches of law. For instance, Civil Code says that 'norms of civil law contained in other laws must conform to the present Code'.[112] Similar rules are found in a number of other codes, including Family, Land and Housing Codes. At the same time, all codes are federal laws. So a federal law containing rules on land should correspond to the Land Code, which, in its turn, should conform to the Civil Code. But the perplexity about it is that the Constitution makes no difference between federal laws, and the Constitutional Court, too, emphatically qualifies them as acts of equal force.[113] This, in fact, annihilates the value of the rules concerning the superiority of codes. In these circumstances, lawyers and courts can and, in practice, do solve the priority issue differently.

110 Decree of the Constitutional Court of 29 June 2004, No. 13-П, on the verification of constitutionality of certain provisions of Arts 7, 15, 107, 243 and 450 of the Criminal Procedure Code of the Russian Federation, *HCC*, no. 4 (2004), p. 95.

111 Article 17(3), Federal Law of 1 April 1996, No. 27-ФЗ, 'On the Individual Personified Account' (in the version of 25 October 2001) against Art 27(3), Federal Law of 15 December 2001, No. 167-ФЗ, 'On Obligatory Retirement Insurance'.

112 *CCRF*, p. 2. The consequences of this provision will be considered in Chapter 6.

113 Ruling of the Constitutional Court of 5 November 1999, No. 182-O, *HCC*, no. 2 (2000), pp. 22–23. See, however, a decree of the Federal Arbitrazh Court for the Northwestern Circuit of 20 November 2000 (unpublished), in which the court refused to apply the rules of the Federal Law 'On Joint-Stock Societies' as being contradictory to the Civil Code, despite their being both *lex posterior* and *lex specialis*.

Gaps or uncertainty in a common law rule or a statutory scheme may force a court to choose between different authorities in order to come to a justifiable solution. It can be a choice between contradicting authorities or between competing lines of precedents. English senior judges do recognise that in some cases they were faced by a real dilemma and had to choose between several legitimate decisions.[114] For instance, in the case of Sudanese hijackers, in which the elusive concept of 'duress' was interpreted, the Court of Appeal had to choose between two incompatible lines of precedents that had equal authority. In the end, the narrow construction of duress was rejected by the Court for being at variance with common sense and morality.[115] Thus, lacking any guide as to how such a conflict of primary rules should be resolved, judges had nothing to do but look for a decision which they thought to be most reasonable.

Ameliorating the law

In court practice, the exercise of moral judgment may take place even if there is neither gap nor conflict between rules or interpretations of equal force. It happens when moral or/and policy implications of a case induce judges to place on it an interpretation which is difficult to justify by recourse to ordinary meaning of the words or parliamentary intention. Nevertheless, it may be preferred by a court deeply concerned with these implications.

This point can be illustrated by a number of cases turning on the meaning of the word 'appropriation' in the Theft Act, 1968 (see p. 38 above). This meaning contrasted with that in the Larceny Act 1916 which required that the property alleged to have been stolen be taken 'without the consent of the owner'. In a number of cases the question arose whether the omission of the words 'without the consent of the owner' in the 1968 Act was deliberate or the statute should be construed as if they were read into it after the word 'appropriates'. Accordingly, two basic schools of thought have emerged. The first contended that the word 'appropriation' has a negative connotation (something inconsistent with the owner's rights, hostile to the interests of the owner or contrary to his wishes or intention or without his authority). The second school tried to prove that the term is a neutral one and does not presuppose any adverse interference with the rights of the owner.

The first case where the matter was examined was *Lawrence v Metropolitan Police Commissioner*.[116] A taxi driver charged an Italian student for £7 though the lawful fare was only 10s6d. He was convicted of theft and appealed on the ground that the money was taken with the consent of the owner.

---

114 A. Paterson, *The Law Lords* (1982), p. 194.

115 *R v Abdul-Hussein; R v Aboud; R v Hasan; R v Nagi; R v Muhssin; R v Hosham* [1999] Crim LR 570.

116 *Lawrence v Metropolitan Police Commissioner* [1972] AC 626.

In the speech of Viscount Dilhorne in the House of Lords, with which other members of the House agreed, it was stated that:

> Belief or the absence of belief that the owner had...consented to the appropriation is relevant to the issue of dishonesty, not to the question whether or not this has been an appropriation. That may occur even though the owner has permitted or consented to the property being taken.[117]

So, the decision in *Lawrence* belonged to the second school of thought.

Twelve years later the House of Lords considered a case (*R v Morris*) where the defendant had taken goods from the shelves in the supermarket, changed labels on them and paid a lesser price at the checkout.[118] In the opinion of Lord Roskill, 'the concept of appropriation...involves not an act expressly or impliedly authorised by the owner but an act by way of adverse interference with or usurpation of those rights'.[119] Lord Roskill's pronouncements belong to the first school. But they might be considered as *obiter*, since in that case the switching of the price labels was unauthorised by the supermarket and it was not necessary for the decision to find out whether an unauthorised act could amount to appropriation.

The next important case was *DPP v Gomez*[120] in which the House had eventually to make a choice between the conflicting views on the meaning of 'appropriation'. The defendant was an assistant manager of a shop. He persuaded the shop manager to agree to sell goods to his accomplice and to accept payment by cheques. But the cheques, as the defendant knew quite well, were, in fact, stolen and had no value. In the Crown Court the defendant was convicted of theft, but the Court of Appeal quashed the conviction. The Court, noting the difficulty of reconciling *Lawrence* and *Morris*, preferred to follow the latter. However, it certified a question for the House of Lords whether the appropriation could take place if the owner consented to the taking of the property, or whether an element of adverse interference with or usurpation of some rights of the owner is needed.

The unanimous view of the House of Lords was that the decisions in *Lawrence* and *Morris* could not be reconciled. But the House divided strongly on the question which of the two decisions should be followed in the case at hand. Two approaches were set out during the debates. The most elaborate analysis of the matter was given by Lord Lowry in his dissent. He carefully explored both intrinsic and extrinsic materials in order to prove that the decision in *Morris* was correct in law and should be followed in the instant case.[121]

---

117   Ibid., at p. 632.
118   *R v Morris* [1984] AC 320.
119   Ibid., at p. 332.
120   *Director of Public Prosecutions v Gomez* [1993] AC 442.
121   Ibid., at p. 475. *Gomez* was considered only a week after the decision in *Pepper v Hart* had authorised recourse to parliamentary materials.

In complete contrast to it the majority of the House of Lords confined themselves to the exploration of the previous precedents. In the opinion of Lord Keith:

> The decision in *Lawrence* was a clear decision of this House upon the construction of the word 'appropriate' in section 1 (1) of the Act, which had stood for 12 years when doubt was thrown upon it by *obiter dicta* in *Morris*. *Lawrence* must be regarded as authoritative and correct, and there is no question of it now being right to depart from it.[122]

This view prevailed in the House of Lords in *Gomez* and was later followed in *Hinks*, where it was decided, by a majority 3:2, that 'appropriation' was a neutral word comprising any assumption by a person of the rights of an owner, even though there was an acceptance of indefeasible gifts of property.[123]

Summing up the hard story of hard cases relating to the meaning of 'appropriation', it should be remarked that irreconcilable statements in *Lawrence* and *Morris* made by the House of Lords in different cases will 'carry equal weight in terms of precedent and either statement may be followed'.[124] There was no gap in the law. It appears to be a classic conflict of interpretations contained in different precedents. Since their legal status was equal (or, perhaps, equally imprecise) the choice between them in subsequent cases had to be made on policy arguments. As Lord Steyn stated in *Hinks*, the narrow definition of 'appropriation' as expressed in *Morris* should be rejected because it placed 'beyond the reach of the criminal law dishonest persons who *should* be found guilty of theft' [emphasis added].[125] Was it the right method of solving hard cases of this kind? Should moral sentiments such as the desire not to let a dishonest person to avoid punishment influence the outcome of a case? It appears to me that the appropriate course for a judge is to take into account *all* possible consequences of his decision. In cases examined above the price to pay for the morally satisfactory result was a conflict with the civil law. As Professor Smith remarked in relation to the decision in *Hinks*, 'a line must be drawn where a conviction of theft would cause a conflict with the civil law – in this case the law of gift'.[126]

Certainly judges are human beings who tend to evaluate not only formal aspects, but also the justice of the case. In doing so, they may ignore (more or less subconsciously) some important but more latent, indirect, or long-term effects of their decisions. Even if a judge is aware of them, it can be difficult for him to pass the decision which is morally unattractive and unjustifiable in

---

122 *Director of Public Prosecutions v Gomez* [1993] AC 442, at p. 464.
123 *R v Hinks* [2000] 3 WLR, at p. 843.
124 Manchester, Salter and Moodie, *Exploring the Law*, p. 434.
125 *R v Hinks* [2000] 3 WLR, at p. 843.
126 The All England Law Reports: Annual Review: 2000 (2001), p. 160.

the eyes of general public. It should not be forgotten, however, that contrary decisions might cause further difficulties and increase the number of hard cases to be faced in the future.

If courts of last resort give up in the face of moral and political difficulties of a case, they do make a new law by wrongly deciding the case which on a purely legal account ought to be taken as an easy one. Such are *contra legem* decisions. To be sure, judges almost never acknowledge that a particular decision has been rendered in defiance of the law. And yet such judgments do occur from time to time.

In recent years, the most striking example of an erroneous interpretation which affected the rights and duties of a large number of people has been the Ruling of the Supreme Court Presidium of 14 July 2004 concerning the taxation of land. Article 8 of the Law 'On the Payment for Land' provided that in rural areas land plots occupied with 'housing fund' should be taxed on a concessionary basis, namely, the rate of tax should be 3 per cent of the normal rate for land plots in urban areas. So the crucial condition for the exemption of a land plot from the full-fledged taxation was the presence of a building which might be encompassed by the concept of 'housing fund'.

The problem arose and came to the attention of courts in 2001 when a citizen Zhukov living near S.-Petersburg received a letter from tax agencies which prescribed him to pay the full tax (that is, 100 per cent) from his land plot on which he had a house under construction. Before 2001 tax agencies collected payments for land according to the reduced rate, but then their policy had changed. They argued that a construction in progress was not yet a part of 'housing fund' for the purposes of taxation. Indeed, there was no definition of housing fund in the Tax Code, but it could be derived from the Housing Code, which defined it as 'dwelling houses situated on the territory of the Russian Federation and also dwelling premises in other buildings' (Art 4). So the question was whether it was permissible to apply this definition to the case at hand given that it was borrowed from another branch of law.

The positive answer to the question seemed unavoidable: Art 11 of the Tax Code says that 'institutes, concepts, and terms of civil, family, and other branches of the legislation of the Russian Federation used in the present Code shall be applied with that meaning in which they are used in these branches of legislation unless provided otherwise by the present Code'.[127] The Tax Code did not provide anything, so the application of the Housing Code definition in such circumstances was unobjectionable. And the first three court decisions upon the suit of Mr Zhukov were in line with that view. His suit and a procurator's protest in his support were dismissed. But the Civil Division of the Supreme Court took, quite unexpectedly, a contrary view. It allowed the protest and reversed the decision of lower courts on the grounds that by virtue of Art 1 of the Tax Code the legislation on taxes and charges 'shall consist of the present

127 Translated in W. E. Butler, *The Tax Code of the Russian Federation* (1999), p. 11.

Code and of federal laws on taxes and charges adopted in accordance with it'.[128] Besides, by virtue of Art 7 (point 3) of the same Code 'all ineradicable doubts, contradictions and ambiguities of the legislation on taxes and charges shall be interpreted in favour of the taxpayer'.[129]

This ruling was clearly wrong, for such a broad interpretation of Art 1 makes Art 11 pointless, so long as the latter expressly permits the application of legal concepts borrowed from other branches of law. What Art 1 actually aimed to prohibit was not the recourse to other laws in search of missing definitions, but the establishing of taxes and charges unprovided by the Tax Code and lesser laws. And there were no ambiguities in that case which might warrant the reference to Art 7.

Concurrently with bringing the case before courts of general jurisdiction Mr Zhukov lodged a complaint to the Constitutional Court which did not fail to articulate its view. Regrettably, the Court's intervention led to unhappy consequences. On the one hand, the Court held that the interpretation and clarification of legal concepts used in the Tax Code was not a job for the Court.[130] On the other hand, it mentioned, almost in passing, the ruling of the Civil Division as being the one which 'has removed the uncertainty in understanding of the contested norm and restored the violated rights of the citizen A. A. Zhukov'.[131] This appendage was at odds with what the Court had said before: it was absolutely unnecessary for the Court, when dismissing the case, in which no constitutional issue had been found, to express any view on the substance of interpretation made by the Civil Division. But the Court did so and thus, intentionally or not, has thrown its weight to Mr Zhukov's cause.

The next player to come into the game was the Presidium of the Supreme Court. At first it felt unbound by the pronouncement of the Constitutional Court, perhaps finding it improper. In December 2003 it endorsed a survey of judicial practice where the negative answer was given to the question whether the reduced rate of payment could be extended to the land with housing construction in progress. In that way the Presidium affirmed that the applicable definition of the 'housing fund' is provided by the Housing Code and recourse to it when settling tax disputes by no means implied that the Housing Code was thereby included into legislation on taxes and charges.[132]

In the end, it is not clear whether the Presidium had known about the holdings of the Civil Division and the Constitutional Court, although an omission of this kind seems unlikely. The review was published in 'The Bulletin of the Supreme

---

128 Translated in W. E. Butler, *The Tax Code of the Russian Federation* (1999), p. 1.
129 Ibid., p. 4. Ruling of the Civil Division of the Supreme Court of 13 February 2003, No. 78-Впр03-3 (unpublished).
130 Ruling of the Constitutional Court of 5 June 2003, No. 276-O, *HCC*, no. 6 (2003), pp. 63–66.
131 Ibid., p. 65.
132 Survey of judicial practice of the Supreme Court of the Russian Federation for the 3rd quarter of the year 2003 (civil cases), *BSC*, no. 3 (2004), p. 29.

Court' in March 2004, and it is no wonder that the Ministry of Taxes was not slow to take an advantage of such an auspicious development. It immediately applied to the Presidium and on 19 May 2004 the latter reversed the ruling of the Civil Division.[133] This might (and ought to) be a conclusive judgment on the case, for there were no prior case in which the Presidium would have reversed its own decision. But this dispute was a special one, and therefore the triumph of tax agencies proved to be premature. Not later than two months thereupon it had to reexamine the issue, for the Deputy Procurator General submitted that the ruling should be reversed in the light of 'newly discovered circumstances' (Art 392 of the Civil Procedure Code). The Presidium followed this unprecedented invitation. It acknowledged that 'in the given case...there has been made a mistake in the application of norms of substantive law, because the concept of "housing fund" is used not in the Tax Code...but in the special Law of the Russian Federation 'On the Payment for Land' (Art 8(5) of the Law). Therefore, the use...of the concept of 'housing fund' in the meaning, in which it is given in Art 4 of the Housing Code...is mistaken'. The rate of taxation should depend on the ultimate use of the land and has nothing to do with the terms of completion of a building and its registration as a housing fund.[134]

This ruling is striking in a number of ways. First, Art 8 of the Law 'On the Payment for Land' contained no definition of 'housing fund' and that is why this definition ought to be found elsewhere. Second, it is very surprising that this change of view was presented as a 'newly discovered' circumstance. There was nothing to discover, for Art 8 was before the eyes of the judges all along. And, third, there was no kind of 'newly discovered' circumstance in Art 392 of the Civil Code which might justify the reversal. There are only four kinds of such circumstances: those essential for the case which were not and could not have been known to the applicant (point 1); knowingly false evidence of a witness or conclusion of an expert, etc (point 2); crimes committed by a party or their representatives or judges in the process of settling the dispute (point 3); the abrogation of an official decision on which the judgment of the court has been based (point 4). None of these grounds had whatever relation to the case at hand. Their list is exhaustive, and it is revealing that the Presidium failed to choose any of them. Instead, it simply referred to Art 392 as a whole!

One may only wonder why judges were so determinate to bend the law to the detriment of the reputation of the court. Of course, their final judgment has satisfied those many citizens who possessed land plots with buildings in progress upon them. Otherwise they would have to pay an incomparably larger amount of tax. Many lawyers were amazed by this judgment; but laymen might

---

133 Ruling of the Presidium of the Supreme Court of 19 May 2004, No. 5пв-04 (unpublished).
134 Ruling of the Presidium of the Supreme Court of 14 July 2004, No. 15пв04пр, *BSC*, no. 12 (2004), pp. 6–7. Seven of nine judges who had rendered the previous judgment were present in the new hearing.

well be happy with it. There is little doubt that members of the Presidium were conscious that their previous decision was right in law. But, if put somewhat cynically, their reply to critics might be this: 'What is right in law is not always the right law, and that is why we have changed our mind as well as the law.' In so doing they boldly produced a piece of judicial legislation which is both outstanding and extremely dubious.

Chapter 2

The scope and limits of judicial law-making

The previous chapter addressed the issue when the application of law by courts grows into judicial creativity and why. But there should be another, external limit – this time with the domain of the legislator. To put it another way, now the question is where does judicial law-making end? What does the area of judicial creativity consist of and what basic factors make courts more or less creative? What are the instruments in the hands of courts?

It seems clear that the conception of the omnipotent legislator is not easy to reconcile with judicial creativity. At a minimum, it makes judges to conceal their contribution to law. That was the case with respect to the pre-revolutionary Russian Senate (which was in fact quite active law-maker),[1] not to speak of the Soviet judiciary. By contrast, American judges seem to be bolder. This is usually accounted for by the special nature of the US Constitution, which restricts the legislature and thereby permits judicial activism.

The prevalence of declaratory theory in legal thinking may also make judges more cautious. Under this theory judges should discover and declare the law but not make it. In its extreme form, this theory tends to completely deny that legal rules can be created. Even legislators are not genuine law-givers; what they actually promulgate is just an expression of *Volksgeist* or natural reason, the rules of which they can declare but not invent. There is a valuable point underlying such conceptions, for they stress a non-arbitrary element in law-creation. In the light of this theory, law-making (that is, deliberate law-creation) seems *per se* undesirable, even if possible. But this impression that the declaratory approach negates judicial law-making is illusory, for the theory is ambivalent: to a certain extent, it tends to smoothen the difference between legislative and judicial powers. It is not accidental that some theories of this kind lead to the conclusion that the praetorian power of judges should play a crucial role in shaping the legal system.

---

1 Wagner wrote that the Ruling Senate possessed 'a power of judicial law-making that was unique both in tsarist Russia and among continental European civilian legal systems' (Wagner, *Marriage, Property and Law in Late Imperial Russia*, p. 41).

Paradoxically, the declaratory theory may be supportive of the phenomenon (if not the very idea) of judge-made law.

The theory itself is by no means uniform. Rather, it is a general approach or a cluster of theories suggesting that the decisions in so-called 'hard cases' (and, particularly, in 'cases of first impression') are to be dictated by some pre-existing norms. The attractiveness of the declaratory approach is largely explained by the way it disposes of the problem of gaps and disappointed expectations. If the law applied in a 'hard case' had existed prior to the facts of the case, then, the argument goes, the decision meets the criteria of legality. This, *inter alia*, is Dworkin's point.[2] But this argument seems to underrate the important question of the *form* in which the rule exists. If it exists in a latent form (as a custom or merely a vague idea of what just conduct in particular circumstances should be), it is not sufficient to guide effectively peoples' behaviour. Otherwise it would be unnecessary for judges and legislators to make precedents and statutes. In practical terms the solution is also unsatisfactory, for there is little chance of convincing a party who lost a trial to accept this reasoning.

Gaps in the law

The denial of the existence of gaps is another weakness of the declaratory approach. The discovery of a gap in legal regulation is widely regarded as the most appropriate occasion for judges to act creatively (or 'to legislate interstitially'). Thus, gap-filling constitutes the first component of the area of judicial law-creation. According to Raz, gaps exist in so-called 'unregulated disputes'. The latter, like regulated disputes, are subject to laws applying to them and guiding the courts as to their solution. But since the law applying to them has gaps, no particular solution to the dispute is required by law though the law may rule out several solutions as inappropriate and give some general guidance concerning the choice.[3]

Many legal theorists concede that the discovery of a gap does not mean that judges should stop at this point and wait for parliamentary intervention.[4] However, it has been observed that the trouble with gaps is 'that a "gap" in this sense is almost inevitably a gap only given some value orientation. Mere silence of the law can be handled by appeal to the maxim that whatever is not prohibited is permitted. To go beyond that requires a view on how the law ought to be; the gap is a gap by virtue of there being no law where law (in a certain tenor) ought to be'.[5] So not only the authority of courts with respect to the legislature is

---

2 Dworkin, *Law's Empire*, p. 356.
3 Raz, *The Authority of Law*, p. 183.
4 R. S. Summers, 'Precedent in the United States (New York State)', in D. N. MacCormick and R. S. Summers (eds.), *Interpreting Precedents: A Comparative Study* (1997), p. 367.
5 Z. Bankowski, N. MacCormick and G. Marshall, 'Precedent in the United Kingdom', in *Interpreting Precedents*, p. 333.

problematic, but also the limits of law itself. In 'cases of first impression', how can judges be sure that the case in question is posited within the law, if there is no rule directly applicable to it?

This question can be answered only with due regard to the fact that law is systemic by nature. Certain norms may operate only in combination with others. It is true with respect to all branches of law, but particularly obvious in the context of public law which consists of what may be called 'the rules of organisation'.[6] For instance, public institutions such as courts may not properly perform their functions prescribed by law in the event of there being a deficit of norms delimiting their competence, duties and the relations with contiguous institutions. Some supplementary norms are required, even though they are not explicitly provided for by statutes or precedents. Only if we think (and as long as we think) that there is a need for a new law can we speak about the gap in the legal system.

It should be noted that the emergence of gaps is not necessarily the result of the new enactments. Sometimes gaps may emerge even if the law remains unchanged. Moreover, it is exactly the lack of change that makes gaps inevitable. Sooner or later, some new situations come into light, which have not been foreseen by the standing law. It is impossible to determine the number of gaps or even to find them until a particular new situation makes them evident.

Some civil law systems have been susceptible to the idea of judicial law-making during recent decades. This is the case in Germany, where the Federal Constitutional Court has, in principle, allowed judge-made law which contradicts the wording of statutes.[7] However, it is still quite common for judges to deny that they fill in the gaps. They argue that what they actually do is just an extension of pre-existing rules to new situations. Theoretically, the difference between an extension and gap-filling seems clear: 'In any instance of (extensive) interpretation it is presupposed that the case to be decided is contemplated by a rule. In any instance of gap-filling it is presupposed that the case to be decided is not contemplated by any rule'.[8]

French judges habitually distinguish between the 'precedent of solution' and the 'precedent of interpretation'. The latter is allowed because it presents not a rule for the solution of future cases, but the best interpretation of an existing rule; the former is not permissible because it amounts to usurpation of the legislative function.[9] In practice, however, the difference between these two concepts is

---

6 Hayek, *Law, Legislation and Liberty*, Vol. 1 (1973), pp. 132–133.

7 R. Alexy and R. Dreier, 'Statutory Interpretation in the Federal Republic of Germany', in D. N. MacCormick and R. S. Summers (eds.), *Interpreting Statutes: A Comparative Study* (1991), pp. 80–81; MacCormick and Summers, 'Precedent in the Federal Republic of Germany', in *Interpreting Precedents*, pp. 25–26.

8 M. La Torre, E. Pattaro and M. Taruffo, 'Statutory Interpretation in Italy', in *Interpreting Precedents*, p. 218.

9 M. Troper, C. Grzegorczyk and J.-L. Gardies, 'Statutory Interpretation in France', in *Interpreting Statutes*, pp. 176–177; see also there M. Troper and C. Grzegorczyk, 'Precedent in France', p. 126.

not clear-cut. Gap-filling can be represented as a case of extensive interpretation, and vice versa. There can be disagreement as to whether the situation was contemplated by the legislator or not, as was actually the case in *R v R (Marital Exemption)*. In the United Kingdom only the 'interpretative' gap-filling is acceptable, but not the 'substantive' one. It means that an interpretation of a statutory text, even though a somewhat strained one, is treated as legitimately preferable because by it a gap is avoided. But 'the difference between interpretative and substantive gap-filling is itself a matter of interpretative controversy'.[10]

All these points can be exemplified and elucidated by the hypothetical Hartian rule – 'No vehicles in the park'.[11] What should pass for 'vehicles' in this context? Besides, what does 'in' mean here? Assume that the rule was passed long ago, before the invention of aircraft. At the time of the enactment the meaning of the word 'vehicles' was clearer than it became upon the invention of the new means of conveyance, which increased indeterminacy and possibly created a gap. The question for a judge is whether airplanes fall within the ambit of the rule or not. If yes, he should prohibit them from using airspace over the park. If no, is it actually a gap and would it be correct and reasonable of him to fill it?

The judge may argue that there is no gap. Although the legislator has not foreseen the invention of aircraft, he could well anticipate that new means of transportation would be invented. If so, the notion of a 'vehicle' is open and extends to 'all the existing kinds of vehicles and all those that may appear in the future'. Nevertheless, the judge has to explore the concept of 'vehicle' in the sense used by the legislator and determine how far it may reach. The judge should decide which 'objective' features are essential for this class of things and whether an airplane has them. These questions are by no means easy. For instance, should the notion be extended only to mechanisms that move by land or may it cover others as well?

Alternatively, the judge may avoid all these doubts by concluding that 'vehicle' is a collective notion which is closed and includes only those things that were known as vehicles at the time of the enactment. The immediate purpose of the legislator was to protect people walking in the park from noise and disturbances made specifically by vehicles *known at that time*. So, the prohibition on 'vehicle' has no bearing upon airplanes, and therefore there is no gap, since what is not prohibited is permitted.

But there are more options open to the judge. Suppose the legislator did not think about the new kinds of vehicles, but his purpose was more general, that is, to make people in the park free from any disturbances. If so, the meaning of the word 'vehicle' in the context of the rule can be extended by analogy to cover

---

10 Z. Bankowski and D. N. MacCormick, 'Statutory Interpretation in the United Kingdom', in *Interpreting Statutes*, p. 362.
11 Hart, *The Concept of Law* (2nd edn., 1994), p. 124.

new inventions. Alternatively, the dispute can be deemed to be unregulated and decided in the light of countervailing considerations of economic profits and damages, on the one hand, and public health, on the other. Or the judge may leave to the legislator to consider all these implications, thereby inviting him to legislate. But the judge should justify the need for a new law in one way or another.

Hart's idea is that legal rules usually consist of a solid and unchangeable core and an amorphous sphere around it, which he called 'the open texture'. There is no doubt that a car is a vehicle (so that this case is within the 'core'), but it can be called into question with respect to airplanes, bicycles, baby carriages and so on. The rule can be broadened or narrowed depending on the principle or approach chosen by the judge. His choice is not predetermined, because principles and values have no absolute weight, only a relative one. As such their mutual merits can be a matter of disagreement, because the hierarchies of values and principles differ among people, including judges. And there seems to be no easy way to distinguish interpretative and gap-filling arguments in every instance, because a value orientation is a necessary precondition of doing it.

Gap-filling and interpretation in hard cases are forms of law-creation and therefore involve judicial discretion. The distinction between judicial law-making and discretion is somewhat blurred. Some scholars distinguish them by saying that discretion is exercised only with respect to the outcome of concrete disputes and does not affect the content of the legal norm applied.[12] Others treat discretion more broadly. In the opinion of Barak, the object of discretion may be the lawful determination of the limits of a norm as well as the application of the norm to a certain set of facts. The first activity is of a general nature and constitutes law-making by virtue of the principle of binding precedent.[13] I believe both definitions of discretion are not mutually exclusive, for either of them can be preferable within a certain context.

It is asserted by some scholars that if there is a rule prescribing how gaps should be filled, there are no lacunae at all. For example, according to Hans Kelsen:

> Even if positive law empowers judges to decide cases according to justice, the judicial decision is an application of valid positive law, because it is empowered by the law; and the postulate of legal positivism, that each concrete case is to be decided on the basis – i.e. by applying – valid positive law, is maintained.[14]

12 A. D. Abushenko, Судебное усмотрение в гражданском и арбитражном процессе [Judicial Discretion in Civil and Arbitrazh Procedure] (2002), p. 104.

13 A. Barak, Судейское усмотрение [Judge's Discretion] (1999), pp. 113–114, 124–125.

14 H. Kelsen, *The General Theory of Norms* (1990), p. 114.

What is applied in such cases, though, is not a primary (or substantive) rule, which is still to be created, but a secondary (or operational) rule.[15] This rule may not positively determine the specific content of primary rules (although it may rule out some alternatives as being incorrect in law), but simply empowers judges to create them when necessary. For example, Swiss law requires the judge in the absence of any rule to create a new one, as though he were the legislator. Similar provisions are found in the codes of Austria, Mexico, Italy and other countries. In so doing the judge has to exercise his discretion. Every lacuna is a challenge to the legal system, which has no ready response to it. It has to be worked out, not merely picked from a list of legal rules already in existence. On the other hand, as Raz rightly noted, 'there are no pure law-creating cases. In every case in which the court makes law it also applies laws restricting and guiding its law-creating activities'.[16] Hence a strict delimitation between law-making and law-application is, whether one likes it or not, unattainable in every case.

Legal analogy

Analogy is the basic tool which judges are expected to employ when filling gaps. To reason by analogy means to apply a similar rule to a similar set of facts. But how can the similarity be proved? In the opinion of Raz, 'argument by analogy is essentially an argument to the effect that if a certain reason is good enough to justify one rule then it is equally good to justify another which similarly follows from it'. The analogy shows that 'the new rule is a conservative one, that it does not introduce new discordant and conflicting purposes or value into the law, that its purpose and the values it promotes are already served by existing rules'.[17] So the basis of analogical reasoning ultimately consists of judgments about purposes and values, which always have an element of subjectivity at the bottom. Despite the use of analogy being considered by some lawyers as a substitute for judicial creativity rather than a law-making instrument, it does not appear to be a strict procedure bound by formal and determinative rules. More than a century ago Muromtsev observed that legal analogy does not coincide with analogy in the strict logical sense of the word, because a genuine analogy draws conclusions from similar to similar, whereas a legal analogy is confined within less strict borders. He also stressed that 'any conclusion as to what the legislator ought to have said, but failed to say for whatever reason... is of fictitious nature. A judge does not discover a hidden thought of the legislator. It is more

---

15   The terminology used was invented by H. L. A. Hart (*The Concept of Law*, 2nd edn., p. 81) and
     L. L. Jaffe (*English and American Judges as Law-Makers* (1969), p. 36).
16   Raz, *The Authority of Law*, p. 195.
17   Ibid., p. 204.

accurate to say that he finishes thinking for him what the legislator himself did not think of'.[18]

In Russia the use of legal analogy is licensed by civil and arbitrazh procedural legislation.[19] Russian judges have recourse to analogy of *lex* frequently. However, the use of *analogia juris* is rarer. On occasion, it is employed by courts as a way to back the conclusion already made by way of analogy of *lex*. In doing so, they additionally refer to the 'general principles and sense' of the appropriate legislation.

Consider one case in which the Supreme Court made use of both *analogia legis* and *analogia juris* to make up a deficiency of legal regulation.[20] Several plaintiffs contested the legality of a decree of the Federal Government. However, the Federal Law 'On the Government of the Russian Federation' (as of 8 January 1998) when principally providing for the possibility of such suits failed to indicate which court should consider such a claim. The position of the Supreme Court was for some time uncertain: it assumed jurisdiction over such claims in some cases[21] and declined it in others. For instance, by ruling of a judge of the Supreme Court, later affirmed by ruling of the Cassation Division of the Court, a case was sent for consideration in the court of first instance on the grounds that only non-normative acts of the Government had been assigned to the Supreme Court by the Civil Procedure Code (Art 116). It should be remarked that the first ruling in the case was rendered on 26 January 1999, and the second, on 3 June 1999, that is, more than one year after the passing of the Law on the Government. Since no previous case in which the Supreme Court had pronounced its opinion on the matter of competence was known, this dispute was doomed to become a leading precedent, for it would be utterly strange if the results of analogous suits in the future would be different. On 7 February 2001 these rulings were reversed by a decree of the Presidium of the Supreme Court. The last found it illogical that a normative act of the Federal Government having a higher status than other acts directly assigned to the competence of the Supreme Court should be considered by a lower instance. In coming to this conclusion, the Presidium used a number of arguments. First, it referred to Art 10(2) of the Civil Procedure Code, which

---

18 S. A. Muromtsev Суд п закон в гражданском праве [The Court and the Law [*Lex*] in Civil Law], *Юридический вестник* [Legal Herald], no. 11 (1880), p. 386. There are more recent opinions among legal scholars backing this line of reasoning (A. Peczenic, 'The Binding Force of Precedents', in D. N. MacCormick and R. S. Summers (eds.), *Interpreting Precedents*, p. 474).

19 Article 10(3), 1964 RSFSR Civil Procedure Code and Art 11(3) of the successive 2002 Code, Arts 12(3) and 13(6) of the 1995 and 2002 Arbitrazh Procedure codes, respectively.

20 Decree of the Presidium of the Supreme Court of 7 February 2001, No. 268пв-2000пр, in the *case TOO 'Energo' and others v The Government of the RF* (unpublished).

21 Decision of the Supreme Court of 2 September 1998, No. ГКПИ 98–412, in the case *The Federation of Independent Trade Unions of Russia and others v the Government of the RF* (unpublished).

permits judges to apply *analogia legis* and *analogia juris*. In the case at hand, the Presidium applied both. In the first place, it pointed out that the law on military courts (in force as of 29 June 1999, Art 9[3]) had provided for contesting normative acts of the government by military personnel in the Military Division of the Supreme Court. This allowed the Presidium to invoke *analogia legis* to substantiate the Supreme Court's jurisdiction in the disputable case. Besides, it also referred to the general *sense and purpose* of the relevant legislation (analogy of *ius*) as well as to the effective protection of rights and freedoms of citizens (Arts 2, 17, 18, 46, Constitution) which is the primary constitutional purpose of justice.

What is remarkable about the reasoning of the court is that its arguments were mutually supportive, each line of argumentation being sufficient to substantiate the solution the Presidium favoured, and yet the decision it rendered was neither unobjectionable nor inescapable. Had the dispute arisen prior to the adoption of the Law of 29 June 1999, the decision had to be justified solely by analogy of *ius*. In the real circumstances, however, it merely provided further support for the conclusion of the Presidium, which was based in the first place on analogy of *lex*. The rationale of invoking the constitutional provisions was the same. Apparently, the Presidium was not absolutely sure of the incontestability of the conclusion; otherwise it would confine itself to a single irrefutable argument instead of invoking several weighty ones. Indeed, there could be objections or alternative decisions, which the outcome of the case in lower instances clearly shows. To begin with, all of the cases tried by the Supreme Court or middle-level courts as trial courts (as a 'court of first instance', in Russian legal usage) were explicitly mentioned by the Civil Procedure Code, so that its competence should be viewed as closed or exhaustive (Arts 114–116). By contrast, the competence of lower courts (of first instance) was described differently: 'Civil cases within the competence of courts, shall be considered by district (city) courts' (Art 113). This means that normally *all* cases should be considered by courts below, except for those explicitly mentioned by law. This reasoning seems particularly forceful in the light of the fact that lower instances, including the Cassation Division, could not yet be guided at the time of consideration by the law on military courts that the Presidium later applied by way of *analogia legis* (cf. the dates of the rulings and the law above).[22] This possibility was simply beyond their reach. However, the Presidium was not reluctant to avail itself of it, although the pure analogy of *lex* in the instant case could not *per se* warrant the conclusion desired and therefore has been coupled with analogy of *jus*.

---

22 Oddly enough, the Presidium reproached the lower courts for their failure to give due regard to the Law on Military Courts. But the ruling of the Cassation Division was made at the time when it was merely a draft.

All the same, perhaps the majority of lawyers would agree that the solution given by the Presidium was preferable from the standpoint of institutional design. What is important in the present context, however, is that there were indeed two solutions to the problem, and the alternative one was legally defensible as well. But even if not, if only one solution was correct, the use of legal analogy was creative nonetheless. There is no reason to presume the existence of any specific legislative intent concerning the jurisdiction of different tiers of the judiciary. It seems more probable that legislators simply missed the problem. Or they could have been of different opinions on the solution implied, but the difference was not articulated for whatever reason, which left the imperfect provision as it is. In any event, there was a gap or, to be more accurate, a deficiency of legal regulation. It was up to the judiciary to produce a complementary rule and thereby add a new bit to the incomplete picture of legal regulation. The judges were bound by the requirement of consistency: such new fragment ought to correspond to other parts already in place. There is little doubt that if the legislature's attention were drawn to this problem, they would instruct judges to solve it precisely the way they did, and the new Civil Procedure Code supports this conclusion (Art 27[1]). The fact remains, however, that there was no such instruction from legislators, so judges had to proceed on their own. Thus the final result was a consequence of the joint efforts of legislators and judges. In rectifying such a flaw by means of analogy, the Presidium was one step ahead of the legislator and did act creatively.

Legal analogy differs from broad interpretation in that the latter purports to bring statutory language in conformity with legislative intent, whereas analogy implies the lack of specific intent. It is up to the judge to accomplish the legislator's design. Even if analogy is explicitly allowed by statutes (as is the case in a number of Russian codes) it does not exclude or diminish its creative nature. The legislator has not predetermined the concrete outcome of the application of analogy. He says nothing as to *what* is the result to be achieved; he only predetermined *how* it should be done.

Hart tells us that there are certain universal rules prohibiting violence, theft and deceit. They constitute the so-called 'minimal content of natural law' (the violation of which should be regarded as *malum in se*).[23] The principle of compensation for damages appears to be universally recognised. Nonetheless, the scope of its application is uncertain and may be significantly extended by analogy. Such are the 'cases of first impression'.[24] In Roman law there was no general principle that every wrong should have a remedy. It was worked out much later by Grotius and Domah, the adepts of natural law theory.[25] But in

---

23 Evil in itself (Lat.). An innately immoral act, regardless of whether it is forbidden by law.
24 On their emergence see: 'A Case of First Impression: Priestley v Fowler', in A. W. B. Simpson, *Leading Cases in the Common Law* (1995), pp. 100–134.
25 K. Zweigert and H. Kotz, *Introduction to Comparative Law*, Vol. 2 (2nd rev. edn., 1992), p. 638.

Roman law one rarely finds any sweeping definitions or all-embracing principles. Javolenus wrote that 'every definition in the civil law is dangerous, for there is hardly one which cannot be subverted'.[26] For Roman jurists, the reasoning by way of examples derived from actual legal practice seemed to be more promising than general definitions. It became trivial to say that the development of common law was similar. As Lord Mansfield said, the common law 'does not consist of particular cases but of general principles, which are listed and expanded by those cases'.[27]

In Rome liability for damages caused to property of another was initially strictly conditioned upon physical actions of the delinquent, as *Lex Aquilia* (III century BC) had prescribed. However, later praetors extended liability by analogy (*actio utilis*) to cover cases of indirect causation of damages. Was it gap-filling reflective of their view of what the law should be, or an interpretation of the existing law? The edicts of praetors insisted on the declaratory nature of their powers (*nova interpretatio juris, praetor jus facere non potest*).[28] Many lawyers would say (and did say) that it was a fiction, a stream of novelties under the thin disguise of loyalty to tradition. In any event, the latent general rule, which underlay and justified both the original norm and its modified version, was essentially the same.

The very existence of legal analogy suggests that even in continental jurisdictions law is not confined to the plain wording of the statutes, but also encompasses a latent or invisible part consisting of rather abstract principles capable of being transformed into concrete norms through judicial decisions in 'hard cases'. These principles cannot be found in legislation, which provides only some clues as to their nature. Therefore, even in civil law countries the area of 'law' (*jus*) is larger than the body of statutory norms. *Analogia juris* enables one to appeal to these implicit principles directly, thereby skipping concrete statutory norms. The expression 'spirit of law' (or legislation) that denotes the basis of this kind of analogy has a strong metaphysical flavour. Is it possible to argue that these general principles and norms are contained in the articles of a statute? If so, why not appeal to them directly? Can they be deduced from legislative provisions in a strict logical way? The answer to these questions I believe should be negative.

Review of normative acts

One comparative study suggests that 'law-making by judicial organs can come about in three different ways: with the establishing of precedents, with declarations

---

26 'Omnis definitio in jure civil pericolosa est, parum est enim ut non subverti possit' (Digest of Justinian. 50. 17. 202). Modern jurists also emphasise this point. As it was noted by Brian Simpson, 'the purpose of the law can never be encapsulated in the rule. Neither life, nor language, permits it' (A. W. B. Simpson, *Leading Cases in the Common Law*, p. 97).

27 *King v Bembridge* (1783) 99 English Reports 679, at p. 681. Cf. W. S. Holdsworth, *Some Lessons from Our Legal History* (1928), p. 18.

28 New interpretation of law; praetor cannot make law (Lat.).

of the illegality or constitutionality of normative acts previously in force, and with the issuing of rules of court'.[29] Although this scheme does not fit the state of affairs in the Russian legal system quite accurately, it is perfectly correct in taking judicial review of legislation as a kind of law-making. Together with gap-filling, it constitutes the basis of judicial law-creation.

It is common for legal theorists to distinguish two types of judicial review of legislation: the concrete review and the abstract one. The concrete (or indirect) judicial review involves the assessment of the validity of a certain norm in the context of the settlement of a particular dispute in which that norm is subject to application. By contrast, in the process of the abstract review, the legislation is challenged directly and the matter of its legality and/or constitutionality constitutes the only essence of the dispute. In the latter case the decision of a court is valid for everyone (*erga omnes*), not only to the parties to the dispute. In Russia general and arbitrazh courts may exercise both kinds of judicial review, whereas the powers of constitutional (or charter) courts at the level of the Federation and its subjects are limited to the abstract review.

Since the activities of the Constitutional Court of the Russian Federation represent a kind of standard of the abstract judicial review within the Russian legal system, it seems plausible to take them as a starting point of our analysis. It should be remarked, however, that our conclusions can be applied to other appellate courts as well. As for the concrete judicial review, it is closely connected to the evolvement of precedents and thus is to be investigated in this context (see pp. 118–120 below).

In Russian legal theory there is an ongoing debate about the nature and significance of Constitutional Court functions. Nersesiants argues that provisions deemed to be unconstitutional are abrogated not by virtue of the Constitutional Court's decision, but only on the grounds of the respective provision of the Constitution which vested the power to review legislation in the Court. Therefore, Court's decisions cannot create norms.[30] This argument is not persuasive. The decrees of the President are also issued in furtherance of constitutional provisions (Art 90, Russian Constitution), but it has never been denied that they are a source of law. Nor was it suggested that the true law-maker in such a case would be the Constitution itself. Nersesiants's contention replicates the Kelsenian argument considered above.[31] Of course, constitutional clauses restrict legislators and judges by creating 'channels' within which they can operate. But if the Constitution authorises the legislature to legislate, it does not follow that the real law-maker is the Constitution, and not the legislative body.[32] When the legislator legislates in order to develop some constitutional norm, there is no trouble in describing it as 'law-making'. If the highest court of this jurisdiction, not the legislator, lays down

29 *Law in the Making: A Comparative Survey* (A. Pizzorusso (ed.), 1988), p. 55.
30 Судебная практика как источник права [Judicial Practice as a Source of Law] (2000), p. 112.
31 See p. 63 above.
32 Cf. Barak, Судейское усмотрение [Judge's Discretion], p. 46, footnote 98.

the same rules which are complied with by the courts below (as is normally the case) how can one deny its creativity? To think differently is tantamount to saying that everything produced by a poet is necessarily poetry, but if a prose writer does the same the result is necessarily prose.

Moreover, 'law' can be broadly conceived as the whole legal system. Accordingly, any State institution whose word is decisive in determining the composition of the system can be viewed as a law-maker. The Russian Constitutional Court does have such power. However, this is not the only sense in which the Court acts as a law-maker.

It is typical to maintain that the Constitutional Court 'is indeed acting as a "negative legislator" when it deems certain laws to lose legal force. But in no case does it create positive norms'.[33] Contrary to this common *cliché* (also originating from the works of Hans Kelsen), the Court can be viewed as a positive law-maker. When a court (constitutional or another) invalidates a norm, it may lead to its automatic replacement with another norm. The kind of the norm which emerges reflects the nature of the norm repealed. So one has here a sort of 'normative symmetry', in which norms of certain types correspond to each other, as shown in the Table 1 below.

As shall be seen from the table, the norms themselves can be reformulated (prohibitions can be turned into instructions, and so forth). But they correspond to each other and may automatically replace each other in case of invalidation. It can be proved by both hypothetical and real cases. Suppose, for instance, that some eccentric legislator has passed a prohibition on making wills, but this was later deemed unconstitutional by a court. There would be no conceivable reason to deny that wills would be permitted by virtue of the court judgment.

The real examples are numerous. Let us consider but one of the Russian Constitutional Court decisions chosen almost at random. In its decree of 17 February 1998 the Constitutional Court passed judgment on Art 31(2) of the

Table 1 Invalidated norms and their substitutes

Types of norms abrogated by a court	Norms emerging instead
Prohibition of action or instruction not to act	Permission to act or not to act
Prohibition of action or an instruction to act	Permission to act or not to act
Permission to act	Prohibition of action or instruction not to act
Permission not to act	Prohibition of in action or instruction to act

33 B. S. Ebzeev, L. V. Lazarev and N. V. Vitruk, Федеральный Конституционный закон 'О Конституционном Суде Российской Федерации': Комментарий [Federal Constitutional Law on the Constitutional Court of the Russian Federation: A Commentary] (1996), p. 246.

USSR Law 'On the Legal Status of Foreign Citizens in the USSR'.[34] The provision in question permitted the detention of foreign citizens and stateless persons for the term necessary for their deportation from the country. The norm was recognised as unconstitutional on the grounds of its incompatibility with the 'equal protection' clauses contained in Arts 22 and 46 of the RF Constitution. Thus the norm in question has been invalidated, but what has emerged instead? Actually, no gap was created by the decision of the Court. What has appeared in the place of this permissive norm is a prohibition against detaining foreign citizens and stateless persons for a term exceeding 48 hours without a judicial decision. Or, alternatively, it can be perceived as an instruction addressed to the relevant authorities not to do so. In any event, a *positive* norm was thus created by the Court's decision.

Moreover, when a norm is invalidated by a duly empowered court, such a decision, upon its coming into legal force, gives birth to a new rule which prohibits the adoption of the same norm in the future, unless a higher statute or the Constitution applied by the court in the given case is changed so as to make it possible.

Therefore, the label of 'negative legislator' does not fit the activities of the Constitutional Court. It is in no way 'negative', and it is in no way a 'legislator', although it does have law-creating powers. It can create positive norms, rights and duties. However, unlike the legislator, the Court is not allowed to address questions it deems to be important on its own initiative, but has to wait until such a question is put by interested persons, State agencies or groups of members of Parliament (Art 125, 1993 Russian Constitution).[35] Furthermore, the norm created by the nullification of a particular rule does not necessarily have *the appropriate degree of specificity.*

On some occasions it can even become an obstacle, restricting the freedom of the court. In one case, for instance, the Constitutional Court reviewed the rules of the RSFSR Civil Code which limited the circle of heirs by operation of law to only those of the first and second priorities.[36] The Court took a somewhat ambiguous position. On the one hand, it pointed out that the norm in question could not be assessed as violating Art 35 of the Russian Constitution ('the right of inheritance shall be guaranteed'). On the other hand, it opined that 'such regulation does not in full measure correspond to the changes in the property relations occurred in connection with the radical reconstruction of the economic system in the Russian Federation. The State which has proclaimed as its purpose the creation of market economy...must ensure, among other things, such a regulation of inheritance law which would promote the strengthening and the

---

34 Decree of 17 February 1998, No. 6-П, concerning Art 31(2) of the Law of the USSR 'On the Legal Status of Foreign Citizens in the USSR' in connection with the petition of Iah'ia Dashti Gaphur, *HCC*, no. 3 (1998), pp. 35–40.

35 Under Art 74(2) of the 1991 Law, the Constitutional Court could address certain issues at its own initiative.

36 Article 532 of the RSFSR Civil Code (see W. E. Butler (ed.), *Russian Civil Legislation* (1999), p. 267).

highest possible development of private property and exclude its unjustified transfer to the State'.[37] It seems to me that recognising the restrictive norm of the old Civil Code as unconstitutional was not a way open to the Court, for it might lead to an absurd and unacceptable result. Since the Constitution itself does not anyhow restrict the circle of heirs who can succeed by the operation of law, the only consequence of the direct application of Art 35 would be calling to inherit everyone capable of proving any degree of kinship with the decedent, however remote. Therefore, the Court had nothing to do but refrain from invalidating the dubious norm, with a concomitant recommendation to the legislator to expand the circle of heirs. This has been made soon thereafter in the new Civil Code (Arts 1142–1145) which extended the right to inherit by the operation of law to the seventh degree of kinship.

In other words, while some norms can be simply replaced by their opposites, others (for instance, electoral laws) are not so self-compensatory. These are, in particular, 'organisational' norms necessary for the proper effectuation of other norms, such as civil and political rights. When such a mechanism is found not to correspond to laws or the Constitution, it can be destroyed without actually providing any alternative mechanism. In other cases, the Court's judgment can fail to take account of a systemic connection between different norms. As a result, a gap may emerge. Therefore, it is desirable that such judicial decisions be followed and reinforced by legislative measures.

Judge Lebedev believes that the view of the Constitutional Court as merely 'a negative legislator' is too narrow because its decisions do create new rights and duties.[38] The decisions of the Court are able to guide the behaviour of natural and juridical persons on the one hand, and law-applying agencies on the other. Therefore, they operate as a source of law. The norms obliging the legislator to repeal the law deemed unconstitutional by the Court[39] are mere lip-service to the legislature's prerogative. Both *de jure* and *de facto*, it does not matter whether or not the legislator has vacated the norm in the aftermath of the Court's judgment. Such a provision is no longer applicable anyway by virtue of Art 79(4) of the Law on the Constitutional Court. Contrary to Judge Lebedev's opinion,[40] even the theoretical distinction between the legislative repeal of a law and the Constitutional Court judgment to the same effect is irrelevant because it has no consequence. Given that a distinctive feature of law is the ability to guide human behaviour, it can be argued that if a rule is no longer able to do so, it is not a law in any conceivable sense. Besides, the decisions of the Court have immediate

---

37 Ruling of the Constitutional Court of 5 October 2000, No. 200-O (unpublished). See on the Court's website at [www.ksrf.ru/doc/opred/o200_00.htm]. The case arose out of disputes concerning the inheritance of Gallina Ulanova (d. 1998), an illustrious ballerina of Bolshoi Theatre.

38 V. M. Lebedev, Судебная власть в современной России [Judicial Power in Modern Russia] (2001), p. 207.

39 Articles 80 and 87, Federal Constitutional Law on Constitutional Court (as amended).

40 Lebedev, Судебная власть в современной России [Judicial Power in Modern Russia], p. 205.

effect (Art 79[2]). Is it not a quality of a legal norm to regulate certain questions immediately?

There is a general feeling that legislative developments regarding the Russian judicial system were given a new impact when Vladimir Putin came to presidency. Among the most notable measures was a series of important amendments to the Law 'On the Constitutional Court of the Russian Federation', signed on 15 December 2001. Their legislative history has been already analysed elsewhere.[41] In the opinion of Trochev, these amendments 'represent an attempt to accommodate Constitutional Court rulings to the civil-law system, which does not recognise "judge-made" law'.[42] Basically, they were intended to ensure compliance with the Court's judgments by establishing concrete terms within which State agencies and officials are to bring the legislative provisions declared void into conformity with the Constitution. Plainly, the federal authorities were concerned that gaps created by the Court's judgments should be filled somehow. The frequent disregard of these judgments, coupled with the reluctance of regional legislatures to create new legal mechanisms instead of ones deemed unconstitutional, has been a constant difficulty during the past decade. In order to get things right, the amendments placed upon the respective authorities the duty to adopt new normative acts in place of those set aside or, in case only part of the normative act was annulled, to amend it accordingly. This should be done within definite terms, which vary depending on different levels and branches of State power. It is noticeable, however, that sanctions for the failure to meet them were provided only with respect to regional authorities.[43] No sanctions were established for possible non-compliance by the Federal Government, State Duma or President.

The previous version of the law (Art 79[4]) read that 'if the deeming of a normative act to be unconstitutional has created a gap in legal regulation, the Constitution of the Russian Federation shall be applied directly'.[44] According to the new version of the Article, the direct effect of the Constitution shall continue until the gap is filled by an act of the appropriate authority. Moreover, the new act should contain provisions declaring the previous act to be repealed. This novelty has inevitably given rise to doubts concerning the force of Constitutional Court decisions. It might seem that unconstitutional provisions are made void not by the Court's judgment, but through a subsequent legislative act. Legally speaking, this is not the case, because other parts of Art 79 remained completely

41 A. Trochev, 'Implementing Russian Constitutional Court Decisions', *East European Constitutional Review*, Vol. 11, no. 1/2 (Winter–Spring, 2002), pp. 95 ff.; See online at [www.law.nyu.edu/eecr/vol11num1_2/features/trochev.html].

42 Ibid.

43 The relevant procedures are found in Arts 9 and 29 of the Federal Law 'On General Principles of the Organisation of Legislative (or Representative) and Executive Agencies of State Power of the subjects of the Russian Federation' of 6 October 1999, No. 184-ФЗ.

44 *RLT*, p. 194.

untouched by amendments. As formerly, they provide that 'a decision of the Constitutional Court of the Russian Federation shall be final, not subject to appeal and shall enter into force immediately after its proclamation' (para 1). Most importantly, it 'shall operate directly and shall not require confirmation by other agencies and officials' (para 2); furthermore, 'acts or individual provisions thereof deemed to be unconstitutional shall lose force' (para 3). What may have changed in the aftermath of the 2001 amendments is the perception of Court decisions by various law-enforcement agencies and officials: they may assume that the rules deemed unconstitutional can operate unless and until formally repealed. Although the danger is real, it has little to do with the wording or true meaning of the law; rather, it relates to the legal culture of officials. As such, the innovation has a strong rationale, which lies in the fact that the direct application of the Constitution is simply insufficient in many instances. Moreover, although the decisions of the Court come into force immediately, the filling of the gaps created cannot be immediate by definition. Given the lack of any terms for doing it, the relevant authorities could keep themselves aloof from the problem.

In spite of the fact that some decisions of the Constitutional Court do not create gaps (or the deficit of legal regulation), it is indeed more reasonable to oblige the relevant authorities to react to *every* case of invalidation of certain norms by the Court. Viewed in this perspective, the December 2001 amendments appear to arise out of practical concerns, and not theoretical considerations about the inadmissibility of judge-made rules in a civil law system.

Although declaratory approach to law is at the heart of constitutional adjudication, the latter fails to be consistent in practice. At first sight, it rests on the presumption that, far from *making* normative acts unconstitutional, the tribunal merely *discovers* their non-conformity to the Constitution. Indeed, if the given provision was unconstitutional, it should be such by its nature, not by virtue of judicial decision. Quite frequently, however, this declaratory doctrine should be balanced against the requirements of legal stability. Under Art 79 of the Law on the Constitutional Court, the acts deemed unconstitutional lose force; judicial and other decisions made pursuant to such acts must be reversed in cases governed by federal law. The moment from which the provision is considered to be void is not explicitly indicated. Some are inclined to interpret Art 79 in the sense that the judgments of the Constitutional Court have 'not a law-confirming but a law-establishing character'.[45] But the possibility of reversal of decisions made on the basis of invalidated norms speaks for the 'law-confirming' nature of the judgments. The term 'federal law' should no doubt apply to procedural codes. However, they are quite inconsistent in this respect. The Criminal Procedure Code treats such a ground for reversal of a decision as a 'new circumstance' (Art 413). That hints at the

45   A. V. Madiarova, Разъяснения Верховного Суда Российской Федерации в механизме уголовно-правового регулирования [Explanations of the Supreme Court of the Russian Federation in the Mechanism of Criminal Law Regulation] (2002), p. 259.

creative nature of Constitutional Court judgments. The Code of Arbitrazh Procedure (2002) also makes provision to this effect, but defines it as 'a newly *discovered* circumstance' (Art 311[6]).[46] Quite surprisingly, the Civil Procedure Code lacks a similar norm,[47] despite being adopted just several months later.

One should also take into account Art 75 (point 12). It allows the Court to postpone the moment when its decision comes into force.[48] It is practically inevitable, for a strict application of the rule of retroactive force may sometimes lead to undesirable effects. An example of such a postponement is found in a Decree of the Constitutional Court, by which the operation of an invalidated legislation concerning obligatory insurance payments was prolonged for 6 months.[49] The Court's concern was about the State budget which might suffer as a result of an immediate invalidation. At the same time, it is hard to deny that the purity of the 'law-confirming' theory may suffer from such a postponement, apparently based on considerations of policy. This also makes the constitutional tribunal look similar to a legislature.

The limits of judicial law-making

The scope and character of restrictions on judicial creativity can vary tremendously from one legal system to another. Even in the common law countries there is no uniform approach to this matter. It is common knowledge that American judges are more active (or, anyway, more inclined to take considerations of policy into account) than their British counterparts. There were various explanations for this phenomenon. In the opinion of Goodhart, in England, where conditions are 'more or less static' the primary concern of the law is not flexibility but certainty, which is best achieved by adherence to precedent, by 'strict construction of statutes and by syllogistic interpretation of the existing rules of law'.[50] As Jaffe has said, 'the self-avowed passivity of the English judges during the last half-century is an understandable response to the political pressures generated by the dynamic force of the emerging social service state' and its abundant legislation. Very often judges were sharply criticised for favouring the social *status quo*.[51] This criticism was threatening to undermine the prestige of their profession and, eventually, has forced most of them to adhere to the doctrine of judicial self-restraint.[52] But criticism of judges for their

---

46 There was no such clause in 1995 Code of Arbitrazh Procedure.
47 The list of 'newly discovered circumstances' is contained in Art 392.
48 Or, at least, it is how the Court itself has construed it: see its Ruling of 14 January 1999, No. 4-O (*HCC*, no. 2 (1999), pp. 48–51) as interpreted by a Ruling of 5 February 2004, No. 78-O (*HCC*, no. 5 (2004), pp. 33–34).
49 Decree of the Constitutional Court of 24 February 1998, No. 7-П, *HCC*, no. 3 (1998), p. 50.
50 A. L. Goodhart, *Essays in Jurisprudence and the Common Law* (1931), pp. 68–69.
51 J. A. G. Griffith, *The Politics of the Judiciary* (5th edn, 1997).
52 Jaffe, *English and American Judges as Law-Makers*, p. 29.

arguably conservative bias was sometimes even stronger in the United States. However, it has not led to a lower degree of activism in the work of the courts.

This boldness of American judiciary compared with their British counterparts can be partially explained by the lack of the doctrine of parliamentary omnipotence in the United States. Although the British Parliament is also effectively restricted by public opinion and constitutional agreements, the legal system is still reluctant to accept the idea of a written constitution and judicial control over statutory law. Another reason can be found in the differences between the ways American and British judges are selected. The popular mandate of the latter seems to be considerably weaker.

British cases of the last decades are rich with pronouncements of judges reflecting on the propriety of judicial law-creation. On the whole, it is customary for British judges to declare that they can make their judgments only on the grounds of law, not policy. In *Lynch v DPP for Northern Ireland* Lord Simon of Glaisdale said:

> I am all for recognising frankly that judges do make law. And I am all for judges exercising this responsibility boldly at the proper time and place – that is, where they can feel confident of having in mind, and correctly weighed, all the implications of their decision, and where matters of social policy are not involved which the collective wisdom of Parliament is better suited to resolve.[53]

His view was echoed by Lord Slynn in another case:

> When considering social issues in particular judges must not substitute their own views to fill gaps. They must consider whether the new facts fall within the parliamentary intention.[54]

A more restrictive view on the matter was set out by Lord Wilberforce in *Royal College of Nursing of the UK v Dept of Health and Social Security*:

> In any event there is one course which the courts cannot take under the law of this country: they cannot fill gaps; they cannot by asking the question, 'What would Parliament have done in this current case, not being one in contemplation, if the facts had been before it?', attempt themselves to supply the answer, if the answer is not to be found in the terms of the Act itself.[55]

---

53 *Lynch v DPP for Northern Ireland* [1975] 1 All ER 913.
54 *Fitzpatrick v Sterling Housing Association Ltd* [1999] 4 All ER 705, at p. 710.
55 *Royal College of Nursing of the UK v Dept of Health and Social Security* [1981] 1 All ER 545, at pp. 564–565.

This position can be criticised for giving no answer as to how gaps should be treated. That is why there seems to be no shortage of contrary opinions. For instance, Lord Reid in *Myers v DPP* expressed himself as follows:

> The common law must be developed to meet changing economic conditions and habits of thought, and I would not be deterred by expressions of opinion in this House in old cases; but there are limits to what we can or should do. If we are to extend the law it must be by the development and application of fundamental principles. We cannot introduce arbitrary conditions or limitations; that must be left to legislation: and if we do in effect change the law, we ought in my opinion only to do that in cases where our decision will produce some finality or certainty.[56]

His words (frequently cited in the opinions of British appellate courts) represent in a nutshell the traditional approach of many English judges to the problem of the proper judicial function and its limits. The crucial term here is *certainty*; it is because the law should be certain that judges should not move ahead of the legislator. They can develop the common law, but in the modern era they cannot create new criminal offences, new kinds of defence, and the like. But, since statutory words frequently have some degree of uncertainty, it is also a duty of courts to decide which facts (especially if the latter are new and unanticipated) may be covered by a particular concept.

The concept of 'certainty' is itself elastic enough, to the extent that competing arguments might well rely on it. This, for instance, was made clear from judicial reasoning in *Knuller*.[57] It was contended on the part of the appellants in that case that *Shaw v DPP*,[58] which confirmed the existence of the offence of conspiracy to corrupt public morals in the common law, created a state of uncertainty as to what behaviour may be found an offence against public morals and therefore it ought to be overruled.[59] The facts of this case were clear, but there were strong doubts as to the clarity of the rule established in *Shaw*. But Lord Reid, in spite of his dissent in *Shaw*, took the view that it is 'in the general interest of certainty' not to overrule the decision, however wrong or anomalous it might be, and any alteration of the law must be left to Parliament.[60] In the end, his conception of 'certainty' gained the upper hand over the necessity (expounded in that case by Lord Diplock) to correct mistakes in the interests of the liberty of the citizen to do what he wants.[61]

---

56 *Myers v DPP* [1964] 2 All ER 881 at pp. 885–886; [1965] AC 1001, at pp. 1021–1022.
57 *Knuller (Publishing, Printing and Promotions) Ltd and others v DPP* [1972] 2 All ER 898 [1973] AC 435.
58 *Shaw v DPP* [1961] 2 All ER 446.
59 *Knuller (Publishing, Printing and Promotions) Ltd and others v DPP* [1973] AC 435, at p. 443.
60 [1972] 2 All ER 898, at p. 903.
61 Ibid., at p. 924.

On other occasions, however, certainty can be outweighed by competing considerations, such as the need for innovations and correction of a previous mistake. Not infrequently, such a need can be met through updating the meaning of statutory words. It is trite to say that both social conditions and legal concepts may change. When are judges allowed to update the meaning of statutory words, if at all, and how should this power be limited?

It is often said that most legal acts are 'always speaking' – a definition first used by Lord Thring (Henry Thring, 1818–1907). According to Bennion, an 'always speaking' act, 'though necessarily embedded in its own time, is nevertheless to be construed in accordance with the need to treat it as current law'. 'It "speaks" from day to day, though always (unless textually amended) in the words of its original drafter'.[62] On the contrary, the number of the acts which can be considered as dated is insignificant. The obscurity of an expression used by the legislature may be regarded as the delegation to courts of the power to elaborate its meaning in accordance with public policy. It was an intention of Parliament that its words should be given the meaning more appropriate to the ever-changing social conditions.[63]

This presumption, however convenient, is not always shared by judges themselves. This issue was raised in the House of Lords in *Fitzpatrick v Sterling Housing Association*.[64] It was a case where an appellant was a homosexual partner of a person who was the 'original tenant' of a flat for the purposes of the right of succession to a statutory tenancy under Sched 1 to the Rent Act 1977. They were living in a close, loving and faithful homosexual relationship. After the death of his partner, Mr Fitzpatrick sought a declaration that he was a person who, immediately before his death, had been living with him 'as his or her wife or husband' for the purposes of para 2(2) of Sched 1, and that he was therefore entitled to succeed to his statutory tenancy as the 'surviving spouse' within the meaning of para 2(1). Alternatively, he contended that he was entitled to succeed to an assured tenancy on the ground set out in para 3(1), namely, that he was a member of the original tenant's 'family' and had resided with him for two years immediately before his death.

In the Court of Appeal, his claims were rejected.[65] Waite LJ said, however, that the judgment was 'out of tune with modern acceptance of the need to avoid any discrimination on the ground of sexual orientation'.[66] But he recognised that he was bound by law as it stood, which made no allowance for the homosexual partners to be considered as spouses or persons who are able to constitute a family.[67] Ward LJ approached the issue of construction in a quite different way.

---

62 F. A. R. Bennion, *Statutory Interpretation: A Code* (2nd edn., 1992), pp. 617–618.

63 Ibid., p. 619.

64 *Fitzpatrick v Sterling Housing Association* [1999] 4 All ER 705.

65 [1997] 4 All ER 991.

66 Ibid., p. 1005.

67 Ibid., p. 1009.

He said that the 1977 Act was an 'act of social engineering' and it must remain contemporaneously able to cope with the inevitable expansion and contradictions of the structure it creates. Therefore, its words had to be construed to bear the meaning they had in contemporary society.

In *Harrogate BC v Simpson*, referred to in the case in question, Watkins LJ had said that 'if Parliament had wished homosexual relationships to be brought into the realm of the lawfully recognised state of a living together of man and wife... it would plainly have so stated'.[68] But Ward LJ objected that, on the contrary, where Parliament wished gender to be expressly determinative, Parliament can and does say so and when it does not, gender is not critical.

Was his argument of any force? It seems that such an approach requires too much from the legislature. It was provided in para 2(2) that 'a person who was living with the original tenant as his or her wife or husband shall be treated as the spouse of the original tenant'. The requirement, that gender is essential, obviously follows from this wording, though it was not plainly stated. How can it be decided who is husband and who is wife in a homosexual partnership? Not surprisingly, this contention on the part of the appellant was rejected by the House. It was held that the words 'husband' and 'wife' were 'gender-specific, connoting a relationship between a man and a woman'.

Much more difficult questions were raised with regards to the meaning of the word 'family'. Could it be extended in order to cover homosexual relationship? On the matter of appropriate construction the views of the Law Lords diverged strongly. Lord Slynn said:

> It is... for the court in the first place to interpret each phrase in its statutory context. To do so is not to usurp Parliament's function; not to do so would be to abdicate the judicial function. If Parliament takes the view that the result is not what is wanted it will change the legislation.[69]

It can be argued, on the other hand, that the legislature may prove to be incapable of reacting every time to decisions of the courts which do not correspond to its intentions. In an extreme case, the function of the legislature would be merely confined to the review of judicial decisions and it would lose any initiative.

Lord Nicholls of Birkenhead asked the question: 'Can the expression "family" legitimately be interpreted in 1999 as having a different and wider meaning than when it was first enacted in 1920 at the time of the first Rent Act'? His own answer was that 'it would be unattractive, to the extent of being unacceptable, to interpret the word "family" in the 1977 Act without regard to these changes'. Parliament itself made this clear in 1988, when amending the Rent Acts. Paragraph 2(3) of

---

68 *Harrogate BC v Simpson* [1984] 17 HLR, at p. 205.
69 *Fitzpatrick v Sterling Housing Association* [1999] 4 All ER 705, at p. 710.

Sched 1 envisages that more than one person may be living with the tenant as a surviving spouse under the extended definition. 'In so enacting the law, Parliament was not expressing a view, either way, on the morality of such relationships'. But it made plain that 'what matters is the factual position. The same must be true of homosexual relationships'.[70] Therefore, the inclusion of a tenant's homosexual partner within the ranks of persons eligible to qualify as members of his family is not a step which should be left to Parliament. In cases such as this the courts 'must always proceed with particular caution and sensitivity'.[71]

Lord Clyde also favoured the innovative approach. He said that 'Parliament has in relation to protected tenancies under the Rent Act 1977 left the word "family" to be applied by the courts without the guidance of statutory definition'. He added that 'the rule of contemporary exposition should be applied only in relation to very old statutes, and the general presumption is that an updating construction is to be applied'.[72]

Possibly, he was right, but the question arises: what can be the social consequences of the innovative judicial decision? If the meaning of the word 'family' is to be extended to cover homosexual partners, would it be fair to foreclose the claims of friends, living together and caring about joint households? *Fitzpatrick* is the case in point, for it is demonstrated that sexual relationships are irrelevant for constituting a family in legal terms. How far were the courts prepared to go in this direction?

The traditional approach to construction was assumed by Lord Hutton in his dissent. He recalled the words of Lord Wilberforce that 'in interpreting an Act of Parliament it is proper...to have regard to the state of affairs existing, and known by Parliament to be existing, at the time. It is a fair presumption that Parliament's policy or intention is directed to that state of affairs'. So long as 'a new state of affairs, or a fresh set of facts bearing on policy, comes into existence, the courts have to consider whether they fall within the parliamentary intention'. When should the answer to this question be positive? In the view of Wilberforce (and Hutton),

> They may be held to do so if they fall within the same genus of facts as those to which the expressed policy has been formulated. They may also be held to do so if there can be detected a clear purpose in the legislation which can only be fulfilled if the extension is made.[73]

Then Lord Hutton remarked that in 1920 the fact of homosexuals living together in permanent relationship was known to Parliament. No new state of

---

70 *Fitzpatrick v Sterling Housing Association* [1999] 4 All ER 705, at p. 722.
71 Ibid., at p. 722.
72 Ibid., at p. 726.
73 *Royal College of Nursing of the UK v Dept of Health and Social Security* [1981] 1 All ER 545, at pp. 564–565.

affairs has come into existence which extends the meaning of the term 'family'.[74] In the view of Lord Hobhouse, to accept the submission of Mr Fitzpatrick would be an exercise of legislation, not interpretation, because the submission was seeking to establish a legal right based upon the advocacy of a social policy, which had not yet been incorporated in legislation.[75] However, despite all these objections, the appeal was allowed by 3 : 2 vote. Characteristically, the construction of parliamentary intention out of the wording of relevant laws served as a basis of the verdict, not the considerations of social policy. Thus, the triumph of the evolutionary view on statute law, however strongly suspect, was by no means evident, because the decision was pictured by the majority of Lords as the most concordant with legislative intent.

At times Russian judges, too, resorted to what some theorists call 'accommodating interpretation', although they did it without eloquent pronouncements typical of common law courts. For instance, a highly controversial decree of the Presidium of the Supreme Soviet adopted on 8 July 1944 prohibited women who gave birth to children out of the bonds of an officially registered wedding from establishing the fact of paternity and seeking alimony from the fathers of their children in judicial proceeding. The decree was reflective of wartime social policies. But as time passed and Soviet society became relatively 'liberal', its injustice was increasingly felt by judges. The decree remained in force until 1968, but courts had effectively repealed it. They proceeded on the basis of an earlier norm of the 1926 Family Code that allowed recovery of alimony from the 'actual upbringer' of the natural child. Nearly all fathers, who took no significant role in bringing up their natural children, were consistently deemed by courts to be such 'upbringers', however stretched this conclusion might seem. Legal doctrine strongly approved this 'accommodating' practice as more consistent with morality (of course, the 'communist' one).[76]

Although examples of such interpretation have always been rare in Soviet and Russian law, it is possible that such occasions may arise more frequently in the future as a consequence of changing attitudes of the judicial community, as well as rapid social and technological evolution. It should be remarked that Russian family law does not contain a definition of family either. Although since 1944 only an officially registered marriage is recognised as legally valid and may serve as a basis of a family, linguistic and demographic norms have changed significantly and encompass non-registered marriages too. No wonder that statistics shows an ongoing and quite considerable increase in the number of 'families' due to the addition of the latter to the former. It is sufficient to say that,

---

74 *Fitzpatrick v Sterling Housing Association* [1999] 4 All ER 705, at p. 740.
75 Ibid., at p. 743.
76 A. F. Cherdantsev, Толкование советского права [Interpretation of Soviet Law] (1979), pp. 106–107.

according to the results of the 2002 census, three millions of married couples were not registered (about 10 per cent from the total number of family couples). But, unlike England, in Russia no considerable attempt to judicialise the problem has been recorded so far: although the legislation is patently obsolete and unjust, it was never challenged in the Constitutional Court.

The means of judicial law-making compared

The methods of achieving just and reasonable decisions which courts possess differ a lot from one legal system to another. This can be exemplified by the decisions of supreme courts of the United States, Great Britain and Russia with regard to the incommensurability of sanctions for the failure to comply with tax or customs regulations. Let us consider first the American case *United States v Bajakadjian*, and then how English courts resolved the problem of incommensurability in case *Inland Revenue Commissioners v Hinchy*.

In the first case the defendant was prosecuted for the failure to report, in violation of a law, the exporting of the sum in cash exceeding $10,000 from the United States.[77] The sanction for such a violation ought to have been the forfeiture of any property involved in such an offence. It this case the sum subject to forfeiture was about $357,000. It was found that the money in question was not intended for a criminal purpose; the respondent had failed to report that he was taking the currency out of the United States because of fear stemming from 'cultural differences': the respondent, who had grown up as a member of the Armenian minority in Syria, had a 'distrust for the Government'. The issue was not about failure to pay any duties with respect to the sum in question; it was just about the failure to inform the authorities concerning the export of cash. These circumstances were taken by courts into account when reducing the amount of forfeiture ($20,000 only). The appeal of the United States against the decisions of lower courts was dismissed by the US Supreme Court with the majority of voices 5 : 4. The Court held that the confiscation of the entire sum would be 'grossly disproportional' to the gravity of the offence and violate the Eighth Amendment to the US Constitution which provides that 'excessive fines [shall not be] imposed'.[78] For these reasons the norm of federal legislation was denied application. It was the first case where this Amendment (or Excessive Fines Clause) was used in such a way. There is no doubt as to the importance of this precedent and its far-reaching consequences, for it questioned the future of a vast range of statutory sanctions (that was the main point of the minority's opinion).[79]

---

77 *United States v Bajakadjian* [1998] 141 L Ed 2d 314.
78 Ibid., at p. 321.
79 Ibid., at p. 344.

The second of the cases mentioned above was considered by the House of Lords and had a much worse outcome for the respondent in the case. He was accused of understating the income from his bank account. The amount of the income tax he had underpaid was a little bit more than 14 pounds. Inland Revenue commissioners brought an action against him under s 25(3) of the Income Tax Act, 1952, which provided that the offender should pay the sum of £20 and 'treble the tax which he ought to be charged'. Importantly, the 1952 Act was a consolidated act so that the origins of the rule in question were to be found in legislative acts of the early nineteenth century. The literal reading of this norm would entail the trebling of the whole sum of income tax payable for the year in question, that is, £418. As well as *Bajakadjian* case, that was the first case of such a kind. An alternative to this tough interpretation might be the trebling of the underpaid tax only, and this construction was used by Lord Diplock in his judgment in the High Court.[80] Diplock accentuated the absurd and unjust consequences flowing from the literal understanding of the norm – theoretically, every mistake, however insignificant, could entail any amount of fine depending on the taxpayer's income. His decision in favour of the defendant was, in general, approved by the Court of Appeal,[81] but then reversed by the unanimous decision of the House of Lords. The Lords agreed that the amount of fine was incongruent to the gravity of the offence, but found the words of the statute quite unambiguous and therefore felt themselves bound by their literal meaning. Lord Reid suggested that the norm has been enacted when the rate of tax was low, and penalties based on the total amount of tax payable were probably not oppressive. In his opinion, the words of the Act were not possible of a more limited construction and therefore they ought to be given effect, 'however unreasonable or unjust the consequences and however strongly we may suspect that this was not the real intention of Parliament'.[82] This case confirms once more that the lack of such a tool as a written constitution or a Bill of Rights might sometimes leave British judges with no choice other than to enforce the literal will of the legislator even though it might cause a manifest injustice.

As shall be seen, at present Russian courts follow a pattern which can be called a middle way between the American and British models, although it is somewhat closer to the former. In one of the surveys of judicial practice confirmed by the Presidium of the Supreme Court one finds an interesting example. The question was raised whether a court is empowered to reduce the amount of penalty imposed for the failure to pay on time customs duties and taxes as envisaged by Art 124 of the Customs Code (0.3 per cent per each day of delay) and Art 75 of the Tax Code (0.1 per cent per each day), if the court found that the amount of penalty is patently incommensurate to the consequences of

---

80 *Inland Revenue Commissioners v Hinchy* [1958] 3 All ER 682.
81 *Inland Revenue Commissioners v Hinchy* [1959] 2 All ER 512.
82 *Inland Revenue Commissioners v Hinchy* [1960] 2 All ER 505, at pp. 509, 512.

the offence. The Supreme Court held that there was a gap in the legislation which ought to be filled by way of analogy with civil law. In its view, a penalty (of fine, forfeit) is one of the means of securing the performance of obligations, whether civil law or tax ones. Therefore, the rules concerning the payment of all such penalties are similar to each other. Consequently, the relations concerning penalties for the delayed payment of taxes or customs duties can, by way of analogy, be regulated by Art 333 of the Civil Code which provides that 'if a penalty subject to payment is clearly incommensurate to the consequences of the violation of the obligation, a court shall have the right to reduce the penalty'.[83] The Supreme Court, however, did not confine itself to saying that the analogy of *lex* is admissible to substantiate the decision. It also used the analogy of *ius* and cited the vague declarations of Art 7 of the Constitution (Russia is 'a social state whose politics is directed to the creation of conditions securing a deserving life and free development of man'). Hence the Court inferred that 'the imposition of a penalty and its recovery should not entail the devastation or exorbitant expenses of the taxpayer...and tax (as well as customs) legislation does not pursue such goals'.[84]

Very soon these pronouncements of the Supreme Court gained precedential importance for lower courts which began to repeat them almost verbatim.[85] But the question must be raised whether the conclusions made by the Supreme Court were legally impeccable? After all, tax and civil law are essentially different branches of law, and it is not occasional that Art 2(3) of the Civil Code contains a general prohibition of such an analogy: 'Civil legislation shall not apply to property relations based on administrative or other power subordination of one party to another, including to tax and other financial and administrative relations, unless provided otherwise by legislation'.[86] And this is the reason why arbitrazh courts usually reject invitations to apply Art 333 of the Civil Code to tax relations.[87]

At the same time, Art 11 (point 1) of the Tax Code stipulated that the institutions, concepts and terms of the civil, family and other branches of legislation used in the Tax Code shall be applied in the meaning in which they are used in that branch of the legislation unless provided otherwise by the Tax Code itself. The definitions of penalty in the civil and tax codes are

---

83 *CCRF*, p. 129.

84 Survey of judicial practice of the Supreme Court of the Russian Federation for the IV quarter of the year 1999 (civil cases), *BSC*, no. 7 (2000), pp. 20–21. The policy of reducing the gravity of sanctions for tax offences has been launched by the Constitutional Court, not the Supreme Court (see the Decree of the Constitutional Court of 12 May 1998, No. 14-П, *HCC*, no. 4 (1998), pp. 41–50).

85 But, characteristically, the source of the opinion was usually omitted.

86 *CCRF*, p. 2.

87 Decree of the Federal Arbitrazh Court for the Eastern Siberian Circuit of 15 February 2002. The same court opined that penalty in the tax legislation is not a forfeit (in Russian: *neustoika*) and is not subject to reduction in the absence of direct permission in the tax law (Decree of 18 September 2001 (unpublished)).

notionally similar because both consider penalties to be a means of securing the performance of obligations (of course, there are some incidental differences of terminology: 'debtor' in the former, 'taxpayer' in the latter, etc). At the same time, there are also important differences that may cast doubt on the identity of these institutions. For instance, the Civil Code identifies a penalty with a fine, whereas in the Tax Code they are unequivocally distinguished (Art 114). It is still more essential that the Tax Code does contain its own definition of penalty but, unlike the civil legislation, does not provide for its reduction. This may warrant the conclusion that an analogy is inappropriate, because the institution of penalty is separately (and exhaustively) defined by the law on taxation and there is no gap. As regards a penalty under the customs legislation, such an analogy is even more dubious there, since the 1993 Customs Code defines a penalty as a measure of responsibility (Art 124).[88]

The question of the nature of penalty under Russian law is complex, but it should not detain us here. It will do that the opinions within the legal community differ and the relevant 'operational' rules as to which substantive norms ought to be applied in such cases were indeterminate. This enabled the Supreme Court to opt for the use of legal analogy, whereas arbitrazh courts did not follow its suit. But what is remarkable about the Supreme Court opinion is the subservient role of the analogy of *jus* with respect to the analogy of *lex*. This is very characteristic of the prevalent methods of adjudication. Obviously, the resort to the Constitution and the general sense of the current legislation was not an all-sufficient basis for the Court's judgment, but just a means to support the conclusion at which the Court had already arrived. It begs the question whether, in the absence of the convenient Art 333 of the Civil Code, its conclusion would have been the same, and whether the Court would be able to work out the same view only on the basis of the analogy of *jus*. The answer is not yet known but, possibly, will be received from future decisions of the Court.

In the United Kingdom new opportunities for judicial law-making can be found in the incipient judicial examination of provisions of domestic law and the adoption of interpretative techniques favoured by European Court of Justice.[89] In the *Litster* case the House of Lords departed from the traditional requirement that specific legislation should be enacted in order to implement rules of the European Communities having only indirect effect. It was held that the courts of the United Kingdom were under a duty to give a purposive construction to the European Communities Regulations in a manner which would accord with the decisions of the European Court of Justice and where necessary to imply words which would achieve that effect.[90]

---

88 These notions are treated as different ones in the Russian arbitrazh practice. Cf. a decree of the Federal Arbitrazh Court for the Central Circuit of 28 February 2000 (unpublished).

89 Manchester, Salter and Moodie, *Exploring the Law*, pp. 91–93.

90 *Litster and others v Fourth Dry Dock & Engineering CO.LTD (in receivership) and another* [1990] 1 AC, at p. 547.

Even more interesting developments are underway following the enactment in 1998 of the Human Rights Act, which was designed in order to give further effect to European Convention rights. It should be noted that some provisions of the Convention and the Human Rights Act have an immediate relation to cases such as *Fitzpatrick*.

The European Convention on Human Rights provides that 'men and women of marriageable age have the right to marry and to found a family, according to the national laws governing the exercise of this right' (Art 12). According to Art 14 (prohibition of discrimination), 'everyone whose rights and freedoms as set forth in this Convention are violated shall have an effective remedy before a national authority notwithstanding that the violation has been committed by persons acting in an official capacity'.

Under s 3(1) of the Human Rights Act, 'so far as it is possible to do so, primary legislation and subordinate legislation must be read and given effect in a way which is compatible with the Convention rights'. Pursuant to s 4(2) if the court is satisfied that the provision is incompatible with a Convention right, it may make a declaration of that incompatibility. It is somewhat similar to the duty of Russian ordinary courts to bring their doubts concerning constitutionality of a norm to the Constitutional Court.

The Convention does not have any legally binding effect under British law and an individual claimant cannot directly invoke it before a British court.[91] This notwithstanding, it seems that the Convention extends the power of the courts to have dialogue with Parliament and take part in shaping legal policy. Although a declaration of incompatibility has no immediate effect upon the legislation or the case in question, it can be a successful mechanism for putting pressure on Parliament to take action to remove the incompatibility.[92] How broadly the courts will exercise this discretionary power remains to be seen. To a great extent, this depends on the view of the small group of judges sitting in courts at the top of the judicial hierarchy. In any event, it is expected that henceforth any doubts about the meaning of statutory norms should be resolved in accordance with the Convention. Russian legislation goes further: it enables courts not to apply a clear norm as well on the grounds of its unconstitutionality.

What has been judicial approach to the matter of incompatibility so far? The decision in the *Fitzpatrick* is instructive in this respect too. On the one hand, Art 12 (right to marry) refers to the sex distinctions ('men and women of marriageable age'), otherwise one would expect the word 'people' or 'persons' to be used. On the other hand, homosexual partners may argue that they are discriminated against in respect of their right to marry. In the Court of Appeal, Ward LJ cited the resolution of the European Parliament on equal rights for homosexuals and lesbians in the European Community of 8 February 1994 to

91 See Manchester, Salter and Moodie, *Exploring the Law*, p. 132.
92 Ibid., p. 135.

sweep away any unequal treatment based on sexual orientation.[93] The same rule may apply to the right to marry for transsexuals.[94]

In Canada any discrimination 'based on race, national or ethnic origin, colour, religion, sex, age or mental or physical disability' is prohibited by s 15 of the Charter of Human Rights. In *Egan v Canada*[95] the matter was whether discrimination based on the grounds of sexual orientation can be compared with discrimination on the grounds of sex. The court was unanimous in holding that sexual orientation was a ground of discrimination. La Forest, J. said that 'sexual orientation is either unchangeable or changeable only at unacceptable personal costs, and so falls within the ambit of s 15 protection as being analogues to the enumerated grounds'.[96] In so extending the law, the court in fact made a political decision favouring minority rights.

The right to make a declaration of incompatibility has significant potential for an increase in the political role of the judiciary, but the final word is reserved for Parliament. Only the legislature can remove incompatible legislation. But can it respond to the judicial challenges without a risk of being overburdened? Previously the judges of British superior courts pointed out in their *dicta* that the matter in question, though to be solved in accordance with the existing law, should nevertheless be considered by Parliament. For example, in *R v Gotts*[97] the question was about availability of duress as a defence to a charge of attempted murder. The answer of the House of Lords was negative. Furthermore, it was said that 'given the climate of violence and terrorism which ordinary law-abiding citizen now have to face Parliament might do well to consider whether the defence of duress should continue to be available in the case of all very serious crimes or whether it ought to be treated as a matter of mitigation rather than defence'.[98] But in this case Parliament failed to take promptly measures to correct the law.

It is not reasonable for courts to anticipate the decision of the legislative body even if the matter is already on the parliamentary agenda. For example, in *Bellinger v Bellinger* that was one of the reasons for the judge to follow existing law in the expectation of the changes to come.[99] Likewise, the Constitutional Court of Russia sometimes declined to give its opinion on the grounds that the issue in question was being considered in Parliament and the preliminary constitutional control is not entrusted to the Court.[100] It also may reject invitations

---

93 [1997] 4 All ER 991, at p. 1018.
94 See *Bellinger v Bellinger and another* [2000] 3 FCR 733; [2002] Fam 150; [2003] 2 WLR 1174. This case led to the House of Lords having issued a declaration of incompatibility, one of the few during the first years of Human Rights Act operation.
95 *Egan v Canada (A-G of Quebec, intervener)* [1995] 124 DLR (4th) 609.
96 Ibid., at p. 619.
97 *R v Gotts* [1992] 1 All ER 832.
98 Ibid., at p. 839 (per Lords Templeman, Jauncey and Browne-Wilkinson).
99 *Bellinger v Bellinger and another* [2000] 3 FCR 733.
100 Ruling of the Constitutional Court of 4 February 1997, No. 14-O (unpublished).

to interpret a constitutional clause, if such an interpretation would, in view of the Court, create a new norm and thus impinge upon the principle of separation of powers.[101] In practice, such interpretations can be requested by those who are frustrated by certain provisions of draft laws and attempt to obstruct their adoption in such a way. It should be added that the Russian Constitution is not considered by the Law on the Constitutional Court as capable of giving an answer to every question, for the Court may refuse an application, if 'it is established that the question resolved by a law, other normative act, or treaty between agencies of State power or by an international treaty … whose constitutionality it is proposed to verify was not resolved in the Constitution of the Russian Federation or by its character and significance is not relegated to constitutional questions' (Art 68).[102] This elastic formula gives the Court a considerable freedom of action in selecting cases.

Some inconclusive remarks

I doubt that it would be sufficient to lay down formal rules guiding judges as to where they should stop and where are they permitted to proceed. I agree with Wood's remark that 'ultimately, there seems to be no easy way to limit the judges' interpretative power except by changing the attitude of judges themselves'.[103] The actual state of affairs depends on a great variety of factors and circumstances which create a unique combination within particular legal system. Much depends on the mood of the judiciary and the legislature and their (un)willingness to preserve the *status quo*, which is always a matter of political compromise. In practical terms, some traditional attitudes and avowed patterns can serve as a more effective guide than abstract principles.

Judicial legislation is only a by-product of the judicial process. It is not (or at least should not be) the deliberate purpose of the judge. His thinking differs from that of a legislator. When filling gaps in the statute he proceeds more in a judicial rather than a legislative way. But his activity does have some political effect in many cases where interests of different groups conflict. Therefore, the legislative function of the judiciary is frequently suspected of being arbitrary, lacking responsibility and restraint. It would be better for judges to remember this general dislike and exercise their subsidiary legislative function with caution, avoiding as much as possible any direct clashes with other branches of power. It is a difficult question whether judges should frankly recognise that they create law or it is better for them to use the mask of 'judicial interpretation' instead of 'judicial legislation' in every case when they legislate. It also depends on traditional attitudes. Even in the common law countries we do not see a uniform approach to

---

101   Ruling of the Constitutional Court of 16 June 1995, No. 67-O (unpublished).
102   *RLT*, p. 189.
103   G. S. Wood, 'Comment', in Scalia, *A Matter of Interpretation*, p. 63.

this matter among the judiciary. But Russian courts were traditionally far more cautious in this respect. It was often maintained that were judges expressly allowed to make law, they would make it more often and to a greater extent than necessary.[104] On the other hand, it can be objected that this view overrates the significance of received conventions and rhetoric and therefore fails to provide a principled decision. In any event, the attitudes of the judiciary may change as time goes by.

At any rate, the real problem is that a judge deciding a 'hard case', regulated by neither statute nor precedent, is nevertheless expected to abide by the law. The ultimate resource he can avail himself of is custom (broadly conceived), that is, a set of ideas of justice and just conduct shared within the community. This source, however, has its own defects. First, its content is often too vague to be of use in every case. The heterogeneity of modern societies makes the ideas of justness vary depending on race, profession, social strata, etc. In such circumstances the judge needs a better guide than custom. For instance, Roman law existed in form of *mores majorum* (that is, custom) long before the Twelve Tables, but proved to be unsatisfactory at a certain point as the social structure became more complex. As a result, written laws were brought into being. Their principal function was to integrate Roman society by making laws whose text could be agreed upon by both patricians and plebeians. Importantly, they could be referred to in courts thereby restricting the arbitrariness of law-appliers. But it is exactly because of the ever-growing complexity of social life that legislation frequently fails to grasp all combinations of facts within its provisions. Therefore, it needs developing and shaping by judges along the lines set up by legislators.

Do legislators themselves always *make* laws? According to Hayek, the rules of common law or private law are made by neither judges nor legislators. From this perspective, the true difference between judges and legislators was misunderstood by legal positivists. They believed the crucial distinction was that legislators had to make (or 'give') laws, whereas judges ought to apply them. Nothing could be more delusive, Hayek argues. For centuries judges found and expressed rules as developed by the collective experience of the community, and they were restricted by public expectations which their decisions had to meet. Legislation (which initially purported to correct the laws found and laid down by judges) is a relatively recent phenomenon.[105]

It is needless to engage in controversy as to whether the law existed before being found or it is invented by judges or legislators for the first time. On either view, Hayek's point is insightful. It allows us to consider the interaction between

---

104 See the opinion of Lord Patrick Devlin in his book *The Judge* (1979), p. 12.

105 Hayek, *Law, Legislation and Liberty*, Vol. 1 (1973), pp. 85–91. A contrast between the 'unconditioned' and unpredictable legislative style of changing law and an incremental judicial method is drawn also by Bruno Leoni in his *Freedom and the Law* (3rd edn., 1991).

legislative and adjudicative ways of rule-making, which should not be contrasted but, rather, viewed as *two different stages of a single process*, namely, the process of the development of legal regulation. The efforts of legislators are not sufficient in a mature legal system to achieve the general purpose of legislation, that is, to effectively govern human behaviour and delimit the domains of individual rights. The creators of the French Civil Code were remarkably conscious of the dangers of making provisions unduly detailed and therefore relied heavily on the role of judges. Portalis once expressed the view that 'with time codes make themselves; strictly speaking nobody makes them'.[106] Some theorists such as Ehrlich or Muromtsev or the adepts of sociological jurisprudence would call it 'law in action' or 'living law'. One should be careful about such terms so long as they imply a contrast between 'living' law, on one hand, and 'dead law', on the other. Statutory law is normally no less 'living' than judge-made; they simply represent two different but equally necessary stages in the development of an effective legal order. The very idea that legislators and judges shape the body of law together is not a novel one in jurisprudence. More than a century ago it was expounded by Oscar Bulow (1837–1907).[107]

Court activity is divided (however unequally) between the application of laws and law-creation. This division of judicial energies between two different kinds of activity (application of pre-existing rules on the one hand and the invention of complementary rules on the other) is, in fact, unavoidable. Reflecting on the relations between norms and the factual order of human actions Hayek noted: 'If we accept a given system of norms without question and discover that in a certain factual situation it does not achieve the result it aims at without some complementary rules, these complementary rules will be required by those already established, although they are not logically entailed by them.'[108] 'Like most other intellectual tasks, that of the judge is not one of logical deduction from a limited number of premises, but one of testing hypotheses at which he has arrived by processes only in part conscious'.[109]

Raz says that every time a decision does not emanate from either a statute or another judicial decision or custom, such decision is a law-making one. There was no law as to the question in hand prior to the decision.[110] It can be maintained I think that often the law is not lacking but, rather, there is a *deficit* or *shortage* of law. Such disputes are 'underregulated'. Of course, the absence of law is possible, if the aforesaid sources supply no clue whatsoever as to how a particular dispute should be settled. But such occasions are extremely rare.

---

106 R. C. Caenegem, *An Historical Introduction to Private Law* (1994), pp. 8, 14.
107 Bulow was a professor of Roman law and civil procedure at the University of Leipzig. His article was translated into English and published as 'Statutory Law and the Judicial Function' in *American Journal of Legal History*, Vol. 39 (January 1995), p. 71 ff.
108 Hayek, *Law, Legislation and Liberty* (1982), p. 105.
109 Ibid., pp. 119–120.
110 Raz, *Ethics in the Public Domain: Essays in the Morality of Law and Politics* (1994), p. 234.

The systemic nature of legal regulation and the drive to consistency and completeness inherent in it allow judges and lawyers to extract lacking elements out of the existing rules in a manner somewhat resembling the way palaeontologists handle the bones of an extinct animal. The criterion of truth is different because the supplementary rules cannot be later discovered in the way the lacking bones can. The correctness of construction should be tested against the criterion of consistency with past legislative and court decisions as well as society's principles.

Accordingly, reasonable activity of judges exercised beyond the limits of mere application of law may be properly called the 'judicial *development* of laws'. This notion emphasises a linkage, continuity and succession between the more abstract legislative provisions and principles of law and the rules laid down by judges aiming to complete what the legislator has left unaccomplished. All the same, an element of novelty is inherent in the term 'developing', but, unlike 'law-making', it does not give rise to objections based on the traditional view on judicial duties.

What really happens in most 'hard cases' is a kind of cooperation between legislators and judges, when the last are to continue and accomplish what was merely outlined by the first. To use the term of art, the judge works as an apprentice of a senior painter, that is, the legislature. The law-giver, much like some painters do, often works out a general outline of the picture and then entrusts his assistants to complete the details. The difference is, however, that legislators frequently have no choice. They cannot envisage everything that will need improvement and completion. Unlike a piece of art, a legislative act is not self-contained: it should be tested against the ever-changing social life.

Chapter 3

The forms of judge-made law in Russia

Sources of law

It was recently suggested that the debate as to whether judicial decisions constitute a source of law in Russia is methodologically futile because one side of the debate proceeds from the premises of juridical dogmatism, whereas the opposite relies on facts of legal practice.[1] Consequently, these two lines of arguments cannot meet and give rise to a meaningful discussion, having produced an excellent example of what Brian Bix defines as 'talking past one another'.[2]

There is a significant grain of truth in this observation. Not denying it, I have to note that even legal dogmatism (that is, an appeal to the existent law) eventually fails to oppose judicial creativity. To start with, there is no conclusive and legislatively established hierarchy of sources of law in the Russian legal system.[3] It is true that Art 120(1) of the Russian Constitution says that 'judges shall be independent and subordinate only to the Constitution of the Russian Federation and a federal law'.[4] However, this constitutional clause does not contain an exhaustive list of sources of Russian law. It does not say that judges should obey normative acts as they obey the Constitution and federal laws. Presidential edicts and other kinds of secondary legislation are not mentioned, although they no doubt constitute applicable law.

According to Art 5(1) of the 1996 Federal Constitutional Law 'On the Judicial System of the Russian Federation', judges are 'subordinate only to the Constitution of the Russian Federation and to a law' (not '*federal* law'); para 3 of the same article provides that 'a court, having established when considering a case the nonconformity of acts of a State or other agency, and likewise of an official, to the Constitution of the Russian Federation, federal constitutional law,

---

1 Abushenko, Судебное усмотрение в гражданском и арбитражном процессе [Judicial Discretion in Civil and Arbitrazh Procedure], p. 29.

2 Bix, *Jurisprudence: Theory and Context* (1996), pp. 17, 28; cf. Bix, *Law, Language, and Legal Determinacy*, p. 59.

3 As is the case in some other post-socialist countries (see, for instance, Art 87 of the Constitution of the Republic of Poland).

4 *RLT*, p. 43 (emphasis added).

federal law, generally-recognised principles of international law, international treaty of the Russian Federation, or constitution (or charter) of a subject of the Russian Federation, shall adopt a decision in accordance with the legal provisions having the greatest legal force'.[5] Clearly, the list of sources of law in Russia should be much longer than provided for in Art 120 of the Constitution. The law on the judicial system is also inconclusive in this respect because, apart from the sources enumerated, there is a variety of 'normative acts', whose conformity to higher-level provisions can also be tested by courts.

This brings us to Art 13 of the Arbitrazh Procedure Code and Art 11 of the Civil Procedure Code. They itemise applicable *normative acts*, but not all sources of law. With respect to normative acts, their provisions are identical and exhaustive.[6] But regarding other sources of law, they are not so uniform and complete. Both codes mention a custom of the business turnover, although it is not a normative act. It is curious that general courts may apply it only in cases provided for by a normative act, whereas arbitrazh courts can do so without restrictions. It should be noted, after all, that the problem of the sources of law is constitutive of a legal system and thus should be a matter of constitutional regulation, not an ordinary legislation.

Therefore, the absence of judicial acts on various lists of applicable norms is not sufficient reason to deny that they are a source of law. There is also a positive argument in their favour. Judge-made rules are often necessary in order to meet fundamental requirements of the Constitution. On the one hand, judges are required to obey the Constitution and a federal law. On the other hand, 'all shall be equal before law and court' (Art 19[1]).[7] That is to say, if a legal norm is not applied uniformly in different courts of the country, or if the Supreme Court or the Supreme Arbitrazh Court neglect their own previous decisions, this may result in a violation of Art 19. As the Constitutional Court pointed out, 'the possibility of arbitrary application of the statute is a violation of an equality of all before the law and court (Art 19[1]) proclaimed by the Constitution'.[8]

According to Art 15(1) of the Constitution, it 'shall have highest juridical force, *direct effect*, and be applied throughout the entire territory of the Russian Federation'.[9] In consequence, the question has emerged as to whether judges make law when exercising their power to apply the Constitution directly. In my view, such application may create new norms provided that it is stable and uniform in all courts. This is possible if a certain understanding of constitutional

---

5 *RLT*, p. 143.
6 But they differ from that of the 1996 Federal Constitutional Law on the Judicial System where the principles of the international law and the international treaties are ranked below the federal laws, whereas codes place the treaties next to the Constitution and higher than federal constitutional laws. Principles of international law are missing in both codes.
7 *RLT*, p. 8.
8 Decree of 25 April 1995, No. 3-П, *HCC*, no. 2/3 (1995), pp. 32–38.
9 *RLT*, p. 7.

provision subject to direct application is approved by the Supreme Court, or when the Constitutional Court defines the content of such provision by virtue of its power to interpret the Constitution.[10] In the latter case such interpretation would be binding upon the legislators should they want to pass a law on the same subject. As for interpretations of the Supreme Court, they will stand until approved or revised by the legislature.

The idea that judges cannot make law when applying the Constitution directly (or, in case of supreme courts, when instructing lower instances how to apply it) is no more defensible than the contention that legislators do not create specific rules, but merely extend the norms of the Constitution. From this standpoint, any legislation (unless it does not patently contradict the basic law of the country) should be viewed as a mere emanation of constitutional provisions. If the Russian legislature would replace one federal law with another (both of them being in conformity with the Constitution), it makes little sense to question the creative nature of the new law. It can be very different from the previous version, although equally 'constitutional'.

It is sometimes submitted that judicial decisions are not sources of Russian law because, unlike legislation, they are not applied directly to legal cases. But this opinion is not true. First of all, it is not the sources of law that are applied by courts or other agencies. 'Source of law' is simply a metaphor; what is actually applied to cases is norms (rules or principles). But this metaphor is helpful and illuminating. Based on it, one may convincingly argue that norms, like rivers, often flow from several 'sources'. When the principle source (that is, legislation) is defective (contradictory or imprecise or whatever) the judicial decision, alongside with the statute, becomes a necessary ingredient of the rule actually applied. In other words, they form the rule together, in one joint action.

In Russian legal language, judge-made rules are usually called 'judicial practice'. However, the opinions of legal scientists differ as to the precise scope of this concept. As early as in 1975 Bratus and Vengerov wrote that 'it is necessary in the strongest terms to reject the idea that judicial practice includes any decision of a people's court, ruling of a cassation or supervisory instance or even a summary of decisions in a particular group of cases'.[11] They denied that 'guiding explanations' of superior courts were a pure form of judicial practice in that sense because they frequently contained mere reminders to the courts as to how the law stands, without actually adding something to the law interpreted. Only those explanations that contain clauses making a legal norm more concrete ('legal positions', as they put it) could correctly meet the concept of 'judicial practice', constituting an intermediate link between an individual judicial decision and the relevant norm.[12]

---

10 Article 125(5) of the Russian Constitution (*RLT*, p. 44).

11 See their article in S. N. Bratus (ed.), Судебная практика в советской правовой системе [Judicial Practice in the Soviet Legal System], p. 8.

12 Ibid., p. 21.

However, their view was not universally accepted even at that time. For instance, Iaroshenko believed that judicial practice did have a creative character and emphasised that decrees of the Supreme Court Plenum (normally based on previous judicial decisions) frequently served as a model for future legislative amendments.[13]

The Supreme Court Chairman Lebedev in his book represents judicial practice as the aggregate of all judicial decisions, only some of them being 'creative' in the strict sense of the word. He identifies three kinds of judicial practice:

1   current practice;
2   precedential practice (decisions capable of having persuasive force);
3   'guiding' practice (explanations of supreme courts addressed to inferior instances).

He argues that only 'guiding' practice should be regarded as a true source of law. As to 'precedential' practice, it does not constitute new legal norms, but normally contains only 'patterns of understanding and application' of legal norms already existent.[14] Similar view has been expressed by the leading law theorist Alekseev.[15]

I believe this to be true only in part. First, 'precedential practice' consists of quite different cases. In complex cases the sole right answer can be found in law, although it requires considerable effort even from experienced lawyers. But in really hard cases no 'right answer' exists. The court ought to render a decision, which should by itself create a legal norm for similar cases in the future. Thus, the real function of precedential practice of the Supreme Court may vacillate between mere 'elucidation' or 'concretisation' of a particular norm on the one hand, and that of 'creating' a new rule, on the other. Although not binding, such decisions are typically regarded as a source of law by courts. Conversely, the decrees of the Plenums of the Supreme Court and the Supreme Arbitrazh Court mostly consist of provisions which add nothing to the content of the norms being explained. Therefore, the difference between 'precedential practice' and 'guiding' is merely formal, not functional.

Interpretive guidelines

These include, in the first place, the 'explanations' issued by the plenums of the Russian supreme courts in the form of decrees. Besides, there are information letters, surveys of judicial practice and answers to the questions from lower courts which are often stripped of the details of specific disputes and thus

---

13 K. V. Iaroshenko, Судебная практика и гражданское право [Judicial Practice and Civil Law], in Судебная практика в советской правовой системе [Judicial Practice in the Soviet Legal System], p. 129.

14 Lebedev, Судебная власть в современной России [Judicial Power in Modern Russia], pp. 187–189.

15 S. S. Alekseev, Теория права [Theory of Law] (1994), pp. 181, 186.

resemble the decrees. The latter, although principally based on concrete judicial decisions, are completely detached from the facts of any particular case and therefore represent a kind of generalisation of court practice. The position of courts (including the Constitutional Court of Russia) is that the decrees of the plenums are a kind of official interpretation, and the respective powers are usually traced to Arts 126 and 127 of the Constitution.[16] At first glance, they are addressed to the court personnel. However, it was argued that they constitute a kind of legal norm inasmuch as they affect the life and behaviour of citizens who come into court.[17]

In the Russian Empire the Ruling Senate customarily issued instructions which were taken as a source of law by courts below. According to Art 815 of the Statute on Civil Procedure, 'all judgments and rulings of the Cassation Departments of the Senate, by which the precise sense of the laws is explained, shall be published for everybody's notice, for guidance to uniform interpretation and application thereof'.[18] The said provision of the Statute was usually cited in support of the Senate's power to issue binding interpretations, although that power was contested by some commentators.[19] So the legislation assigned a double purpose to Senate's judgments: apart from settling concrete disputes, some of them were expected to guide the application of laws. In fact, such instructional decisions were a mixture of a precedent and an official interpretation addressed to all courts. Since 1877 the cases raising issues of general importance were to be considered by the relevant department of the Senate *en banc*, whereas ordinary disputes were settled by sections of the departments.[20]

This practice was subsequently embraced and (to a great extent) reformed by the supreme judicial organs of the Soviet State. Unlike Senate's rulings, their guidelines were phrased in an abstract fashion, without references to concrete disputes. Since then this form of judicial interpretation became the principal one for many decades. It is noteworthy that interpretive guidelines have an important advantage over classical precedent: they allow courts to address any issue at any time, instead of waiting until it comes before them as a concrete dispute. This makes them a powerful tool of judicial law-making.

Perhaps, one of the reasons why Soviet supreme courts were not permitted to interpret laws by way of concrete decisions was the control over courts exercised by the Communist Party officials. It was simply impossible for them to screen and approve many hundreds of decisions rendered in concrete disputes. This brings us

---

16 See, for instance, the Decree of the Constitutional Court of 17 December 1996, No. 20-П, *HCC*, no. 5 (1996), p. 23.

17 See O. S. Ioffe, Советское гражданское право [Soviet Civil Law] (1967), p. 44.

18 G. V. Bertgold (comp.), Устав гражданского судопроизводства [Statute on Civil Procedure] (1915), p. 173.

19 See in particular E. V. Vas'kovskii, Руководство к толкованию и применению законов [Manual for Interpretation and Application of Laws] (1997; 1st edn. – 1902).

20 I. M. Tiutriumov (comp.), Устав гражданского судопроизводства [The Statute of Civil Proceedings] (1912), pp. 1165–1166.

to an issue which was given a significant attention in the Western studies of Soviet law: to what extent can the content of such guiding interpretations be ascribed to the courts themselves? To put it simply, it was doubted that 'legislative' innovations of the Soviet supreme courts were initiated by judges themselves and not by Communist Party organs. Wagner unequivocally denied the law-creating significance of 'guiding explanations' on the following grounds: the Senate Cassation Departments, he said, 'acted as autonomous judicial bodies, however, the "guiding decisions" of the post-1938 USSR Supreme Court were always vetted, and often drafted, by state and party officials'.[21] That said, the role of the supreme courts of the USSR and RSFSR was marginal, for they were merely driving belts of the regime. But it raises the question of the purpose of this circumvention. Why could permanent legislative organs (the presidiums of the Supreme Soviets of the USSR and RSFSR) not, when necessary, correct and specify legal provisions by themselves?

Two answers may be suggested. First, these bodies were filled with high-ranking Communist Party officials who had too many duties and were not trained in legal matters to engage in such work. Second, the issuance of authentic interpretations by legislative bodies themselves endangered the prestige of the Soviet State, since this would reveal the imperfection of legislative acts. The guiding explanations, in their turn, were considered by law as a mere interpretation of such acts, not as the 'correction of mistakes'. The pretext for their issuance was quite different, that is, the necessity to inform judges of new legal developments and prevent *mistakes of the courts*.

Unlike Wagner, other authors were less categorical in their assertions on this issue. Ioffe and Maggs emphasised the legislative function of the Supreme Court and remarked that Soviet courts were given that function because of their political reliability.[22] It is true that the decrees of the Central Committee of the Communist Party and the Soviet Government were frequently mentioned and cited in guiding explanations. However, in the opinion of Barry and Barner-Barry, 'to emphasise this point alone would be to suggest that the Plenum's role is limited to transmitting the political will to the legal sphere. This is not the only thing it does, and the large number of decrees lacking political references indicates that there are different aspects to the Plenum's functions'. All the same, they found that examples of genuine legislative activity were rare in criminal law and can better be found in civil law or the field of judicial administration,[23] partially because 'civil law appears to have been more successfully removed

---

21 Wagner, 'Civil Law in Late Imperial Russia', in *Reforming Justice in Russia*, p. 43. Peter Solomon seems to share this opinion (see Solomon, *Soviet Criminal Justice under Stalin* (1996), pp. 416–418).

22 O. S. Ioffe and P. B. Maggs, *Soviet Law in Theory and Practice* (1983), p. 303.

23 D. D. Barry and C. Barner-Barry, 'The USSR Supreme Court and the Systematisation of Soviet Criminal Law', in D. D. Barry, F. J. M. Feldbrugge and D. Lasok (eds.), *Codification in the Communist World* (1975), pp. 15–16.

from the political arena than criminal law, so the Plenum can more easily play the role of a disinterested interpreter of existing legal norms'.[24]

What was the legal status of decrees under Soviet law and how did it change in modern Russian legislation? After the 1917 revolutions there were five generations of laws on the structure and powers of courts, new laws being adopted every 15–20 years. Quite naturally, every law brought some changes to the legal framework within which the supreme courts had to operate. The first generation was initiated by the establishment of the so-called Supreme Judicial Control within the RSFSR People's Commissariat of Justice (10 March 1921). It was the forerunner of the Supreme Court, which was created next year. The USSR Supreme Court was set up soon thereafter (July 1923). It was empowered to issue 'guiding explanations' (*rukovodiashie raz'iashenia*) for supreme courts of union republics.[25] The term 'explanations' suggests that their purpose was conceived to be the elucidation of the meaning of legal norms.

However, the Law 'On Court Structure of the USSR, Union and Autonomous Republics' of 16 August 1938 (the basic act of the 'second generation') employed (Art 75) a substantially stronger term, namely, 'guiding directives' (*rukovodiashie ukazania*). Quite probably, this terminological change was reflective of a more centralised and less 'legalistic' approach to the administration of justice so characteristic of Stalinism. One should take into account that in the Russian language the word *ukazania*, as opposed to *raz'iasnenia*, sounds more authoritarian. Even more importantly, the first term does not connote being necessarily based on a certain legal act subject to 'elucidation' or 'explanation'. Also, it does not imply being backed by any kind of argumentation or discourse. Due to these connotations, it could be regarded as a self-contained source of law. No wonder that legal doctrine during the last years of Stalin's rule was inclined to view Supreme Court pronouncements as being such. It is also of importance that the RSFSR Supreme Court was deprived of this function. It started to issue instructions for lower courts again as late as the 1960s.

The 1957 Statute of the Supreme Court of the USSR (the core act of the third 'generation') abandoned this authoritarian terminology. The decrees were again called 'guiding explanations' (Art 9).[26] The same was done with respect to the

---

24 D. D. Barry and C. Barner-Barry, 'The USSR Supreme Court and Guiding Explanations on Civil Law', p. 83. This view also found support in works of John Hazard ('Understanding Soviet Law without the Cases', *Soviet Studies*, Vol. VII, no. 2 (1955), p. 121), Bernard Rudden ('The Role of the Courts and Judicial Style under the Soviet Civil Codes', in *Codification in the Communist World* (1975), p. 319), and F. J. M. Feldbrugge (*Russian Law: the End of the Soviet System and the Role of Law* (1993), p. 26).

25 Article 43 of the USSR Constitution (31 January 1924).

26 In very rare cases the Plenum of the USSR Supreme Court passed judgments, which were officially declared to have the force of a guiding explanation (S. N. Bratus (ed.), Судебная практика в советской правовой системе [Judicial Practice in the Soviet Legal System], p. 57). To my knowledge, there were no such examples with respect to the Supreme Court of the RSFSR. One reason is that its Plenum could not consider individual disputes.

RSFSR Law 'On Court Structure' (27 October 1960). But neither the 1938 Law nor its successor made any mention of the binding force of the Supreme Court decrees.

For the first time the term 'binding' (*obiazatel'nyi*) was used as late as in 1979 in the Law on the Supreme Court of the USSR (the fourth generation of judicial laws). Article 3 of the Law provided that the Plenum of the USSR Supreme Court shall give guiding explanations binding upon courts, other agencies and officials applying the law which has been interpreted (or 'explained'). This definition was replicated in the 1981 RSFSR Law 'On Court Structure' (Art 56(1)), still in force). It could be taken as a strong (although by no means explicit) reinforcement of the law-creative function of the court.

This term is lacking, however, in the post-Soviet Federal Constitutional Law 'On the Judicial System of the Russian Federation' (23 October 1996), which belongs to the last generation of laws on the structure of the judiciary. Besides, the draft Federal Law 'On Normative Legal Acts in the Russian Federation' (which was adopted at first reading in the State Duma in 1996 and is still pending) does not mention decrees of the Supreme Court and the Supreme Arbitrazh Court among normative acts. But this generation of laws is far from complete. The draft law 'On the Supreme Court of the Russian Federation' whose Art 17(2) makes the decrees binding is not yet adopted. At the same time, the draft Federal Constitutional Law 'On Courts of General Jurisdiction in the Russian Federation' (proposed by the President, not the Supreme Court) lacks provisions to that effect. Much more important fact, however, is that the 1995 Federal Constitutional Law 'On Arbitrazh Courts in the Russian Federation' has already provided for binding force of the decrees of the Plenum of the Supreme Arbitrazh Court with respect to inferior courts (Art 13). Moreover, the 2002 Code of Arbitrazh Procedure allows courts to make reference to decrees of the Plenum in their judgments (Art 170), thereby acknowledging that they can constitute the legal basis of court decisions. But the 2002 Code of Civil Procedure does not go so far. It neither allows nor prohibits such references.

It should be added that neither the 1977 USSR Constitution nor the 1993 Russian Constitution made such decrees binding upon lower courts. But, as was seen, this did not prevent particular laws on court system from having provisions to that effect. All the same, it remains unclear whether the rule of the 1981 Law applies to the Supreme Court of the Russian Federation, given that this law predates the present Constitution. If it does apply, then the Supreme Court decrees are still binding on courts below; if it does not, there would be an asymmetry between the powers of the courts of last resort in general and the arbitrazh system. This discrepancy can be accounted for by the difference in jurisdiction of the arbitrazh and general courts. Whereas the former settle economic disputes based on civil legislation, the latter deal with criminal cases too. It was frequently argued that judicial creativity in criminal matters is incompatible with the principle of legality because norms of the criminal law can be specified only by the Criminal Code.[27] This does not mean that judge-made rules were completely unknown to Russian criminal law. Rather, the opposite is true. But, in light of this theory, it is understandable that the legislature was reluctant to admit the bindingness of decrees of the highest court of general jurisdiction. As a practical matter, decrees of the Supreme Court, even those that deal with criminal law, are still thought by most practitioners (including judges) to have normative force.[28]

The said hesitations might explain why arbitrazh courts make references to decrees more readily. Among many thousands of decisions available on KoncultantPlus electronic database some portion contains such references. How large is this portion with regard to different courts? The Table 2 below convincingly demonstrates that Supreme Court is more timid than the top judicial instances of arbitrazh system.

A question to be asked in connection with the interpretive decrees is whether they are creative. This issue came to the fore in late 1940 and has been frequently debated since. On the whole, Soviet legal doctrine tended to reject the idea that any of the Supreme Court rulings (first, in concrete cases and, second, their generalisation in form of the 'guiding explanations') could be considered as a source of law. The cautiousness of scholars was mainly accounted for by their reluctance to doubt the exclusive legislative authority of the parliamentary body, the Supreme Soviet, which, according to the Soviet ideology, was the only State agency empowered to make laws and express the people's will in that way.

This ideological fiction could not, of course, fully preclude the analysis of realities in the area of law-creation. In Soviet legal literature opposite views on

Table 2 The share of decisions with references to the decrees of the plenums (%)

Year	Presidium of the Supreme Arbitrazh Court	Federal Arbitrazh Courts	Supreme Court (Presidium and all division)
1996	2.82	3.05	6.31
1997	3.06	4.90	7.16
1998	3.75	5.15	7.04
1999	3.58	7.33	4.50
2000	4.12	6.13	3.79
2001	4.41	7.32	5.58
2002	7.24	6.90	4.54
2003	8.91	6.64	2.29
2004	9.16	7.59	2.44
2005	11.21	9.88	2.71

27 See Madiarova, Разъяснения Верховного Суда Российской Федерации в механизме уголовно-правового регулирования [Explanations of the Supreme Court of the Russian Federation in the Mechanism of Criminal Law Regulation], p. 295.

28 Ibid., p. 34.

the subject were expressed by Vil'nianskii in the late 1940s, who argued that judicial practice did constitute a source of law,[29] and sometime later by Novitskii, who denied this.[30] On the whole, the latter opinion seemed dominant, although not absolutely. But in Western studies on the activity of the USSR and RSFSR supreme courts the 'realistic' approach prevailed. The overwhelming majority of those scholars who studied the matter from abroad were convinced that decrees of the Supreme Court constituted a source of law. As Ioffe and Maggs remarked, the Soviet courts 'are entrusted with considerable "legislative" powers to fill the gaps in the often sketchy Soviet legislation', and in particular 'the USSR Supreme Court combines judicial and legislative functions'.[31] The similar points were made by Butler, who noted the 'creative and unusual role' of judicial practice in the development of law, and also by Rudden, who concluded: 'The courts, whether or not they have normative power, act as if they do.'[32]

An interesting example of how the Supreme Court 'interpretation' of a set of legal provisions has produced a new norm subsequently incorporated into legislation is the development of the presumption of innocence in Soviet law. For the first time in Soviet legal history this principle was formulated in 'guiding explanations' of the USSR Supreme Court. According to Art 160 of the 1977 USSR Constitution, 'no one may be adjudged guilty of a crime and subjected to punishment as a criminal except by the sentence of a court and in conformity with the law'. It was rightly noted that this provision could not be actually given the meaning of presumption of innocence, for it established only an exclusive right of a court to pass the verdict of guilty. That is why the Supreme Court had to employ a complex logical and systematic interpretation of Art 160 of the Constitution and criminal procedure law in connection with the relevant provisions of international human rights law. As a result, the norm stipulating presumption of innocence was introduced into Soviet law.[33]

The analysis of the past and present operation of the plenums' decrees draws us to the conclusion that they constitute a kind of subordinate (or 'delegated') normative acts and simultaneously a subsidiary source of law. These characteristics are different: whereas the subsidiary function relates to their substantive purpose, that is, to fill gaps in both primary and secondary legislation, their subordinate nature means that they can be overcome by the decisions of the appropriate legislative agencies at any time. Although it has been

29 S. I. Vil'nianskii, Значение судебной практики в гражданском праве [Significance of Judicial Practice in Civil Law], Ученые труды Всесоюзного института юридических наук [Scientific Reports of All-Union Institute of Legal Sciences], Vol. IX (1947).

30 Novitskii, Источники советского гражданского права [The Sources of Soviet Civil Law], p. 134.

31 Ioffe and Maggs, Soviet Law in Theory and Practice, pp. 303, 305.

32 Butler, Soviet Law (1st edn., 1983), p. 49; Rudden, 'The Role of the Courts and Judicial Style', p. 321. See also Butler, 'Necessary Defence, Judge-Made Law, and Soviet Man', pp. 99–130.

33 Lebedev, Судебная власть в современной России [Judicial Power in Modern Russia], pp. 190, 202. See also J. Quigley, 'The Presumption of Innocence in the Russian Constitution', Parker School Journal of East European Law, no. 3 (1994) 329, esp. pp. 330–332.

maintained that there is still no answer to whether decrees should be aligned with normative acts or not,[34] the legislative recognition of their normative capacity is already underway, and courts frequently refer to them in their decisions.[35]

Although the decrees are not law-creating acts in their entirety, the same is true as regards those legislative acts which replicate the norms of other laws. The difference is a matter of degree, not quality. But some provisions of the decrees are novel: they deal with problems having two or more solutions, each of them being not contrary to law. If logical deductions can be creative, this also applies to concretising provisions contained in Supreme Court guidelines. Otherwise one must inevitably deny the creative nature of subordinate and even primary legislation on the grounds that it is a mere emanation or logical extension of higher sources of law.

It was argued that there is an important difference between the court explanations and ministerial normative acts: the violation of the latter usually entails sanctions provided for in the acts themselves or in other norms to which these acts refer.[36] In this respect, the explanations are incomplete (or 'imperfect'). One can object, however, there is an abundance of statutory provisions which do not entail sanctions; what is more, *lex imperfecta* is a *lex*, despite being *imperfecta*. Moreover, judicial decrees also entail sanctions, although implicit. The persons who failed to comply with them run the risk of losing the trial or getting a result essentially different from what they had hoped for. Most often, sanctions for the disregard of these judge-made norms are the same as provided in more general or analogous norms, from which they were deduced by way of creative interpretation. Of course, judges are capable of ignoring rules made by higher courts. In Soviet law there were no formal sanctions which would require lower judges to comply with Supreme Court guidelines. Nor are such sanctions provided by Russian legislation. In practice, Soviet judges were simply running the risk of being not re-elected for the following term or, at a minimum, not promoted to a higher position because of the large number of reversed cases. Another sanction can be reversal on appeal, which is quite efficacious. But, most importantly, the same sanction applies if a judge neglects any other source of law.[37] So there is no difference between judge-made rules and subordinate legislation in this respect.

---

34 Madiarova, Разъяснения Верховного суда Российской Федерации в механизме уголовно-правового регулирования [Explanations of the Supreme Court of the Russian Federation in the Mechanism of Criminal Law Regulation], p. 81.

35 See, for instance, the Decree of the Presidium of the SAC of 21 January 2003, No. 8095/02, *Вестник Высшего Арбитражного Суда Российской Федерации* [Herald of the Supreme Arbitrazh Court of the Russian Federation; hereinafter: *HSAC*], no. 6 (2003), pp. 43–45. Two examples are cited in a Survey of the Practice of the Supreme Court for the 3rd Quarter of the Year 2001, *BSC*, no. 4 (2002), pp. 17, 21. There are also hundreds of unpublished decisions which can be found in electronic databases.

36 Bratus and Vengerov in S. N. Bratus (ed.), Судебная практика в советской правовой системе [Judicial Practice in the Soviet Legal System], pp. 26–27.

37 Apart from extreme cases dealt with by Art 305 of the Criminal Code.

The process of recognising decrees as a source of law could conceivably pass through three stages. The first is legislative consolidation of their binding force; the second is permission to refer to them as a ground for court decisions in individual disputes; the third step would be to recognise non-compliance with them as a ground for reversal of such decisions. The first and second steps do not necessarily entail the third, since references to the decree can be viewed as making the decision more persuasive or giving it further support. Up to now, Russian legislation has reached the second stage, but only with regard to arbitrazh courts. The process was completed in Polish law of the socialist era, where the non-compliance of judges with directives of the Supreme Court was explicitly recognised as a ground for retrial or reconsideration of their decision (during the years 1962–1989). But Soviet and Russian legislators refrained from this.

The next question is whether the power of highest courts to issue binding explanations is contrary to the constitutional principle of judicial independence. The opinions within the legal community vary. In 1993 the status of 'guiding explanations' was debated at considerable length at the Constitutional Conference whose task was to draft a new constitution. There was a vivid exchange of views between law professors, top officials and judges in which they voiced their opinions quite unreservedly.

The debate was opened by the then chairmen of the supreme courts, Veniamin Iakovlev and Viacheslav Lebedev, who insisted on the binding force of the explanations issued by their courts. But the constitutional judge Tamara Morshchakova objected: 'It is necessary to understand what we want. [Do we want] the court be subordinate to the law or not? May the supreme judicial agency of any branch of judiciary give its explanations? It may, of course, but their significance cannot be binding.'[38]

Lebedev replied immediately: 'This idea is good, especially today courts are mad on it – complete independence, it's very good. But the point is that today . . . in this situation when we have a scrappy legislation, the explanations of a superior court . . . are simply necessary. It is judges who ask for it.' His argument was carried further by Iakovlev: 'We do not say that we have precedent, but that these explanations have such a character, it is clear. I think, if there are no such acts of judicial interpretation by the supreme court instances on the basis of [judicial] practice, we shall indeed have very grave consequences.' And then he added, quite excitedly: 'I know that . . . the decrees of the Supreme Arbitrazh Court Plenum bearing exactly such a character, do have a tremendous value for all arbitrazh courts. Tremendous! They always ask us for explanations on the basis of generalisation of disputes on privatisation and so forth – the

38 Конституционное совещание Стенограммы Материалы Документы 29 апреля–10 ноября 1993г 1993г. [The Constitutional Conference. Verbatim Transcripts. Materials. Documents. 29 April–10 November 1993], Vol. 13 (1995), pp. 109–110 (meeting of 23 June 1993, S. A. Filatov, presiding).

cases are absolutely new, the practice is just being formed. Therefore I think it is a dangerous thing – to reject them.'[39]

Chief judges received backing from Boris Topornin (the Director of the Institute of State and Law of the Russian Academy of Sciences):

> The main question – the principled one – is whether we depart from the former system and turn to the use of precedents in our judicial practice? If these decisions are simply explanations, then they are mere consultations or advices, but not acts, not documents, which a court may refer to when adopting a future decision. The point is...that it is necessary to make so that these judicial explanations or decisions or advices or recommendations could be used by courts as grounds for making their judgments in the future, as a precedent.[40]

But the advocates of binding force for the decrees faced a strong opposition from those who disliked the idea: Tamara Morshchakova, Sergei Filatov (the Head of Administration of the Russian President) and Alexander Iakovlev (a leading expert on criminal law). The latter advanced a compromise formula – to permit the highest courts to issue explanations without mentioning their bindingness in the Constitution – and evolved his suggestion thus:

> Certainly, no sentence can be based on the decision of the Plenum. A rule of a law should necessarily be present here. But rare sentence goes without the judge's opinion being supported by reference to a decree of the Plenum. Consequently, the decree of the Plenum does not have the authority of power, but it has the power of an authority. [...] That is why this formula – 'and shall adopt explanations regarding questions of judicial practice' – just mirrors, to my mind, the position which the Plenum does currently enjoy and will enjoy in our practice. On the one hand, its decision is not a source of law in pure form, but, on the other hand, nobody denies that it embodies the synthesis of judicial practice and is always reflected in sentences and decisions. This formula, in my view, is a good one.[41]

Topornin, however, was still dissatisfied:

> We must now say either 'yes' or 'no'. We are saying neither 'yes' nor 'no', leaving it to interpretation, to practice. But we, nevertheless, should say 'yes'. Since we speak of the development of law...we need, in addition to a decree and a law which cannot envisage many occurrences, have explanations, interpretations, or precedents, which would interpret our current practice.[42]

39 Ibid., pp. 111–112.
40 Ibid., p. 113.
41 Ibid.
42 Ibid., pp. 113–114.

The debate continued for a while along the same lines. Filatov and Morshchakova kept on saying that judges should obey only the Constitution and laws, that guiding explanations deprive judges of their individuality, etc.[43] In his extensive response Veniamin Iakovlev relied on the need for uniformity which is needed because 'the application of law ... is an utterly complex thing' and therefore a law cannot contain 'absolutely precise criteria for solution of millions of concrete situations differing one from another'. He continued: 'One can label it with different names. One can call it acts of judicial interpretation, or guiding explanations, possibly a precedent. These things are somewhat different, but the essence is same. The law is necessarily subject to interpretation when applied to various distinct situations. But there should be some leeway in interpretation, it should not happen that one court interprets the law in one way, the other court does it other way round, and the third interprets in its own original way and nothing remains of the law.' He conceded, though, that the explanations might be called 'authoritative' instead of 'binding'.[44]

The opponents, however, remained unconvinced. The representative of the President, Alexander Kotenkov, reminded stubbornly that 'judges are independent and subordinate only to the law and they cannot be submitted to any explanations'. Filatov concurred: 'It is a judge who is responsible for his actions, who does not put the blame upon his being compelled to do [certain things]. I think, it is correct.' In the end, the compromised formula was approved. Its author, Alexander Iakovlev, summed up the discussion: 'They will be binding anyway. Every clever judge will obey them.'[45]

A later attempt of some members of the Conference to delete the mention of the explanations from the final draft of the Constitution was successfully rebutted by two leading lawyers – Anatolii Sobchak and Marat Baglai.[46] The former emphasised that 'in all judicial systems the highest courts give such explanations, but in a different form', that is, in the form of precedents. Baglai agreed: 'Judicial practice is a source of law, legal stability cannot exist without it.'[47] Thus this formulation eventually became a part of the Constitution.

---

43 Конституционное совещание Стенограммы Материалы Документы 29 апреля–10 ноября 1993г 1993г. [The Constitutional Conference. Verbatim Transcripts. Materials. Documents. 29 April–10 November 1993], Vol. 13 (1995), pp. 114–115.

44 Ibid., p. 115.

45 Ibid., p. 116.

46 Anatolii Sobchak (d. 2000) was a professor of law and the mayor of Petersburg in 1991–1996. He is thought to be among the main sponsors of Vladimir Putin's career. Marat Baglai, also a professor of law, became the Chairman of the Constitutional Court in 1997. He held this post till 2003.

47 Конституционное совещание Стенограммы Материалы Документы 29 апреля–10 ноября 1993 г. [The Constitutional Conference. Verbatim Transcripts. Materials. Documents. 29 April–10 November 1993], Vol. 20 (1996), pp. 387, 389 (meeting of 30 October 1993, A. A. Sobchak, presiding).

In my view, the binding force of Supreme Court explanations can be reconciled with the principle of independence of judges.[48] One may wonder what should be the purpose of the explanations if they are not binding? Why should the Supreme Court's position be more persuasive for a judge than, say, the lawyers' opinion? Simply because the former could reverse the decision on appeal and thereby impose its view of the law? This might be qualified as pressure on judges which is expressly outlawed by the Law 'On the Judicial System' (Art 5).[49] On the other hand, binding force does not amount to pressure because there is no inducement to pass a certain decision or sentence. Paradoxically, but in these circumstances the best approach may be the explicit recognition of guiding explanations as a source of law.

As for the impingement upon of judicial independence, it can be noted that judges may refuse to implement the provisions of a Supreme Court decree if they find it contrary to law. In this respect they are similar to normative acts, because, unlike the Constitution, lesser laws are not absolutely binding upon judges. If judges find a law unconstitutional, they must refuse it application. Likewise, if a court makes a judgment in a particular case which runs counter to the decree, the only thing required of the court would be to set out the reasons for such deviation. It is difficult to see how the duty to expose the reasons for disagreement would diminish the independence of judges. Moreover, it will be more difficult for superior courts to overturn such a decision, for they would have to openly refute the arguments of the lower court. Whether or not Russian judges would feel constrained in the face of the express bindingness of decrees does not depend on the legal status of the latter. It largely depends on the institutional reforms of the judiciary and changes in the judges' mentality.

If the plenums' decrees are, in fact, a kind of subordinate legislation, this necessarily entails a possibility of their review. At present no body has a right to examine their legality and constitutionality. There is no problem with respect to reviewing them when settling concrete disputes, due to the formula of Art 120(2) of the Constitution: 'A court, having established when considering a case the failure of an act of a State or other agency to conform to a law shall adopt a decision in accordance with the law.'[50] Yet the abstract review of decrees is impossible, and this is inconsistent with their binding force. Their provisions should be subject to judicial examination and invalidation in the event of their non-conformity to higher sources of law.

According to the first law on the Russian Constitutional Court (1991), this tribunal could check the constitutionality of the decrees of the supreme courts (Arts 32[5] and 66). But the law of 1994 excluded this power from the Court's

---

48 Lebedev, Судебная власть в современной России [Judicial Power in Modern Russia], pp. 197–198.

49 *RLT*, p. 143.

50 *RLT*, p. 42.

competence. It became unclear whether these decrees are, as formerly, subject to review or not. A positive answer seems more convincing, for the Constitutional Court is still entitled to verify the constitutionality of laws evaluating 'the meaning imparted to it by an official or other interpretation or existing law enforcement practice' (Art 74, present Law).[51] So, today they are subject to *indirect* control of the Constitutional Court. Consequently, it seems logical to subject them to direct control following recognition of the decrees of the Supreme Court as acts of subordinate legislation. Article 3 of the Law on the Constitutional Court provides that subordinate legislation of such highest organs of the State as the President, the Soviet of the Federation, the State Duma and the Federal Government are subject to review for constitutionality. But the decrees of the supreme courts are not included. Are decrees of the Supreme Arbitrazh Court a kind of subordinate legislation, given that they are already binding on courts? Is it doubtful that what is binding on courts settling a dispute is equally applicable to parties to such dispute? If yes, it seems illogical that they are exempt from constitutional review.

There should be a legal opportunity to challenge them on the ground of non-conformity with federal laws as well. For now this is impossible, although such attempts were recorded. Citizen Mironov challenged certain provisions of point 26(3) of the Supreme Court Plenum Decree of 22 December 1992 on labour law. The contested provisions were indeed a striking example of how the Supreme Court developed the law by issuing supplementary rules which were effectively complied with by lower courts.[52] Mironov challenged them in the Supreme Court, for the latter is empowered to deem normative acts of the federal level inoperative. He lost, but filed an appeal against this ruling in the Cassation Division of the Supreme Court (the second instance in such cases). The Division rejected the appeal, but, notably, not on the grounds that the decree was not a normative act. Instead, it ruled that the Constitution 'does not vest in the courts of general jurisdiction the powers concerning verification of the legality of the decrees of the Plenum of the Supreme Court of the Russian Federation on questions of interpretation of judicial practice. Since a federal constitutional law which would provide for the possibility and establish the procedure of appeal against explanations of the Plenum...has not yet been adopted, Mironov's claims fall outside the scope of the court's jurisdiction'.[53] Just a little earlier in *Efimov*'s case the Supreme Court refused to review a decree of the Supreme Arbitrazh Court Plenum on the same grounds.[54] The applicant lodged a complaint in the Constitutional Court which held that, although the review of 'guiding explanations' was not envisaged by the legislation in force, it did not

---

51 *RLT*, p. 192.
52 See next chapter for details.
53 Ruling of 25 May 2000, No. KAC00-202, in the case of Mironov (unpublished).
54 Ruling of the Supreme Court of 24 April 2000, No. 00ГКПИ-368, in the case of Efimov (unpublished).

preclude the applicant from challenging in the constitutional tribunal the norms of the law explained in those decrees.[55] But often the real issue is their conformity to the law, not the Constitution. This circumvential way – challenging the law with a full awareness of its conformity to the Constitution – seems quite awkward and inconvenient. The applicant is supposed to apply to the Constitutional Court in the hope of getting from it certain pronouncements (in fact, a kind of *obiter dictum*) as to how the law *should not* be interpreted, and then try to convince an ordinary court to reconsider the case in the new light. But, given that the decrees of the plenums cannot be nullified by the Constitutional Court, it is far from certain that an ordinary court would reopen the case decided on their basis. In a later case the Constitutional Court refused to rule on the constitutionality of Art 13 of the law on arbitrazh courts by saying that this article regulates the relations between the Plenum of the Supreme Arbitrazh Court and other arbitrazh courts and therefore 'the rights and freedoms of the applicant are not directly affected by it'.[56]

It seems that Russian highest courts do their best to avoid the issue. Therefore, at present no court can review the decrees of plenums. Nonetheless, it is a long-standing practice to publish them in collections of *normative acts*. And they are not mere application of laws, nor are they instructions to judges as to how to apply them. They do affect the rights of citizens. Some of them may govern certain issues for decades. To give just one example: it was not clear who fall into the category of children and dependants of the deceased 'not having labour capacity' for the purposes of Art 535 of the 1964 Civil Code which entitled such persons to an obligatory participatory share in inheritance. Thus far the answer has been given only by the Decree of the USSR Supreme Court Plenum in 1966.[57] And it is still applied under Art 1139 of the new Civil Code which is equally vague in respect of this issue.[58]

So long as subordination to a law is conceived as being concurrently subordinate to lesser normative acts which develop the law, it would make sense to formally attach a normative status to all interpretive decrees of the plenums (at any rate, in civil cases) and simultaneously provide for their review to ensure their conformity to the law. Until it is done, their ambivalent and disputable status will persist. As a result, they find themselves in a 'grey zone' of uncertainty. It is particularly true with respect to the decrees of the Supreme Court: without being clearly binding, they *de facto* operate in that way. In other words, although having the 'rights' of subordinate legislative acts, they are immune from 'responsibilities' and requirements which are concomitant to such 'rights'.

---

55 Ruling of the Constitutional Court of 14 June 2001, No. 159-O (unpublished).

56 Point 4, Ruling of the Constitutional Court of 4 July 2002, No. 200-O, *HCC*, no. 1 (2003), p. 81.

57 Decree of the Plenum of the USSR Supreme Court of 1 July 1966, No. 6, 'On Judicial Practice with Regard to the Cases about Inheritance', Бюллетень Верховного Суда СССР [Bulletin of the USSR Supreme Court], no. 4 (1966), p. 21.

58 See Butler, *Russian Civil Legislation*, pp. 661–662, and *CCRF*, p. 421.

Conversely, the deprivation of interpretive decrees of their binding status is not a viable solution, given that their force is by nature independent of what is prescribed by laws on judicial system. Most probably, it will result in nothing more than a flood of declarations about the freedom of judges to interpret laws in the way he or she thinks best, etc, but not in the lessening of their real effect. If, alternatively, the very power to issue these guidelines, to which courts have accustomed, would be withdrawn from the supreme courts, it will require even more radical changes, first of all an accelerated development of the law of precedent. One should realise that in Russia and other post-Soviet countries the explanations of supreme courts assume the role which in other legal systems is left for precedents. Although (as shall be seen below) the question – 'whether precedents or explanations?' – is a false dilemma, because they do not exclude each other, it seems reasonable to preserve the existing balance between different kinds of judge-made law in the near future.

Irrespective of whether or not making decrees formally binding would help to inferior courts, it is definitely important to do so in order to enable both natural and juridical persons to contest their legality and constitutionality. While exempt from judicial review, they enjoy a privileged position in the Russian legal system, since they do guide the court practice on the one hand, and are outside the ambit of judicial review, on the other. But the procedures for their review require further consideration. If the questions of their *constitutionality* can be entrusted to the Constitutional Court without difficulties, it remains unclear by whom their *legality* could be reviewed. But there is little doubt that a solution will be found one way or the other.

Rules of courts

Among all forms of judicial law-making the issuance of court rules is the most straightforward and uncontroversial. It might be questioned whether such rules can always claim the status of legal rules in Russia, given that they are not necessarily subject to official publication. But some basic regulations of this kind are published and must be followed not only by the staff of the courts concerned, but also by litigants and their representatives because the 'internal' activities of courts cannot be strictly distinguished from others. The issuance of such rules is a special form of gap-filling. The peculiarity of such gaps lies in the fact that they were intentionally left open by the legislator, who explicitly authorised certain judicial bodies to fill them in.

The examples of such rules are few, but remarkable. These are the 'Regulations of Arbitrazh Courts of the Russian Federation' (last amended 8 April 2004) confirmed by the Plenum of the Supreme Arbitrazh Court[59] and the 'Regulations of the Constitutional Court of the Russian Federation' adopted on

---

59   The current version was published in *HSAC*, no. 3 (2003), pp. 6–23; no. 6 (2004), pp. 12–15.

1 March 1995.[60] They were adopted on the basis of Art 13 of the Federal Constitutional Law on arbitrazh courts and Art 3(7) of the Federal Constitutional Law on the Constitutional Court, respectively.[61] There is no equivalent document in the general judicial system because the legislative acts empowering the Supreme Court to issue such regulations are still pending.

However, there is one legal act which allowed the Supreme Court to regulate a particular subject by way of directives binding upon lower courts. This is the Federal Law 'On People's Assessors of Federal Courts of General Jurisdiction in the Russian Federation'. It empowered the Supreme Court to determine the procedure by which assessors for lower courts should be selected (Arts 5[2], 6[1], 7[2]). For reasons, which are not quite clear, this was done not by the Plenum, but through a decree of the Presidium of the Court.[62]

Precedents

Precedents emerge not only in court practice, but also in the activities of administrative agencies. The origins of precedents lie in the Chinese legal tradition at the time of the Sung dynasty. Characteristically, the oldest precedents were more administrative rather than judicial in character. They were 'the decisions of the central legal authorities on individual cases, in reaching legal decisions'.[63]

In Russian legal history the making of precedents was first evidenced as early as in the sixteenth–seventeenth centuries in the activities of the highest governmental organ, Boyar Duma, which can be roughly compared with Privy Council in England of the same period. The 1550 *Sudebnik* – an early Russian 'code' drawing upon the experience of dispute resolution – in Art 98 required that all new and unforeseen cases, upon being solved by the tsar and the Duma, shall be included into *Sudebnik*. The eminent Russian historian, Vasilii Kliuchevskii, has recounted a number of cases where Boyar Duma in its capacity of the highest governmental and judicial agency was developing law and deriving rules for the future time out of concrete disputes. Kliuchevskii unhesitatingly calls such decisions 'precedents'.[64]

---

60 See at [http://www.ksrf.ru/about/index.htm].

61 *RLT*, pp. 160, 214.

62 Decree of 14 January 2000 'On the Procedure for Selection of People's Assessors of Federal Courts of General Jurisdiction', *BSC*, no. 2 (2001), pp. 6–7. People's assessors were laymen who participated in court proceedings on a par with a professional judge. This institution was originally designed by Bolsheviks and has been abolished as late as in 2002. Their real influence on decision-making was negligible.

63 *The New Encyclopædia Britannica* (15th edn., 2002), Vol. 16, p. 104. On the origins of precedent see also: Nanping Liu, *Judicial Interpretation in China. Opinions of the Supreme People's Court* (1997), pp. 34–35.

64 V. O. Kliuchevskii, Боярская Дума Древней Руси [Boyars' Duma of the Ancient Russia] (1902), pp. 475 ff. See also: K. V. Petrov, «Прецедент» в средневековом русском праве (XVI–XVII вв.) ['Precedent' in the Medieval Russian Law (XVI–XVII centuries)], in Государство и право [State and Law], no. 4 (2005), pp. 78–83.

Obviously, making precedents was a native practice, not borrowed from the East or West. It evolved out of practical needs of the administration of justice, and for a long time was not regarded as something problematic. Apparently, it was the rise of Petrine 'regular state' governed by legislative rules imposed 'from above' as well as the attempts to form a separate judicial branch of government under Katherine II that eventually undermined the legitimacy of precedents and made it impossible to create norms through adjudication.

It is widely accepted that 'precedents are prior decisions that function as models for later decisions'.[65] Are precedents characteristic of some legal systems and completely alien to others? The principle of *stare decisis*, as found in the classic common law tradition, can be conceived as a form of a broader principle inherent in the judicial function as such. It is conventional wisdom that consistency and uniformity are among the most valuable traits of adjudication which litigants and society at large can expect from judges. Some degree of 'precedentiality' is intrinsic to the judicial function, regardless of the formal status of judicial decisions in a given legal system. It is remarkable that there was no prohibition in Soviet law against judicial precedent. This denial of precedent was merely a doctrinal position of Soviet jurists.[66] Therefore, the feeling of many observers that, despite the lack of formal binding force, Soviet judges did respect previous decisions in making their own is well-grounded.

As far as precedents in civil law countries are concerned, their binding force has always been the crucial issue. Traditionally, only binding precedents were viewed as precedents in the proper sense. They were a kind of general standard, which any judicial decision ought to attain in order to be regarded as precedent. Obviously, 'binding force' is not a divisible or graded concept, whereas 'persuasive force', on the contrary, is relative and can be a matter of degree. The current trend in the common law countries leads to a weakening of the binding force of precedents. The turning point was the 1966 Practice Statement of the House of Lords.[67] Therefore, these decisions are no longer universally binding; they retain only persuasive force for the House of Lords itself, however strong this force might be. It is no wonder that today comparative lawyers, rather than treat the normative force of precedents in 'yes-or-no' manner, scale them as follows:

(a) binding precedents;
(b) not binding but persuasive;
(c) providing further support;
(d) illustrative.[68]

---

65 D. N. MacCormick and R. S. Summers, 'Introduction', in *Interpreting Precedents*, p. 1.
66 Butler, *Russian Law* (2nd edn., 2003), p. 94.
67 *Practice Statement: Judicial Precedent* [1966] 3 All ER 77.
68 A. Peszenik, 'The Binding Force of Precedent', in D. N. MacCormick and R. S. Summers (eds.), *Interpreting Precedents*, p. 461.

From this perspective the decisions of supreme courts in Russia are not formally binding, but capable of having persuasive force or providing further support. As has been already said, in the Russian legal system, not all sources of law are absolutely (or indefeasibly) binding upon courts. Only the Constitution is regarded as absolutely binding; other sources are not. Therefore, precedents also cannot be denied normative force simply because they are not formally binding. This reason is no longer sufficient. If the formal binding force of the precedent means that future decisions must follow it or be subject to reversal on appeal, it is tantamount to saying that the highest-level courts are not formally bound by their previous decisions, for no appeal lies from the highest court.[69]

It also answers the question whether a persuasive precedent can be a source of law. Since 1966 precedents are no longer binding on the highest British court,[70] yet they constitute a part of English law. With respect to precedents in the Russian supreme courts the trend is exactly the opposite: precedents are not formally binding yet (the exception of judicial review will be considered below). Thus, despite many important differences in the operation of precedents within mature legal systems, the phenomenon itself is universal.

Strictly binding precedents have, under certain circumstances, fewer chances to survive than merely persuasive ones. There is no point in overruling a precedent if it can simply be departed from[71] and so saved from complete destruction. By contrast, strictly binding precedents cannot be departed from but only overruled, which leads to their exclusion from the legal system.

Even a persuasive precedent, in the absence of other normative resources capable of defeating or outweighing its force, may work as virtually binding. Moreover, a precedent can simultaneously be binding upon one court and merely persuasive for another, depending on the status of the court that laid it down, its jurisdiction, and relation to the court which applies the precedent. If the normative force of a precedent may vary under different circumstances, it follows that its normative force is not its 'internal quality'.

Ivanov wrote that in Russia judges are subordinate only to the Constitution and to a federal law, but in England they are bound by precedents.[72] This view is simplistic. Many branches of law in England are shaped by the legislature. But even in this area judges do create precedents when construing statutory norms, and other judges follow them when applying the same norms afterwards. Therefore, the question 'whether to follow statutes or precedents?' is mistaken. Judges may be guided by statutes and precedents at the same time. Precedents clarify

---

69 Ibid., p. 462.

70 Cf. the opinions of Lords Denning and Wilberforce and Professor Julius Stone in G. Sturgess and P. Chubb (eds.), *Judging the World: Law and Politics in the World's Leading Courts* (1988), p. 16. They argued that 'there is no absolutely binding precedent'.

71 A. Peszenik, 'The Binding Force of Precedent', in *Interpreting Precedents*, p. 463.

72 See his article in Судебная практика как источник права [Judicial Practice As a Source of Law], p. 124.

the content of laws, make them more concrete and precise, and effectively govern courts and laymen as to how they should understand a certain legal act.

Sometimes it is impossible to apply an elastic and inherently evaluative statutory norm uniformly without looking into relevant case law. For instance, Art 3 of the 2001 Russian Labour Code contains two norms that are hard to reconcile by purely abstract reasoning: Art 3(2) prohibits any preferences not connected with the professional qualities of an employee, whereas the next paragraph provides that the establishment of distinctions, exceptions, preferences, and restrictions of employee rights shall not constitute discrimination if they flow from the requirements peculiar to a particular type of labour provided by a federal law, or are conditioned by a special concern of the State concerning persons needing heightened social or legal defence.[73]

Historically, particular decisions of the USSR Supreme Court were commonly regarded as precedents.[74] The *Martsyniuk* case of 1940 is a case in point. For the first time in Soviet legal history it recognised the possibility of compensation for harm caused as a result of the rescue of 'socialist property'. The decision was reached on the basis of Art 131 of the 1936 USSR Constitution. This attitude was affirmed by another decision of the Court in 1949.[75] It was customary for advocates in Russia to refer to previous judicial decisions in their argumentation during court hearings.[76]

In modern times the development of precedents was given a further lease of life by the practice of direct application of the Russian Constitution by regular courts on the grounds of Art 15(1). A decree of the Plenum of the Supreme Court adopted on 31 October 1995 has focused courts on the necessity of giving the Constitution direct effect in all cases when necessary.[77]

Point 2 of the decree enumerates circumstances when direct application of the Constitution is expected. In particular, it is required when:

- a court comes to the conclusion that a federal act enacted prior to the entry into force of the 1993 Constitution is contrary to it;
- a court comes to the opinion that a federal act, although adopted after this date, does not conform to the relevant provisions of the Constitution;
- a law or other normative act adopted by a subject of the Federation on questions of joint competence of the Federation and its subjects is contrary to the federal Constitution, given that the federal act which ought to regulate the legal relations considered by the court is lacking.[78]

---

73 Labour Code of the Russian Federation, *Sudebnik*, Vol. VII (2002), pp. 37–38.
74 W. E. Butler, 'Judicial Precedent as a Source of Russian Law', in J. A. R. Nafziger and S. C. Symeonides (eds.), *Law and Justice in a Multistate World* (2002), pp. 584–586.
75 S. N. Bratus (ed.), Судебная практика в советской правовой системе [Judicial Practice in the Soviet Legal System], pp. 49, 111–112.
76 Butler, 'Judicial Precedent as a Source of Russian Law', p. 584.
77 Decree of the Plenum of the Supreme Court of 31 October 1995, *BSC*, no. 1 (1996), pp. 1–5.
78 Ibid., p. 3.

This decree created a new basis for judicial law-making. This contention may seem doubtful, for the decree instructs judges how to apply the Constitution directly, but not how to lay down new legal *standards*. But there is a linkage between the powers of courts to apply the Constitution and the precedential value of such decisions. If a federal law or other normative act is absent or is found by a court to be contrary to the Constitution, the court may face a deficiency in legal regulation which should be somehow filled. This does not mean to say that every case of direct application of the Constitution will become a precedent. A law not corresponding to the Constitution is still considered to have legal force, even though a court in a particular dispute has refused to apply it. Only if such decision becomes a pattern to which future judicial decisions will comply (*jurisprudence constante*) does it amount to law-creation.

Point 3, also very important, provides that 'in case of uncertainty as to the question whether the law applied or subject to application in a concrete dispute corresponds to the Constitution of the Russian Federation, a court...shall have recourse to the Constitutional Court of the Russian Federation with an inquiry about the constitutionality of this law'.[79] This point makes clear that the power of courts to apply the Constitution directly is residual. It is an ultimate resource to be used only in the absence of any reasonable doubt.

Currently Russian courts of general jurisdiction (but not arbitrazh courts) have a choice whether to deny the application of a law found to be unconstitutional in a particular dispute or to bring the matter to the Constitutional Court.[80] In the first case, the refusal to apply a certain normative act on the grounds of unconstitutionality or illegality means its invalidation for the parties to a concrete dispute, not *erga omnes*. However, there is a requirement intrinsic to the judicial function to treat like cases alike or, as the Supreme Court usually puts it, 'to ensure the unity of judicial practice'. It would be quite strange if some courts were to ignore such judgments of other courts, even if they are not formally bound by the latter. It is up to the supreme courts to impose general standards by choosing one way or another to ensure the desirable uniformity. There are examples of it. The 'Bulletin' provides an extensive abstract of a decision of the Presidium of the Tiumen regional court which refused to apply para 1(2) of Art 135 of the Family Code. The provision of the Code was deemed not to correspond to Art 55(3) of the Constitution containing the test of admissibility of restrictions on the rights and freedoms of man and the citizen.[81] By publishing the abstract in its official journal, the Supreme Court gave unequivocal support to this ruling and invited lower courts to follow it in similar cases. It is also

---

79 Ibid., pp. 3–4.
80 On the use by Russian courts of the power to apply the Constitution directly see: P. Krug, 'The Russian Federation Supreme Court and Constitutional Practice in the Courts of General Jurisdiction: Recent Developments', *Review of Central and East European Law*, no. 2 (2000), pp. 129 ff.
81 Decree of the Presidium of the Tiumen Regional Court in the case of spouses V., *BSC*, no. 4 (2003), p. 14.

noticeable that this precedent was made by an intermediary court, not by the Supreme Court itself.

In a similar way, the decisions of higher courts in which they refer to the generally recognised principles and norms of international law may work as precedents in future cases. The definition of such principles and norms was provided by the Supreme Court Plenum:

> As generally-recognised principles of international law one should understand the fundamental imperative norms of international law adopted and recognised by the international community of states, the deviation from which is inadmissible. Among the generally-recognised principles of international law are, in particular, the principle of general respect of human rights and that of good-faith performance of international obligations. As a generally-recognised norm of international law one should understand a rule of behaviour adopted and recognised by the international community of states as a whole as being legally mandatory. The content of the indicated principles and norms of international law can be exposed, in particular, in the documents of the United Nations and their specialised institutions.[82]

Evidently, they are not necessarily sanctioned by the national legislator. If so, courts may have some latitude in their application and construction which makes their decisions to that effect a kind of precedent of interpretation. The Supreme Court is silent as to whether courts must deny application to domestic enactments in the event of their being contrary to the principles of international law, or the latter are subject to subsidiary application only (for instance, when domestic provisions are ambiguous or not specific enough).[83] Yet the priority of those principles seems logical and is confirmed by a ruling of the Constitutional Court.[84] This Court frequently refers to such principles and norms and thus determines which of them must be viewed as a part of Russian law. Sometimes it goes so far that exceeds the limits of Art 15(4) of the Constitution and makes references to European law.[85]

The position as to whether court decisions are grounded in the norms of international treaties is more uncertain. The Supreme Court Plenum admits the 'direct and immediate effect' of international treaties.[86] At the same time,

---

82 Point 1, Decree of the Plenum of the Supreme Court of 10 October 2003, No. 5, *BSC*, no. 12 (2003), p. 4.

83 Cf. point 5 of its Decree of 31 October 1995, No. 8, *BSC*, no. 1 (1996), p. 4.

84 Ruling of the Constitutional Court of 3 July 1997, No. 87-O, *HCC*, no. 5 (1997), p. 33.

85 More details can be found in B. Zimnenko, Международное право в судебной практике России [International Law in the Russian Court Practice], *Российская юстиция* [Russian Justice], no. 9 (2003), pp. 6–10.

86 Point 5, Decree of the Plenum of the Supreme Court of 10 October 2003, No. 5, *BSC*, no. 12 (2003), p. 5.

the international treaties whose performance requires changes of federal laws currently in force or the adoption of new ones, or the treaties establishing other rules than those provided by a law need ratification in the form of a federal law.[87] Therefore, it seems that if a contradiction arises it should be settled by the application of the respective federal law which ratified them. But there is no guarantee that such a law is readily available in case of every contradiction which may arise at some point in the future. There can be conflicts between an existing law and a newly signed international treaty missed by the legislator in the same way as contradictions between other kinds of enactments escape his notice. Or a federal law can be changed without due regard to international treaties on the same subject, in which case a court will face a dilemma whether or not to deny application to such a law. Neither the legislation in force nor the Supreme Court Plenum provides a clear solution to it. Again, the operational rules do not determine the choice of substantive norms with sufficient precision.

From the standpoint of their functions and origin, the body of precedents in Russian law is divisible into four categories:

1 precedents of interpretation and gap-filling;
2 precedents arising out of judicial review;
3 precedents of discretion;
4 law-finding precedents.

Precedents of interpretation are probably the most common. Precedents of gap-filling also fall into this broad category, since in a statute-based legal system it is technically possible to justify any decision by way of legal analogy from a statutory norm. When the most senior Russian judge, Nina Sergeeva, was asked whether she could remember any single case of reversal of a decision on the grounds of its irrationality or injustice, her response was: 'No; it is impossible'.[88] However, there were actually cases in which statutory law was bent by judges as a result of its injustice.[89] During the era of rapid inflation the Presidium of the Supreme Court once decreed that a credit contract obligation fixed in the US dollars should be performed in roubles, but the amount due should be changed to

---

87 Articles 14–15, Federal Law of 15 July 1995, No. 101-ФЗ, 'On International Treaties of the Russian Federation' (*RLT*, p. 776).
88 The question was asked by the Constitutional Court Judge Anatolii Kononov (see V. M. Savitskii (ed.), Судебный контроль и права человека [Judicial Review and Human Rights] (1996), p. 91). N. S. Sergeeva was a Deputy Chairman of the Supreme Court in 1957–2003.
89 A few examples are given in A. Fedotov, Возможно ли применение contra legem в демократическом правовом государстве [Is the Application of *Contra Legem* Possible in a Democratic Rule-of-Law State?], Журнал российского права [Journal of Russian Law], no. 8 (2002), pp. 92–99.

accord with the currency exchange rate.[90] This judgment was a sheer compromise between the requirements of law and justice. However, considerations of justice are never explicitly admitted by Russian judges, for any decision should be traced to a certain norm, however abstract or vague or remote. Accordingly, gap-filling precedents are difficult to distinguish from those of interpretation. Their force may be virtually binding (in this respect published decisions of the presidiums of the supreme courts seem to be the case in point) or merely persuasive, with different degrees of force. Some are of such a nature that it is simply impossible to imagine how they can be ignored or departed from without the risk of undermining public confidence in the courts.[91] In general, it should be noted that 'precedents of interpretation' are too tightly entwined with the content of the norms being interpreted, so that they can hardly be ignored in the process of adjudication unless such disregard is motivated by weighty reasons.

Judicial review precedents, when applied, are strictly binding upon courts: if it is proved that a provision is analogous to or based upon the rule already invalidated, such a provision is subject to immediate invalidation on these grounds by a court ruling. Although some legal scholars have reservations concerning the idea that judicial review creates precedents in the proper sense,[92] the opposite view is more prevalent.[93] The present author shares this view. Consider, for instance, general features of precedent as outlined by Podol'skaia. A decision of the Constitutional Court would meet all essential requirements she sets out.[94] It is binding upon the entire court system, its legal force is even higher than that of a law, it has both retroactive and prospective effect, decides the question of law, not fact, and is subject to publication. The only objection might be that a constitutional case is a singular one, so that exactly the same dispute will not come before the same court in the future. However, provisions analogous to those already vacated or countenanced may be considered by the Court, and there is an implicit duty of the Court to treat them the same way, unless they can be reasonably distinguished. The passing of a legal act and its supposed similarity to the one previously held to be unconstitutional constitute the facts of

90 Decree in the case *B. v Mezhotraslevoi Kommercheskii Bank* (excerpt), *BSC*, no. 12 (1996), pp. 8–9. Inflation can be a powerful inspiration for judicial activism, as the case of Germany in the 1920s shows. See J. E. Herget and S. Wallace, 'The German Free Law Movement', p. 418.

91 See the example of such precedent concerning the competence of different tiers of the judicial system in Chapter 2, pp. 65–66 above.

92 A. Pesczenik, 'The Binding Force of Precedent', in D. N. MacCormick and R. S. Summers (eds.), *Interpreting Precedents*, p. 477.

93 Z. Bankowski, D. N. MacCormick, L. Morawski and A. R. Miguel, 'Rationales for Precedent', in D. N. MacCormick and R. S. Summers (eds.), *Interpreting Precedents*, p. 485.

94 N. A. Podol'skaia, К вопросу о понятии прецедента как источника права (общетеоретический аспект) [To the Issue of Precedent as Being a Source of Law (General Theoretical Aspect)], in Судебная практика как источник права [Judicial Practice as a Source of Law] (2000), pp. 149–152.

a new case, whereas the applicable law is the Constitution and the previous decision of the Court, to which the new ruling should conform.

Let us exemplify it by the decree of the Constitutional Court of 6 July 1998.[95] The Court deemed unconstitutional the rule of Art 325 of the RSFSR Criminal Procedure Code which prohibited appeals against sentences passed by the Supreme Court as a court of first instance. In its decision the Constitutional Court has obliged the legislator to make amendments to that effect into the Criminal Procedure Code. The legislator did this and even more by granting the right to appeal against the decisions of the Supreme Court in both criminal and civil cases. Accordingly, a new (Cassational) division was instituted within the Supreme Court. However, the arbitrazh procedure remained untouched, and it is still impossible to appeal against the decisions of the Supreme Arbitrazh Court acting as a court of first instance (Art 181 of the 2002 Arbitrazh Procedure Code). Why only two of the three procedural codes have been amended is difficult to explain. There is little doubt that if parties are deprived of the opportunity of cassational appeal in an arbitrazh case, such deprivation equally infringes upon their right to judicial protection guaranteed by Art 46 of the Constitution. But for our inquiry it is much more important that in the event of Art 181 being challenged in the Constitutional Court it should be invalidated on the grounds of the precedent made by the Court in its 1998 Decree. The facts of such hypothetical case – the existence of the norm forbidding cassational appeals – would be absolutely similar to those which have been previously examined by the Court. The applicable law would also be the same, that is, Art 46 of the Constitution as interpreted by the 1998 Decree, and the Court will be bound by its former conclusions. To cut a long story short, what is 'tried' in cases of judicial review of normative acts is norms, and they are tried on the basis of rules of a higher level, so that there is no difference with reasoning by analogy in cases in which 'ordinary' precedents are applied. The Constitutional Court says that ordinary courts can establish the invalidity of regional laws analogous to the ones that have already been invalidated by the Constitutional Court. In so doing, they must 'rest their decisions' upon its judgment, which hereby provides the only basis for settling such disputes.[96] The same must to be true with regard to all court decisions made in the process of abstract review of normative acts. In late 2005 the need for such precedents was acknowledged by the Supreme Court in its draft code of administrative proceedings, in which, according to Chief Justice Lebedev, the previous rulings on the legality of various regulations are supposed to serve as 'model' cases applicable to analogous regulations in future disputes.

---

95 The Decree of the Constitutional Court of 6 July 1998, No. 21-П, on Art 325(5) of the Criminal Procedure Code of the RSFSR, *HCC*, no. 6 (1998), pp. 5–9.

96 Point 4, reasoned part of the Decree of the Constitutional Court of 11 April 2000, No. 6-П, *HCC*, no. 4 (2000), pp. 18–19.

The decisions of the Constitutional Court are applied by regular courts too.[97] In one case the Cassation Division of the Supreme Court ruled that the court of first instance was wrong when it refused to apply the legal positions of the Constitutional Court, contained in its decree of 1 April 1997. This decree, the Division held, 'has no doubt material significance' for the case in question because the norms being verified were analogous to those invalidated by the decree.[98] The decisions of the Constitutional Court enjoy the highest degree of normative force and can be overruled in some special cases only by the Court itself in the plenary session.[99]

According to the arbitrazh and civil procedure codes (Arts 194[7] and 248, respectively), if there is already a previous judicial decision on the conformity of the challenged normative act to an act of higher legal force, the proceeding should be terminated by a court ruling. Although these clauses may appear as conferring precedential value on such decision, this impression is not correct because the act in question would be the same, not analogues one.

Precedents of discretion are not and should not be binding, but they may have strong persuasive force. If, for instance, the Supreme Court, upon examining the facts of a case, awards a certain amount of contributory compensation for moral harm incurred, the plaintiffs in a similar position may expect that judges will not deviate unreasonably from this pattern. An example of such decision can be found in ruling of the presidium of a regional court which found insufficient the amount of contributory compensation for moral harm[100] (15,000 roubles) awarded by a district court to the plaintiff whose only daughter perished as a result of the negligence of the respondent. The Presidium satisfied her claim in full by awarding 100,000. The Supreme Court upheld the decision by publishing it in the 'Bulletin'.[101] Thus, although not binding, a decision involving the discretionary power of a court necessarily creates expectations that the same pattern will be followed in the future.[102]

Precedents of law-finding are rare species in the Russian legal environment, as far as the present author is aware. But the way for them to come into existence

---

97 Numerous examples can be found in P. B. Maggs, 'Constitutional Commercial Cases in the Courts', see online at: [http://home.law.uiuc.edu/~pmaggs/concom.htm].

98 Ruling of 19 June 2001, No. KAC 01-208. Cf. the decision of the Supreme Court of 2 September 1998, No. ГКПИ 98–412, in the case *The Federation of Independent Trade Unions of Russia and others v The Government of the RF* (both unpublished).

99 See Art 73 of the Law on the Constitutional Court (*RLT*, p. 191).

100 For more information on the concept of 'moral harm' see in Chapters 4 and 5 below, pp. 149, 200.

101 Survey of Judicial Practice of the Supreme Court of the RF for the 4th Quarter of the Year 2002, *BSC*, no. 7 (2003), p. 22. The sum awarded was roughly equivalent to 3,300 US dollars. In another case the same amount was awarded to a victim of police violence merely because his belief in justice and State had been shaken (the Ruling of the Civil Division of the Supreme Court of 30 July 2004, No. 56-Г04-18, *BSC*, no. 2 (2005), p. 10). There appears to be no judicial standards for calculating moral harm, although many lawyers suggested certain methods of assessment.

102 See Barak, Судейское усмотрение [Judge's Discretion], p. 124.

is open under current law. By precedents of this kind I mean decisions in which a court (especially a higher court) would certify and confirm the existence of a 'custom of the business turnover' under Art 5(1) of the Russian Civil Code, which provides that such a custom 'shall be deemed a rule of behavior which has been formed and extensively applied in any domain of entrepreneurial activity and is not provided for by legislation irrespective of whether it has been fixed in any document'.[103] Such judicial confirmation may operate as a persuasive precedent and I believe may be used as a proof of its existence in future cases. This possibility has been stipulated by point 4 of a joint decree of the plenums of the Supreme Court and the Supreme Arbitrazh Court.[104] Interestingly, an analogous provision is found in pre-revolutionary legislation. Statute of Civil Proceeding (as amended in 1912) provided that 'when resolving questions concerning the existence of customs, the court may take into consideration . . . previous decisions on similar cases'.

The highest courts themselves have not yet used such an opportunity, but there are the decisions of intermediate courts confirming the existence of certain customs. In one case, for instance, a cassational court had to resolve the question whether the defendant (an individual entrepreneur) was entitled to use the domain name 'www.kodak.ru', which was so similar with the firm name of the plaintiff – the 'Kodak' Company – that it could be confused with it and thus allowed the defendant to entice potential clients of 'Kodak'. The defendant argued that under Art 54 of the Civil Code the firm name should contain two indissoluble parts: an indication of its organisational-legal form and its name, and only such combination enjoys judicial protection. This argument was in keeping with the existing case law,[105] but was not accepted by the circuit court which in fact made an exception to the established rule: 'In accordance with . . . the customs of the civil turnover, an indication to the organisational-legal form is not used in domain names', because the firms with well-known names are accustomed to use only a short distinctive element of the full name, its arbitrary part which is familiar to most of the customers who are unaware of the form in which the company interesting to them has been incorporated.[106]

Then the court noted that 'since the relations emerging in connection to the use of a domain name on the Internet are not regulated by the RF legislation,

---

103 *CCRF*, p. 3.
104 Decree of 1 July 1996, No. 6/8, 'On Certain Questions Connected with the Application of Part One of the Civil Code of the Russian Federation', *HSAC*, no. 9 (1996), p. 6 (Translated by W. E. Butler in *Russian Civil Legislation*, p. 547).
105 Decree of the Presidium of the SAC of 9 February 1999, No. 7570/98 (unpublished).
106 Decree of the Federal Arbitrazh Court for the Moscow Circuit of 25 January 2001, No. KA-0/6520–00. By a decree of the same court of 2 June 2003, No. КГ-А41/3503-03, it has been affirmed that the regulations on the registration of domain names in the zone RU issued by the Russian Scientific Research Institute for the Development of Social Networks constitute a custom of the business turnover.

these relations, nevertheless, need judicial protection in case of a violation of rights of the owner of the firm name'. It is remarkable that the court found a gap in the legislation but not in the law in general. This fact is worth of special noting because the difference between the law-finding precedents and the gap-filling ones is that the former should find out a pre-existing rule, whereas the latter emerge in cases in which no law can be found. Although in practice the line can be difficult to ascertain, the very difference is essential for the purposes of classification.

As was noted before, the bulk of precedents in the common law countries are created by courts in the course of statutory interpretation. The judicial decisions rendered by various courts are obliged to interpret the same statutory provisions alike. But what is the position in Russia, where judicial decisions do not have formal binding force? Is it sensible to suggest that cases in which judges have to make a choice between two or more legitimate interpretations of a statutory norm are rarer in civil law jurisdictions? As was noted long ago by Lazarevskii, judges in continental Europe when establishing a new principle should give it the form of something derived from a law, that is, the form of interpretation.[107] In other words, they deal with specific problems arising from vague or contradictory legal texts by stretching the statutory provisions so as to conceal them. This, perhaps, is one reason why extensive reasoning is so uncommon in Russian court decisions, and no dissent is published (except for the Constitutional Court). This 'no problem' style of adjudication does not allow the alternatives open to the court to be unveiled. However, it cannot completely eliminate the unavoidable problems of legal interpretation.

If decisions of higher courts are not universally recognised as precedents even though typically followed, this inevitably leads to a lesser degree of uniformity in judicial practice. There is also an increase of disappointed expectations of litigants who relied on decisions in cases reasonably analogous to theirs, but unexpectedly have got quite a different outcome. Therefore, the scope of judicial arbitrariness seems greater in the absence of judicial decisions of higher courts as full-fledged precedents. On the whole, following precedents should increase the predictability of judicial decisions.

In Russia the practice of courts has been long governed by decrees of the plenums of the supreme courts. It can be argued that if such decrees have normative force, there is little reason to deny the similar force of concrete decisions from the same courts, given that the former are mostly based on the latter.[108] There are also other kinds of supreme courts' guidelines (surveys, answers, etc) which explicitly refer to particular cases and are widely regarded as virtually binding, however loose their formal status might be.

---

107 N. I. Lazarevskii, Судебная и административная практика как источник права [Judicial and Administrative Practice as a Source of Law], *Вестник гражданского права* [Herald of Civil Law], no. 1 (1916).

108 This was particularly clear with respect to the Plenum of the USSR Supreme Court, which was the final instance for concrete disputes and issued guiding explanations at the same time.

However, could precedents be better than the guiding explanations? The question comes down to the long controversy as to whether 'abstract' or general norms of codified law have any advantage over case law. The variety of philosophical and jurisprudential problems arising from this are beyond the scope of this study. Suffice it to note that concrete decisions of the supreme courts of USSR and RSFSR and of State Arbitrazh have been published for decades. Plainly, there ought to be some purpose to this. Apparently, it would be impractical to convene the Plenum and issue explanatory decrees on every single point of law, however small it might be. But such points are too many to be easily neglected.

How often are precedents used in the everyday practice of courts? In the absence of a complete information only some preliminary conclusions are possible. It is reported that it was customary for advocates in the USSR to cite previous decisions when arguing before a court.[109] The available surveys, although fragmentary, suggest an extremely high rate of compliance of Soviet judges with decisions of the USSR Supreme Court, including those which were thought to be patently wrong.[110] And in modern Russia the collections of case law and law reports enjoy great popularity and are in constant demand in bookshops. This can be accounted for in two ways. First, 'judicial practice' is considered by lawyers to be a source of law whatever the formal hierarchy of the sources might be. The other explanation suggests that case law (or 'law in action') is simply the best aid to learn the statutory law. Most probably, both reasons contribute to this popularity, but the relative significance of each factor is unknown.

An investigation into massive collections of court decisions available on electronic databases makes an impression that the arbitrazh courts feel free to refer to the decisions of superior instances, especially the Supreme Arbitrazh Court Presidium, whereas general courts do it less willingly. Commonly, when using certain acts of the Supreme Court they avoid referring to them directly. The Chairman of the Supreme Court, Viacheslav Lebedev, complains that 'the stout non-recognition of judicial precedent as a source of law frequently makes the courts...reluctant to refer in their judgments to the decisions of the Constitutional Court of the RF or the Supreme Court of the RF'.[111] This makes the decision unconvincing, especially if the parties were unaware of the respective decisions of the highest courts and, at the same time, the lower court (as is frequently the case) does not offer a comprehensive interpretation of the constitutional or statutory provisions to which it refers.[112]

---

109 See W. E. Butler, 'Judicial Precedent as a Source of Russian Law', J. A. R. Nafziger and S. C. Symeonides (eds.), *Law and Justice in a Multistate World*, p. 584.

110 See A. K. Bezina and V. I. Nikitinskii in S. N. Bratus (ed.), Судебная практика в советской правовой системе [Judicial Practice in the Soviet Legal System], pp. 170–171.

111 Lebedev, Судебная власмь в современной России [Judicial Power in Modern Russia], p. 210.

112 Ibid.

Such reluctance to cite precedents is very typical of many courts of general jurisdiction, including the Supreme Court itself. One of its surveys of judicial practice provides a good example. There the Court upheld the opinion of a lower court that 'since an unlawful normative act infringes upon... the interests of the citizen or legal person during the entire period of operation of the given act, the term for submitting a complaint to a court should not be calculated from the day of the act's coming into force. Such an act can be contested at any time during its operation for the purpose of preventing negative consequences in the future, as well as for the suppression of a continuing violation of civil rights'.[113] This *ratio* has been reiterated verbatim in a number of later decisions but, characteristically, without any mention whatsoever of its source.[114] Such is the traditional Russian attitude to precedent at work: it does exist and, what is more, is widely used at all levels of the court system but in a somewhat diffident and underground way.

There are, however, 'conservatives' among judges: in some arbitrazh decisions the invitations from a party to follow previous decisions were rejected on the grounds that 'the law of precedent in the Russian Federation is not established'.[115] It is difficult to understand whether such a rejection is a matter of principle or simply a convenient way to disregard a precedent which displeases a particular judge. It is perhaps not occasional that the highest courts are wary enough and avoid such pronouncements. Fortunately, the examples of 'conservatism' are far outnumbered by those of judicial 'liberalism' with respect to precedent. By now many dozens of decisions have been made public (through legal databases) in which arbitrazh courts cited relevant judgments, especially those of the Supreme Arbitrazh Court Presidium, to substantiate their view of law. In some cases courts had to analyse them in depth. For instance, the Federal Arbitrazh Court for the Moscow circuit has once had to make a choice between two conflicting precedents. It preferred the later one.[116] In another instance this court pointed out to the necessity to follow the view of the Supreme Arbitrazh Court Presidium, because the decisions of the latter must 'be considered as a formation of judicial practice influencing the stability of judicial decisions at their consideration by

---

113 'Some Questions of Judicial Practice in Civil Cases', *BSC*, no. 8 (1998), p. 15.

114 Cf. a Survey of the Judicial Practice of the Supreme Court of the Russian Federation for the 1st Quarter of the year 1998 (in civil cases)' (*BSC*, no. 9 (1998), pp. 9–10), the decisions of the Supreme Court of 22 June 1999, No. ГКПИ 99–114 (published in excerpts, *BSC*, no. 10 (2000), p. 1) and of 13 August 2002, No. ГКПИ 2002-522, 523 и 529, and also the Ruling of the Civil Division of the Supreme Court of 17 November 2000, No. 5-Г00-119 (unpublished).

115 Decree of the Federal Arbitrazh Court for the Volgo-Viatskii Circuit of 30 September 1999. See also the decrees: of the Federal Arbitrazh Court for the Northwestern Circuit of 28 August 2001 and of 26 June 2003; of the Federal Arbitrazh Court for the Volgo-Viatskii Circuit of 26 February 2003; of the Federal Arbitrazh Court for the Moscow Circuit of 3 October 2002; of the Federal Arbitrazh Court for the Western Siberian Circuit of 14 January 2002, of 24 December 2002, and of 24 April 2003. All the decisions were not published.

116 Decree of the Federal Arbitrazh Court for the Moscow Circuit of 21 May 2003 (unpublished).

way of supervision'.[117] The most 'progressive' courts dare to refer to the decisions of equal courts which in their view represent *jurisprudence constante*.[118] To be sure, the lack of a consistent approach to the value of precedents must not be tolerated, because it undermines the principle of equality before the law and the court. It flourishes only due to the uncertainty as to the normative status of precedential decisions.

It should be noted that a very careful regard to judgments of the highest courts is typical not of judges alone. The federal tax agencies whose importance in the modern Russian State is difficult to overrate are equally sensitive. They routinely monitor the practice of arbitrazh courts and adjust their own behaviour to judicial policies. As a practical matter, *if* court decisions back the position of tax agencies, the latter readily assign them the value of precedents. This may be seen, for instance, from the following instruction:

> The Ministry of the Russian Federation for Taxes and Charges is forwarding for your information and use in work the decree of the Presidium of the Supreme Arbitrazh Court of the Russian Federation of 14 June 2001 N 3419/00 [...]. Bring the decree indicated to the notice of the inferior tax agencies and ensure the preparation of appeals by the inferior tax agencies against the judicial acts adopted by arbitrazh courts not in favour of tax agencies in cases analogous to the one considered by the Presidium of the Supreme Arbitrazh Court.[119]

An interesting point relating to precedents can be found in the reasoned part of a Constitutional Court Decree of 27 January 1993 dealing with the question of compensation to employers in cases of illegal dismissal. The decree explicitly instructed regular courts when settling such disputes to follow the ruling of the Supreme Court Civil Division of 6 April 1992 made in a concrete case.[120] However, the present Constitutional Court (since 1995) has changed direction. In its controversial decree of 16 June 1998 (to be discussed below), the Court

---

117 Decree of the Federal Arbitrazh Court for the Moscow Circuit of 14 April 2003 (unpublished). The same opinion is expressed in the decrees of the Federal Arbitrazh Court for the Povolzhskii Circuit of 17 August 1999, and of the Federal Arbitrazh Court for the Northern Caucasian Circuit of 26 March 2001, of 2 August 2004 (unpublished).

118 In an unpublished decree of the Federal Arbitrazh Court for the Moscow Circuit of 18 January 2005 judges referred to 6 decisions of 3 other circuit courts which provided further support for their holding.

119 Letter of the Ministry for Taxes and Charges of 1 August 2001 (unpublished). It is noteworthy that the Ministry believes the Decree to be a precedent even though it has never been officially published. Similar prescriptions are found in the Ministry's letters of 12 November 2003 and of 11 February 2002 (also unpublished) concerning the decrees of the Presidium of the SAC in which the court upheld the position of tax agencies. It is characteristic that all these letters were about precedents relating to oil excises – a very important source of State revenue.

120 Decree of 27 January 1993, No. 1-П, with regard to the law-application practice of limitation of the period of paid enforced down-time in the event of illegal dismissal, *HCC*, no. 2/3 (1993), p. 62.

declared that decisions of courts of general jurisdiction and arbitrazh courts are not binding on other courts in other cases because the courts shall independently interpret relevant legal provisions. Nor are such decisions subject to official publication, which (by virtue of Art 15(3) of the Constitution of the Russian Federation) makes them inapplicable and not binding on other law-applying agencies. The possibility of publishing some decisions is not, in the view of constitutional judges, a sufficient guarantee for realisation of the aforesaid constitutional norm.[121]

However, these views run counter to recent trends in Russian procedural legislation. According to the 2002 Code of Civil Procedure (Art 377[3]), the Presidium of the Supreme Court may examine and reverse rulings by the Civil and Military Divisions of the Supreme Court rendered by way of supervision if they violate 'the uniformity of judicial practice'. A similar ground for reversal is provided for by Art 304 of the 2002 Arbitrazh Procedure Code. Additionally, the decrees (that is, decisions on individual cases) of the Presidium of the Supreme Arbitrazh Court must be published in its 'Herald'.[122]

Many lawyers believe that the concept of 'uniformity' is too imprecise, even mysterious. Therefore, the Presidium of the Supreme Court attempted clarification. In one decision where applicants submitted the breach of uniformity on the part of the Civil Division, the Presidium ruled that with respect to the Civil Division such a breach would be rendering a decision which would be inconsistent with the decrees of the Plenum or Presidium, rulings of the Cassational Division or Civil Division itself, as well as the surveys and 'answers' issued by the Supreme Court.[123] So far there was no clarification of this concept with regard to arbitrazh courts. In any event, these innovations imply that the significance of judgments of the highest courts transcends the limits of particular cases, in which they were rendered.

Judicial usage

The lack of established practice in citing precedents in Russian courts has probably encouraged the formation of such peculiar form of judge-made law as judicial custom (or 'usage'). For the purposes of the present work, 'judicial custom' means a rule found neither in acts of primary or secondary legislation nor in decisions or decrees of the highest court of the given system, but, nevertheless, enforced by courts in quite a consistent fashion.

It is sometimes difficult to identify these customs or trace back their origins, which is why they usually escape the attention of academic lawyers. However,

---

121 Decree of 16 June 1998, No. 19-П, *HCC*, no. 5 (1998), p. 55.
122 By virtue of Art 307(3) of the Code. The civil procedure legislation still refrains from making provision to that effect.
123 Decree of the Presidium of the Supreme Court of 23 March 2005 N 25-ПВ04, *BSC*, no. 9 (2005).

brief observations concerning the existence of judicial usages were made as early as in the 1860s by D. I. Meier in his influential work on Russian civil law.[124] His assessment was quite positive: he believed such usages to be of help to the legislator who might well convert them into laws. But in later times this topic seems to have been disregarded. To my knowledge, judicial customs were not explored in Russian legal literature of the twentieth century. At best, they were sometimes referred to in passing. One author mentioned them disapprovingly by saying that such 'shadow customs' of the judiciary either oppose 'the official law' or use it as a legal smokescreen.[125] All the same, every practitioner would concede that there are a number of settled practices (but not rules in the formal sense) which are uniformly enforced by courts. Such attitudes or customary interpretations in labour law area will be examined below. But they can also be discovered in other branches of law, both substantive and procedural.

At a first glance, such practices may look like 'living law' in a sense, but it is hardly correct to contrast them with statutory norms (at least in every case). Rather than impeding their operation, such usages constitute a kind of modification or complication. In Constitutional Court jurisprudence they are labelled as the 'usages of law-application' (*obyknoveniia pravoprimenitel'noi praktiki*). In fairness it should be added that this label has a somewhat broader meaning than 'judicial usage' as defined here, for it may equally embrace those judge-made rules which originate in concrete decrees of different supreme courts. At the same time, it may refer to any regular practices discernible within a particular court system irrespective of their origin.

The first Constitutional Court statute (1991) paid more attention to this phenomenon than the present one, which mentions 'law-application practice' just briefly in Art 74(2). But some analysis of the first statute seems relevant, because the Constitutional Court has repeatedly referred to this practice even in judgments made under new law. The 1991 law dealt with this issue at considerable length in a number of articles. The court was empowered to verify 'constitutionality of law-application practice' (Art 1[2]); in examining a legal act, the Court had to have in view not only its literal meaning but also the 'settled practice of its application' (Art 32[1]); and Chapter 3 (Arts 66–73) was wholly devoted to the procedure for their review. An unsuccessful attempt to define such usage was made in Art 66(2), which provided that 'a decision is considered to be taken in accordance with a usage, when from the standpoint of the existing law-application practice the circumstances of the case established in the form in which they were established by this decision should receive the same juridical qualification and entail the same juridical consequences as were

---

124 D. I. Meier, Русское гражданское право [Russian Civil Law] (2001), pp. 58–59. The book was published for the first time in 1861–1862.

125 See V. M. Baranov in Iu.A. Tikhomirov (comp), Судебная власть в России: роль судебной практики [Judicial Power in Russia: The Role of Judicial Practice], p. 45.

defined by this decision'. This confused formulation does not help to draw a line between judicial usage, on one hand, and an individual decision which was simply wrong, on the other. Article 67(7) and (12) required a plaintiff to indicate the normative acts, decisions or explanations which substantiate the contested law-application usage, *if* they were published, as well as any other proof that the contested decisions represent such a custom. Furthermore, by Art 66(3) the legislator admitted that the Constitutional Court may consider an act of law-application, although not made in accordance with a usage, but capable of creating a usage of law-application practice by virtue of its character and significance. As clearly follows from Arts 8(5) and 21(1–6) of the Law, the expression 'an act of law-application' means something different from instructions or explanations of supreme courts. Therefore, it can be regarded as shorthand for individual administrative and judicial decisions capable of guiding courts in future cases. In other words, it was legislative recognition of the existence of precedents in Russian law or, at a minimum, the possibility of their existence.

The tradition was continued by Art 74(2) of the present Law on the Constitutional Court which permits the Court when making judgments to take into account a settled law-enforcement practice. According to the opinion of the Court itself, for establishing the existence of such a practice, the complete unanimity of law-appliers is not required. For instance, several decisions of the Presidium of the Supreme Arbitrazh Court may amount to a settled practice, even though some lower courts disagree with them.[126]

Thus, the 'usage of law-application' practice in the sense of the Constitutional Court jurisprudence can originate either in certain normative or quasi-normative acts or in individual decisions (precedents). Or its origin may be simply unknown, although its very existence undeniable. Only cases of the last kind constitute what I call 'judicial usage'. One example will illustrate this point. In every Russian court of first instance one will face the practice of filing so-called 'brief cassational appeal' by litigants aggrieved by the court's decision. This institution is not provided for by *any* legislative act or Supreme Court decree,[127] but nonetheless is virtually universal and unavoidable. Normally, such an appeal is merely a declaration of the litigant's disagreement with the decision, accompanied with the request for its reversal. The purpose of the 'brief appeal' is to allow judges to have more time (in practice, as much as they want) for writing a reasoned decision after making a judgment.

---

126 Decree of the Constitutional Court of 12 October 1998, No. 24-П, *HCC*, no. 1 (1999), pp. 10–17.

127 It has been mentioned in passing by the Supreme Court Presidium in two criminal cases – in the decree of 25 July 2001, No. 406п01, on the case of Kirpichnikov (unpublished) and also in the Decree of 21 June 2000, No. 42п2000, on the case of Aiupov (excerpts) in *BSC*, no. 1 (2001), p. 15). In scholarly literature it has received a negative assessment (see an article by E. Borisova in *Российская юстиция* [Russian Justice], no. 3 (2003), p. 29.

The term for submitting a cassational appeal is 10 days after the rendering of the judgment.[128] At the same time, the judge is obliged by law to compose such reasons immediately after the rendering of the decision. Only in 'exceptional cases' can it be delayed for up to three days (Art 203, 1964 Code).[129] In practice, this requirement is rarely met: all cases can be exceptional for judges. In Moscow courts the time taken by a judge in a civil case to draw up this document varies between one week and several months. Only thereafter may the litigants submit, within the term specified, a full cassational appeal, which should be written with the reasoned decision in hand and is expected to contain the grounds for disagreement therewith. This court usage allows judges to know in advance, by the time of giving their reasons, which of their decisions are appealed against by a party, and to write accordingly. Coupled with the absence of verbatim transcripts of court sessions, the bad state of official court minutes (and the common practice of amending the *post factum* in a way desirable for judges), this usage may effectively hamper an appeal against the decision and eventually force the complainant to abandon the case. Quite apart from any moral or legal evaluation of such practice, it is doubtless that here we have a certain kind of judge-made rule, which is universally applied, printed and brought to everybody's notice in the courts' premises, and virtually inescapable.

Another famous judicial custom is that of leaving children with their mother and not father in case of a dispute between divorced spouses. This line is pursued by courts without due regard to any circumstances which might be of relevance, such as the desire of the child, the financial position of each parent, and so forth. Their adherence to this policy is not impelled by legislation which leaves the matter entirely to judge's discretion (Art 24, Family Code), and is usually accounted for by the popular belief that the bonds of a child with mother are necessarily stronger, and also by the fact that the vast majority of judges in family cases are women.

---

128 Article 284, 1964 Code of Civil Procedure and Art 338, successive Code of 2002.
129 Five days under the 2002 Civil Procedure Code (Art 199).

Chapter 4

Judicial policies

To the extent courts are able to choose among several ways of interpretation and application of laws one can speak of the policies of the judiciary. A nagging problem for the Russian judiciary is to ensure 'the unity of judicial practice', that is, to work out an integral approach of different courts to the same legal issues. The chronic failure of Russian courts to treat like cases alike placed this problem to the forefront of the activities of Russian highest courts.

The problem of conflicting decisions is often raised in the United States, mainly due to the fact that their legal system in general and the judicial system in particular is much less centralised than that of England. Federal courts of appeals frequently took different views on the same legal issues. This, however, is not considered to be a great evil and the reason for the Supreme Court to reverse those decisions which it thinks faulty. Quite the opposite, as was said in *Hart v Massanari*, 'the courts of appeals, and even the lower courts of other circuits, may decline to follow the rule we announce – and often do. This ability to develop different interpretations of the law among the circuits is considered a strength of our system. It allows experimentation with different approaches to the same legal problem, so that when the Supreme Court eventually reviews the issue it has the benefit of "percolation" within the lower courts'.[1] That is why the US Supreme Court does not usually hasten to intervene in order to ensure the uniformity of case law and sometimes refuses to grant certiorari on an issue, so it will have the benefit of a variety of views from the inferior courts before that issue comes for final solution. It makes the lower courts a kind of 'laboratories' for testing and experimenting, whereas the Supreme Court works, to a considerable degree, not as a mere final court 'receiving' cases from below, but as an active 'top manager' capable of exercising control over the development of the system as a whole.

In Russia the lack of uniformity is often displayed, however, within the jurisdiction of one court. How endemic, in the absence of a well-developed doctrine of precedent, this problem can be is well exemplified by a whole array of legal problems solved differently by various courts or even by one and the same court. Let us take just two examples of many.

---

1 *Hart v Massanari* [2001] 266 F3d 1174.

On 25 August 2003 a three-judges panel of the Federal Arbitrazh Court for the Northwestern Circuit (which is widely regarded as the most 'advanced' circuit court) held that granting property on lease does not amount to the realisation of services for the purposes of taxation. In coming to this conclusion, it declined to follow the reasoning of a Supreme Court precedent which had previously upheld the contrary interpretation. Still, having stated their view of the law so clearly, the judges felt at liberty to change their mind whenever they want. Just one week later, on 1 September, the Court rendered a decision on the analogous case, and this time its holding was exactly the opposite. Now it was convinced that the granting of lease was indeed a service and thus was subject to taxation.[2] The most striking fact is that in the latter decision two judges of three were from the former case. To my knowledge, these avowedly inconsistent rulings have not received any significant coverage, perhaps for not being extraordinary or scandalous enough.

From bad to worse, on a number of occasions the same circuit court had to consider whether the refusal of a law-enforcement agency to report to tax administration the data concerning the earnings of its employees was an offence. The perplexity was that defendants had routinely justified the refusal by following instructions of a superior agency (namely, the Ministry of Interior) which had forbidden to report that data because it allegedly constituted a State secret. On the first occasion, the court held the defendant not answerable for the failure to report, because a necessary prerequisite of responsibility is guilt, whereas the agency was duty-bound to comply with the instruction and thus could not be held guilty. On the second and third occasions, however, it found it guilty on the grounds that the list of circumstances excluding responsibility (Art 111 of the Tax Code) is exhaustive and the adherence to instructions was not included therein. At the same time, the court found such an adherence to be a mitigating circumstance and therefore reduced the amount of fine many times less.[3] Again, all the decisions were rendered by the same judges over two months! Furthermore, on another occasion a differently constituted panel of this court found another mitigating circumstance, namely, the fact that the police agency was financed by the State budget.[4] On the other hand, there are court decisions that imposed full liability in such cases.[5] Such variations may well account for the obsession of Russian superior courts with the enforcement of like attitudes to like cases.

---

2 The decrees of the Federal Arbitrazh Court for the Northwestern Circuit of 25 August 2003, No. A26–1286/03-25 and of 1 September 2003, No. A56-5809/03. Cf. the Decision of the Supreme Court of 24 February 1999 ГКПИ 98-808, 809 (unpublished; see legal databases or online at the Court's website: [www.fas.spb.ru/base/arb_base.phtml]).

3 Decrees of the Federal Arbitrazh Court for the Northwestern Circuit of 16 May 2003, of 17 July 2003, and of 30 September 2003 (unpublished).

4 Decree of the Federal Arbitrazh Court for the Northwestern Circuit of 12 January 2004 (unpublished).

5 Decree of the Federal Arbitrazh Court for the Far East Circuit of 16 June 2003 (unpublished).

Partly, this problem became permanent because the borderlines between the domains of various branches of judiciary are vague and their relations are not settled properly. That is why delimitation of their competence remained a controversial issue on the court and legislative agenda for a long time. But even though some attempts to define their domains were partial success, the lack of concerted policy on the part of the courts, which kept on applying the same legal rules differently, remains unresolved. We shall consider some examples of this kind below.

The difficult fate of judicial review

The development of judicial review of legislative acts is perhaps the best demonstration of difficulties flowing from the institutional isolation of higher judicial instances. As we have seen, the judicial review of legislation is an important opportunity for courts to make law. Besides, the details of the jurisdictional battles between courts are *per se* distinguished examples of judicial involvement in law-creating activity in the areas insufficiently regulated by laws.

The power of the judiciary to invalidate laws has had a difficult history in modern Russia. For a long time the relevant legislation was a mosaic, and some important details are still unsettled. Although over the 1990s certain kinds of normative acts were made challengeable under specific conditions,[6] until recently there was no explicit rule that *all* normative acts shall be subject to judicial review, although this principle could be read into Art 46 of the Constitution concerning the guarantee of judicial defence of rights.

There are a number of pending legislative proposals put forward by higher courts in late 1990s that aim to develop the power of judicial review. In the first place, there were two separate draft laws on the powers of courts of general jurisdiction and arbitrazh courts, respectively, to rule on the validity of normative acts.[7] In order to be adopted, such laws required the approval of the Soviet of the Federation consisting of the regional representatives who are usually reluctant to subject regional legislation to judicial scrutiny. Besides, it is unclear whether Art 128(3) of the Constitution does imply that powers of judicial review

---

6 This possibility mainly depended on which agency issued the act in question, who can bring a suit against it (for instance, a procurator only), or the subject of the act (for example, Art 138(2) of the Tax Code specifically provided for the possibility of challenging the normative acts of the tax agencies in the arbitrazh court following the rules of arbitrazh procedure). The relevant legislation includes, among others, the 1964 Civil Procedure Code (Chapter 24, enacted by the Law of the RF of 28 April 1993, and also Art 116), the 1992 Federal Law 'On the Procuracy of the Russian Federation', the 1997 Federal Constitutional Law 'On the Government of the Russian Federation'. This legislation was basically superseded by the 2002 procedural codes.

7 The draft law on the powers of arbitrazh courts was revoked by the Supreme Arbitrazh Court on 18 September 2003, whereas the law on the review of legislation by general courts was declined by the Soviet of Federation and withdrawn in early 2004.

of legislation should be regulated by a federal constitutional law. If it does, a doubt may be cast upon the decisions already taken by general and arbitrazh courts by way of judicial review. If, however, such powers can be entrusted to courts in the form of a federal law, it seems superfluous to adopt special laws, given that the powers of judicial review have been already elaborated in the recent codes of civil and arbitrazh procedure (Chapters 24 and 23, respectively) which enjoy the status of federal laws. In the Constitutional Court interpretation, the issue is to be regulated by constitutional laws. However, the Court has refused to invalidate the existent regulations other than upon a request from the agencies and persons empowered to bring it.[8] As shall be seen below, such a request was brought by the Federal Government in late 2003.

An idea of administrative courts as a specialised branch of judicial system is a long-standing topic of discussion in the Russian legal community. However, the practical solutions are still to be seen. In the draft Federal Law 'On Federal Administrative Courts in the Russian Federation'[9] it is envisaged that the newly created Administrative Division of the Supreme Court as a first-instance court would consider cases where normative and non-normative acts of the President and the Government of Russian Federation are contested (Art 4). Nothing was said about other federal agencies and their acts.[10] Article 5 states that the federal district court (the intermediate court of the supposed system of administrative adjudication) shall consider challenges to normative acts at the level of the subjects of the Federation and normative acts of the federal executive agencies (para 2[1] and [2]). It seems, however, quite illogical to endow the *intermediate* courts with the power to verify the normative acts of *federal* agencies.

It should be added that there was little logic in the adoption of the basic Russian laws on the judiciary. As a result, the legislative basis of judicial review is unstable. Art 128(3) of the Russian Constitution requires that 'the powers, procedure for the formation, and activity of the Constitutional Court of the Russian Federation, Supreme Court of the Russian Federation, Supreme Arbitrazh Court of the Russian Federation, and other federal courts shall be established by a federal constitutional law'.[11] Pursuant to it, laws on the Constitutional Court (1994), on arbitrazh courts (1995) and on judicial system as a whole (1996) were adopted. However, the draft federal constitutional law on the courts of general jurisdiction, proposed by the President, has been pending in the State Duma since 1998. Moreover, the Supreme Court proposed a draft statute on military courts, which was passed into law on 23 June 1999. Since military courts constitute a part of the system of the courts of general jurisdiction, the very logic

---

8 Ruling of the Constitutional Court of 4 March 1999, No. 31-O, on the interpretation of the Decree of the Constitutional Court of 16 June 1998, *HCC*, no. 3 (1999), pp. 64–66.

9 Which was proposed by the Supreme Court and approved by the State Duma at first reading on 22 November 2000.

10 The same in Art 5, draft Federal Constitutional Law 'On the Supreme Court of the Russian Federation'.

11 *RLT*, p. 45.

of adoption of the laws on the judiciary has been disturbed. Therefore, the draft law 'On the Courts of General Jurisdiction' has eventually little chance of being adopted, given that many of its provisions were anticipated by other laws (for instance, by the Federal Law 'On Justices of the Peace in the Russian Federation' of 17 December 1998). As for the separate Federal Constitutional Law 'On the Supreme Court of the Russian Federation' whose draft has been submitted by the Supreme Court itself, the adoption of such a law is not envisaged by the Constitution.

This badly coordinated legislative activity can partially explain the slow development of the area of judicial review. There have been too many competing and overlapping legislative proposals aimed at regulating the same subject. However, they have finally been overridden by recent procedural codes. In the 2002 codes of arbitrazh and civil procedures the rules for contesting normative acts are elaborated in greater detail than in the draft special laws on that subject.[12]

Not all the contingencies are anticipated by the codes, however, and their provisions differ in important details. For instance, in the Code of Arbitrazh Procedure the decision of any arbitrazh court deeming a certain provision inoperative comes into force immediately (Art 195[4]), although (with the exception of the decisions of the Supreme Arbitrazh Court) it is subject to cassational appeal, whereas under the Civil Procedure Code such a decision comes into force only upon the expiry of the term provided for cassational appeal (Arts 209, 253[3]). But the arbitrazh procedure is more cautious in another respect: it makes such provision inapplicable from the moment when the decision on its illegality is rendered (Art 195[5]),[13] whereas its counterpart deems the provision inoperative from the very moment of its *adoption* or from *another time* indicated by the court (Art 253[2]). So, the decisions of the general courts can have retroactive force, but it is not expressly provided that this is a ground for reversal of the judgments made on the basis of the norms abrogated.

Both codes provide that the court is not bound by the arguments of the claimant and may exceed the limits of the appeal in order to determine the lawfulness of the challenged provision as a whole.[14] Moreover, the Civil Procedure Code provides for the deeming inapplicable of those normative acts which are not directly challenged but nevertheless are based on the acts set aside, or which replicate their contents (Art 253[3]), although no procedure is provided for determination of their equivalence. Its arbitrazh counterpart does not contain such provision at all. But it does attempt to avoid gaps in the law by way of obliging the respective agencies and officials to bring the inoperative

---

12 Chapters 4 and 23, and Chapters 3, 23 and 24, respectively.
13 A similar rule is found in the RSFSR Civil Procedure Code (Art 239[8]), as amended in 1993, while the former code on arbitrazh procedure (1995) did not make provision to that effect.
14 Article 195(4), Arbitrazh Procedure Code; Art 246(3), Civil Procedure Code.

provisions into conformity with the acts having higher legal force (Art 195[5]). No parallel is found in the Civil Procedure Code. The lack of any provision to this effect is surely not in line with recent developments in the contiguous area of constitutional adjudication.

The frontier between these domains is difficult to draw, which at some point has led to jurisdictional rivalry between the Supreme Court and the Constitutional Court. A landmark decision was the Constitutional Court Decree of 16 June 1998.[15] That was a binding interpretation of Arts 125, 126, 127 of the Constitution, relating to the powers of different branches of the Russian judiciary. The Court pronounced that laws should operate uniformly, and that contradictory interpretations of constitutional norms by different courts are impermissible. The area of direct application of the Constitution by ordinary courts must be confined to cases in which there is no particular law concretising a constitutional norm. If such a law does exist, but it is supposed to be contrary to the Constitution, the court is not simply empowered but is *obliged* to bring the matter to the Constitutional Court.[16] Hereby a doubt was cast upon the legitimacy of a contrary position contained in the decree of the Supreme Court Plenum of 31 October 1995.[17]

All the same, the Constitutional Court conceded that the powers of courts to verify the *legality* of normative acts as well as the appropriate procedures could be established by a federal constitutional law, as follows from Arts 71, 118(3) and 128 of the Constitution. However, until it is done, they are not empowered to engage in this kind of judicial review. A judge does have the power not to apply a statute and may resort to a constitutional norm instead, but after that he is *obliged* to put the question of (un)constitutionality before the constitutional tribunal.[18]

Two judges, Nikolai Vitruk and Ghadis Ghadzhiev, submitted dissenting opinions. Both dissents embraced the idea of unrestricted judicial protection of any rights of citizens as established by the Constitution. Vitruk pointed out that the Court had exceeded the limits of examination by confusing the questions of constitutionality and *legality* of normative acts, the latter issue being beyond the Constitutional Court competence. The decree had also failed to explain which courts could verify the constitutionality of normative acts of federal ministries and the subjects of the Federation. This omission ran counter to Arts 18, 45 and 46 of the Constitution, providing for judicial protection of any right. Moreover,

---

15 Decree of 16 June 1998, No. 19-П, concerning the verification of the constitutionality of some provisions of Arts 125, 126 and 127 of the Constitution of the Russian Federation, *HCC*, no. 5 (1998), pp. 51–66.

16 Ibid., pp. 56–57.

17 Decree of the Plenum of the Supreme Court of 31 October 1995, No. 8, 'On Certain Questions of the Application by Courts of the Constitution of the Russian Federation When Effectuating Justice', *BSC*, no. 1 (1996), pp. 1–5. See also p. 114.

18 Ibid., pp. 58–59.

Art 5(3) of the Federal Constitutional Law 'On Judicial System of the Russian Federation' says that in cases of non-conformity between legal acts of different levels (including the Constitution) a court shall adopt a decision in accordance with the legal provisions having the greatest legal force. The law does not obligate the court to have recourse to the constitutional tribunal.[19]

Ghadzhiev believed that the case was, in fact, a jurisdictional dispute between the Constitutional Court and the Plenum of the Supreme Court, and by solving it the former had breached the general principle that nobody can be a judge in his own case. Article 46 of the Constitution does not require any special procedure to have been established in order to make the examination of the legality of normative acts possible. Therefore, the rules of civil procedure should apply. He concluded by saying that 'the findings of courts (especially higher courts) about the contradiction of a legal norm to the Constitution of the Russian Federation do not mean deeming it invalid. But such decisions of courts signify the emergence of judicial law whose development is extremely necessary for the Russian legal system in order to overcome positivistic approaches'.[20]

It is likely that the dissents were somehow taken into account, for shortly afterwards the Constitutional Court changed its position, as follows from the Decree of 11 April 2000.[21] In that case the Supreme Court Civil Division initiated the motion of constitutionality with respect to certain provisions of the Federal Law 'On the Procuracy' (1992), which provided for judicial invalidation of regional statutes at the initiative of the procurator, if they were found to be inconsistent with federal laws.

This time the Constitutional Court drew a line between the questions of constitutionality and legality as well as between the notions of *invalidity* and deeming *inoperative*. It conceded that regular courts could verify issues as to the conformity of legislation of the subjects of the Federation to federal laws (but not to the Constitution). However, courts cannot declare regional laws to be invalid, but only not subject to a further application, that is, inoperative. Whereas an invalid law is to lose force from the moment of its issuance, the laws deemed to be inoperative by ordinary courts should not be applied from the moment of the judicial decision coming into force.[22] The questions of the *constitutionality* of regional laws can be verified by the Constitutional Court only. Therefore, deeming such normative acts to be inoperative does not *per se* exclude verification by the Constitutional Court which is the only court enabled either to invalidate them or to affirm their constitutionality. This implied that these acts could somehow retain legal force despite being inoperative!

---

19 Ibid., pp. 62–63.
20 Ibid., pp. 64–66. It is worth reminding that continental versions of positivism are reputed to be denying the judges' contribution into law.
21 Decree of 11 April 2000, No. 6-П, concerning Art 1(1), Art 21(1) and Art 22(3) of the Federal Law 'On the Procuracy of the Russian Federation' in connection with the request of the Civil Division of the Supreme Court of the Russian Federation, *HCC*, no. 4 (2000), pp. 15–29.
22 Ibid., pp. 19, 22–23.

Obviously, it was a matter of principle for the Constitutional Court not to give up its exclusive power to invalidate laws. It tried to reserve an exclusive right to make the final decision as to which of two mutually inconsistent laws (the federal one or that of the subject of the Federation) conforms better to the federal Constitution.[23] But the Court acknowledged that the conformity of regional laws to a federal law can be verified by ordinary courts pursuant to Chapter 24 of the RSFSR Civil Procedure Code. This seemed to be a retreat from its previous position.[24]

The Supreme Court Presidium was not slow to avail itself of this turn in Constitutional Court practice. On 11 October 2000, presided over by first deputy chairman Vladimir Radchenko, it reversed the decision of the Civil Division of the Supreme Court on the legality of a Moscow City law regulating the emission of harmful substances.[25] That law was contested on the grounds of its non-conformity to the RSFSR Law 'On Protection of Natural Environment'. But the Civil Division of the Supreme Court ruled that the matter was outside the general courts' jurisdiction. Notably, in coming to its conclusion the Civil Division held, with reference to the Constitutional Court Decree of 16 June 1998, that no federal constitutional law had empowered general courts to review regional laws. However, the Presidium reversed the ruling. In so doing, it referred to the Decree of 11 April 2000, in which the Constitutional Court recognised that such a power of general courts could not depend on the adoption of a federal constitutional law. The Presidium reminded that the law of the subject deemed to be contrary to the federal legislation should be amended by the appropriate legislature so as to bring it into conformity with the federal law. The case was remanded to the Civil Division for new consideration.

As was recently shown, the Decree of 16 June 1998 had not terminated the review of normative acts by the Supreme Court.[26] Its impact was purely statistical: the share of cases in which the last assumed jurisdiction has temporarily dropped from 65 per cent to 42 per cent only. No wonder that from May 2000 this caseload increased tremendously to reach the current level of 83 per cent.[27] It is significant that in one case considered just a few weeks after the aforesaid

23 Decree of the Plenum of the Supreme Court of 31 October 1995, No. 8, 'On Certain Questions of the Application by Courts of the Constitution of the Russian Federation When Effectuating Justice', *BSC*, no. 1 (1996), pp. 23, 25. The Constitutional Court admitted (referring to Art 27 of the Law on the Judicial System) that constitutional (or charter) courts of the subjects of the Russian Federation could verify the conformity of the regional laws to federal ones. However, that Article says nothing about federal laws. Only the questions of conformity of regional normative acts to the regional constitutions or charters have been mentioned there.

24 Cf. point 7 of the reasoned part of the Decree of 16 June 1998, *HCC*, no. 5 (1998), pp. 57–58.

25 Decree of the Presidium of the Supreme Court of 11 October 2000, No. 170пв2000пр, on the petition of Demidova (unpublished).

26 A. L. Burkov, Борьба за власть между Конституционным Судом РФ и Верховным Судом РФ: пострадают ли права человека? [Struggle for Power between the Constitutional Court of the RF and the Supreme Court of the RF: Will Human Rights Suffer?], *Российский судья* [Russian Judge], no. 11 (2002), pp. 35–39.

27 Ibid., p. 39.

Constitutional Court decree the Supreme Court invalidated an act of the Federal Government *from the moment of its adoption* on the grounds of necessity to restore in full the citizens' rights violated by the act.[28]

Moreover, the Supreme Court of Russia is insistent, as formerly, that general courts are not obliged, in cases of the supposed unconstitutionality of legal norms, to bring the matter to the Constitutional Court (see Art 11, 2002 Civil Procedure Code), whereas Art 13 of the Arbitrazh Procedure Code imposed such a duty upon arbitrazh courts.

The next turn of jurisdictional battles occurred in 2002–2004. On 28 March 2002 the Supreme Court adopted a decision concerning the illegality (or invalidity) of certain provisions of the Decree of the Government of the Russian Federation of 22 August 1992 № 632. That decree regulated the payments for environmental pollution, waste products and other kinds of harmful influences. The Supreme Court came to the conclusion that 'in violation of Art 17 of the Tax Code of the Russian Federation all essential elements of the indicated tax payment have been defined not by a federal law, but by the decree of the Government of the Russian Federation and the normative acts of the federal agencies of the executive power'. On 4 July 2002 this decision was affirmed by the ruling of the Cassational Division of the Supreme Court. In view of the future developments, it seems curious that in both proceedings the representatives of the Government did not deny that the payments in question were federal taxes.[29]

Nevertheless, a few months thereupon the Government challenged these judgments in the Constitutional Court. The applicant contended that the payments for environmental pollution did not possess the necessary attributes of tax obligations in the constitutional sense and therefore ought not to be enacted by a law. Hence, the Decree № 632 had been issued in accordance with the constitutional powers of the Government. That was a consequential switch of argument, because the issue of *illegality* of the normative act was thus replaced with the question of its *constitutionality*.

Before going further it should be noted that by then the Constitutional Court had already revealed an attitude which might have encouraged the Government's application. By its Decree of 4 April 2002 the Court assumed the right to make final judgment on the conformity of regional laws to the federal Constitution and *federal laws*. This expansion of the notion of constitutionality was justified by the statement that checking the conformity of a regional act to a federal one 'is always constitutionally substantiated by the delimitation of competence between the Russian Federation and its subjects as consolidated by

28 Decision of the Supreme Court of the Russian Federation of 2 September 1998, No. ГКПИ 98-412, in the case *The Federation of Independent Trade Unions of Russia v the Government of the Russian Federation* (unpublished).

29 Decision of the Supreme Court of 28 March 2002, No. ГКПИ 2002–178, and the Ruling of the Cassational Division of the Supreme Court of 4 June 2002, No. KAC 02-232 (unpublished).

the Constitution'.[30] Therefore, if regional authorities failed to bring an act whose illegality was established by an ordinary court in conformity with the federal legislation, the matter should be brought to the Constitutional Court before using the procedure of federal intervention against regional authorities who are guilty of that failure.[31] Although the decree is very vague on the questions who and at which stage of the conflict must apply to the constitutional tribunal and why the right to do so has been effectively turned into an obligation, the trend of the Constitutional Court jurisprudence became nonetheless evident.

It is not surprising, therefore, that its next step was the extension of the same attitude to the acts of the Federal Government. In the ruling issued by the Constitutional Court on 10 December 2002, the latter sided with the Government by confirming the constitutionality of the Decree № 632.[32] Although it is not our purpose to analyse in detail the Court's arguments concerning the possibility of non-tax payments in the form of the so-called 'fiscal dues', one should take note of the Judge Gadzhiev's dissent. He opined that the key constitutional norm – Art 57 – was equivocal and did not answer with sufficient precision whether such dues were permissible or not.[33] If the judge was right, there was a leeway of choice available to the Constitutional Court, and the outcome of the dispute was not fully dictated with the Constitution itself. But it is more significant that this ruling had a far-reaching effect upon the development of judicial review of legislative acts. Importantly, the Court considered the dispute as a constitutional one (on the assumption that the matter concerned the constitutional powers of the Government). By doing this, the Constitutional Court assumed the role of an arbiter empowered to pronounce the final judgment on such issues. By the same token, the Constitutional Court has changed the criteria of admissibility concerning the consideration of cases. The dissenting judge Gadzhiev rightly reminded that the request concerning the constitutionality of a normative act is admissible only if a federal agency of State power refused its application and execution on the grounds of its unconstitutionality, but the applicant believed it to be subject to application.[34] But 'in the present case the Supreme Court of the Russian Federation...did not execute and did not apply the decree of the Government' and also did not make a decision to deny it application on the grounds of its unconstitutionality.[35] That is to say, the Constitutional Court went beyond the limits of its original competence and acted *ultra vires*.

---

30 Decree of the Constitutional Court of 4 April 2002, No. 8-П, concerning the Federal Law 'On General Principles of the Organisation of Legislative (or Representative) and Executive Agencies of State Power of the Russian Federation', *HCC*, no. 5 (2002), p. 8.

31 Points 2.1 and 4 of the Decree (ibid., pp. 7–8, 18).

32 Ruling of the Constitutional Court of 10 December 2002, No. 284-O, *HCC*, no. 2 (2003), pp. 67–80.

33 *HCC*, no. 3 (2003), p. 70.

34 See Art 85 of the present Law on the Constitutional Court (*RLT*, p. 196).

35 *HCC*, no. 3 (2003), p. 69.

Not only have the criteria of admissibility undergone a change, but also the concept of 'legislation'. Article 16(3) of the Law 'On the Protection of the Natural Environment'[36] stipulated that the procedure for the calculation and the exaction of payments for negative influence upon environment shall be established by the legislation of the Russian Federation. In the view of the Constitutional Court, 'legislation' in this context implied not only federal laws, but also other normative acts, including those of the Government if adopted in accordance with the laws. Potentially, such construction would not exclude the matter being regulated not only by the Government decrees, but also by the acts of subordinate executive agencies. Indeed, point 2 of the Decree No. 632 delegated the right to establish the basic rates of environmental payments to the Ministry of the Protection of Environment and Natural Resources, which did not fail to use this power. That became a ground for a new application to the Supreme Court concerning the Decree No. 632 made by the Joint-Stock Society *Kol`skaia gorno-metallurgicheskaia kompaniia* (the applicant in the original case as well).[37] It proved to be partially successful, for the Supreme Court deemed inoperative some provisions of the Decree, including point 2. The arbitrazh courts which ought to resolve disputes regarding environmental payments were obviously embarrassed by the struggle. For instance, the Federal Arbitrazh court for the Urals Circuit changed its view on the lawfulness of those payments four times during 2 month period![38]

This series of decisions was the most overt demonstration of the struggle for competence and powers between two highest courts and ultimately led to the adoption of the Decree of the Constitutional Court of 27 January 2004, in which the latter made a decisive attempt to achieve preponderant position by securing for itself the final say in all key judicial review cases.[39] This time the Federal Government contested those provisions of the Civil Procedure Code which provided for the power of the Supreme Court to recognise as inoperative the normative acts of the Government. The applicant believed that the review of such acts (so long as the Government's duty to issue them was directly prescribed by a law) with respect to their conformity to federal laws necessarily implies their evaluation in the light of the constitutional principles of separation of powers and delimitation of competence between federal legislative and executive bodies. Therefore, the only tribunal entitled to make such evaluation was the Constitutional Court of the Russian Federation.

The Constitutional Court proceeded by saying that the contested provisions of the Civil Procedure Code should be interpreted in a manner which would allow

---

36 Federal Law of 10 December 2002, No. 7-ФЗ, 'On the Protection of the Environment'.
37 Decision of the Supreme Court of 12 February 2003, No. ГКПИ 03–49, and the ruling of the Cassational Division of the Supreme Court of 15 May 2003, No. КАС 03-167 (unpublished).
38 See its decrees: of 15 October 2002, of 5 November 2002, of 12 November 2002, of 2 December 2002, and of 4 January 2003 (unpublished).
39 Decree of the Constitutional Court of 27 January 2004, No. 1-П, *HCC*, no. 2 (2004), pp. 3–21 (with the dissent of Judge A. Kononov).

the Supreme Court to exercise the review of the acts of the Government only if it does not affect the issues of their constitutionality or the constitutionality of the federal law on which they were based. Otherwise their verification is a job for the Constitutional Court. Moreover, since by virtue of Art 125(2a) of the Constitution the verification of the constitutionality of the normative acts of the Government is placed upon the Constitutional Court, the latter is also entitled to check their conformity to other constitutional clauses, including Art 115, which says that the acts of the Government shall not contradict to the federal laws and decrees of the President.[40]

It should be acknowledged that this approach goes too far. Article 115 does not say that it is for the Constitutional Court to ensure the subordination of the governmental decrees to federal laws and presidential edicts. To be sure, many constitutional clauses are quite abstract and sometimes imprecise, which enables one, if necessary, to tie them to any dispute. But it is hardly correct to think that the concept of a 'constitutional matter' should be so amorphous and potentially all-embracing.

Besides, the Constitutional Court opined that if a federal law empowers the Government to regulate a certain issue, it may entail the review of the constitutionality of the law as well.[41] This, of course, can be exercised only by the Constitutional Court. If the Supreme Court doubts the constitutionality of an appropriate federal law when checking the legality of a governmental regulation, it must apply to the Constitutional Court. But when the Supreme Court has no such doubts, it does have power to render a judgment, but this may not prevent both the law and the subordinate act of the Government from being reviewed by the Constitutional Court, if the applicant, contrary to the Supreme Court judgment, thinks the decree of the Government to be correct in law.[42]

It is evident that, as far as the review of principal acts of secondary legislation, is concerned, the Constitutional Court took a superior position with respect to the Supreme Court and (by default) the Supreme Arbitrazh Court. But what has been left for them? In the opinion of constitutional judges, the Supreme Court has to ensure the execution of their decisions by finding invalid normative acts which are analogical to those which have been deemed invalid by previous decisions of the Constitutional Court. But, once again, such decisions of the Supreme Court can be later verified by the constitutional tribunal, if the Government thinks it necessary.[43] It should be added that the Constitutional Court passed over in silence the question of terms within which the Government

---

40 Decree of the Constitutional Court of 27 January 2004, No. 1-П, *HCC*, no. 2 (2004), p. 8.
41 Ibid., pp. 8–9.
42 Ibid., p. 11.
43 Some time before the same opinion has been expressed by the Constitutional Court in relation to the power of general courts to review the conformity of regional constitutions and charters to federal laws (cf. the Decree of the Constitutional Court of 18 July 2003, No. 13-П, *HCC*, no. 5 (2003), pp. 15–29).

should either to apply to the Constitutional Court or to remove the regulation which failed to pass the Supreme Court examination.

In view of the Constitutional Court, the Civil Procedure Code is not the appropriate legal act to consolidate the powers of courts in the area of judicial review, for such disputes are administrative by nature and, besides, the Code has a status of a federal law only. Therefore, the legislator failed to comply with the requirements of Art 128(3) of the Constitution and some Constitutional Court decrees. But the Constitutional Court has refrained from nullification of corresponding provisions of the Civil Procedure Code, because it might undermine the whole basis of judicial review in general courts. At the same time, it pointed out that the process of adoption of the federal constitutional law on the powers of general courts had been unjustifiably delayed. Previously made judgments of Supreme Court on the validity of legal acts of the Government were left in force, provided that they are not challenged and reversed in the Constitutional Court.[44]

The practical consequences of the Decree are still to be assessed, but there is little doubt that they may affect not only the decrees of the Government, but other categories of normative acts as well, if the Constitutional Court finds there a question of constitutional significance. It is too early to say whether the Constitutional Court will be able to cope with its increased caseload. The Court has done its best to protect the governmental decrees from being challenged and simultaneously expanded its competence at the expense of the Supreme Court. Besides, it enhances its interpretive authority by issuing many decisions which, rather than vacating a contested rule, gave it a 'constitutional' interpretation binding upon all law-appliers. Such decisions 'with a positive content' allow the Court to act in a creative fashion, even though the provisions in question are left in force, thus making judicial review a still more powerful tool in the hands of constitutional judges.

The Decree of 27 January 2004 indirectly calls forth the revision of the similar norms of the Arbitrazh Procedure Code. But the past experience of constitutional proceedings in Russia shows that the application of Court's attitudes (or its 'legal positions', in Russian legal parlance) by way of analogy is not always an easy thing. Therefore, an asymmetry between the powers of general and arbitrazh courts created by the Decree may well take root. Perhaps, it is still too early to declare a winner in this struggle for powers.

Some issues of judicial review remain unsettled or even stand untouched by law and doctrine. For instance, it is unclear which courts should ensure the conformity of federal laws to federal *constitutional* laws given that the latter enjoy a higher status in the hierarchy of legal acts. Pursuant to Art 76(3) of the Constitution, federal laws should not contradict federal constitutional laws.[45]

44 *HCC*, no. 2 (2004), p. 16.
45 *RLT*, p. 25.

This matter is still more complicated by the constitutional clause which makes the rules of international law superior with respect to domestic law (obviously, except the Constitution itself). This clause extends to the federal constitutional laws as well. At the same time, in case of a conflict between the rules of an international treaty and those of a domestic law (not excluding constitutional laws), the treaty has to be ratified in the form of a federal law.[46] Consequently, in some circumstances a federal law may have greater force than a federal constitutional law!

In Soviet time many issues were regulated by ministerial instructions, not laws. Plenty of them have never been published. But Art 15 of the Russian Constitution forbids the application of normative acts which touch upon the rights and freedoms of man and the citizen, if such acts have not been published for general information. Does this norm relate only to acts adopted before 12 December 1993? The literal reading of the clause may suggest the positive answer, but the Supreme Court has ruled that this date was indeed a watershed, and so the acts adopted before may persist provided that they do not contradict the laws based on the current Constitution.[47] This appears to be a politically informed decision which has saved a large body of Soviet regulations that are still applied. Otherwise they ought to have been rapidly replaced which might give enormous difficulty to the executive. As for the unpublished acts adopted after 1993, the policy of the Supreme Court is simply inconsistent: in some cases it deemed them *ipso facto* inapplicable and therefore not subject to judicial review, whereas on other occasions it did review them.[48] In the end, the latter approach seems to be more sound, because it is for the court to determine whether any rights and freedoms of citizens could have been affected by an act in question, which is a crucial point for deciding the issue of its applicability. But some time later the Court invented a middle-way solution: it declared that such acts must be reviewed in the procedure provided for the review of non-normative (or individual) acts which, unlike normative acts, affect the rights of concrete persons.[49] In other words, they should be checked by district courts, not the Supreme Court. It goes contrary to the common feeling of the vast majority of lawyers who believe that the review of secondary legislation requires special expertise and in future must be entrusted to special administrative courts. Instead, the Supreme Court conferred the duty (or the right) to verify the legality of federal regulations, including those issued by the President and the Government, to lowest courts.

46 See Art 15(1) of the Federal Law of 15 July 1995, No. 101-ФЗ, 'On International Treaties of the Russian Federation'.
47 Decision of the Supreme Court of 16 October 2001, No. ВКПИ 01-66 (unpublished).
48 Compare the Ruling of the Supreme Court of 28 June 2002, No. ГКПИ 02-686 (unpublished), with its Decision of 21 March 2001, ГКПИ 00-1366, *BSC*, no. 12 (2001), p. 3.
49 Survey of Judicial Practice of the Supreme Court of the Russian Federation for the 3rd Quarter of the year 2003 (Civil Cases), *BSC*, no. 3 (2004), p. 21.

Overlap and discrepancy in court practice

There is a considerable overlap in the competences of general and arbitrazh courts, as there are many occasions on which they have to apply the same laws, particularly the civil legislation. Therefore, it seems apposite to address some discrepancies in their interpretations of the Civil Code provisions in order to see how the cooperation between different branches of the judiciary works (or, rather, fails).

One discordance is found in the defence of rights of good-faith acquirers of property in light of the Civil Code. Pursuant to Art 167(1), 'an invalid transaction shall not entail legal consequences, except for those which are connected with its invalidity, and shall be invalid from the moment of its conclusion'.[50] Paragraph 2 of the same Article provides that 'in the event of the invalidity of the transaction, each of the parties shall be obliged to return to the other everything received according to the transaction, and if it is impossible to return that received in kind (including when that received is expressed in the use of property, work fulfilled, or service provided), to compensate its value in money, unless other consequences of the invalidity of the transaction have been provided by a law'.[51]

Article 302(1) deals with demanding and obtaining property from a good-faith acquirer:

> If property has been acquired for compensation from a person who did not have the right to alienate it, of which the acquirer did not know and could not have known (good-faith acquirer), then the owner shall have the right to demand and obtain this property from the acquirer when the property has been lost by the owner or person to whom the property was transferred by the owner in possession, or stolen from one or the other, or left the possession thereof by means other than the will thereof.[52]

Thus, the mechanism of restitution (Art 167) does not depend on the good faith of the acquirer, whereas the mechanism of vindication does take it into account (Art 302). The general courts, however, were in the habit of giving preference to Art 167. For instance, if a purchase-sale transaction of an apartment was accompanied by violations of the rules of housing law, then such transaction was deemed invalid by a court upon the suit of interested persons, and bilateral restitution was inevitable. The number of transactions which could be thus deemed invalid due to this judicial custom was large. The privatisation of the housing fund in the early 1990s was abundant with violations of norms

---

50 *CCRF*, p. 74.

51 Ibid., p. 97.

52 Ibid., p. 158. The issue is also analysed in N. Shestakova, 'Transactions under the Russian Civil Code: Invalidity and the Protection of Rights', *Review of Central and East European Law*, no. 5/6 (1998) 429.

protecting the rights of minor family members. Quite frequently, these dwelling apartments changed owners again and again, so that the last acquirer in the chain could have scarcely known about the invalidity of a previous transaction.

Arbitrazh practice took a different path. On the grounds of Art 302 the demands of owners were regularly dismissed by arbitrazh courts.[53] This attitude towards the problem was consolidated by the Plenum of the Supreme Arbitrazh Court.[54]

The Constitutional Court tried to resolve this controversy between the two branches of the judiciary. It should be noted that its policy of defending the rights of good-faith acquirers started with the Decree of 14 May 1999, as interpreted by the ruling of 27 November 2001, in which the Court confirmed the possibility to possess the cars and other property imported from abroad with violation of the rules of customs clearance, if these goods were acquired in good-faith.[55] Nevertheless, it was still unclear what the nature of the right of a good-faith acquirer to property, that is, whether he was the owner or not. In the latter case vindication of it by customs agencies from the hands of the infringer and subsequent confiscation would be possible under Art 380 of the Customs Code.

In the Decree of 21 April 2003 the Constitutional Court upheld the position of the arbitrazh courts.[56] It held that the norms in question were interpreted by general and arbitrazh courts differently, which lead to a conflict of constitutional rights being exercised by the owner and good-faith acquirer through these norms. The Constitutional Court refused to deem Art 167 to be contrary to the Constitution, but tried to interpret it in such a way as to harmonise it with Art 302, and strike a certain balance between competing claims and rights. The Court declared that if property rights to a disputable thing arise on the grounds provided by law and belong to persons other than the owner, the protection by the State should be extended to these rights as well, and the rights of good-faith acquirers are just such. Therefore, the federal legislator should provide for such regulation of property

---

53 See, for instance, the Decree of the Presidium of the SAC of 22 May 2001, No. 1940/00, in the case of Aviation Company 'Volga' (*HSAC*, no. 9 (2001), pp. 41–42), and also the decree of the Federal Arbitrazh Court of the Moscow Circuit of 12 September 2001 at [www.orc.ru/~legist/obzors12.html]. Cf. point 7, Information Letter of the Presidium of the SAC of 21 April 1998, No. 33, a 'Survey of Practice of Resolving of Disputes on Transactions Connected with the Placement and Turnover of Stocks', *HSAC*, no. 6 (1998), pp. 82–93.

54 Decree of the Plenum of the SAC of 25 February 1998, No. 8, 'On Certain Questions of the Practice of Resolving the Disputes Connected to the Defence of the Right of Ownership and Other Rights to a Thing', *HSAC*, no. 10 (1998), pp. 14–21.

55 Decree of 14 May 1999 No. 8-П concerning Arts 131(1) and 380(1) of the Customs Code, *HCC*, no. 4 (1999), pp. 50–61. Ruling of 27 November 2001, No. 202-О, on official interpretation of the Decree of the Constitutional Court of 14 May 1999, *HCC*, no. 2 (2002), pp. 67–70.

56 Decree of 21 April 2003, No. 6-П, concerning Art 167(1) and (2) of the Civil Code, *HCC*, no. 3 (2003), pp. 54–61.

rights, which would grant a defence to good-faith participants of civil turnover. In the event of a dispute, the owner must present evidence that the property in question had left his possession (or the possession of a person to whom it had been transferred by the owner) by virtue of the circumstances enumerated in Art 302. The acquirer, in turn, should prove that he acquired the property for compensation and he could not have known that the property was acquired from the person who did not enjoy the right to alienate it. Additionally, the acquirer cannot be deemed in good faith, if at the moment of conclusion of the transaction for money there were claims of third persons with respect to the property in dispute, of which he was aware, and if such claims were later deemed lawful in the established procedure.[57] It is remarkable that here the Constitutional Court merely reproduced almost verbatim the provisions of point 24 of the Decree of the Plenum of the Supreme Arbitrazh Court of 25 February 1998.[58]

It may be argued, however, that this construction does not fit well certain principles of civil legislation. Article 10 of the Civil Code runs: 'In instances when a law makes the defence of civil rights dependent upon whether these rights have been effectuated reasonably and in good faith, the reasonableness of the actions and the good faith of the participants of civil law relations shall be presupposed'.[59] This presumption of good faith of the acquirer means that the person that received a property under a transaction for compensation need not prove that he did not know about its belonging not to the seller but to another person. It is exactly the supposed owner who must prove the opposite. In fact, it was a novelty introduced by the Constitutional Court and the Supreme Arbitrazh Court, since the burden of proof was placed not in accordance with the Civil Code.

The Court went on to say that when under a contract for compensation the property is acquired from the person who did not have the right to alienate it, the owner is empowered, in accordance with Art 302, to bring a suit and evict the property from the illegal possession of a person who has acquired it ('vindication', or *rei vindicatio*). If, however, the owner brings a suit concerning the invalidation of the transaction and application of the consequences of its invalidity in the form of return of the property to him (Arts 166–167, Civil Code), but the court will find that the purchaser is a good-faith acquirer, the action should be dismissed. This opinion coincides with point 25 of the aforesaid decree of the Supreme Arbitrazh Court.

In coming to its conclusions, the Constitutional Court used a complex, but not flawless argumentation. It remarked that Art 168 of the Civil Code provides, as a general rule, that a transaction not corresponding to the requirements of a law or other legal acts shall be void unless the law provides other consequences for

57 Ibid., pp. 58–59.
58 *HSAC*, no. 10 (1998), pp. 14–21.
59 *CCRF*, p. 5.

the violation.[60] The Court concluded, therefore, that the rules concerning general consequences of invalidity of transactions do not extend to the transaction violating a law, so long as the law provides for other consequences of such violation. Good-faith acquisition in the sense of Art 302 is possible only when the property is acquired not from the owner, but from a person who did not have the right to alienate this property. Therefore, the consequence of such transaction will be not bilateral restitution, but the return of the property from another's illegal possession, that is, vindication. So, the rights of a person who thinks himself to be the owner of the property in question are not to be defended by way of bringing a suit against the good-faith acquirer through the legal mechanism established by Art 167 (paras 1 and 2) of the Civil Code. Such defence is possible only by way of allowing the action of vindication, if the grounds provided for by Art 302 are available which allow the eviction of property even from a good-faith acquirer, that is, the lack of compensation for its acquisition and the property's leaving the possession of the owner by means other than his will. Consequently, by virtue of this logic Art 302 takes precedence over Art 167. But it has been already noted that the fact that good-faith acquisition presupposes the alienation of the property by an unempowered person does not imply that bilateral restitution cannot be the consequence of a transaction concluded by such a person and only the owner is entitled to seek restitution.[61] Such an inference drawn by the Constitutional Court contradicts Art 166(2) of the Civil Code (which entitles 'any interested person' to demand the application of the consequences of the void transaction) and is a novelty not resting upon the law.

The decision of the Constitutional Court did not resolve all doubts. For instance, the Court excluded the attempts of a bad-faith seller of apartment to get it back through court proceedings. But it is a well-known fact that many decisions concerning the invalidity of transactions are made by courts upon the suits of third persons whose rights were violated as a result of alienation of these apartments. In some cases (especially if these third persons are minors) the proceedings are initiated by the respective procurators. The Constitutional Court did not touch this problem, so that the risk for a purchaser to lose the acquired property still remains, for the courts of general jurisdiction are inclined to defend the interests of minors in any circumstances. Besides, it now becomes possible 'to laundry' the apartments bought in violation of the provisions of a law by artificially creating good faith through a chain of transactions.

In the legal literature attention was drawn to the strained argumentation of the Court in this case. The references to the Constitution looked artificial, and it was even doubted whether it falls within its competence.[62] Indeed, nothing has been

---

60 *CCRF*, p. 75.

61 D. O. Tuzov, Конституционный суд о защите добросовестного приобретателя [The Constitutional Court about the Protection of the Good-Faith Acquirer], *Законодательство* [Legislation], no. 10 (2003), p.11.

62 Ibid., p. 9.

known so far about the 'constitutional' rights of good-faith acquirers. No provision of the Russian Constitution mentions them. It is true that Court's reasoning was based on the Civil Code rather than the Constitution. But it is hardly accidental that the Court twice referred to its Art 55(1) which says that 'the enumeration in the Constitution of the Russian Federation of basic rights and freedoms must not be interpreted as a denial or diminution of other generally-recognised rights and freedoms of man and the citizen'.[63] This rule enables Court to articulate new rights that are not mentioned in the Constitution and thus expand Court's jurisdiction. Theoretically, the rights of the good-faith acquirer, although unfamiliar to the previous legislation, may fall into this category. It is quite another matter that the pronouncements of the Constitutional Court regarding their contents and means of enforcement are indeed insufficiently well-defined. It is not clear, for instance, whether these rights were put on the same footing as the owners' rights. On the one hand, the Court could not simply equate them with the owners because those who do not pass the test of Art 302 can lose their property upon the owner's suit. This made some commentators suggest that the Court drew a line between owners and 'other' persons, good-faith acquirers being among the latter. But it seems to me that those acquirers who do pass the test gain the owner's rights as a result of dismissing the suit of the previous owner, because the transaction on which basis the property has been acquired (say, purchase-sale transaction or gift) is thus deemed valid. Nothing in the decree would exclude such an interpretation. In any event, this is the case where further clarification is necessary.

Another dissimilarity between policies of general and arbitrazh courts relates to the question whether the contributory compensation of moral harm may be awarded to juridical persons as well as to natural ones. The relevant provisions of the Civil Code are not quite consistent in this respect. On the one hand, Art 151 says that 'if moral harm has been caused to a citizen (physical or moral suffering) by actions violating his personal nonproperty rights or infringing on other nonmaterial benefits belonging to a citizen...the court may impose on the offender the duty of monetary contributory compensation of the said harm'. Non-material benefits include, *inter alia*, 'life and health, the dignity of the person, personal inviolability, honour and good name, business reputation, inviolability of private life, personal and family secrecy, the right of free movement, and choice of place of sojourn and residence, the right to name, the right of authorship'.[64] Of them, at least business reputation can belong to both natural and juridical persons. The problem is complicated even greater by Art 152(5). It makes provision for compensation to a citizen of losses and *moral harm* caused by the dissemination of information defaming his honour, dignity

---

63 *RLT*, p. 17.
64 *CCRF*, p. 69.

or business reputation. Paragraph 7 of the same Article says that 'the rules of the present Article concerning the defence of business reputation of a citizen respectively shall apply to the defence of the business reputation of a juridical person'.[65] Hereby the provision concerning moral harm was included, whether intentionally or not.

Arbitrazh and ordinary courts took opposite views on this subject. Arbitrazh courts believe that moral and/or physical sufferings which constitute moral harm may be caused only to a natural person. In a number of decrees of the Presidium of the Supreme Arbitrazh Court it is maintained that, inasmuch as a juridical person cannot experience such sufferings, no moral harm can be caused to it.[66] Although lower arbitrazh courts had previously awarded contributory compensation of moral harm to juridical persons, their decisions were invariably reversed by the Presidium.

General courts approached the matter in a different way. In the Decree of the Plenum of 20 December 1994 the Supreme Court said that 'rules regulating contributory compensation of moral harm in connection with the dissemination of information defaming the business reputation of a citizen, shall be applied also in the event of the dissemination of such information in relation to a juridical person'.[67] In 2005 this position was confirmed once more.[68] It was not suggested, however, that juridical persons may have honour or dignity.

A similar position has been taken by the International Commercial Arbitration Court attached to the Chamber of Commerce and Industry of the Russian Federation. It permits this kind of compensation to juridical persons.[69] Nevertheless, the arbitrazh courts had been reluctant to follow the lead so far. Moreover, they believe that inasmuch as the consideration of disputes between citizens is the domain of the general courts, a citizen-entrepreneur also is not entitled to such compensation from these courts.

Some leading lawyers and judges think that the concept of moral harm may extend to juridical persons. Sadikov argues that such civil law categories as fault, good faith, fraud, threat and the like do apply to juridical persons. Therefore, he

---

65 Ibid., p. 70.
66 Decrees of 1 December 1998, No. 813/98, in the case of open joint-stock society 'Krosno' (*HSAC*, no. 2 (1999), pp. 83–86), of 5 August 1997, No. 1509/97, in the case of limited responsibility society 'Zhilspetsmontazh' (*HSAC*, no. 12 (1997), pp. 63–64), and of 24 February 1998, No. 1785/97, in the case of closed joint-stock society 'Alevar' (*HSAC*, no. 6 (1998), pp. 42–43).
67 Point 5, Decree of the Plenum of the Supreme Court of 20 December 1994, No. 10, 'Some Questions of Application of Legislation on Contributory Compensation of Moral Harm', *BSC*, no. 3 (1995), p. 10.
68 Point 15, Decree of the Plenum of the Supreme Court of 24 February 2005, No. 3, 'On Judicial Practice Regarding Cases of About the Protection of Honour and Dignity of Citizens and Also of Business Reputation of Citizens and Legal Persons', *BSC*, no. 4 (2005), p. 7.
69 O. N. Sadikov in Комментарий судебно-арбитражной практики [Commentary on Judicial and Arbitrazh Practice], Vol. 5 (1998), p. 65.

sees no reason why 'sufferings' cannot be assigned to them too.[70] Although this position has been a subject of scholarly criticism,[71] the matter remains unsettled.

Dissemination and availability of judgments

Whereas forms and procedure for the publication of Constitutional Court judgments are determined by law in sufficient detail[72] and decisions themselves are not numerous, the situation is different with respect to other courts of last resort. Relevant legislation is scanty and often repetitive. The question is regulated by a handful of legal provisions and internal rules of courts.[73] On the whole, certain aspects of relations between courts of higher and lower instances are difficult to learn for an outsider.

At present the range of documents of interpretive nature issued by the Supreme Court and the Supreme Arbitrazh Court includes:

1 Decrees of the plenums. The interpretive decrees are normally published in the court periodicals without any abridgment. Besides, they are subsequently reproduced in numerous unofficial publications. More 'technical' decrees (relative to draft legislative proposals on behalf of courts or on the issues of internal court administration, etc), are not published, but for the most part are available on the court official websites.

2 Surveys of judicial practice over a certain period or concerning a particular subject. The subject-oriented surveys from the Supreme Court are not frequent. They are issued on behalf of the respective divisions and mainly consist of their rulings and answers to the questions of courts, but may include the decrees of the Presidium too. Conversely, the periodic surveys are quite regular and include extracts from Supreme Court judgments for a certain period (usually quarterly). Curiously, despite being affirmed by the Presidium, they usually contain few of its decrees. For the most part, they include rulings of the divisions of the Supreme Court and presidiums of intermediate courts rendered by way of supervision. In the end, it seems unlikely that the surveys endorsed by the Presidium enjoy a higher status. All the judgments cited there are supplied with an ordinal number and the number of the original ruling.

---

70 Ibid., p. 66. See also V. M. Zhuikov, Возмещение морального вреда [Compensation of Moral Harm], *BSC*, no. 11 (1994), p. 8.

71 I. A. Tarassenko in Комментарий судебно-арбитражной практики [Commentary on Judicial and Arbitrazh Practice], Vol. 5 (1998), p. 69.

72 Articles 76, 78, Federal Constitutional Law 'On the Constitutional Court of the Russian Federation'.

73 The laws on arbitrazh courts (1995), on the judicial system of the RF (1996) and on the judicial structure of the RSFSR (1981), as well as 2002 civil and arbitrazh procedure codes are the laws in question. See also the Regulations of Arbitrazh Courts, *HSAC*, no. 3 (2003), pp. 6–23.

Likewise, the Supreme Arbitrazh Court also disseminates surveys but they always cover a particular subject, not period. Some address a certain legal issue without reference to concrete disputes, while others do refer to details of concrete cases and are structured as a digest of case law. The surveys are disseminated in the form of 'information letters' endorsed by the Presidium. A typical introduction is 'the Presidium has examined the question and informs courts about recommendations worked out'. Although in principle they are deemed to be not binding, merely persuasive, the arbitrazh courts are careful enough not to challenge these letters openly in their decisions.[74] Like normative acts and decrees of the plenums, the information letters are amended to accommodate changes in relevant legislation which they purport to explain. By October 2006, the Supreme Court had issued 115 information letters.

The surveys of judicial practice of both highest courts usually contain very few facts of original cases or even none. Here is an example of such a judgment: 'By virtue of the principle of separation of powers the court cannot oblige the legislative organ of a subject of the Federation to change, to amend, or to adopt a law or bring it into conformity with another normative act, having greater legal force. It can only verify its conformity to federal legislation.'[75] The names of the parties are omitted, and no cue as to the real circumstances of the dispute is given. Therefore, it is difficult to regard them as precedents proper.[76] At best, they occupy an intermediate position between the decrees of the plenums and concrete decisions. All the same, these surveys are always published in the court periodicals.

3 *Concrete decisions of highest courts.* Among them the most important are the decrees of the presidiums. Both presidiums hold their cessions every week and have roughly equal output, but the number of available decisions differs considerably. At present, only the decrees of the Supreme Arbitrazh Court Presidium are necessarily published. They are virtually unabridged. Those of the Supreme Court Presidium are published selectively and sometimes abridged. The same is true regarding the rulings of the divisions of the Supreme Court as well as the decisions of the Supreme Court upon the legality of normative acts. But some of them are available in full on the Court website.

Exceptionally, the Supreme Court Presidium can render decrees on general questions of judicial policy. These resemble 'information letters' in the system of arbitrazh courts. For instance, on 27 December 2002 the Presidium adopted a decree 'On Consideration by Courts of the Russian Federation of Cases with the Participation of Joint-Stock Societies'. In this document, drawn in an unusually

---

74 For instance, the chairman of the Federal Arbitrazh Court for the Moscow Circuit Liudmila Maikova called information letters binding as well as concrete decisions of the Presidium. See her interview at [www.consultant.ru/news/interview/maykova.html].

75 Ruling No. 82-Г01-9, *BSC*, no. 8 (2002), p. 14.

76 Cf. Z. Bankowski, D. N. MacCormick, L. Morawski, A. R. Miguel, 'Rationales For Precedent', in *Interpreting Precedents*, p. 488.

angry manner, the Presidium described in detail a number of cases in which the courts committed the 'most flagrant violations of the norms of procedural law' and demanded that disciplinary sanctions be applied to judges found guilty of breaching them.[77]

4 *Endorsed judgments of inferior courts.* Select decisions of the courts immediately below the Supreme Court and the Supreme Arbitrazh Court are published in their journals (always in excerpts), as an example of correct interpretations.

In the final analysis, it appears that in the system of arbitrazh courts the dissemination of decisions and interaction between the highest court and the inferior ones is much better adjusted.

The examination of the availability of judicial decisions in electronic form shows that the highest courts of Russia have official websites, which are quite informative. At the same time, lower courts having their own websites are few. As of May 2005, only 21 of 89 regional courts of general jurisdiction which are immediately below the Supreme Court had their own websites. By contrast, as many as 44 of 89 regional arbitrazh courts in the subjects of the Federation had websites, and 9 of 10 cassation courts. Things are far better with respect to the Supreme Court and the Supreme Arbitrazh Court. Both have online versions of their monthly journals (or law reports).[78] Besides, their websites have extensive databases served by 'Garant', the leading company in this area. They contain more documents than the law reports. It is important to note that electronic versions of decisions are unabridged. The former Chairman of the Supreme Arbitrazh Court, Veniamin Iakovlev, and his successor, Anton Ivanov, have repeatedly announced the accessibility of all judicial decisions through legal databases 'ConsultantPlus', 'Garant' and 'Kodeks', and subsequently through the Internet to be their ultimate goal. With respect to the cassational courts this purpose has been largely achieved, not to mention the Supreme Arbitrazh Court. As for the Supreme Court, only some of its judgments, not excepting those of the Presidium, are available in electronic form to general public. The position in relation to decisions of lower courts is still much worse.

The development of information technologies begs the question of whether decisions available only in electronic form can be rightly regarded as precedents. Should judges be expected to know them and take them into account? Given that judicial decisions, although capable of containing supplementary legal norms,

---

77 Decree of 27 December, No. 27 пв02 (unpublished). The unusual tone of the Decree can be explained by the inveteracy of the problem. Remarkably, the Decree cites the opinion of the Russian President, Vladimir Putin, that the judicial system can be discredited when different courts deliver contradictory judgments in the same cases (which was indeed a recurrent practice during recent years as a result of stockholders battles. *A.V.*).

78 The 'Bulletin of the Supreme Court' is available on the Court's official website at [http://www.supcourt.ru/vs_docs.php] (free access). The 'Herald of the Supreme Arbitrazh Court' can be seen online at: [www.vestnik.ru/] (access is restricted).

are not technically 'normative acts', there seems to be no issue of their applicability in light of Art 15(3) of the Russian Constitution. Assuming as we do that judicial decisions of higher courts may serve as a guidance and, in fact, a subsidiary (or derivative) source of law for lower courts, there is no need for them to be officially published (although this may be highly desirable) in order to have normative force. The analogy with customs of business turnover, which do constitute a source of Russian civil law, seems appropriate. Under Art 5(1) of the Civil Code, a rule of behaviour may be deemed to be such a custom 'irrespective of whether it has been fixed in any document'.[79] It follows that, in principle, Russian law does allow the application of rules which are neither published nor even fixed in a written form.

The issue of publication of court decisions as well as the significance of those which remain unpublished draws attention of the legal community across various jurisdictions. In the United States before mid-1960s almost all decisions of the federal courts had been published. As a consequence, virtually every decision was capable of becoming a precedent. However, beginning with 1970s the courts' caseload has grown tremendously, and at a certain point courts started to select cases for publication.[80] They decided by themselves whether a case ought to be published or not, and in this respect their practices became closer to the ones of the Soviet and Russian courts where only select publication of decisions has always been (and still is) a rule, no matter how different the reasons for (non-)publication might be in those legal systems. In very much the same way, many decisions of the English higher courts also fell into the ranks of unpublished. So, in 1986 only 39 per cent of the decisions of the Court of Appeal have been published. Although there is no formal prohibition against using unpublished decisions as precedents, the absence of publication makes such a use unlikely.[81] In the United States, on the contrary, the response to this situation was the adoption by the federal courts of an appeal of the new procedural rules which expressly forbade parties to refer to unpublished decisions. Thereby their status as precedents was called into question. On the average, only 20 per cent of decisions of federal courts are officially published nowadays.[82] But at some point the development of information technologies has created the necessary prerequisites for revision of these attitudes and for returning to unpublished decisions their nearly lost status of precedents. That was because

---

79 *CCRF*, p. 3.

80 P. Pether in her excellent study of the problem argues, however, that unpublication was a reaction of courts against appeals from marginalised litigants – prisoners and civil rights appellants. She believes that caseload was just a plausible excuse (P. Pether, 'Inequitable Injunctions: The Scandal of Private Judging in the U.S. Courts', *Stanford Law Review*, Vol. 56, no. 6 (2004), p. 1440).

81 R. J. Martineau, *Appellate Justice in England and the United States: A Comparative Analysis* (1990), pp. 107, 150.

82 The US Supreme Court was exempt from this calculation, for all its opinions are subject to publication (about 100 each year).

the leading electronic databases such as WestLaw and Lexis-Nexis provided an instantaneous access to a great number of judicial decisions many of which had never been published. As a result, currently litigants and their advocates can easily find relevant decisions which could have been unknown or inaccessible to them before. In fact, the traditional distinction between published and unpublished decisions became somewhat smoothed out, if not obliterated completely. The very notion of an *unpublished* decision partakes of a paradox since many of such decisions have become available for public. This completely new situation that took shape during 1990s has given rise to a new turn of debates within the US legal community concerning the role of unpublished decisions.

The peace was broken by the holding of the United States Court of Appeal for the Eighth Circuit in *Anastasoff v United States* (2000), in which it found unconstitutional its own rule which prohibited the bar from citing unpublished opinions.[83] The decision in *Anastasoff* triggered heated debates and a torrent of literature concerning the practices of unpublishing and 'depublishing' exercised by courts. Another court of equal status, United States Court of Appeals for the Ninth Circuit, refused to follow the line and in *Hart v Massanari* offered a criticism of the view taken by the former court.[84] It came to the conclusion that the prohibition against citing unpublished opinions was not unconstitutional and 'so long as the earlier authority is acknowledged and considered, courts are deemed to have complied with their common law responsibilities'.[85] Giving up the practice of select publication might have, in the opinion of the court, the most dramatic consequences: 'Federal judges have a responsibility to keep the body of law cohesive and understandable, and not muddy the water with a needless torrent of published opinions'.[86] A special emphasis was put on practical difficulties: it would have been a very time-consuming thing to prepare all court dispositions for publication and therefore will require an increase in the number of judges by something like a factor of five to allocate to each judge a manageable number of opinions each year.[87]

---

83 *Anastasoff v United States of America* [2000] 223 F3d 898.

84 Hart v Massanari [2001] 266 F3d 1155.

85 Ibid., p. 1157. It should be acknowledged that the court in *Hart v Massanari* found itself in a somewhat different position. Whereas the rule challenged in *Anastasoff* said that 'unpublished opinions are not precedent', the rule of the Ninth Circuit was not quite the same. It provided that 'unpublished dispositions and orders of this Court are not *binding* precedent' which does not deny their *persuasive* authority. According to one interpretation, the decision in *Anastasoff* intended to gain a similar status for unpublished decisions within the jurisdiction of the Eighth Circuit, but not to make them binding precedents as was understood by critics (see P. J. Price, 'Precedent and Judicial Power after the Founding', *Boston College Law Review*, Vol. 42 (2001), p. 81).

86 Ibid. The complaints that the body of cases was 'as the rolling of a snowball, it increaseth in bulk in every age, until it becomes utterly unmanageable' were heard from English lawyers as early as in 1671! (cited in J. I. Braun, 'Eighth Circuit Decision Intensifies Debate over Publication and Citation of Appellate Opinions', *Judicature*, Vol. 84 (2000), p. 91.)

87 Ibid., p. 1179.

It was not only the judiciary that was split by the arguments of the Judge Richard Arnold in *Anastasoff*. His opinion found support from one fraction of academic lawyers but aroused an equally strong dislike of the rest. The sharpest criticism was incurred by the way he tried to substantiate the unconstitutionality of the prohibitive rule. Interestingly, he found it contrary to Art 3 of the US Constitution which relates to the power of the judiciary, but did not attempt to appeal to the principle of equality before the law, which requires to treat like cases alike. This principle is not articulated in the Constitution as a general rule, but can be read into the provisions of s 1 of the Fourteenth Amendment which says about the equal protection of laws, in a systemic relation with 'due process of law' clause of the Fifth Amendment.[88] It should be noted that Russian Constitution, unlike the American one, is more explicit in this respect. It does contain the principle of equality before the law (Art 19[1]), and this enables one to argue that the emphatic disregard of some Russian judges of the decisions of the same, equal, or higher courts is against the Constitution, as long as the law is differently interpreted and applied in like cases.

Selective publication has long-standing roots in the Russian legal past. During late imperial era the Ruling Senate used to distinguish its important decisions which were thus marked for publication from routine rulings which were not. The distinguishing was entirely within the discretion of the Senate. The ratio of published decisions was roughly estimated as 5 per cent of the total number of settled disputes, the average annual caseload being about 7,500 cases before 1901.[89] At the same time, there was no prohibition against citing unpublished opinions. Moreover, it was a legislatively prescribed duty of the judge who reported a particular case to draw the attention of the bench to previous decisions of the Senate in similar cases (Art 919, Statute of Criminal Proceedings). Under Statute of Civil Proceedings (Art 804[2], enacted in 1877) the decision of the Senate had to refer to cassational decisions taken into consideration as well as to statutes. All the more it was common for litigants to cite Senate's precedents including unpublished ones. In relation to unpublished rulings the position of the Senate was that courts were not bound by them, but they could take such rulings into consideration.[90] That is to say, the non-publication did not preclude citation, and the reasons of non-publication had more to do with the large number of rulings than an attempt to conceal 'inconvenient' precedents. In fact, contradictions between published rulings were not rare at all.

---

88 J. A. Strongman, 'Unpublished Opinions, Precedent, and the Fifth Amendment: Why Denying Unpublished Opinions Precedential Value is Unconstitutional', *Kansas Law Review*, Vol. 50 (November, 2001), pp. 195 ff.

89 N. S. Tagantsev, Русское уголовное право (Общая часть) [Russian Criminal Law (General Part)], Part 1 (1902).

90 I. M. Tiutriumov (comp.), устав гражданского судопроизводства [The Statute of Civil Proceedings] (1912), pp. 1169, 1190.

Unlike Britain, in Russia and the USA courts may exercise control over the process of reporting. They can decide which judgments should become available to the public and which should not. This practice of select publication at judges' discretion undermines their accountability and releases them from the disciplining effect of producing reasoned opinions.[91] It also diminishes the transparency of their work. It appears, however, that nowadays the accessibility of Russian court decisions has little effect on their quality. In other words, accessible decisions are often as poorly reasoned as 'secret' ones. Moreover, they are usually scarce of facts. Judges invest too little time and effort in writing decisions. The net result is that through the prism of texts some cases may look similar, but in fact they are not. If all facts were provided, such cases might have proved to be clearly distinguishable. The poor quality of decision writing contrasts strikingly with those novel and highly sophisticated search techniques that some leading electronic databases in Russia may offer. These techniques are based on complex linguistic methods and allow users to extract a line of essentially similar judgments by simply clicking a button above the text of a decision. Theoretically, such mechanisms allow higher courts to screen the body of decisional law and eliminate inconsistencies, thus keeping it coherent. But the efficiency of these technologies is seriously reduced by the poor quality of the data which they are invented for. That is why, in spite of the availability of decisions, similarly placed litigants may still be treated unevenly without actually having a chance to know about it. So, the access to decisions is just a part of the problem; the other equally important and perhaps more difficult part is the quality of reasoning. Whereas the former is being solved with considerable success, there is still too much to be desired with respect to the latter.

Judicial dissent

Judicial dissent is quite special phenomenon within Russian law. If the difference between the families of legal systems is that of style,[92] then judicial dissent is a discordant note in Russian law, for it breaks austere Romano-Germanic 'design' of the latter. At a first glance, it comes as a phrase from another novel which has been somehow gotten into an alien context. That said, this legal phenomenon was brought into Russia quite long ago and succeeded in taking root there. Its stubborn adaptation to an unfriendly environment calls into question the very possibility to achieve insularity and homogeneity of a national legal system. What is more, such uniformity becomes particularly difficult to achieve in our age – the age when styles conflate and extremes converge.

There is very little reflection on the dissenting opinions of judges in Russian legal scholarship. It contrasts sharply with the role they play in common law jurisprudence. The difference of judicial styles – terse and syllogistic in Europe,

---

91 Pether, 'Inequitable Injunctions', pp. 1483, 1522.
92 See more in K. Zweigert and H. Kotz, *Introduction to Comparative Law*, Vol. 1, para 5 (any edition).

open-minded and pluralistic in England and the US – surely plays a part in this division. But it is clear the rise of judge-made law and the admission of judicial dissent are interactive and mutually supportive developments.

Although it is correctly thought that in common law countries, in contrast to continental jurisdictions, the right of judges to dissent is deeply rooted, it does not mean to say that there were no attempts to restrict it. In England the publication of dissents became an established practice not earlier than by the middle of the nineteenth century, and even in the United States there was no lack of debates concerning the rationale and usefulness of dissents. However, it is the United States where this practice eventually flourished more that anywhere else. It was observed that the style of dissents in English appellate courts is more restrained, and the percentage of dissenting opinions in the House of Lords is significantly lower than in the US Supreme Court.[93]

The existence of dissents proves in the most visible way that different views among judges on difficult points of interpretation are common and, in fact, unavoidable. That is why the publication of dissenting opinions has always had powerful opponents who wanted judges to behave (at least, in public) as a single entity. Open dissents, they insisted, might threaten the authority of courts by unveiling the personalistic nature of judicial decisions and thus undermine the belief in their 'objectivity'. But there have always been practical reasons that pulled in the opposite direction and impelled legislators and courts to make some concessions.

In courts the submission of dissents in writing was established by Katherine the Great (1762–1796) in her *Institutions for the Government of Provinces* (1775).[94] They addressed dissents in Arts 184, 326, and 370 when dealing with proceedings in different courts. The wording of these provisions is identical. They say that 'since any decision of a case shall not be made otherwise but strictly by virtue of statutes and the words of a law and, consequently, a disagreement in decisions should not be; but if somewhere, contrary to expectations, in a decision of a civil case the division of judges' voices will turn out', such a disagreement 'shall be entered into special minutes, which shall not be disclosed other than when the case was obtained on demand for revision in the Chamber', that is, in the higher court.

These provisions laid down the foundations of the subsequent Russian/Soviet legislative and (to a large extent) doctrinal attitudes to judicial dissent. The basic principles are three:

1   Dissent is an undesirable and even abnormal thing, but it is unavoidable and therefore must be tolerated.
2   As a rule, dissents must be kept secret from parties and the general public.

---

93 J. Alder, 'Dissents in Courts of Last Resort: Tragic Choices?', *Oxford Journal of Legal Studies*, Vol. 20 (2000), Footnotes 87, 88, 125.
94 Ibid., p. 170.

3   The only useful function of written dissents is to assist superior courts in revising the decisions that gave rise to disagreement (that is, an auxiliary function).

These principles did not, however, remain unshaken in later times. Only the first one was not directly challenged in the future, whereas the latter two proved to be an easier target for various kinds of criticism. It seems that legislators were not unaware of their vulnerability and this perhaps accounts for the gaps and reticence that were so characteristic of future legal policies. The question was who ought to have access to dissents. In general, the most common position was uncertainty – legislators neither prohibited the general public from reading them nor explicitly permitted such access. Legislators felt comfortable in such position, because it allowed them to shift the burden of a difficult issue to higher courts which thus received significant room for their discretion. However, neither the Ruling Senate nor Soviet Courts were happy to assume responsibility, so court regulations remained cursory and incomplete.[95]

However, on 3 April 1987 the USSR Supreme Court decreed that, if there is a dissenting opinion of a judge or people's assessor in a civil case, parties can get access to it as well as to other documents in the file of the case.[96] Perhaps, this remarkable judicial gloss was inspired by the policy of *glasnost.* In any event, that was the first outright permission for litigants to access dissents in Russian and Soviet law. But it did not allow the general public to know the content of dissents and thus did not reach the standards of transparency typical of some other jurisdictions such as the United States.

The norm introduced in 1987 survived the demise of the Soviet Union and the abolition of its Supreme Court. It lost force not long before the new Civil Procedure Code entered into force, without being substituted by another norm.[97] But it succeeded in shaping a legal doctrine that favoured access to dissents in civil proceedings. The commentaries on the new Civil Procedure Code (2002) continue to insist that parties do have the right to read the dissents.[98]

By contrast, criminal procedure seems to follow a different line – dissents are never avowed to the parties and are accessible only to higher judges (although

---

95 For more details see A. N. Vereshchagin, 'Dissents in Russian Courts', in *Forging a Common Legal Destiny: Liber Amicorum in Honour of W.E. Butler* (2005), pp. 315 ff.

96 See the Point 1-1, Decree of the Plenum of the Supreme Court of the USSR of 1 December 1983, No. 10 (as amended by the Decree of 3 April 1987, No. 3), *Бюллетень Верховного Суда СССР* [Bulletin of the USSR Supreme Court], no. 3 (1987), p. 19.

97 Decree of 1 December 1983 was repealed as a whole by the Decree of the Plenum of the Russian Supreme Court of 10 October 2001, No. 11, *BSC*, no. 12 (2001), p. 1.

98 Cf. the opinion of the G. A. Zhilin, the Judge of the Russian Constitutional Court, in G. A. Zhilin (ed.), *Комментарий к Гражданскому процессуальному кодексу Российской Федерации (постатейный)* [A Clause-by-Clause Commentary on the Civil Procedure Code of the Russian Federation] (2nd edn., 2004), p. 46.

this prohibition is entirely based on practices, not laws). It is quite surprising, therefore, that arbitrazh procedure, despite its natural linkage with the civil procedure, has opted for the criminal law approach. The 1995 Arbitrazh Procedure Code was quite severe for dissents. It provided that a dissenting opinion of a judge is joined to the case, but it shall not be announced, and parties shall not have the right to know it (Art 15, point 1). But only the prohibition against announcement survived the new revision of arbitrazh procedure in 2002, whereas the words about the parties' access have been dropped.[99] On the other hand, no direct permission to reveal the content of dissents to parties has been introduced either. As for the new Civil Procedure Code, its expressions are equally vague (Art 15). In the final analysis, one may doubt that prohibitive interpretation can be reconciled with the right of parties to be acquainted with the documents of the case (Art 41 of the 2002 Arbitrazh Procedure Code; cf. Art 35 of the 2002 Civil Procedure Code). Rather, the systemic construction of the relevant provisions suggests that Russian procedural legislation does not outlaw the access to dissenting opinions, although it tries to discourage it (first of all, by failing to elaborate a procedure for such access).

In reality, it is the Supreme Arbitrazh Court, in its capacity of a 'secondary legislator', not the federal legislator himself, which banned access to dissenting opinions. Point 44 of the Regulations of the arbitrazh courts says: 'Judges taking part in the consideration of a case in courts of all instances are obliged to familiarise themselves with a dissenting opinion. Other persons shall not be informed about the dissenting opinion of a judge and its content.' This rule makes the situation exactly the opposite to the one which exists in legal systems which are more propitious to dissenting opinions. The latter usually attach more value to the dissents in courts of last resort, and it is not a mere coincidence that dissents are more frequent in appellate courts, for they are staffed with the most experienced judges who decide the most difficult cases capable of influencing judicial practice across the appropriate jurisdiction. As we have seen, in the Russian arbitrazh courts the role of dissents is confined to their being an aid for senior judges in revising cases from lower courts. The paradox about this position is that it makes the opinions of top judges the least valuable, if not completely useless, since no further appeals lie to anywhere![100]

The practice of publishing dissents in modern Russia is limited to the area of constitutional proceedings. The legislation on the Constitutional Court draws a line between a 'dissenting opinion' proper (*osoboe mnenie*) and a mere 'opinion' (*mnenie*). In the present law on Constitutional Court the latter are called

---

99 See Art 20 of the 2002 Arbitrazh Procedure Code.

100 In a conversation with the author, the former Chief Justice Veniamin Jakovlev admitted that the rule has been changed quite consciously, as a result of internal discussions within the Supreme Arbitrazh Court. He said that he never wrote dissents, and they were very rare in the Presidium during his presidency (interview with Iakovlev on 25 July 2006).

'the opinions concerning disagreement with a majority of judges' and designed for cases when a judge voted for the essence of the final decision of the Court, but was outvoted with respect to some minor question or the reasoning of the decision (Art 76). Obviously, this is an equivalent to the 'concurring opinions' of common law courts. At the same time, such 'opinions' are considered by law as a special form of dissent. In the Constitutional Court practice they are rare. It is for judges themselves to choose the label – either 'dissent' or 'concurrence' – for their opinions. There are no rules as to the form and style of opinions. Although the law on the federal Constitutional Court does not forbid joint dissent, it has never happened in practice. Therefore, we never know whether a particular dissent is just a voice crying out in the wilderness or it found support among some fraction of the Court. For whatever reason, it became customary that every judge wrote on his or her own behalf instead of giving open support to another dissenter.

For a long time the process of publication of dissents from the Constitutional Court was disordered. As a rule, they were published with respective decisions in the 'Herald' of the Court and frequently in other official periodicals. Quite often, the publication in the 'Herald' was belated and, in case of other periodicals, incomplete. The amendments of 15 December 2001 to the Law on Constitutional Court made the publication of dissenting opinions in its journal compulsory. It should be noted that a literal interpretation of the new version of Art 76 does not imply that publication in other official periodicals is inadmissible. But in practice this amendment was understood as purporting to suppress the excessive dissemination of dissents. Quite possibly, it was the real purpose of the amendment, for it was in line with the political aim of strengthening the authority of the Court.[101] As a result, the official periodicals, other than the 'Herald', ceased publishing the dissents. But it is doubtful that the goal could be achieved in this way, because judges' opinions can be easily found in unofficial legal databases such as 'Garant' and 'ConsultantPlus'. The number of their users far exceeds the number of readers which those periodicals might have.

The calculation made by the present author shows that during the years 1992–2005 there were 185 dissenting opinions from the Constitutional Court that were made available to the public through various periodicals and the Internet. Out of them, 149 opinions related to the decrees of the Court, 7 to its conclusions, 27 to its rulings and 2 accompanied its 'decisions' (in 1993). It is no wonder that rulings, being the most routine and numerous kinds of decisions (about 3–5 hundred each year) have the least potential for provoking dissent.

---

101 Interestingly, this amendment is not found in the initial draft of the law and there is no reference to it in the stenographic record of any of the three readings on the law in State Duma (28 June, 22 and 28 November 2001). See [www.akdi.ru/gd/PLEN_Z/2001/06/s28-06_d.htm]. Perhaps, it was included by the committee in charge of the law before the second or third readings. It is not unlikely that it escaped notice of many parliamentarians who voted for the law as a whole. In any event, no legislative intent as to this amendment has ever been articulated.

It is very interesting to explore the dynamics of dissents in the Constitutional Court decrees over the years.[102] An annual level of dissenting activity can be measured in two steps. First, we need to count the number of judges' participations in making decrees. This number is taken to be 100 per cent. Then we shall calculate the number of actual dissents and find out their correlation with the number of participations. In so doing we assume that every judge present in a case enjoys the right to express an individual opinion. Therefore, the number of judges who took part in rendering decrees during a certain year shows how many chances to dissent there were. The number and percentage of actual dissents will show how many chances have been used. This will be the rate of dissenting activity for the year in question, and by comparing the annual rates one may observe changes in the trend.[103]

The result may be seen from the following Table 3:

Table 3 Statistics of dissents in the Russian Constitutional Court, 1992–2004

Year	Total number of decrees	Number and percentage of decrees with dissents		Dissents in all decisions of the court	Dissents in decrees	Judges' participations in adoption of decrees	Annual rate of dissenting activity (%)
1992	9	6	66.6	8	8	106	7.55
1993	20	9	38.9	19	17	217	7.83
1995	17	9	52.9	23	22	185	11.89
1996	21	10	47.6	15	15	197	7.61
1997	21	11	52.4	19	19	215	8.84
1998	28	11	39.3	22	15	270	5.55
1999	19	4	21.1	7	6	193	3.11
2000	15	5	33.3	9	8	166	4.82
2001	17	6	35.3	11	7	165	4.24
2002	17	5	29.4	10	8	173	4.62
2003	20	4	20.0	8	8	223	3.59
2004	19	7	36.8	13	9	199	4.52
2005	14	7	50.0	21	14	144	9.72
Total	237	94	—	185	156	2453	—
Average	—	7.23	39.7	14.23	12	188.7	6.36

102 For the purposes of our analysis conclusions are included into the figure of decrees. There were only two conclusions in the history of the Court, both made in 1993 and both on hot issues of the then political agenda. The first was on 23 March (3 dissents) and the second on 21 September (4 dissents).

103 One may wonder how the overall number of participations can be 100 per cent, since dissent is the right of a minority and, if all judges dissent, with whom do they then disagree, then? But, first, a concurrent opinion is considered as a form of dissent and, secondly, a judge may disagree with some points in a *per curiam* decision of the Court and support others. Therefore, it is theoretically possible that every judge in a case writes an individual opinion.

This table is the most comprehensive statistical survey of dissents in the Russian Constitutional Court.[104] But what do these figures show? The average annual rate of dissent for the entire period is 6.36 per cent. This means that judges used 6.36 per cent of their opportunities to render an individual opinion. In 1992–1997 the yearly rates were constantly higher, but afterwards they dropped and later on never reached the average score. Although it may seem that the first year of decline was 1998, this is not quite true, for one should take into account the record number of dissents (seven) in rulings rendered that year. Therefore, the real divide was the year 1999. The declining trend as to the annual number of dissenting opinions endorses this conclusion as well. During the period 1999–2003 the largest annual number was 11, whereas during the five preceding years it had never been less than 15. Although 13 individual opinions in 2004 might seem to be an improvement, in reality it is not. Rather, the contrary is true, for 8 out of 9 full-fledged dissents of 2004 have been written by one justice only, Anatolii Kononov! (This, by the way, is the record individual number of dissents during one year). So this moderate increase may be rightly seen as a result of the desperate effort of a single judge to oppose the general tendency towards unanimity. However, this attempt could be a certain success, given a significant raising of the rate in 2005.

There is one more (and perhaps an easier) way to explore the dissenting activity of the Russian Constitutional Court. We shall count how many judges wrote individual opinions during a certain year and, additionally, how many judges dissented more than once. To put it another way, the question is how large was the group of dissenting judges within the Court? Did it increase over the years or not? The answer can be gained from Table 4.[105]

Notice the sharp line between years 1998 and 1999 in terms of the number of dissenting judges. Indeed, the share of dissenters in the composition of the Court decreased from 51.3 per cent on the average during the years 1995–1998 to 23.3 per cent over subsequent six years. By the same token, the percentage of judges who dissented more than once during a single year has also halved (on the average, it was 27.6 per cent in 1995–1998 and just 11.4 per cent in 1999–2004).

This data draws us to the conclusion that the 'golden era' of dissents was in the early period of the Court history, particularly during the first year of its work under the new Constitution.[106] But the period after 1998 witnesses a conspicuous decline. These phenomena can be accounted for in a number of ways.

---

104 Curiously, the Constitutional Court itself seems to have no reliable statistics of dissents. The figures published by *Rossiiskaia Iustitsia*, a joint periodical of Russian highest courts (no. 1 (2001), pp. 43–44) on the occasion of the tenth anniversary of the Court, are not quite correct.

105 It should be noted that in 1992–1993 there were 13 judges who were actually sitting on the Court (2 more seats remained vacant), whereas since 1994 the Court is comprised of 19 judges.

106 That is, in 1995. In the year 1994 the Court did not work and made no judgments.

Table 4 The share of dissenting judges within the court

Year	The number of dissenting judges	Their percentage	The number of judges who dissented repeatedly	Their percentage
1992	6	46.2	1	7.7
1993	5	38.5	4	30.8
1995	10	52.6	6	31.6
1996	9	47.4	3	15.8
1997	10	52.6	5	26.3
1998	10	52.6	7	36.8
1999	5	26.3	2	10.5
2000	5	26.3	2	10.5
2001	6	31.6	2	10.5
2002	4	21.1	3	15.8
2003	5	26.3	2	10.5
2004	3	15.8	2	10.5
2005	7	36.8	5	26.3
Average (%)	6.62	37.1	3.54	19.2

First of all, it should be noted that the figures above are reflective of *open* dissent only. There can be strong disagreements that would remain unknown to the general public. To write a dissenting opinion is a right, not a duty, of the judge who voted against the decision of the majority. Therefore, the reduction of written dissents is not necessarily the result of growing unanimity and common judicial philosophy of the members of the Court.

One can imagine at least three factors capable of affecting the sad fate of dissenting opinions in the most influential Russian court. The first factor is the growing caseload, which leaves judges little time to write individual opinions. But it would be contrary to the well-known facts to suggest that judicial work in mid-1990s was much easier than now. In fact, the financing of judicial institutions has considerably improved after 2000, and the Constitutional Court was not an exception. Every judge has legal clerks who help to cope with the increasing number of applications. And, last but not least, to write several opinions per year is not a great burden anyway.

The second factor might be a change in the character of the reviewed legislation. One may argue that it became more 'technical' compared with mid-1990s, when a number of overtly 'political' acts came before the Court.[107] But this could scarcely have a decisive impact upon the dissenting activity of judges. There is no doubt that the 'purely legal' implications of a case are no less capable of giving rise to dissension than 'political' ones.

---

107 Characteristically, the greatest number of dissents to date (eight) was in one of the first cases considered by the Court upon the renewal of its work. It was the famous 'Chechnya case' (judgment made on 31 July 1995).

In order to explain this decline it should be remembered that the writing of individual opinions based upon a legal philosophy of a certain kind has never been an important task for judges of Soviet or Russian supreme courts. It is more a 'matter of taste', than a requirement of tradition. It is remarkable that the dissenting activities of the Constitutional Court judges vary tremendously. The majority of dissents have been written by four judges only – Anatolii Kononov (44), Nickolai Vitruk (34 opinions), Ghadis Ghadzhiev (21) and Tamara Morshchakova (16). Together, these 'great dissenters' have written almost 2/3 of all individual opinions to date (62 per cent).[108] At the same time, some judges wrote very few opinions or never dissented at all.[109] Given these inequalities and the restrictions imposed upon the dissemination of judges' opinions, the crucial factor appears to be a general turn of judicial and legislative policies discouraging open dissent among Russian judges, especially those of the Constitutional Court.

At the same time there are weighty reasons to sustain it. It is obvious that the ancient practice of open dissents in common law countries was far from having a detrimental effect upon the authority of the courts. Quite the contrary, it constitutes a part of the general atmosphere of openness, individual responsibility and intellectual freedom that are so characteristic of their work and make an invaluable contribution to public confidence in the courts. This fact requires explanation on the part of those who, for whatever reason, are prejudiced against the practice of open dissents. In modern jurisprudence the existence of dissents is viewed as a consequence of the fact that judges of appellate courts confront choices between incommensurable principles and approaches which compete with each other. Since these principles are eventually rooted in value judgments, any of them claim respect. The coexistence of such principles and values (flowing, for instance, from the demands of man as an autonomous person and, on the other hand, as a social being) is considered to be a part and parcel of liberal democracy.[110] Dissenting opinions uncover those principles and promote useful debates within the legal community, thus helping the legislature and society at large to make an informed choice between them. And in this respect a minority opinion can be no less valuable than that of the majority. There is evidence that some members of the Russian judicial community are prepared to defend the practice of dissents before their colleagues. In one of the recent

---

108 Vitruk and Morshchakova no longer serve on the Court. They have retired because of the age limit. On the whole, the composition of the Constitutional Court is expected to become more stable due to the Federal Constitutional Law of 4 April 2005, No. 2-ФКЗ, which raised the age limit and made it uniform for all judges (70 years). This may prolong the existing patterns within the Court, including the number of regular dissenters.

109 To be sure, it is possible that they are the real leaders of the Court whose opinions are normally expressed in its final judgments. Or they simply do not share the views of the present author concerning the worth of public dissents.

110 Alder, 'Dissents in Courts of Last Resort', pp. 223–224.

Constitutional Court cases Judge G. Ghadzhiev opined that society at large is interested in the information concerning the nature and profundity of theoretical discussions. Then he cited the US Supreme Court Justice A. Scalia who said that the system of dissenting and concurring opinions makes the Supreme Court the central arena of modern legal debates and turns its decisions into an annotated history of American legal philosophy.[111]

Moreover, the availability of dissents to the public would have two important advantages: first, it makes the majority of judges better feel their responsibility for the decision than is the case in the event of anonymity of opinions, and may protect the individual reputation of dissenters, when court decision is unwise; second, they bring the shortages of the law to the attention of legislators. Therefore, it seems quite natural that in the course of time many continental jurisdictions became susceptible to the idea of publication of dissents (Norway, Finland, Sweden, Switzerland, Germany, Portugal, Greece) or, at a minimum, of their openness (Spain). One may hope that the role of dissents, especially those in courts of last resort, for the future of the Russian legal system will be reassessed. It is also important to emphasise that, in the absence of a legislative ban, the prospects of their publication will depend mostly upon the attitudes of senior judges, that is to say, upon the politics of the higher courts.

The internal structure of highest courts

Up to now the activities of the Supreme and Supreme Arbitrazh courts of Russia were very rarely assessed in terms of their ability to perform the functions, which in aggregate can be called 'judicial politics'. In part, it is explained by the fact that the system of arbitrazh courts whose role is preeminent for economic life took its present shape not earlier than in mid-1990s. Our inquiry is not intended to explore all ramifications of this large theme, but only suggest some observations concerning institutional aspects of those functions.

It appears that, on the whole, the Presidium of the Supreme Arbitrazh Court enjoys more power and plays a more active part within its own system than does its counterpart – the Presidium of the Supreme Court. Numerically speaking, the former issues more documents capable of affecting the practice of lower courts than does the latter. The latest version of the Regulations of arbitrazh courts (as of 30 December 2002)[112] attempts to further centralise the arbitrazh system, making the Presidium the only authority with respect to all controversial questions of judicial practice and its chairmen (or chief justice) the key figure determining the composition of the Presidium, judicial divisions and benches of the Supreme Arbitrazh Court (Arts 19, 24, 62–69).[113] It gives more attention to elaborating

---

111 Decree of the Constitutional Court of 17 June 2004, No. 12-П (Judge G. Ghadzhiev, concurring), *HCC*, no. 4 (2004), p. 88.

112 *HSAC*, no. 3 (2003), pp. 6–23.

113 Ibid., pp. 9, 10, 16–17.

a procedure for issuing surveys and explanations of judicial practice by courts, which was regulated but slightly in the original version (1996). Now it requires that any surveys by lower judicial instances be submitted to the Supreme Arbitrazh Court and, if publication in any form is envisaged, received the preliminary approval by its Presidium. Any decisions concerning the deeming of normative acts to be illegal should also be submitted to the Supreme Arbitrazh Court for publication in its 'Herald' (Art 46).[114] Such procedures are still lacking in the system of general courts.

The role of the Chairman of the Supreme Arbitrazh Court within the system also appears to be stronger. Before 2002 he was the only person allowed to bring protests to the Presidium against the decisions of the Supreme Arbitrazh Court as a court of first instance. The 1998 amendments to the Regulations still more enhanced his powers. He may determine the composition of the benches of the Court (while in the Supreme Court this is done by the heads of judicial divisions). Individual judges may be elected to the Presidium by the Plenum of the Supreme Arbitrazh Court only upon the Chairman's recommendation. According to the Regulations (in the version of 20 July 1998), they should be elected by *open ballot* for a term of one year with due regard to the principle of rotation (Art 69).[115] The Federal Constitutional Law of 4 July 2003 increased this term to two years with the possibility of re-election.[116] In practice the use of rotation was far from sweeping. Apparently, no judge has been elected on the temporary basis in 1998–2004. There is no fixed limit on the number of judges in the Presidium. The comparison of available data concerning its composition in April 1996 and January 2005 shows that it expanded from 15 judges to 18.[117] Almost all of them were members *ex officio* (the Chairman, his six deputies and the chairman of the benches). It should be noted that the chairmen of the benches are confirmed in office by the Plenum upon the recommendation of the Chairman. These are permanent members; besides, judges who present individual cases to the Presidium (they are called 'reporters') act as its members at their consideration. The composition of the Presidium was quite stable under Veniamin Iakovlev (1991–2005). Only two vacancies were filled between 1996 and 2005. However, his resignation had an immediate impact upon the composition of the Presidium – within less than two years five new judges were added, while seven members of the 'old team' retired.

---

114 Ibid., p. 14.
115 *HSAC*, no. 10 (1998), p. 22.
116 Art 15(2) of the Federal Constitutional Law 'On Arbitrazh Courts in the Russian Federation' (in the version of 4 July 2003). The regulations were amended appropriately on 8 April 2004.
117 Strangely, the composition of the Presidium was not given in the reported decisions or any official publications years 1997–2003. It is still impossible to find a complete list of its members in any open source. So the present author had to glean information from concrete decisions.

By contrast, all members of the Presidium of the Supreme Court are confirmed in office by *secret ballot* of the upper chamber of Parliament – the Soviet of the Federation, not by the Plenum of the Court. They are just 13, and their term of office is not determined by law. The more stable and compact composition makes its members (at least, potentially) more independent and authoritative figures than is the case with respect to the Supreme Arbitrazh Court. Between 1994 and 2003 five seats were filled with new persons, whereas since 2003 seven vacancies emerged.

Nevertheless, the Presidium of the Supreme Arbitrazh Court seems to enjoy a greater role in governing the system than its counterpart. It holds sessions at least once a week and is capable of managing a formidable caseload.[118] One more peculiarity of internal structure of the Supreme Arbitrazh Court is that judicial divisions play a relatively insignificant part there. Their activities are very superficially described by law. Characteristically, the 2002 Arbitrazh Procedure Code makes no mention of them. By contrast, the 1981 law on court structure (as amended) speaks about the divisions of the Supreme Court in much greater detail than the 1995 law on arbitrazh courts does with respect to those of the Supreme Arbitrazh Court. These distinctions can be accounted for by the more compact structure of the arbitrazh judiciary. It allows the Presidium to consider the majority of important cases. The two divisions of the Court do not consider cases by way of cassation or supervision. Mostly, they engage in preliminary examination of applications for the Presidium. Cassation belongs entirely to intermediary courts, whereas the supervisory function is the exclusive domain of the Presidium. By comparison, the function of cassation within the system of general courts is divided among three instances (intermediary courts, the divisions of the Supreme Court for civil, criminal and military cases and, finally, its Cassation Division). The supervisory function is also effectuated by three instances (presidiums of intermediary courts, three divisions of the Supreme Court and its Presidium).

For a long time the Chairman of the Supreme Arbitrazh Court was Veniamin Iakovlev (b. 1932) who was in fact the creator of the arbitrazh system. He was quite susceptible to the idea of judge-made law in the form of both 'explanations' and precedents.[119] On 1 February 2005 he was succeeded by Anton Ivanov (b. 1967), a relatively unknown young lawyer from S.-Petersburg, who never served on courts.

---

118 To be sure, the number of settled disputes is not always a good indicator of a genuine activity. Recent statistics shows than under the new arbitrazh procedure the number of cases for the Presidium is three times less than before (see B. Ia. Polonskii, Экономическое правосудие: единство правоприменения [The Economic Justice: the Unity of Law-Application], Законодательство [Legislation], no. 5 (2003), p. 50). But this is not a reason to believe that the significance of its interpretations has diminished. Rather, contrary would be true.

119 In his interview published in Государство и право [State and Law], no. 6 (2003), p.11, he said that judicial precedent can be recognised as a source of Russian law, but added a traditional reservation that its role cannot be 'the key one'.

In mass media his appointment was connected to his being a university mate of Dmitrii Medvedev, the then Head of Administration of the Russian President. It is noteworthy that Ivanov's application for this prominent position was the only one, whereas there were five candidates for the vacant seat of the chairman of the Arbitrazh Court of the Moscow City, which is a first-instance court. Despite initial skepticism with respect to this appointment, his first steps were those of a clever and innovative administrator. Although the final judgment would of course be premature, it is evident that he is frustrated by the low quality of the legislation which courts have to apply, and also the lack of interaction and feedback between the Supreme Arbitrazh Court and the legislative bodies. Therefore, his main concerns were the reduction of the heavy caseload by means of the development of pre-trial and alternative ways of settling disputes and the improvement of legislation through bringing difficulties arising at the examination of disputes by the Presidium to the attention of legislative bodies.[120] Also, he gave an additional impetus to the Court's interpretive work by issuing more guidelines on controversial points of law than was the case under Iakovlev. In a quite unprecedented move, their drafts are published in advance on the Court's website, with all the alternative views and contemplations of the drafters avowed, the creative role of the Court thus being unmasked.[121] The court sessions are increasingly becoming more accessible to the general public, the publication of electronic versions of all cassational decisions is an immediate goal, and there is little doubt that in the very near future all arbitrazh courts get their websites.

In the final analysis, the arbitrazh branch of the Russian judiciary appears to be more centralised and, respectively, the role of the Supreme Arbitrazh Court is pervasive. Even more importantly, this court seems to have succeeded in developing – partly through legislation and partly through the internal rules of the system – a better legal and organisational framework for its law-making activities than the Supreme Court currently has. Therefore, the fact that since the year 2003 the Supreme Arbitrazh Court began to consider the 'violation of the practice of law-application' by the decisions of lower instances as a distinct ground for their reversal comes as little surprise to an observer.[122]

---

120 His speech at a conference in the Institute of Legislation and Comparative Legal Studies attached to the Government of the Russian Federation, published in *Журнал российского права* [Journal of Russian Law], no. 4 (2005), pp. 4 ff.

121 In a conversation with the present author (25 July 2006), Iakovlev spoke disapprovingly on this practice of his successors.

122 See, for instance, an array of decrees of the Presidium of the SAC: of 1 April 2003, No. 10114/02; of 13 May 2003, No. 9985/02; of 20 May 2003, No. 288/03; of 27 May 2003, No. 7584/00 (*HSAC*, no. 8 (2003), pp. 20–22; no. 10 (2003), pp. 14, 23, 47).

Chapter 5

Russian labour law and the courts

A case study

In this chapter I shall explore the role of courts in shaping the legal framework of relations between employers and individual workers in post-Soviet Russia, with particular attention to the interplay between different levels and branches of the judiciary. The primary focus will be on controversial points of law relating to the conclusion and termination of labour contracts, especially unfair dismissals (in Russian terminology, 'dissolution of a labour contract without legal grounds'), for such cases create the largest number of disputes in regular courts of all instances and some eventually give rise to proceedings in the Constitutional Court. In Russia, labour disputes concerning dismissals hinge on the question whether there was a 'legal grounds' for it (or a 'just cause', in British legal parlance) and having a job position is conceptualised as a right. It makes them very similar to British practices and unlike those of the United States where the predominant issue is discrimination and employers have broad latitude in hiring and firing so long as their decisions are non-discriminatory.[1]

On 1 February 2002 a new Labour Code of the Russian Federation became effective. From that time on the 1971 RSFSR Code of Laws on Labour (KZoT)[2] is a thing of the past. In the years before adoption of the new code its predecessor was the subject of sharp criticism in public and scholarly debates. The gist of this criticism can be confined to the idea that the 30-year-old code was an obsolete document of the socialist era incapable of providing an adequate framework for labour relations in a market economy.

In fact, given numerous amendments, for the last 10 years before its repeal one had its updated version. It can be said that by 2001 the KZoT differed in its initial wording as much as a human being would differ from himself at a distance of three decades. However, changes in the KZoT were not, on the whole, as significant as those which occurred in social and political life.

The labour law reform in the USSR was launched as early as 1988 by changing the original wording of Art 5 of the KZoT. That Article prohibited an

---

1 H. M. Kritzer, 'Courts, Justice, and Politics in England', in *Courts, Law, and Politics in Comparative Perspective*, pp. 132, 135. Cf. also Jacob's remarks in the chapter on the United States (Ibid., p. 51).

2 In Russian *Kodeks zakonov o trude*, hereinafter: KZoT.

improvement of an employee's position through labour contract beyond the ceiling provided for by legislation. In such a way the freedom of contract of employment lacking in earlier socialist legislation was allowed. The pace of changes in the labour law area was particularly rapid until 1993, that is, in the most dramatic period of transition of the Soviet-type state economy to new market methods. The Russian judiciary did not stand aloof from these developments, but made a notable contribution by adjusting legal rules to the new circumstances, mostly through the efforts of the Constitutional Court and the Supreme Court (labour disputes in Russia are assigned to the jurisdiction of general courts). In many respects the optimal starting date for our inquiry is the year 1992, in which large-scale economic reforms were launched and, as a consequence, the court practice also started to change. Several decrees of the newly established Constitutional Court were devoted to labour law matters, and in December 1992 the Plenum of the Supreme Court issued its most fundamental decree, which remained in force for more than 11 years.[3]

Labour law and civil law

The Russian economic reforms made under the slogans of liberalism led to a revision of the special status which labour law had enjoyed in the Soviet legal system. To put it a bit loosely, the basic trend of the change was the approaching of labour law principles to those of civil law. This is the underlying issue of many developments in labour law area in post-Soviet Russia and of scholarly debates.

Both branches of law have contractual principles at their heart, but there are a number of distinctions as well. In the Russian legal writings the key distinction is assumed to be the subordination of the employee to the employer and to the internal regulations established by the latter. Nothing similar is found in the civil law which is grounded upon the equality of the parties to a contract. But the employer and its worker, the doctrine says, are not equal at all – the position of the employer in this relationship is no doubt stronger. Proceeding on this assumption, the doctrine of labour law requires an enhanced protection for the worker, with the resultant prevalence of mandatory norms in the labour law domain, in contrast to the non-mandatory regulation in the civil law. This is how the received doctrinal position looks like, if set out *in compacto*.

All the same, it became a target for criticism at a certain point. The reason is obvious – the State has abandoned, at least partially, the tough socialist model of labour regulation. Accordingly, the role of the non-mandatory rules has increased. In a more or less explicit form, critics assume that the labour law is not an autonomous branch of law, but only a part of the civil law, the labour contract being just a special kind of the contract of services contemplated by the

---

3 On 17 March 2004 it has been replaced by a new Decree of the Plenum, No. 6, 'On the Application by Courts of the Russian Federation of the Labour Code of the Russian Federation', *BSC*, no. 6 (2004), pp. 2–18.

Russian Civil Code. M. M. Braginski, a senior specialist on civil law, has deployed a theory which emphasised the vanishing of seemingly unshakable distinctions between labour and civil law contracts, such as the object of the contract, its term, etc.[4]

The objections on the part of conservative labour lawyers are the following. They argue that human labour is more than just a commodity or an 'object of property rights'. It is a social value. Besides, it is maintained that an ordinary worker is not free when making a labour contract, since the supply of labour force across the world is usually larger than demand. Therefore, an average worker is more interested in the conclusion of the contract than an 'average' employer.[5] Another point of defence is the lack of the 'autonomy of will' of the parties to the contract – in some cases the employer is obliged to conclude (or renew) a labour contract. That is why the degree of State intervention into the labour relations is necessarily deeper than into the civil ones. An additional difference is found in the special role of trade unions which has no analogy in civil law. It is postulated that any doubts in labour disputes should be interpreted in favour of the worker.[6]

There is some force in these objections, but they do not resolve the issue nevertheless. They are premised on the belief that the labour force is divided into two unequal parts – a high-skilled 'elite' and an ordinary 'mass', and if the former may realise their needs and ambitions within civil law contracts, the latter are completely helpless in the face of the potential employer and therefore need an enhanced social protection which the civil law cannot afford them. However, in reality the degree of both professional skill and the level of market demand as to their skills vary endlessly. They do not concentrate on two poles apart, but constitute a continuum with a great variety of degrees between the extremes. Furthermore, the modern individualised society is characterised by the decline of trade unions. The increasing number of workers, in particular 'white collars', appear on the labour market individually and give preference to civil contracts compared to labour ones. Contrary to the belief of some scholars, it is not typical for workers in labour disputes to seek in court the continuation of work in their former work place. In many cases a compensation for the loss of job (an inherently civil law institution) would suit them better than the reinstatement in their former job. The real problem is the absence of such compensation in the Russian labour law, although it is common in the Western Europe. The obligation to conclude a contract is not a distinct feature of the labour law, for it is not alien to civil law as well (see Arts 421 and 445, Civil Code).[7] The presumption

---

4 M. M. Braginskii, Договор подряда и подобные ему договоры [The Contract of Independent Work and the Contracts Similar to It] (1999).

5 B. R. Karabel'nikov, Трудовые отношения в акционерных обществах [Labour Relations in Joint-Stock Societies] (2001), p. 84.

6 See S. A. Ivanov in Судебная практика как источник права [Judicial Practice as a Source of Law] (2000), p. 119.

7 *CCRF*, pp. 156, 164.

as to the interpretation of any doubts in favour of the worker is not shared by many lawyers and judges and is not expressly authorised by the letter of the law.

On the whole, it is noticeable that the majority of arguments for sustaining the autonomous status of labour law is difficult to reconcile with fundamental tenets of economic theories which treat labour and capital as complementary factors of production. This, however, is a large and interdisciplinary topic which should be left for another day. It will suffice to note here that the modern time witnessed a steadfast penetration of civil law institutions (such as the compensation for moral harm) into the Russian labour law. One may conclude, therefore, that, while preserving some quality distinctions, the difference between the civil and labour law is increasingly becoming a matter of degree. A marked contribution into this transformation was made by some decisions of courts.

It is typically said that the Supreme Court, particularly its Civil Division, adheres to the concept of 'the broad sphere' of labour legislation. The truth of this observation can be exemplified by a number of landmark cases in which Supreme Court judges were inclined to extend the norms of labour law to situations that *could* (but not necessarily *must*) fall within the domain of labour law. One of the earliest was *Ariadna* case, where the courts faced the problem of delimiting areas of civil and labour law.[8] In that case the plaintiffs were workers of a state-owned barbershop. They took part in its reorganisation into the limited responsibility society 'Ariadna', thus acquiring the status of founders and participants of the new company. All the same, they continued working there, but six weeks later were dismissed by decision of the general meeting of participants. They sued the society for non-payment of earnings. They lost in the inferior courts which failed to find labour relations between them and the society, but were successful in appealing to the Supreme Court. The Civil Division noted that according to the RSFSR Law 'On Enterprises and Entrepreneurial Activity' (Art 26) the relations between a worker and an enterprise arising on the basis of the contract of membership in an economic partnership should be regulated by civil legislation and constitutive documents of the partnership. The court took this clause as a compelling argument to sustain the view that the law clearly distinguishes between relations based on labour and those based on membership. Moreover, in spite of the lack of evidence that the reorganisation did take place, it applied Art 29(2) of the KZoT, which provided for the continuation of the labour relations in the event of a reorganisation.

In another case the Supreme Court reversed the decisions of lower courts, which failed to discover *de facto* labour relations.[9] Kirichenko, the plaintiff, was an expert fulfilling a specific task commissioned to him by the vice-president of the closed joint-stock society 'Areopag EX Ltd.' on premises belonging to the

---

8 Ruling in the case *Gladkih, Kuznetsova and others v Ariadna* (excerpt), *BSC*, no. 4 (1993), pp. 3–4.

9 Ruling of 15 December 1998 in the case *Kirichenko v Areopag EX Ltd* (excerpt), *BSC*, no. 5 (1999), p. 4.

society. In this case the Civil Division found for the plaintiff by invoking Art 18(3) of the KZoT, which provides that 'actual admittance to work shall be considered as the conclusion of a labour contract regardless of whether the employment was properly formalised'. In order to classify the relations as labour ones, the Supreme Court was perfectly satisfied with such factual grounds as evidence that the supposed employee was issued a pass by the vice-president and was paid remuneration for work. Also, the Supreme Court judges presumed that labour relations that arose between Kirichenko and 'Areopag EX Ltd.' should be qualified as a contract concluded for an indefinite period, and hereby declared the plaintiff to be entitled to average earnings for the whole period from the end of his work up to the rendering of the final judicial decision, despite the fact that the work in question was a specific assignment. However, according to Art 17 of the KZoT, the contract of employment can be concluded either for an indefinite period or for a determined period but not exceeding five years or *for the period of fulfilment of specified work*. Among these alternatives, the court chose the one most favourable for the employee.

It should be noted that for a long time it was unsettled as to when a certain type of contract should prevail. The question was resolved by the Law of 25 September 1992 'On Changes and Additions to the Code of Laws on Labour of RSFSR' that added Art 17(2) to the KZoT. It provided that a fixed-term employment contract should be concluded in cases when labour relations could not be established for an indefinite term, given the nature of the supposed work or the conditions of its fulfilment or the interests of the employee, and also in instances directly provided for by a law. In all other cases a contract for an indefinite period shall be concluded.

In Supreme Court practice these provisions were given a liberal interpretation. In *Sharapova* case[10] the Civil Division ruled that if a labour contract with an employee was terminated on the grounds of expiration after entry into force of the Law of 25 September 1992 and the employee contested such dismissal, the legality of the termination of the labour contract should be tested against the provisions of Art 17(2) of the KZoT. This ruling merely enforced the instruction contained in point 10 of the Decree of the Supreme Court Plenum of 22 December 1992. However, the difficulty with this position of the Supreme Court is that it was not the moment of termination of the contract, but rather the moment of its conclusion that should be a starting point for the judicial decision. In that particular instance, the labour contract was concluded prior to the enactment of Art 17(2). For this reason that Article was not applicable. But the Supreme Court has extended the area of application of that clause by instructing courts to assess the legality of the termination of the contracts of employment even though they were concluded *before* 25 September 1992. A decision of the Constitutional Court stating that only the legislator might extend

10 Ruling of 24 October 1997 in the case of Sharapova (excerpt), *BSC*, no. 4 (1998), pp. 4–5.

the operation of a law to a preceding period, while no retroactive force had been given to the Law of 25 September 1992, was effectively ignored.[11]

Rigid delimitation between civil and labour law is still a hallmark of the Supreme Court attitude, although some concessions were made. One of them was the reference in 2004 Plenum decree on labour law to the possibility of the 'abuse of rights' on the part of the employee – a purely legal concept borrowed from the Civil Code. In the case of an abuse of rights (such as concealing some essential facts capable of affecting a dismissal case) the employee could be denied legal protection. This opinion of the higher instance, though, did not preclude the Civil Division from holding in a later case that civil law concepts, including the abuse of rights, are not applicable to employment disputes.[12]

Theft as ground for dismissal

An interesting example of parallel (but not equally successful) efforts of the highest Russian courts to resolve a controversial point of law is the issue of legality of dismissal for theft of State or public property (para 1(8), Art 33 of the KZoT). Under literal interpretation, this norm did not cover the property of private businesses. In the case *S. v Open Joint-Stock Society 'Eletskii Tabak'* considered by the courts of general jurisdiction, the plaintiff (a loader who had stolen 24.5 kg of tobacco belonging to the joint-stock society) claimed himself to be unfairly dismissed and sought reinstatement in work, payment of his average earnings during the time of enforced down-time and contributory compensation for moral harm. In the court of first instance the dismissal of the plaintiff was recognised as lawful by virtue of para 1(8) of Art 33 of the KZoT, but this judgment was appealed against and later reversed by the decision of the cassational instance. However, the ruling of the Supreme Court Civil Division reversed it again. In its opinion, although the termination of a labour contract for theft of property owned by economic partnerships or societies was not provided for by para 8 of Art 33(1) of the Code, this provision nonetheless did correspond to Art 8(2) of the Russian Constitution, which guarantees equal protection for private, State, municipal and other forms of ownership. 'Therefore, the establishment of any privileges by the legislator and law-enforcement agencies for a particular form of economic activity and form of ownership is inadmissible.'[13] As long as para 1(8) of Art 33 of the Code is not yet brought into conformity with Art 8 of the Constitution, it should be applied with due regard to the content of the said constitutional clause.

Strangely enough, in a similar case with the same combination of facts which was reported in the 1999 survey of Supreme Court practice on labour disputes,

---

11 Decision of the Constitutional Court of 13 May 1993, No. 35-P3-5/3, 'On the Petition of M. N. Puzanova' (unpublished).

12 Ruling of 7 July 2006, No. 93-B06-1 (unpublished).

13 Ruling of 27 December 1999, No. 77-B99пр-30 in the case *S. v Open Joint-Stock Society 'Eletskii Tabak'*, in Комментарий судебной практики [Commentary on Judicial Practice], Vol. 6 (2000), p. 114.

the Civil Division came to the opposite conclusion. Tarassov was working as a car-driver for the company 'Udmurtneft'. By order of 14 February 1997 he was dismissed for the theft of property in his work place. He then challenged his dismissal in the court. When considering his claim the Supreme Court Civil Division found for the plaintiff. In doing so, it explained that 'termination of a labour agreement (or contract) at the initiative of the administration (management) of the employer for the theft of the property owned by economic partnerships or societies was not provided for by paragraph 1(8) of Art 33 of the Code of Laws on Labour of the Russian Federation'.[14] As for the norm contained in Art 8(2) of the Constitution providing that in the Russian Federation private, State, municipal and other forms of ownership shall be equally recognised and defended, it 'does not vest in courts the power to independently establish the ways of protecting property rights and to expand the list of the grounds of termination of the labour agreement (or contract) provided for by the law for theft of the State or public property, extending it to cases of theft of property relating to other forms of ownership'.[15] This ruling was obviously at odds with the constitutional principles and also failed to allow for new economic realities. It can be accounted for by the fact that different judges within the Supreme Court Civil Division are too often reluctant, for whatever reason, to treat like cases alike, contrary to what might be expected. But in such principled matters the lack of consistency in adjudication looks truly odd.

Apparently, many courts of general jurisdiction gave preference to the strict (or 'literal') interpretation of the controversial Art 33(8). At the end of the day, it was the Constitutional Court of Russia that had to deal with the question, which the current practice of the Supreme Court had so flagrantly failed to resolve. In the ruling of 8 February 2001 the Court pointed out that all of the forms of ownership should be equally protected. The right of the employer to dissolution of the labour contract with the employee should not depend upon the form of the enterprise to which the stolen property of the enterprise belonged.[16] The Constitutional Court ruled that para 1(8) of Art 33 of the KZoT 'did not and does not imply either restrictions of the powers of employers and interests of proprietors or inequalities of rights of citizens in the sphere of employment'. A contrary interpretation would contradict the principle of justness consolidated in the preamble to the Constitution as well as its Arts 8, 19(1) and (2), 45(2) and 55(3), and contravene the principles of contractual relations, namely, the freedom of labour contract with regard to its conclusion and good-faith performance by the parties of the contractual obligations assumed by them.[17]

14 Ruling in the case *Tarassov v Udmurtneft*, in 'Some Questions of Judicial Practice in Civil Cases', *BSC*, no. 10 (1999), p. 19.

15 Ibid.

16 Ruling of 8 February 2001, No. 33-O, with regard to para 1(8) of Art 33 of the KZoT, *HCC*, no. 3 (2001), p. 71.

17 Ibid., p. 73.

The attitude of the Constitutional Court to this case was clearly law-creative, and this triggered the dissents of two judges – Zhilin and Khokhriakova. The Court has indeed created a new norm with a broader content compared with the previous one. Both dissenters insisted that disciplinary responsibility in the form of dismissal is not subject to a liberal interpretation and the correction of the defects of the norm is a job for the legislature.[18] But whereas Judge Zhilin saw the way out not in the 'constitutional' interpretation of the norm, but in its striking aside, Judge Hohriakova believed the issue to be outside the Court's competence.

Anyway, in line with these court decisions, the federal legislator worded the relevant provision of the 2001 Labour Code (para 6(4), Art 81). It provides that 'commission at place of work of stealing (including petty) of another's property, waste, intentional destruction or damaging thereof'[19] may serve as a basis for dissolution of the contract of employment. It is noticeable that, whether intentionally or not, the legislator has gone even further than the Constitutional Court. This provision was formulated in such a way that covers not only stealing of the employer's property, but also the stealing of *any* property whatsoever.

Age limitations as grounds for dismissal

On 4 February 1992 the Constitutional Court rendered a decree concerning the law-application practice of dissolution of an employment contract on the grounds provided for by para 1^1 of Art 33 of the KZoT. According to it, the achievement of pension age and the right to a full old-age pension was a basis for dissolution of the contract. At the time of consideration, the 1978 Constitution of the RSFSR was still in force. The contested provision of the Code was deemed not to correspond to a number of constitutional clauses and international treaties in the area of employment, in particular, Art 2(2) of the 1966 International Covenant on Economic, Social and Cultural Rights concerning the duty of the State to guarantee that rights will be exercised without discrimination of any kind.[20]

As was said in the decree, the courts of general jurisdiction, when considering labour disputes on dissolution of labour contracts on this ground, tend to assume that the fact of attainment by an employee of pension age and his acquisition of the right to receive a full old-age pension (which follows from the literal meaning of Art 33(1^1) may be sufficient proof of the legality of his dismissal. This explanation was also given to the courts in Decree of the Plenum of the

---

18 Ruling of 8 February 2001, No. 33-O, with regard to para 1(8) of Art 33 of the KZoT, *HCC*, no. 3 (2001), pp. 75–78.

19 Labour Code of the Russian Federation, *Sudebnik*, Vol. VII (2002), p. 87.

20 Decree 4 February 1992 concerning the constitutionality of law-application practice of dissolution of labour contract on the grounds provided for by para 1^1 of Art 33 of the KZoT, *HCC*, no. 1 (1993), pp. 26–39.

USSR Supreme Court of 26 April 1984.[21] Thus, when considering the claims of Al'tgovzen and Stadnikova (applicants in the present case), as well as in other cases about reinstating in work the persons dismissed with reference to para 1[1] of Art 33 of the KZoT, the courts have not assessed whether the norm in question was subject to application in view of the meaning of the Constitution.[22]

Moreover, the Court held that such custom of law-application practice contradicts the duty of State agencies and officials to observe the Constitution established by Art 4. In fact, this constitutional clause requires direct application by courts if there is a contradiction between constitutional norms and other laws. Courts are also obliged to assess the law subject to application from the standpoint of its conformity to principles and norms of international law, since the necessity of faithful performance of obligations flowing therefrom is recognised by the Constitution and, moreover, the Declaration of Rights and Freedoms of Man and Citizen of 22 November 1991 specifying these constitutional norms has established, in full conformity with them, that generally recognised international norms relating to human rights directly give rise to rights and duties of Russian citizens.

It is worth noting that the decisions of the courts of general jurisdiction by which Al'tgovzen and Stadnikova were refused protection of their constitutional right to labour were rendered after the opinion of the USSR Constitutional Supervision Committee of 4 April 1991, which declared para 1[1] of Art 33 of the KZoT to be unconstitutional. By virtue of Art 124 of the 1977 USSR Constitution (as amended), the adoption of such opinion made the provision in question inapplicable. In this case, however, the general courts ignored the Committee opinion – no wonder, given the deficit of authority and short existence of this body (1990–1991). The Constitutional Court has been more successful in making the courts and legislators comply with its decisions. In this decree the Court pointed out that the Supreme Soviet of the Russian Federation (the then legislative agency) '*should* [emphasis added] consider the question of the necessity to repeal the provision provided for by para 1[1] of Art 33 of the RSFSR Code of Laws on Labour'.[23] Moreover, until repealed, it was not to be applied. The Law of 12 March 1992 has excluded the said provision from the KZoT.

This line of judicial law-making was sustained by the Court after the adoption of the 1993 Constitution. On 6 July 1995 it declared upon the appeal of the Major-General V. M. Minakov, a policeman, the provision of para 2 of Art 19(7) of the Law of the RSFSR 'On the Police' to be not in conformity with Arts 19(1)

21 Decree of the Plenum of the Supreme Court of the USSR of 26 April 1984, No. 3, 'On Application by Courts of the Legislation Regulating the Conclusion, Change and Termination of the Labour Contract' (in the version of decrees of the Plenum of 6 April 1988, 30 November 1990 and 8 October 1991), Бюллетень Верховного Суда СССР [Bulletin of the USSR Supreme Court], no. 3 (1984), pp. 24–32; no. 3 (1988), pp. 1–7; Вестник Верховного Суда СССР [Herald of the USSR Supreme Court], no. 2 (1991), pp. 15–20.

22 *HCC*, no. 1 (1993), p. 33.

23 Ibid., p. 35.

and 46(1) of the 1993 Constitution to the extent to which they were viewed by law-enforcement agencies as allowing the dismissal of an employee at the initiative of the head of the law-enforcement agency on the grounds of expiration of term of service giving the right to pension, without the consent of the employee and without a substantiation of the reasons confirming the impossibility of further service that could be verified by a court.[24] The articles of the Constitution to which the Court has referred in its decision guarantee the equality of citizens before law and court (Art 19) and judicial defence of rights and freedoms to each person (Art 46).

The dissenting opinion of Judge Kononov delivered in that session contains a number of interesting points as to where the proper frontier between special and general labour law standards, as well as between the functions of the Constitutional Court and law-maker ought to be drawn. Kononov argued that the 1958 International Labour Organisation Convention No. 111 concerning discrimination in respect of employment and occupation does not treat as discrimination any distinction, non-admission or preference made with regard to a certain work insofar as it is founded on its specific demands. And it is exactly this position that was expressed in the aforementioned Decree of the Constitutional Court of 4 February 1992. The Constitutional Court had then pointed out that the age criterion for the termination of the labour relations is impermissible, unless it is conditioned upon the nature and specific features of the work fulfilled.[25]

In Kononov's opinion, police service does presuppose such specific demands, thereby distinguishing it from general labour law standards. If age limits for police service were admissible, as the Court acknowledged in the present case, a similar role, he believed, should belong to the duration of service itself. It is justified by tough requirements as to the discipline, professional suitability, intellectual, physical and volitional qualities of the person working in the police, and also by the arduous and extreme conditions of service. The duration of service is precisely such a specific demand. Therefore, the analogies drawn by the Court majority with both labour and pension legislation, as well as with the legislation on state service, seemed to him incorrect.[26]

He went on to say that the Constitutional Court 'has deemed, in principle, the right of the head of a law-enforcement agency to dismiss a police worker because of duration of his service giving the right to pension, without his consent, to be not contrary to the Constitution of the Russian Federation. By doing this, contrary to the assertions contained in the reasoned part of the

---

24 Decree of 6 June 1995, No. 7-П, concerning the constitutionality of item 2 of Art 19(7) of the Law of the RSFSR of 18 April 1991 'On Militia', *HCC*, no. 2/3 (1995), pp. 57–66.

25 Decree of 4 February 1992, *HCC*, no. 1 (1993), pp. 32–34.

26 Decree of 6 June 1995, No. 8-П, *HCC*, no. 2/3 (1995), pp. 64–65. This interpretation of the Decree can be disputed, so far as it could be understood as prohibiting dismissal at the initiative of the head, if the employee's consent is lacking, irrespective of whether the dismissal was reasoned or not.

Decree, the specificity of the given requirement for police service was also recognised.'[27] So the Constitutional Court limited this right of the police administration by conditioning it upon 'substantiation of the reasons reconfirming the impossibility of further service which might be verified by a court'.[28] But the legislation on the police in force at that time did not provide for such conditions. In Kononov's opinion, the Constitutional Court has effectively exceeded the limits of its jurisdiction and thus substituted itself for the law-maker. It has actually created a new basis for dismissal of police employees, which at the same time is difficult to apply in practice because of the uncertainty of its definition.

A few years later a similar issue concerning the legality of dismissal from law-enforcement agencies on the grounds of attainment of the maximum age arose again, this time before the Supreme Court. 'Regulations on Service in Agencies of the Ministry of Internal Affairs' of 23 December 1992 (Art 59) established the age limit (45 years) for employees. Those who attained the maximum age were subject to dismissal. It was provided, however, that 'in the interests of service, in presence of a positive attestation and absence of medical contra-indications, the employees of a law-enforcement agency as an individual matter and with their consent *may be* left in service over the established maximum age for a term of up to 5 years'.

The Civil Division of the Supreme Court has obviously interpreted the words 'may be left' as 'having the right to be left'. At the same time, the expressions used in the law could be understood to indicate a discretionary right granted to the administration of the law-enforcement agency to use an employee who achieved the maximum age, provided that the aforesaid conditions were met.

The Supreme Court ruled that:

> Dismissal at the initiative of the chief without the consent of the employee and without an indication of the reasons reconfirming the impossibility of further service, does not correspond to the Constitution of the Russian Federation. The norm on dismissal upon the attainment of the maximum age is, in essence, a guarantee of the rights of an employee of law-enforcement agencies on continuation of service in the event of his fitness by state of health and conscientious execution of his duties in the past. By the administration's substantiation of the impossibility of continuation of employee service the probability of arbitrary actions of the head [of the agency] not conforming to the interests of service is eliminated.[29]

---

27 Ibid., p. 65.
28 *HCC*, no. 2/3 (1995), p. 64.
29 Ruling No. 46-B-01пр-2 (excerpt), in a Survey of the Supreme Court's Practice in Civil Cases for the 2nd Quarter of the year 2001, *BSC*, no. 12 (2001), p. 17.

Consequently, according to the interpretation given by both the Constitutional Court and the Supreme Court the administration of a law-enforcement agency no longer can dismiss an employee if his term of service has expired or the maximum age been achieved, unless it is capable of giving *other* reasons for his dismissal. In both cases the interpretations given by courts were, at best, only *admissible*, but not indisputable. It appears to me that these judicial decisions went far beyond the wording of the law and narrowed the discretion given by the legislator to the respective authorities. Perhaps what has originally been thought to be an exception (that is, the continuation of service after the age limit is achieved) was thus effectively transformed into a rule, while the right of administration was, vice versa, turned into an obligation. The policy underlying all these decisions was that of expanding the rights of the employee as much as possible. When so doing, the judges were neither siding with the legislator nor promoting his purpose, nor could they rely on grammatical interpretation of the legislative text.

Still, some provisions analogous to those deemed unconstitutional have survived, among them para 2(1) of Art 25 of the Federal Law 'On Fundamental Principles of State Service in the Russian Federation' (1996). It allows the head of a State agency to dismiss a state employee if the last had achieved the maximum age established for his office. Once it was considered by the Constitutional Court, but left in force as non-discriminatory.[30] The lasting existence of such norms shows that the application of Constitutional Court judgments by way of analogy is not an easily predictable thing.

Dismissal of socially protected employees

Here we address, first of all, the guarantees for employees holding positions as trade-union officials laid down by the KZoT (Art 235). Those guarantees included a prohibition against the dismissal of such employees at the initiative of administration without the consent of an appropriate trade-union agency (Art 235[2]). This immunity is retained for trade-union officials for two years after the termination of their powers (Art 235[5]). Needless to say, the norm favouring a certain category of employees by securing their jobs (the consent of the trade union to dismissal of their colleagues was, of course, a rarity) was deeply embedded in Soviet labour legislation and could create serious difficulties for employers in a market economy. In fact, they were unable to fire workers who committed disciplinary violations. However, the Supreme Court was not slow to enforce this obsolete norm during the recent years.[31]

---

30 Ruling of the Constitutional Court of 3 October 2002, No. 233-O, *HCC*, no. 3 (2003), pp. 62–67.

31 Ruling in the case *Kashaiuk v AOOT Holding Company 'Dalmoreproduct'* and on the meaning of Art 235(2), KZoT (excerpt) in 'Some Questions of Judicial Practice in Civil Cases', *BSC*, no. 10 (1999), pp. 17–18; Ruling of 4 September 2000, No. 41-впр00-20, in the case *B. v Factory 'Zernogradskii'*, *BSC*, no. 3 (2001), p. 11.

To be sure, the Supreme Court was not in the best position to eliminate such legal flaws for the simple reason that the appropriate legislation was beyond its reach. Unlike the Constitutional Court, it is incapable of invalidating provisions of federal laws. However, it could refuse to apply them (and hereby encourage the lower courts to do the same) if they were found contrary to the Constitution. If this policy were uniformly applied in similar cases, it could produce a kind of judge-made law, a judicial precedent, that could not be ignored easily by the courts down the hierarchy, despite the lack of formal binding force. But the Supreme Court did not dare to take initiative. Merely an isolated, cautious attempt to mitigate the difficulties created by the obsolete law could be found in its interpretative opinion that Art 235(2) applies only to a trade-union official who organises the work of the trade-union members working with him at the same enterprise, represents them and is involved in the defence of their labour rights within the limits of powers granted to him. If he is *the only* member of the given trade union in a particular enterprise, being elected for explanatory and organisational work for the purpose of involving workers into membership of the given trade union, the consent of the higher trade-union organisation that elected him to this position is not required.[32]

Apparently, the Supreme Court has construed the legislative provision narrowly by giving Art 235 a purposive interpretation, which is not in harmony with its literal meaning. The Court proceeded from its own suggestion concerning the purpose of this norm, having understood it as a means of protecting trade-union officers and activists engaged in the organisation of the work of trade union and in the defence of labour rights. If their activity is confined to enlisting employees in the trade union, it is not sufficient to grant them a guarantee against dismissal. However, recruiting could be viewed (most importantly, by the employer himself) as merely a first step towards the full-fledged trade-union activity. That is why there is no clear line between such things. The restrictive interpretation given by the Supreme Court can be viewed as a novelty which does not follow directly from the wording of Art 235.

The question of additional guarantees given by the KZoT to certain categories of employees has eventually come to the attention of the Constitutional Court.[33] It had to verify the constitutionality of Arts 170(2) and 235(2) of the KZoT and Art 25(3) of the Federal Law 'On Trade Unions, Their Rights, and Guarantees of Activity'. Article 170(2) of the Code contained a prohibition against the dismissal of employees who had children having the status of 'disabled' or 'disabled from childhood' and had not attained the age of 18 in the event of the commission of a disciplinary offence which, according to a law, might serve as grounds for dissolution of the contract of employment at the employer's initiative.

---

32 *Kashaiuk v 'Dalmoreproduct'*, *BSC*, no. 10 (1999), pp. 17–18.

33 Decree of 24 January 2002, No. 3-П, concerning Art 170(2) and Art 235(2) of the KZoT and para 3 of Art 25(3) of the Federal Law 'On Trade Unions, Their Rights, and Guarantees of Activity', *HCC*, no. 3 (2002), pp. 24–31.

The question submitted for consideration of the Court is interesting because the task before it was, by nature, a creative one. The Court ought to achieve the best (or fairest) combination of various conflicting values, each of them having support in certain Articles of the Constitution. The Court pointed out that the legislator 'has no right to establish such limitations which lead to distortion of the essence of freedom of economic (or entrepreneurial) activity'.[34] But, according to the literal meaning of the disputed provision of Art 170(2) in systemic connection with Arts 213 and 214 of the KZoT of the Russian Federation, and also according to the meaning attached thereto in court practice, the dismissal of the employee having a child who is disabled, or disabled from childhood under the age of 18 years, is theoretically impossible as a statutory measure of disciplinary punishment, and dissolution of the labour contract with him is considered as unlawful from the very beginning.[35]

The Court continued by saying that when placing upon the employer the duty to receive the consent of the trade-union agency to dismissal, the legislator at the same time failed to provide for the duty of this agency to state its reasons if such consent is not given. Therefore, the validity of the dissolution of the contract with an employee who has committed a disciplinary offence at the initiative of the employer is decided, in fact, not by the court, but the trade-union agency representing only one party to the dispute. In the opinion of the Court, the norms in question represented a disproportionate limitation of rights of the employer as a party to the contract of employment and (simultaneously) as a subject of economic activity and the owner, and therefore did not correspond to the Constitution.[36]

Irrespective of whether the efforts of the Court aimed at the transformation of the relations between the worker and the employer were deliberate, the effect of the abrogation of these obsolete legislative provisions came as an important contribution to Russian labour law and an essential assistance to business. It should be noted that the Constitutional Court when deciding the issue was aware that the legislator had already expressed its view in the new Labour Code which was about to come into force. This Code contains a special list of grounds for dismissal of socially protected workers (considerably shorter than the general list of grounds for dismissal) in Arts 261(3) and 374(1).[37] So the exception has been preserved, but in a reduced form. The invalidation of the outdated labour law norms by the Constitutional Court decision was a more radical solution, but a short-lived one, for Art 374 of the Labour Code was a partial restoration of the invalidated guarantees. For instance, the consent of the trade-union agency

34 Decree of 24 January 2002, No. 3-П, concerning Art 170(2) and Art 235(2) of the KZoT and para 3 of Art 25(3) of the Federal Law 'On Trade Unions, Their Rights, and Guarantees of Activity', *HCC*, no. 3 (2002), p. 27.

35 Ibid., p. 29.

36 Ibid., pp. 29–30.

37 Labour Code of the Russian Federation, *Sudebnik*, Vol. 7 (2002), pp. 195, 255.

is now required in case of dismissal for the repeated non-performance of duties. However, an attempt to challenge the new rules in the Constitutional Court has failed.[38] Having refused to invalidate them, the Court, however, has assigned to the trade-union agency the burden of proof that the real reason for dismissal was indeed the trade-union activities of the employee.

As for the Supreme Court contribution, it has recently given courts the right to approve the dismissal of workers having special guarantees against dismissal (for instance, trade-union activists), if the latter have hidden that they enjoyed such protection and the employer has consequently failed to perform the appropriate formal procedures for their dismissal. The Supreme Court suggested that such a conduct of the employee should be qualified as violating the general legal principle that an abuse of rights cannot be admitted.[39]

Additional grounds for dismissal

Here we turn to the question of additional grounds for dissolution of a labour contract under Art 254 of the KZoT. The problem that arose in practice most frequently was the interpretation of para 2 of this Article. This paragraph was introduced by Federal Law of 25 September 1995. It provided that 'additional grounds for the termination of a labour contract of certain categories of employees may be established by legislation in the event of a violation of the established rules of employment and in others cases'. How should the word 'legislation' be understood here? On occasion courts were inclined to treat the term 'legislation' broadly, so that it was able to encompass even such subordinate normative acts as 'Regulations on Service at the Agencies of the Ministry of Internal Affairs', likewise establishing additional grounds for dismissal. This practice was deemed unlawful by the Supreme Court.[40]

At the same time, the question whether such additional grounds could be established by legislative acts of subjects of the Federation seems to be more complex. Unfortunately, the KZoT has employed a very elastic term 'legislation', instead of, for instance, the more concrete term 'federal laws'.

The Supreme Court answer to that question (not always in line with the previous decisions of lower courts) is unequivocal: 'By "legislation" this norm means federal laws'. Therefore, 'the dismissal from work or service on grounds introduced by normative acts lower than federal laws is illegal'.[41] According to

---

38 Ruling of the Constitutional Court of 4 December 2003, No. 421-O, concerning Art 374 of the Labour Code of the Russian Federation, *HCC*, no. 3 (2004), pp. 12–15.

39 Point 27, Decree of the Supreme Court of 17 March 2004, *BSC*, no. 6 (2004), p. 9.

40 Three examples of this kind are found in the 'Bulletin': a Ruling of 9 April 1998 in the case *Shchenin v Minister of Internal Affairs of Udmurt Republic* (excerpt) and a Ruling in the case of Khudiakov (undated, excerpt), *BSC*, no. 10 (1998), pp. 2–3 and 18–19; a Ruling with regard to the meaning of Art 254(2) of the KZoT in 'Some Questions of Judicial Practice in Civil Cases', *BSC*, no. 10 (1999), pp. 15–16.

41 *BSC*, no. 10 (1999), pp. 15–16.

Art 76 of the 1993 Constitution, with regard to the subjects of joint jurisdiction of the Russian Federation and its subjects federal laws are adopted and also laws and other normative legal acts of subjects of the Federation. The latter may not be contrary to the federal laws adopted on questions of joint jurisdiction of the Federation and its subjects. In the event of a contradiction between a federal law and another act issued in the Russian Federation the federal law should prevail.[42]

In principle, it could be argued that the list of grounds for dismissal is not exhaustive and any legislation introducing new grounds for it should be treated as *labour* legislation, which 'shall consist of the present Code and other acts of labour legislation of the Russian Federation and *republics in the Russian Federation*' (Art 4(1) of the KZoT in the version of the Law of 25 September 1992; emphasis added). Indeed, it does not seem improbable that originally this norm was given this meaning in those particular circumstances where national republics were still allowed 'to take as much sovereignty as they want to'.[43] However, this political trend had come to an end by the late 1990s. Also, it should be noted that this provision of the Code treated republics as a privileged club in comparison with Russia's other constituent entities. Therefore, it is not surprising that the federal judiciary was not inclined to favour them at the expense of the federal legislator's prerogatives.

For instance, Art 37(5) of the Labour Code of Bashkiria provided for dissolution of a labour contract with an employee in connection with the refusal of a new owner of the enterprise to renew the contract with the employee irrespective of whether or not a reduction of the work force in the enterprise took place. It is quite natural that this particular norm was deemed invalid as violating para 2 of Art 29 of the KZoT. Furthermore, the Civil Division of the Supreme Court of the RF disagreed with the conclusion of the Presidium of the Supreme Court of Bashkiria that by virtue of Arts 4 and 254(2) of the KZoT additional grounds of dissolution of the labour contract with an employee could be established by acts of labour legislation of the subjects of the Federation. In coming to this conclusion, the Division set forward the following argument. The dissolution of the labour contract with an employee in connection with the refusal of a new owner to renew the contract is restricting the right of citizens to labour as consolidated by para 3 of Art 37 of the Russian Constitution, whereas by virtue of Art 55(3) of the Constitution the rights and freedoms of man and citizen may be limited only by a federal law. But the federal law in question (KZoT) does not contain such ground for dissolution of a labour contract.[44]

---

42 *BSC*, no. 10 (1999), pp. 15–16.
43 The famous phrase which is said to have been repeatedly used by Boris Yeltsin during his visits to Bashkiria and Tataria in August 1990.
44 Ruling of 12 May 1998 in the case *Sorokin v Administration of Neftekamsk* (excerpt), *BSC*, no. 10 (1998), pp. 1–2.

Thus, the Supreme Court was inclined to construe Art 254(2) of the Code in light of the federal Constitution. However, it is not the right to labour as such, but only 'the right to labour in conditions which meet the requirements of safety and hygiene' that is consolidated by Art 37(3) of the Constitution.[45] This ambiguously worded (and, perhaps, deliberately so) constitutional provision sounds very distinctive from the classical (socialist) concept of that right and cannot *per se* warrant any conclusion as to what the right to labour means and how it should be protected in Russia. Under the 1966 International Covenant on Social, Economic and Cultural Rights the right to work 'includes the right of everyone to the opportunity to gain his living by work which he freely chooses or accepts', a similar formula being used by Art 2 of the KZoT in the version of 25 September 1995. ('Each shall have the right to labour, which he freely chooses or to which he freely agrees.') This is essentially a declarative right, which is devoid of concrete substance in and of itself. The degree of its elasticity (and the freedom judges may exercise due to it) is well illustrated by the case concerning the 1989 Statute on Conditions of Combining Jobs. The Cassation Division of the Supreme Court has found the restrictions they imposed on the number of jobs one person could simultaneously hold to be in violation of the right to labour, whereas the restrictions on the duration of work (not more than half of that at the basic job) were found lawful, since this duration was not determined by the Constitution or federal laws.[46] An unreasoned refusal to recognise a person as unemployed is regarded by the Civil Division as a violation of the right to labour, which may entail the contributory compensation of moral harm.[47] Therefore, there is no way to understand it 'literally', which means that it is open to a variety of constructions.

It is hardly surprising to discover that different levels of the Supreme Court disagreed on Art 254(2) as well. For example, as early as May 2001 the Supreme Court in its capacity as a court of first instance considered the legality of an additional ground for dismissal provided for by point 18 of the 'Statute on Discipline of the Workers of Railway Transport'. It was an act of subordinate legislation confirmed by the Federal Government. The Court confirmed the legality of the contested provisions, deeming them to be not contrary to Art 254(2) of the Code. The Cassation Division of the Supreme Court (the second instance for this particular case) arrived at the same conclusion. In the end, it was the supervisory instance, the Presidium of the Court, that deemed the contested provision to be inoperative by reference to arguments once used by the Civil Division itself.[48]

---

45 *RLT*, p. 13.
46 See Ruling of 14 August 2001 on point 2(2) and (3) of the 'Regulations on Conditions of Combining Jobs', No. KAC 01-299 (unpublished).
47 See a 'Survey of Judicial Practice of the Supreme Court of the RF for the 2nd Quarter of the year 1999 (in civil cases)', *BSC*, no. 1 (2000), p. 13.
48 Decree of the Presidium of the Supreme Court of 3 July 2002, No. 256пв-01, on the petition of Seregina concerning the illegality of point 18 of the 'Statute on Discipline of the Workers of the Railway Transport of the RF' (unpublished).

It is difficult to imagine how the experienced judges of the Court, especially those sitting in the Cassation Division, could be unaware of those decisions and arguments. If, nevertheless, they chose as they did, it should be accounted for by some considerations of principle, not by negligence (*per incuriam*) or lack of training.

Perhaps all these contradictory interpretations of Art 254(2) revealed in judicial practice made the federal law-giver specify in the 2001 Labour Code that 'a labour contract may be terminated also on other grounds provided for by the present Code and other *federal laws*' (Art 77(2); emphasis added).[49] So the position of the Supreme Court Presidium eventually received legislative approval.

Some of those grounds were later challenged in the Constitutional Court. On 15 March 2005 it upheld the constitutionality of the provision of Art 278 of the Labour Code that permitted to dismiss the head of an organisation by the decision of an owner without setting out the reasons for the dismissal.[50] That provision was an important exception to the general rule according to which the sacking of an employee should be reasoned. The Court rejected the idea that this exception amounted to discrimination. Unlike its holding in Minakov's case, this time the Court found that the category of workers in question (that is, the heads of organisations) do have a specific status compared with other employees, and so the establishing of special rules for their dismissal was justified. This was a noticeable Court's move towards making its theory of discrimination. There is also another aspect to the case: the Court prescribed that the legislator had to provide for the minimal amount of compensation for top-managers dismissed in that way, for this amount should not be regulated by labour contract only (as had been stipulated by Art 279). Therefore, until the Code is amended, Art 181 should apply by way of analogy, which entitles such top-managers to three average monthly earnings in case of a pre-term dismissal in connection with a change of owner of the organisation.[51] It may be expected that more satisfactory compensation for top-managers following this decree will facilitate the relations between them and the owners, for compensation is no doubt more effective a remedy than reinstatement in job sought by the applicants.

But who is the owner? The Supreme Court decreed that even though 100 per cent of shares in a company have been sold to different persons (or person) it does not provide grounds for the dismissal of top-managers because the owner of the property remains the same, that is, the organisation itself (Decree of the Plenum of the Supreme Court of 17 March 2004, point 32). Under Russian law shareholders do not have a right to organisation's property; they only have a right

---

49 Labour Code of the Russian Federation, *Sudebnik*, Vol. VII (2002), p. 85.
50 Ibid., p. 201; Decree of the Constitutional Court of 15 March 2005, No. 3-П, on the case of verification of constitutionality of the provisions of point 2 of Art 278 and Art 279 of the Labour Code of the Russian Federation and of the second item of Art 69(4) of the Federal Law 'On Joint-Stock Societies', *HCC*, no. 3 (2005), pp. 5–19.
51 Labour Code of the Russian Federation, *Sudebnik*, Vol. VII (2002), p. 141.

to demand from the company the discharge of obligations based on the fact of their having shares in this company (paying dividends, for example). What amounts to the change of ownership, then? The Supreme Court opined that it is the cases of privatisation or nationalisation of the property of the organisation in question or the transfer of property (for instance, an enterprise) among federal and regional or local governments. This interpretation is very timid and formalistic all the way through. It hardly conforms to what legislators actually intended to enact, and makes the dismissal of top-managers by new acquirer of controlling stock more difficult. Needless to say, it will hardly improve the investment climate in Russia.

Some other controversial issues concerning dismissals

It frequently happens that an employee is dismissed by reference to lawful grounds for dissolution of the labour contract and yet the dismissal may not be considered legal, because certain preceding facts were not duly taken into account. In Art 33([3] and [4]) of the KZoT (dissolution of labour contract at the initiative of employer) the term 'justifiable reasons' as an excuse for misconduct was mentioned. Paragraph 3 specifically referred to the 'systematical' (repetitive) failure of the employee to perform the duties assigned to him by the labour contract, whereas the following paragraph addressed the absence from work as a basis for dismissal. In both cases the lack of 'justifiable reasons' for such misconduct is required for the sanction in the form of dismissal to be applied. What reasons, though, shall be regarded as 'justifiable'?

To be sure, it would be unreasonable on the part of the legislator to produce an exhaustive list of such reasons. However, the range of venial contingencies may be determined by way of judicial precedents.

In the case of joint-stock society 'Moskvich', the Civil Division of the Moscow City Court decided that if an employer fails to pay remuneration to his employee, the latter may cease working. The duty of the employer to pay remuneration for labour is consolidated by Art 77 of the KZoT, and follows also from Arts 2, 15, 37 and 96 of the Constitution. Moreover, Art 12 of the Civil Code, which may, according to Art 10(3) of the Code of Civil Procedure, be applied to labour relations by way of analogy, implies the right of an employee to defend his essential interests by his own actions.[52] Therefore, the Moscow City Court classified actions of the claimant as self-defence of a right.[53] It is illustrative that a rule to that effect was later incorporated into the 2001 Labour Code of Russia (Art 142[2]), stipulating that 'in the event of delay of

---

52 *CCRF*, pp. 5–6.
53 Ruling of the Moscow City Court in the case of joint-stock society 'Moskvich', in Комментарий судебной практики [Commentary on Judicial Practice], Vol. 5 (1999), pp. 124–125.

payment of earnings for a period of more than 15 days a worker shall have the right, having notified the employer in written form, to suspend work for the entire period until payment of the delayed amount'.[54] Besides, Art 379 makes provision for self-defence of labour rights.[55] In another case the Supreme Court has ruled that the refusal of the employee to execute an order because of its illegality is lawful, and, therefore, may not entail disciplinary sanction.[56]

In the Decree of the Plenum of the Supreme Court of 22 December 1992 judges were urged to find out whether the administration, when dismissing an employee, took into account 'the gravity of the committed offence, circumstances under which it has been committed, and also the preceding behavior of the employee [and his] attitude towards labour' (point 26[2]).[57] At first glance, this instruction to lower courts is based on the provision of Art 136(7) of the KZoT, which says that *an organ* considering a labour dispute (a Commission for Labour Disputes or a court) *has a right* to take into account the aforesaid circumstances. But there is a difference between *empowering* an arbiter to the dispute to take them into account (as the law says) and *obliging* the employer (that is, one of the parties to the labour conflict) to do so, as the Supreme Court has construed the norm.[58] The last construction seems to be more reflective of the employee's interests, as is the case with respect to many Supreme Court explanations and decrees. But it was omitted by the federal legislator when adopting the 2001 Labour Code.[59]

It is not uncommon in real life for employers to put their workers under pressure to write an application for dismissal at their own wish (as if in accordance with Art 80, Labour Code or, prior to 1 February 2002, Art 31, KZoT).[60] To that effect, the same decree of the Plenum of the Supreme Court has introduced a norm according to which 'dissolution of a contract at the initiative of the employee is permissible only in instances when the submission of the application for dismissal was his voluntary declaration of intent. If the plaintiff asserts that the administration has forced him to file an application for dismissal at his own will, it is a duty of the court to verify carefully these arguments of the plaintiff'.[61] This option was not previously open for courts by the KZoT

---

54 Labour Code of the Russian Federation, *Sudebnik*, Vol. VII (2002), p. 122.

55 Ibid., p. 257.

56 Decree of 11 September 1996 in the case *Lazhe v Bykov Aviation Enterprise* (excerpt), *BSC*, no. 2 (1997), p. 4.

57 Decree of the Plenum of the Supreme Court of 22 December 1992, No. 16, 'On Certain Questions of Application by Courts of the Russian Federation of Legislation When Settling Labour Disputes', *BSC*, no. 3 (1993), p. 6.

58 In concrete decisions the Supreme Court strongly insists on these circumstances being taken into account not just formally (see the Decree of the Presidium of the Supreme Court of 15 November 2000, No. 86пв 2000, in the case of Deviatkina (unpublished; see 'Consultant Plus' database)).

59 Article 193, Labour Code of the Russian Federation, *Sudebnik*, Vol. VII (2002), p. 146.

60 Labour Code of the Russian Federation, *Sudebnik*, Vol. VII (2002), p. 86.

61 Point 15(1) of the Decree, *BSC*, no. 3 (1993), p. 3.

or other acts. Here, as in some other cases, the Supreme Court has developed legislative norms and shown an obvious desire to embrace not only the formal, but also the factual side of a particular case. In any event, this supplementary norm envisaging what is sometimes called 'constructive dismissal' neither contradicts nor directly follows from legislation and thus should be viewed as an example of creative interpretation.

Still more examples of this kind are found in judicial acts relating to the procedure for the application of disciplinary sanctions, including dismissal, at the employer's initiative. Under Arts 136 and 193 of the KZoT and the 2001 Labour Code, respectively, such punishment shall be applied not later than one month from the day of discovery of the disciplinary offence, and not later than six months from the day of its commission.[62] The laws are silent as to what counts as the moment of eliciting the offence and, consequently, the beginning of the one-month term. Therefore, the Plenum decreed that it should be the day when the person to whom the worker is subordinated by way of service came to know about the offence regardless of whether or not he has the right to impose disciplinary sanctions.[63] It should be observed that the decree does not explain what to do in the situation when the aforesaid person is absent for a long time (say, because of being ill or on leave). In practice, this may significantly extend the term provided for by the law and thus undermine the employee's position. The legality of this supplementary judge-made provision has been once challenged in the Supreme Court itself, but the Cassation Division refused to assume jurisdiction.[64]

One peculiarity of the dismissal procedure in Russia is that prior to the application of a disciplinary sanction the employer is expected to request from the employee an explanation in writing. Therefore, in the event of a worker's absence over a long period of time for an unknown reason the managers of the employer must wait until they receive such an explanation and be able to ascertain whether there were any justifiable reasons for the absence or not. Otherwise, the dismissal is illegal. Notionally, this waiting may last indefinitely and may well exceed the terms for imposition of disciplinary sanctions contained in the Code. To overcome this difficulty, the courts found a way around by introducing the concept of 'lasting' or 'prolonged' shirking, unprovided for by any normative acts of general application. They assumed that in such cases the day of eliciting the violation is not the first, but the last day of illegal absence from work. This is a kind of judicial custom which was developed by lower courts independently of the legislator or the Supreme Court and was later supported by some legal commentators.[65] In practice, it failed to prevent some uncertainties

---

62 Ibid., p. 142.
63 Point 26(3), Decree of the Plenum of the Supreme Court of 22 December 1992, *BSC*, no. 3 (1993), p. 6.
64 Ruling of 25 May 2000, No. KAC00-202, in the case of Mironov (see Chapter 3 above, p. 108).
65 Iu. P. Orlovskii (ed.), Комментарий к Трудовому Кодексу РФ [Commentary on the Labour Code of the Russian Federation] (2002), p. 428.

and manipulations which may take place as soon as the employer is not under an obligation to take, within a reasonable period, formal steps to discover the reasons for an absence. If, for instance, the worker fails to appear in person, the employer is free to request an explanation by mail whenever he wants and impose sanctions thereafter. In issuing the order of dismissal, he may disregard the requirement of Art 193 of the Labour Code, for the worker's absence is deemed to be 'prolonged'. What counts as the day of its discovery and the starting point for the one-month period in this case? Not the day of actual discovery, but the day when the employer decides, at his discretion, to terminate the time of presumed shirking by issuance of the said order. This may serve as an opportunity for abuses, because the employer could refrain from any measures in order to postpone the moment when the labour dispute arises, or to aggravate the worker's violation in the eyes of the court. This problem was highlighted by a case reported in the Decree of the Plenum of the USSR Supreme Court of 13 November 1984, in which the Court recognised the dismissal of the plaintiff as unlawful because the one-month period was elapsed by the management of the employer. The Plenum rejected the argument of the defendant that the day of discovery is the day when the explanation was requested from the worker, not the day of actual eliciting of her absence from work place. The Court simply pointed out that one-month period had enabled the employer to find out the reasons for absence and dissolve the labour contract with the employee.[66] The routine practice of courts took, though, a different path.

Legal consequences of deeming the dismissal unlawful

Under Russian labour law, the principal consequence of deeming a dismissal to be illegal is reinstatement of the employee in his former job. However, it may happen only in the event that his desire is such. If the dismissal was illegal, but the employee does not want to be reinstated, the court should oblige the employer to change the discrediting formula of dismissal in his labour book to dismissal at the worker's own will and to award a compensation of average earnings during the enforced down-time.

The role of courts in elaborating this area of labour law is remarkable. Originally, the legislation on this question was rather inconsistent. For instance, Art 211(4) of the KZoT enacted in February 1988 provided for a one-year term, whereas Art 90(4) of Fundamental Principles of Legislation of the USSR and Union Republics on Labour (in the version of 12 May 1991) for a two-year term, after the expiry of which appeals of citizens to reverse by way of judicial supervision either the judicial decrees which had entered into force or the

---

66 Decree of the Plenum of the USSR Supreme Court of 13 November 1984 in the case of Sh., *Бюллетень Верховного Суда СССР* [Bulletin of the Supreme Court of the USSR], no. 1 (1985), pp. 32–33.

decisions of the superior agencies refusing to reinstate them in work could not be accepted.

In a decree of 23 June 1992 the Constitutional Court held that Russian civil procedure legislation did not establish the terms during which citizens have the right to appeal against court decisions on all categories of civil cases including labour disputes, which had entered into force (Art 1(1), 1964 RSFSR Code of Civil Procedure). Therefore, the presence of such prohibitory periods of limitations in labour legislation not only ignored the possibility of judicial errors but, in fact, also deprived the courts of the right to correct them. By this deviation from the norms of civil procedure the opportunities of workers and employees to protect their labour rights by way of supervisory judicial procedure were diminished.[67]

Hence, in view of the conflict between norms of the RSFSR Civil Procedure Code and those of the KZoT, it was the provisions of the former that were subject to application in such cases, as being more consistent with the Constitution. In order to prove its conclusion that the 'custom of law-application practice' devised on the basis of the challenged provisions (including a Decree of the USSR Supreme Court) was unconstitutional, the Court invoked an array of constitutional clauses and principles, however abstract and remotely related to the case in hand: Arts 14 (just conditions of hiring and firing), 31 (rights and freedoms of man are a supreme value), 34 (equality before law), 53 (right to labour), 61 (right of each to defend his rights, freedoms and lawful interests by all means which are not contrary to a law).

It clearly follows from this decree that the contested provisions should not be considered as *lex specialis* with respect to the Civil Procedure Code, despite the Fundamental Principles being a higher legal act than the Code and, in addition, a *lex posterior*, for Art 90 of the Principles was amended later. The Constitutional Court also noted that the Plenum of USSR Supreme Court had exceeded the limits of its power when extending the rules concerning the term of appeal to relations which had arisen prior to 4 February 1988. By this the USSR Supreme Court had, in effect, changed the law and made these provisions retroactive, despite the right to give an official interpretation of a law being an exclusive prerogative of the legislature (Art 109, para 1(8) of the 1977 Constitution).

However, the Court did not consider in detail the relations between barring terms and limitations. It could be suggested that in the legislator's design the terms for defence of a right by way of supervision were basically playing the same part as normally the periods of limitation (whose constitutionality has never been challenged) normally do, that is, to ensure the stability of legal relations in the area of employment and strike a certain balance between contradictory interests and rights. For it is possible that an employee previously dismissed could be reinstated by a court in his former job many years after

---

67 Decree of 23 June 1992, No. 8-П, concerning the law-application practice of reinstatement in job, *HCC*, no. 2/3 (1993), pp. 45–46.

his dismissal, which might seriously affect the interests of the employer's business and his new workers.

As a matter of fact, the real problem with Russian labour legislation is that it is still obsolete, despite the significant changes since 1992. Unlike the labour legislation of most European countries,[68] it does not allow monetary compensation for unfair dismissal. The right of the worker to such compensation is provided by neither the 1971 Code nor its successor. At the same time, it is beyond the reach of the judiciary to introduce a new type of sanction for illegal dismissal. This is definitely a task for legislators, not judges. As we shall see, only contributory compensation for moral harm in the event of unfair dismissal has been provided for by the post-Soviet legislators. But it is of little help because such compensation is usually tiny and its role is that of merely a subsidiary sanction attached to the major ones, that is, reinstatement in the former job and payment of average earnings for the entire period of absence. By now there was no sign that the courts were inclined to increase the amount of contributory compensation if the plaintiff did not want to be reinstated. And correctly so, because it is hard to perceive how the moral harm could be aggravated by such unwillingness. In any event, the 1992 Constitutional Court decree was not, all in all, as favourable to the needs of business and a market economy as its subsequent decrees and rulings. In particular, it failed to draw the attention of legislative bodies to possible ways of changing the obsolete legislation. But, to make the picture complete, it should be observed that it was issued in summer 1992 when the economic conditions of the population were extremely harsh and inflation was rapid.

By this decision the Constitutional Court also changed the routine practice of considering appeals of citizens. Quite frequently in the past, when considering such petitions, officials having the right to bring protests against judicial decisions used to respond to applicants by a mere reference to the absence of any grounds for bringing them. Moreover, the appeals were not considered by the collegiate composition of the court, and no procedural decision was delivered thereon. In the view of the Constitutional Court, such practice was impermissible, so long as labour legislation did not contain exemptions from the principle of collegiality for the judicial consideration of labour disputes relating to reinstatement in job.[69]

Another rule deemed by the Constitutional Court to be not corresponding to the Constitution concerned the limitation of the period for which average earnings for enforced down-time should be paid in the event of illegal dismissal.[70] This limitation had a long history. It was established for the first time in 1938, when 20-day period regardless of the actual duration of enforced down-time was

---

68   I. Ia. Kiselev, Сравнительное и международное трудовое право [Comparative and International Labour Law] (1999), p. 163.

69   Decree of 23 June 1992, No. 4-П, *HCC*, no. 2/3 (1993), p. 47.

70   Decree of 27 January 1993, No. 1-П, *HCC*, no. 2/3 (1993), pp. 53–64.

provided for by legislation. Subsequently, the period of enforced down-time subject to payment was increased up to 3 months by the Fundamental Principles of the Legislation on Labour of 15 July 1970 and then up to 1 year by virtue of USSR Laws of 11 March and 12 May 1991. A one-year period of payment was also provided for by Arts 213 and 216 of the KZoT (in the version of 25 September 1992). The Constitutional Court pointed out that these legal prescriptions were not subject to application, because the full compensation of damage caused to a person by unlawful actions of agencies of State power and their officials is one of the rights of man and citizen.[71]

It usually takes an unduly long time for unfairly dismissed employees to enforce their rights in Russian courts because of the courts' failure to meet procedural deadlines. As a result, the employer has frequently to overpay for an extended period of enforced down-time if the court finds for the worker. For instance, among persons who appealed to the Constitutional Court in the present case there was one S. Mazanov, whose actual duration of absence from work exceeded 12 years! Therefore, the question arose whether the employer should compensate for the entire period of enforced down-time, which had been extended without his fault, and also whether, in view of the rapid inflation, the amount paid should be increased proportionately.

In the decree of the Constitutional Court, 'the employer as the party violated groundlessly the conditions of the labour contract by depriving the employee of the possibility of performing labour function and receiving remuneration for work, should compensate the employee reinstated in work the damage caused by an unfair dismissal in full, *but within the limits of the established terms of resolution of these cases by the agencies for consideration of labour disputes*' [emphasis added].[72] But in practice, the decree goes, 'the full compensation of damage is not ensured even in those cases when courts make a decision on the indexation of average earnings for payment during a long-term enforced down-time and impose the appropriate responsibility upon the employer instead of the State. Due to the fact that this duty does not flow from a contractual responsibility and is an obligation to compensate that part of the damage which the employer did not cause, he frequently refuses to perform it. The law-application practice filling the gaps in labour legislation in such a way violates the principles of justness and legal equality and therefore cannot be considered constitutional'.[73]

How should the amount of compensation be determined? The legislator and the Court disagreed on this issue. In the Constitutional Court's opinion, such compensation could be regarded as lost earnings for work which might be performed by the employee but, owing to his unlawful dismissal through the employer's fault, has not been done by him.[74] In addition, the constitutional

---

71 *HCC*, no. 2/3 (1993), p. 60.
72 Ibid., p. 61.
73 Ibid., p. 62.
74 Ibid., p. 61.

tribunal obligated the legislature of the day, the Supreme Soviet of Russia, to determine the procedure for such compensation.[75] But the legislator has provided only for *average* earnings for the period of enforced down-time (Art 213 of the KZoT in the version of 17 March 1997). The Supreme Court also was of the opinion that these earnings should be calculated on the basis of the last two calendar months of work.[76] This attitude entitles workers for a lesser amount of payments compared with the 'civil law based' approach of the Constitutional Court, because it does not allow for the possibility that the regular salary for the position from which an employee was illegally dismissed might have significantly increased during the period of the enforced down-time.

The Constitutional Court apparently distinguished three parts of the damage incurred, the first arising out of the dismissal itself, the second being the result of inflation, and the third one caused by a delayed judicial consideration. The employer was deemed liable only for the first. However, when the problem of an increase in the amount of compensation caused by delayed consideration of a labour dispute came to the attention of regular courts, they offered a different solution. In one case of this kind the Civil Division imposed the duty to pay the whole amount upon the employer on the ground that it was because of his wrongdoing that the unlawful dismissal had taken place.[77] When discussing this judgment, A. I. Stavtseva noted that it seems expedient to give an answer to the question whether the State should compensate a part of expenses for payment for enforced down-time, if it was because of the court's failure to resolve a particular labour dispute on time the period of enforced down-time had been extended.[78]

At the end of the day, not all the applicants to the Constitutional Court of 1993 found a satisfactory response from the ordinary courts, so that two of them, Mazanov and Shulzhenko, had to seek a remedy in the constitutional tribunal once again. In the confirming ruling of 15 June 1995 the Court lamented that 'the practice recognised as unconstitutional has not changed'.[79] As formerly, the courts when settling labour disputes continued to be guided by inapplicable rules of Art 213(2), and not by norms of the Civil Code and Arts 46 and 53 of the 1993 Constitution. The rights of employers also suffered from such

---

75 *HCC*, no. 2/3 (1993), p. 64.
76 Point 50, Decree of the Plenum of the Supreme Court of 22 December 1992, *BSC*, no. 3 (1993), p. 11.
77 Ruling No. 48 Г93–1, in Комментарий судебной практики [Commentary on Judicial Practice], no. 2 (1995), p. 17.
78 Ibid., p. 18.
79 Ruling of 15 June 1995, No. 29-O, concerning Art 213(2) of the KZoT of the Russian Federation in connection with petitions of citizens G. I. Shulzhenko and S. A. Mazanov, *HCC*, no. 2/3 (1995), p. 68. It was partially accounted for by defects of the 1991 law on the Constitutional Court, which did not provide for direct effect of its judgments.

law-application practice, for they were not guaranteed against liability for damage incurred without their fault as a result of continuous non-restoration of rights of the unlawfully dismissed. The Constitutional Court held that, although under 1994 statute it is no longer capable of reviewing the constitutionality of law-application practice, it might take account of the tendencies of law-application, following its Art 74(2). Therefore, the evaluation of the constitutionality of Art 213(2) of the KZoT, given by the Decree of 27 January 1993, remains in force.

In one respect the Court seems to abandon its previous position by cautiously saying that the precise amount of compensation is not a constitutional question,[80] and inviting the legislature itself to determine it and thereby fill the gap.[81] The legislative response came as an amendment to Art 213(2) of the KZoT by a law of 17 March 1997. According to the new wording of the clause, an illegally dismissed worker is entitled to the sum of his *average* earnings during the entire period of enforced down-time.[82] This formula was later incorporated in the new Labour Code (Art 394[2]).[83] It follows that the only payer of the whole amount is still the employer, not the State. The legislature seems to adhere to the position of the Supreme Court, with all its deficiencies, but not that of the Constitutional Court, which admitted that the employer should not be liable for the entire amount of average earnings in cases of the delayed judicial consideration. At the same time, the problem of indexation, which can be the chief concern of workers in such cases, remained unresolved.

Again, it is easy to see that the real problem is the backwardness of Russian labour law, which does not allow compensation for unfair dismissal as such. Therefore, it is difficult for an employer to calculate the 'price' of employee's probable dismissal if it were deemed illegal by a court. This uncertainty prevents employers from running any risk even in those cases in which there seems to be sufficient ground for dismissal. In such circumstances, even strict compliance with procedural terms by courts also would not help much, for the time difference between judicial consideration in different instances is significant, thus increasing the amount of compensation. If an employee was reinstated in work by the supervisory court instance, one can argue that it is because of the mistakes of lower courts that the employer should pay additional compensation. Paradoxically, if it were the trial court or cassational court that had ruled against

---

80 Ibid., p. 69.
81 See, however, the dissent of Judge Kononov (Ibid., pp. 71–72). He believed the Court failed to justify its retreat.
82 Shulzhenko case was reconsidered on 9 October 1997 (*HCC*, no. 1 (1998), pp. 53–54) by the Supreme Court Civil Division on the grounds of the new law, not the 1992 Decree. The plaintiff was awarded a full compensation for previous years. In fact, the Division gave the legislative amendment a retroactive affect. The ruling of the Division was unsuccessfully challenged by the Deputy Chairman of the Supreme Court (Decree of the Supreme Court Presidium of 17 June 1998, No. 32пв98, unpublished; see 'Consultant Plus' database).
83 Labour Code of the Russian Federation, *Sudebnik*, Vol. VII (2002), p. 264.

the employer, he could save money. The situation could be quite different if a legislatively determined sum of compensation for dismissal, completely detached from the question of time, were at stake. So long as it is not introduced, there is little incentive for Russian employers to prefer formal labour relations to the 'shadow market' of labour force. The unregulated area will continue to grow, and no court is able to help.

Although the consequences of deeming dismissal to be illegal are generally regulated in considerable detail by legislation and decisions of the highest courts, there are some points calling for further elaboration, such as the procedure for implementation of the court decision. It is not quite clear what 'immediate execution' of the decision on reinstatement in work is supposed to mean (Art 396, Labour Code and Art 345, Civil Procedure Code). Is it a right or a duty of the worker to come back to his former workplace without any delay? What would be the consequences if he were slow to do so?

Current legislation on this issue is drawn in such a way that one could think that all the decisions on reinstatement in job must be enforced through formal channels (that is, through judicial bailiff-executors). In practice, however, things are different. Employers can and usually do issue an order of reinstatement even without seeing the writ of execution. But the employer is not obliged to notify the employee about it. If, for whatever reason, the latter is slow to present the writ or to ask the court to suspend the execution of its decision, it may count as shirking and create the grounds for new dismissal. At the same time, the judicial acts subject to immediate execution are enumerated in Art 211 of the present Civil Procedure Code (corresponding to Art 211 of the preceding code). There one can find decisions on the recovery of alimony and award of payments for labour, which in no case can be viewed as obliging the recoveror to start executive proceedings immediately. Also, when speaking about immediate execution, the Federal Law 'On an Execution Proceeding' (Arts 13, 14, 73, 74) addresses the judicial bailiff-executor, not the worker. Article 14 of the Law provides that documents of execution issued on the basis of judicial acts of courts of general jurisdiction can be presented for execution within three years (para 1[1]). In the event of immediate execution, this term starts on the day following the rendering of the decision (para 2[1]).[84] The suggestion that an unfairly dismissed worker can return to his workplace at any moment during three years may sound strange, but it does flow from the letter of the law.[85] That is why court practice proceeds on the assumption that the worker is *obliged* to execute the judicial act as soon as possible. Therefore, if any dispute arises, delay on the part of the worker is normally considered as his reluctance to actually take up the job. To be sure, this inference can be easily justified by

84 See *RLT*, p. 260.
85 Cf. V. V. Iarkov (ed.), Гражданское судопроизводство. Особенности рассмотрения отдельных категорий дел [Civil Proceeding. Peculiarities of Consideration of Individual Categories of Cases] (2001), p. 246.

common sense and practical convenience. Nevertheless, it means that certain aspects of execution proceedings are effectively regulated by court customs and informal practices, rather than by laws.[86]

Unlawful dismissal and moral harm

Contributory compensation for 'moral harm' is one probable consequence of deeming a dismissal unlawful. For the first time such compensation in monetary form was envisaged for by the USSR Law of 12 June 1990 'On the Press and Other Mass Media'. Soon thereafter the question was raised concerning the admissibility of such contributory compensation in other areas also. Article 131 of the Fundamental Principles of Civil Legislation of the USSR and Republics of 31 May 1991 provided for liability for moral harm caused to a citizen by unlawful actions even in those cases when a law contains no special indication as to the possibility of contributory compensation thereof.

However, it had little effect on the practice of the courts of general jurisdiction, which seemed reluctant to apply this norm to labour relations. Moreover, before 17 March 1997 the KZoT did not contain norms relating to this kind of compensation. But, according to Art 1(3) of the Fundamental Principles, norms of civil legislation could be applied to labour relations if the latter were not regulated by labour legislation. The Fundamental Principles were no longer applicable after 1 January 1995, when Part 1 of the 1994 Civil Code became effective. This part of the Code contains Art 151(1), which provides for monetary contributory compensation of moral harm caused to a citizen 'by actions violating his personal nonproperty rights or infringing upon other nonmaterial benefits belonging to a citizen, and also in other instances provided for by a law'. Labour rights were not explicitly mentioned on the list of non-material benefits (Art 150, the Code) but the list was not exhaustive, ending with the formula 'other personal nonproperty rights and other nonmaterial benefits'.[87] So, the question was basically whether it is permissible for courts to extend the civil law rules so as to transplant this civil law institution to labour law. In other words, it remained to judges to decide whether the gap in labour legislation could be filled by way of analogy or, on the contrary, the absence of specific provisions to that effect in the KZoT coupled with the lack of legislative attempts to make them should be taken as a proof of the impermissibility of contributory compensation of moral harm.

Apparently, the Supreme Court believed that labour law did contain a gap and, if so, it was up to the Court to provide a remedy. Inasmuch as there were no provisions on contributory compensation of moral harm in Russian labour

---

86 It was the USSR Supreme Court that addressed for the last time the execution of decisions on the reinstatement in job in a 1968 Decree, No. 5 (*Бюллетень Верховного Суда СССР* [Bulletin of the USSR Supreme Court], no. 3 (1968), p. 18), but these issues were not touched upon.
87 *CCRF*, p. 69.

legislation, the courts when deciding labour disputes should be guided by analogous norms of the Civil Code. Given that the federal legislator has subsequently legalised the judicial position on the question of moral harm, it could be argued that a gap in the law did exist. But we shall see that, although following in the wake of the judiciary, the legislator has approved only part of that which the Supreme Court had already done, and thus cast doubt on the legitimacy of the rest.

The cornerstone of the moral harm issue is the Decree of the Plenum of the Supreme Court of 20 December 1994.[88] It starts with an acknowledgement that 'the variety of legislative acts regulating the relations connected to the causing of moral harm, the various terms of their entry into force, and also the adoption of the Part 1 of the Civil Code of the Russian Federation whose entry into force will commence from 1 January 1995, give rise to questions requiring solution'.[89] With the aim of streamlining this variety of norms, the Plenum has given a number of clarifications. These basically come down to the following:

First, the Plenum has offered a definition of moral harm. The courts were invited to understand it as moral or physical sufferings caused by actions (or failure to act), impinging upon non-material benefits (life, health, dignity of a person, business reputation, inviolability of private life, personal and family secrecy, etc) belonging to a citizen from birth or by virtue of a law, or violating his personal non-property rights (the right to use his name, author's right and other such rights provided by laws), or infringing upon property rights of a citizen.[90] The Supreme Court has decreed that moral harm may consist, by way of example, of moral sufferings connected with the loss of relatives, impossibility of continuing an active public life, *loss of work*, divulgence of family or medical secrecy, dissemination of information not corresponding to truth and defaming good name, dignity, or business reputation of a citizen, temporary restriction or deprivation of any rights, physical pain connected with mutilation or other damage caused to health, and the like.

Second, the courts were instructed to find out how the fact of causing of moral or physical sufferings to the plaintiff could be confirmed, under which circumstances and by which actions (or failure to act) they were caused, the degree of the causer's guilt, which moral or physical sufferings were endured by the victim, in which sum or other material form he estimates the contributory compensation, and other circumstances essential for resolution of the concrete dispute.[91]

---

88 Decree of the Plenum of the Supreme Court of the Russian Federation of 20 December 1994, No. 10, 'Some Questions of Application of Legislation on Contributory Compensation of Moral Harm', *BSC*, no. 3 (1995), pp. 9–11.

89 Ibid., p. 9.

90 Ibid.

91 Ibid.

With regard to guiding *criteria* for determining the degree of moral harm, the Plenum has conferred upon judges a virtually unrestricted freedom of discretion: 'The degree of moral or physical sufferings is assessed by the court in view of the actual facts of causing moral harm, specific features of the victim and other concrete circumstances proving the extent of sufferings endured by him'.[92] This explanation adds little to what has been already said in Art 151 of the Civil Code. Given the obvious difficulty of producing formal criteria in such questions, it is expected that published precedents of the Supreme Court might ensure uniformity of judicial practice. However, the number of such precedents is not yet sufficient to narrow the limits of discretion exercised by lower courts.

Point 4 of the Decree provided an incomplete list of grounds for contributory compensation in the area of employment, such as 'an unlawful dismissal, transfer to another job, ungrounded application of disciplinary punishment, refusal to transfer to another job according to medical recommendations, and the like'.[93] The Supreme Court addressed in considerable detail the question why, in the light of existing norms, such extension of the rule about contributory compensation of moral harm could be justified. Article 131 of the Fundamental Principles of Civil Legislation had established responsibility for moral harm caused to a citizen by wrongful acts even if no law contained special provisions to that effect. According to Art 1(3) of the Fundamental Principles, it was permissible to apply Art 131 to labour relations, since the relations connected to contributory compensation of moral harm are not regulated by labour legislation.[94]

Is it correct to take the provisions of this decree (or at least some of them) as examples of judicial law-making? In other words, could there be any doubt that the civil law obligation of compensation of moral harm under Art 151 of the Civil Code could be applied to labour relations? When contending that the question was not regulated by Russian labour legislation, the Supreme Court, at the same time, instructed judges to find out 'whether legislation admits the possibility of contributory compensation of moral harm with regard to the given kind of legal relations' and provides for its conditions and the relevant procedure.[95]

This paragraph hardly relates to Art 151 of the Civil Code, which does not explicitly cover the area of labour law and, moreover, provides nearly nothing with regard to conditions and the procedure for such compensation. Strictly speaking, judges might conclude that they have nothing to do but refuse to award contributory compensation for moral harm arising out of labour disputes. They *might*, but, as was seen, in other paragraphs the Supreme Court has unequivocally extended the

---

92 Ibid., p. 10.
93 Ibid. It is interesting that the Supreme Court does not allow for compensation of moral harm caused by an unlawfully applied administrative arrest, although it may well be considered as a 'temporary restriction or deprivation of some rights' (*BSC*, no. 6 (1995), pp. 2–3).
94 Ibid., pp. 9–10.
95 Ibid., p. 9.

rules about contributory compensation of moral harm to the area of labour law. It is fair to suggest that the Court thought the right to labour to be one of these benefits. Quite apart from the uncertainty of this right (which, besides, is not explicitly mentioned among non-material benefits under Art 150 of the Civil Code), it is difficult to perceive how, for instance, a disciplinary punishment could violate this right. By taking such a position, the Court has certainly made its own contribution to Russian labour law.

After some delay, the legislator followed the lead of the judiciary by adding to Art 213 of the KZoT a new provision (para 5) which reads that 'in the event of dismissal without lawful grounds or with a violation of the established procedure for dismissal or unlawful transfer to another work a court has the right, upon the demand of the employee, to render a decision to award an employee monetary contributory compensation for moral harm caused to him by the actions indicated' (introduced by Federal Law of 17 March 1997). But here the list of grounds is somewhat shorter that in point 4 of the Decree. At once the question arose of whether the contributory compensation in such cases as, for instance, an unlawful disciplinary punishment was permissible any longer or not. Ivanov thinks that contributory compensation is permissible, since one should proceed from the 'social approach' under which the employee should be given benefit of any doubt arising from interpretation.[96] However, it appears to me that the question here is not so much how a legal rule ought to be interpreted but, rather, whether it exists at all. Stavtseva believes the question of contributory compensation in such cases to be open and suggests that it is up to the Supreme Court Plenum to make things clear.[97] The Supreme Court contemplated for seven long years and eventually decreed that compensation applies in all cases of harm caused to the employee by the employer's wrongdoing.[98]

The difficulties the Supreme Court would have to face here are quite understandable. Mostly they have a bearing upon some fundamental but touchy points in the imperfect relations between the courts and the federal legislator. For courts, to mask their norm-creative activity by analogy from one branch of law to another is a habitual thing, but to develop the law in an open manner, whatever justifications could be given (say, forgetfulness of the legislator), is too ambitious a task. Suppose it is expressly acknowledged that an unlawful disciplinary punishment no longer entails contributory compensation of moral harm. This would be to say that its existence in the past took place due to judicial law-making (no matter whether deliberate or not), which, however, subsequently failed to meet the legislative test. Certainly, it can be asserted that analogy based on Art 151 of the Civil Code is still working and, in principle, guarantees

96 See his article in Судебная практика как источник права [Judicial Practice as a Source of Law] (2000), p. 119.
97 A. I. Stavtseva in Комментарий судебной практики [Commentary on Judicial Practice], Vol. 5 (1999), p. 142.
98 Point 63, Decree of the Plenum of Supreme Court of 17 March 2004, No. 6, *BSC*, no. 6 (2004), p. 18.

contributory compensation of moral harm in all cases of infringement upon the rights of an employee by his employer's fault. But it would not be quite respectful with regard to the legislator: one may wonder why the new provision was added to Art 213 of the KZoT and then repeated almost verbatim in the new code. His reluctance to expand the list may be regarded as a conscious limitation of compensation to those cases that only involved an unlawful dismissal or transfer to other work.

Perhaps the legislator's attitude may be accounted for by the fact that most disciplinary punishments, in contrast to unlawful dismissal and transfer to other work, are not subject to immediate consideration in courts. For them a preliminary extrajudicial procedure by way of the commissions for labour disputes or the State labour inspectorate has been established (Art 210, KZoT; Arts 193, 390, 391, the 2001 Labour Code). But these agencies cannot award contributory compensation for moral harm. If every unlawful disciplinary punishment would entail such compensation, this might result in frequent appeals to courts as the only agency capable of awarding it.

It should be noted that the 2001 Labour Code has obviously attempted to clarify this matter. There is a new clause (Art 237) which reads that 'moral harm caused to a worker by unlawful actions or failure to act of an employer shall be compensated to a worker in monetary form in amounts to be determined by agreement of the parties to the labour contract. In the event of the arising of a dispute the fact of causing moral harm to a worker and the amount of compensation thereof shall be determined by a court irrespective of the property damage subject to compensation'.[99] Given that this article is placed in Chapter 38, which is entirely devoted to the material responsibility of the employer with respect to the employee, one can argue that it relates to those violations only that impinge upon property interests of the employee, thus leaving aside non-property interests, and does not apply to disciplinary punishments other than dismissal, as they do not entail material damage (Art 234, Labour Code). Or, at least, it does not warrant the award of the contributory compensation for all kinds of wrongdoing.

Another controversial point of law is whether deeming the dismissal to be unlawful should necessarily entail the contributory compensation of moral harm or whether it is the discretion of the court to award it. In point 4 of the Supreme Court Decree of 20 December 1994 it is said that 'the court *has the right* to oblige the employer to compensate moral, physical sufferings caused to the employee'.[100] Article 213(5) of the KZoT (as amended in 1997) also provided that the court 'has the right *upon the demand of the employee*' to adopt such a decision. But does it have the right not to do so and confine itself to deeming the dismissal unlawful and obliging the employer to pay off the average earnings for the period of enforced down-time? Are the words 'has a right' (*vprave*) supposed

99 Labour Code of the Russian Federation, *Sudebnik*, Vol. 7 (2002), p. 184.
100 *BSC*, no. 6 (1995), p. 2.

to refer to the freedom of discretion of the judge in such matters, or should they be better understood as a right granted to them by law and simultaneously a duty of the judge to apply this sanction, if the dismissal is recognised as unlawful? The first interpretation seems more persuasive if the literal meaning of these provisions is followed. Therefore, the inferior courts often refused to award compensation when deeming dismissals unlawful.

However, it may be asked whether an unlawful dismissal without causing moral suffering is possible? Legal doctrine and the judges split sharply on this matter. It is not rare to find contradictory opinions within the same circle of scholars or practitioners. For instance, one unofficial survey of judicial practice suggests that from the contents of Art 213 of the KZoT 'the conclusion follows that the very fact of unlawful dismissal causes moral harm to the employee'. With reference to this presumption of moral harm the Presidium of the Irkutsk Regional Court reversed the decision of a lower court in 1999.[101] All the same, in another review published on the same website, one can find a completely different analysis. It is said that the courts in fact rely on the presumption of causation of moral harm by unlawful actions (and not only in labour disputes), which is not permissible.[102]

More surprisingly, not only modern scholarship but also the Supreme Court Civil Division failed to be consistent with regard to the moral harm issue in labour disputes. On the one hand, among its recent decisions there is one which may play the part of a leading case on the issue.[103] An employee dismissed from a law-enforcement agency on the ground of 'a flagrant violation of discipline' succeeded in suing the employer in the Moscow City Court. The discrediting formulation of his dismissal was changed for dismissal 'at his own will', and he was awarded the amount of his average earnings for the respective period plus legal costs and contributory compensation of moral harm. The Civil Division of the Supreme Court left the decision in force with an indication that 'when satisfying such a claim the court has also no ground for refusal ... with regard to the contributory compensation of moral harm'. In the opinion of the Civil Division, 'the unlawful dismissal entails causation of moral suffering to the employee. The degree of physical or moral sufferings may form a basis for determining by the court of the amount of the monetary contributory compensation of moral harm'.[104] Thus, according to this *ratio decidendi* of the Civil Division, the judge could exercise discretion only with respect to the amount of compensation, but not with respect to the question whether the plaintiff should be awarded it or not, provided that dismissal itself was recognised as unlawful.

---

101 The survey was issued by the Legal Institute of Irkutsk State University. See at [http://clinic.lawinstitut.ru/studies/sudpraktik/obzor6.html].

102 See at [http://clinic.lawinstitut.ru/studies/sudpraktik/obzor28.html].

103 Ruling in the case of Perov, published in 'Some Questions of Judicial Practice in Civil Cases', *BSC*, no. 10 (1999), p. 17.

104 It is not clear whether the principle of obligatory contributory compensation in view of the court should cover cases in which dismissal was held unlawful only due to procedural violations on the part of employer.

Hence one could infer that causation of moral harm does not constitute, in the view of the Civil Division, a separate subject of proof in such cases.[105] But there is a contradictory ruling of the Division of the same year. An unlawfully sacked employee instituted an action seeking for moral harm. Her action was dismissed by the Civil Division on the ground that procedural terms had been lapsed. Its reasoning was supplemented with a pronouncement that it is the right, not a duty, of the court to adopt a decision concerning contributory compensation of moral harm. This, however, was only *obiter* which did not affect the outcome of the case.[106]

That was not yet the end of the story, for a fresh ruling of Civil Division has confirmed that 'in the event of a violation of nonmaterial benefits by illegal actions of State agencies the causation of moral harm is presumed and only the amount of monetary compensation is subject to proof'.[107] Although it is this position that seems to have taken the upper hand, the controversy about the alleged inevitability of moral harm demonstrates that working out of a consistent line of precedents is not necessarily an easy task for Russian senior judges. The surveys of judicial decisions of lower courts in Russia suggest that usually they do oblige the employer to compensate moral harm caused by illegal dismissal. However, the amounts of such compensations are tiny in nearly all cases, and it is not rare to come across a decision to award 300 roubles ($10) or so.

To sum up, two questions should be answered. First, what kind of judicial policy is revealed in decisions of the highest courts on labour law matters, if any? Second, to what extent do lower courts respect the decisions of the Supreme Court?

As for the first question, it appears to me that the Constitutional Court since 1995 has shown a trend more favourable to the needs of a market economy whereas many Supreme Court rulings did not. The latter court was, by and large, too timid and reluctant to refuse enforcement to obsolete rules even though it was possible to do so. This is in line with the observation that in all doubtful cases the Supreme Court tends to assume that it is the employee, not the employer, who is on the right side of the law.[108] But this observation catches only

---

105 According to Art 50 of the Civil Procedure Code, 'each party must prove those circumstances to which it refers as a substantiation of its demands and objections'. But it does not mean that moral harm should be proved separately in every case. In many cases mental sufferings are not demonstrable, although it is fair to suggest that the victim should endure them. Some lawyers argue that the concept of moral harm may apply also to juridical persons (see pp. 149–151 above). In such cases, what kind of evidence is expected to prove that the victim had experienced a disease or a state of exacerbation?

106 Ruling of 29 October 1999, No. 49-B99ПР-17, in the case of Riahina. This decision was not published in the 'Bulletin'.

107 Ruling of 28 November 2000, No. 5-B00-227, in the case *R. and A. v Moscow Government and Department of Finance* [Excerpt], *BSC*, no. 3 (2003), pp. 6–7.

108 B. R. Karabel'nikov, Трудовые отношения в акционерных обществах [Labour Relations in Joint-Stock Societies], p. 96. This does not mean that lower courts necessarily share this presumption. Rather, the opposite was true during late Soviet period. See an impressive account of real practices of trial courts in labour disputes in K. Hendley, *Trying to Make Law Matter: Legal Reform and Labour Law in the Soviet Union* (1996).

a part of the picture. To make it complete, it should be stressed that in Russia judges of inferior courts are mostly concerned with formalities. So long as the aim of labour law formalities is to make the employers' life difficult and protect the employee, and not the contrary, the observation is true. But the same formalities can work either way, whereas the judges' vital interest is to compile a formally impeccable file of the case, not to reach a just and lawful decision. For instance, there are lots of employees, such as university teachers and the like, who are formally required by law to be constantly present at their workplace, but in reality they work there just part-time, so long as there is neither need nor conditions for a full-time work. Usually their chiefs shut eyes to this long-standing practice of absenteeism, but at any time it can be conveniently turned against an employee whom they want to get rid of. He or she may be sacked for 'the violation of labour discipline' or at least intimidated in that way. In courts the arguments of dismissed fall on deaf ears – judges never venture to put aside the formalities and look at the real substance of such disputes. And the Supreme Court does not encourage them to evince more flexibility and boldness in cases where they are really able to overcome the effect of obsolete legal rules and thus bridge the gap between 'law in books' and real life.

Sadly, the direct application of constitutional provisions, although encouraged by the 1995 decree of the Supreme Court Plenum, largely remains unused by general courts. This makes one wonder whether judicial guidelines supposedly intended to influence the practice of courts below are indeed taken seriously by both superior and inferior judges. It is difficult to answer this question without a comprehensive survey of the practice of lower courts. Russia has a career judiciary, and the main concern of many (if not most) judges is the avoidance of reversal of their judgments by higher instances and improvement of judicial statistics. To be sure, they may ignore the Supreme Court's practice only in cases which have little chance to come to its attention. It can be suggested, therefore, that the efficacy of Supreme Court precedents eventually depends on the probability of appeal. If it is low, judges feel freer to ignore relevant precedents. Unfortunately, the number of such cases is far from being insignificant, given lengthy terms of appellate proceedings, difficulties with getting legal aid, etc. Moreover, the situation is aggravated by the Supreme Court's failure to issue consistent judgments on similar cases and thereby provide clear guidance for inferior courts. An important change may come, however, through the implementation of the 2002 Civil Procedure Code (effective from 1 February 2003), which entrusts to the Presidium of the Supreme Court the power to consider appeals against the rulings of the Civil Division, provided that these rulings violate the unity of judicial practice (Art 377). Evidently, the authors of the law (proposed by the Supreme Court) felt that the situation had to be improved.

Chapter 6

Joint-stock societies and arbitrazh courts

A case study

In this chapter I will focus on the contribution of arbitrazh courts to joint-stock societies law. Unlike labour law, it is a relatively recent phenomenon within the Russian legal system. The basic relevant legislation includes the 1995 Federal Law 'On Joint-Stock Societies' (FLJSS), as repeatedly amended afterwards, the most important and massive amendments being those adopted on 7 August 2001,[1] the 1996 Federal Law 'On Securities Market' (as amended) and, of course, the Civil Code. Besides, subordinate legal acts issued by the Federal Securities Commission are also of importance. In general, the regulation on joint-stock societies is complex and sometimes highly 'technical'. Although the details cannot be described here,[2] it is important to note that there are open and closed joint-stock societies, the basic distinction being the way in which their stocks are distributed and disposed of. The stocks of the open joint-stock society are subject to open subscription and the stockholders may dispose of them in the way they want to, whereas the number of stockholders of a closed society can not exceed 50 and they have a preferential right to acquire the stocks from their fellow stockholder if they are put up for sale. Besides, the open joint-stock societies should publish annual book-keeping and financial reports, which is not a duty for the closed ones.

Russian procedural legislation assigns disputes arising out of the activities of joint-stock societies to the jurisdiction of arbitrazh courts, which comprise a special branch of the Russian judicial system. However, delimitation of jurisdictions was a touchy point during the 1990s, and a clear line was ultimately drawn as late as 2002 by the new procedural codes. Till then, arbitrazh procedural legislation did not provide for contesting normative legal acts. Accordingly, the task of verification of their legality was assumed by the general courts. Therefore, some of their rulings are still of importance for stockholders in Russia and will be touched upon below.

---

1 Hereinafter: FLJSS. For an older version of the Federal Law 'On Joint-Stock Societies' see W. E. Butler and M. E. Gashi-Butler (eds. and comp.), *Russian Company Law. Basic legislation* (3rd edn., 2000) [hereinafter: *RCL*] and the most recent version is published in W. E. Butler (ed. and transl.), *Russian Company and Commercial Legislation* (2003) [hereinafter: *RCCL*].

2 For further details see Butler, *Russian Law* (2003), pp. 448–455.

Constitutional Court jurisprudence until recently was virtually non-existent. However, during the year 2003 two decrees concerning joint-stock societies were adopted. Besides, the Court was once invited to check the constitutionality of Art 80 of the FLJSS, but ruled that the petition failed to meet the criteria of admissibility.[3] The Supreme Court was also involved in the development of this area of law through issuing decrees jointly with the Plenum of the Supreme Arbitrazh Court.[4] Nevertheless, the role of the latter court, and particularly its Presidium, appears to be the dominant one, and it is no exaggeration to say that this area of Russian law was mainly developed through judgments and interpretive guidelines of the Supreme Arbitrazh Court.

Creation of a society and its charter capital

Courts faced difficulties at the very moment of the enactment of the FLJSS, for its Art 94(2) provided: 'The constitutive documents of societies not brought into conformity with the present Federal Law before 1 July 1996 shall be considered to be invalid.'[5] The joint decree of the plenums of supreme courts of 5 February 1998 tried to relax this draconian requirement. The plenums decreed that in the course of preparation of a case for judicial proceedings a judge may propose to a society to remove the divergences within the law found in its constitutive documents or charter by way of making necessary changes and additions that should be registered in the established procedure. An arbitrazh court may also postpone the consideration of a pending case and propose that the society eliminate the divergences within a period which the court may grant pursuant to Art 120 of the 1995 Arbitrazh Procedure Code. Until the amendments are made, the activities of such societies are regulated exclusively by norms of legislation, not the charter. It should be noted, however, that Art 94(2) uses the expression 'shall be considered to be invalid' instead of more flexible 'may be deemed invalid by a court'. Evidently, the position of the Supreme Court gave more latitude to judges in treating such cases than the legislator apparently intended to give.[6] It is characteristic that the decree itself pointed out that the

---

3 Ruling of 6 December 2001, No. 255-O, on the refusal to accept for consideration the complaints of citizens V. N. Ezhov and Iu. A. Varzughina, *HCC*, no. 2 (2002), pp. 80–81.

4 There were four joint decrees of the plenums of the Supreme Court and the SAC: the Decree of 1 July 1996, No. 6/8, 'On Certain Questions Connected to the Application of Part 1 of the Civil Code of the Russian Federation', the Decree of 2 April 1997, No. 4/8, 'On Certain Questions of Application of the Federal Law "On Joint-Stock Societies,"' and the Decree of 5 February 1998, No. 4/2, 'On Application of Article 94(3) of the Federal Law "On Joint-Stock Societies,"' *HSAC*, no. 9 (1996), pp. 5–19; no. 6 (1997), pp. 11–18; no. 4 (1998), pp. 35–36. The second one has been subsequently replaced by a new one under the same title (*HSAC*, no. 1 (2004), pp. 5–12).

5 *RCL*, p. 375.

6 The legislator acknowledged the difficulty by extending the term till 1 July 1997 in the Federal Law of 13 June 1996. This remedy proved to be insufficient and the situation apparently required the intervention of supreme courts.

activity of a society whose constitutive documents are invalid should be regarded as effectuated in violation of the law.[7]

Another question was whether it was necessary to conclude a purchase-sale contract with the owners of fractional stocks (that is, parts of 'normal' stocks which gave their owners the proportionate amount of rights as against ordinary stockholders). In the opinion of Gallina Shapkina (a judge of the Supreme Arbitrazh Court), the existence of such stocks is incongruent with a basic principle of the joint-stock form of entrepreneurial activity, that is, the indivisibility of stocks, which makes these societies distinct from other commercial structures.[8] Article 74(1) of the FLJSS (in the original version) provided that if consolidation of stocks leads to the formation of fractional stocks, the latter shall be subject to purchase by the society at the market value.[9] Arguably, this norm contradicts Art 209(1) the Civil Code, which says that 'the rights of possession, use, and disposition of his property shall belong to the owner'.[10] Since a fractional stock is an object of civil rights, and the consent of the owner is essential for its alienation. It is important to note that notionally the Civil Code takes precedence over the FLJSS. According to Art 3(2) of the Code, 'norms of civil law contained in other laws must conform to the present Code'.[11]

This issue has been further elaborated in the court cases of the firm 'Kadet-Establishment'. The disputes arose from the consolidation of stocks of two oil companies of the Tiumen region and involved a local oil magnate Viktor Palii who was reportedly in control of 'Kadet-Establishment'. This Liechtenstein-based firm was a minority stockholder of those companies. In the process of consolidation the stocks belonging to 'Kadet' were converted into one fractional stock. It was registered in a special account of a registrar who, after the companies had paid in the necessary sum of money, entered the fractional stock of 'Kadet' into the individual account of the companies.

To make the picture complete, it should be added that at the time of the dispute Palii was under pressure from the Procuracy which suspected him of money laundering. 'Kadet' won in the arbitrazh court of the first instance which found that 'the fractional stocks subject to purchase by virtue of Art. 74 of the Federal Law "On Joint-Stock Societies" ought to have been sold by the possessor to the Society, that is, a purchase-sale transaction ought to have been concluded between them. [. . .] In the event of the refusal of the possessor of fractional stocks to sell them to the Society, the latter had to apply to the court with the demand to compel him to perform the requirement of the law'. Since there was neither contract nor judicial decision to that effect, the registration of

---

7 Point 1 of the Decree, *HSAC*, no. 4 (1998), p. 35.
8 G. S. Shapkina, Новое в российском акционерном законодательстве [The New in Russian Joint-Stock Society Legislation] (2002), p. 9.
9 *Russian Company Law*, p. 359.
10 *CCRF*, p. 88.
11 Ibid., p. 2.

stocks was deemed unlawful and it was ordered to re-enter the firm into the register of stockholders.[12] It is characteristic that the court said nothing as to whether the rule obliging the owners to sell fractional stocks was concordant with the Civil Code, but arrived at its decision about the illegality of the transaction in a more formal way. The decision was upheld by the appellate and cassational arbitrazh courts, but reversed in the Supreme Arbitrazh Court, which said that the purchase of fractional stocks is a duty of the issuer of stocks provided by the law and therefore the consent of the possessor to their alienation is unnecessary. Hence the view of the lower court concerning the necessity of concluding a purchase-sale contract with the owners of fractional stocks was wrong.[13] In so doing the Presidium also abstained from delving into the issue of the supposed conflict of norms.

In parallel to these litigations, a similar suit of Palii himself was dragging through general courts. There the story of arbitrazh proceedings was neatly emulated: the suit was allowed by lower courts whose decisions were finally reversed by the Supreme Court Civil Division upon the submission from a Deputy Procurator-General.[14] Needless to say, the argumentation of the parties and courts' reasoning were simply reiterated. The decisions of the supreme courts were not, however, the last page in this story. When formulating their holdings on the issue, these courts ought to have known that they were out of line with the new approach of the federal legislator. The rule concerning the obligatory purchase of the fractional stocks has been dropped from amended version of the law on joint-stock societies, although the existence of such stocks has been admitted again.[15] It is small wonder that 'Kadet-Establishment', together with more than 40 other applicants, appealed against point 1 of Art 74 of the previous version to the Constitutional Court. In their opinion, the duty to sell fractional stocks was contrary to Arts 17, 35(3) and 55(3) of the Constitution, as well as to the norms of the Civil Court which placed stocks among the objects of civil rights.[16] During the debates in the Court session, the representatives of the applicant put a particular emphasis on the fact that by amending the Law the legislator had acknowledged the imperfectness of the rule in question. The Constitutional Court, however, refrained from the consideration of the supposed contradiction between the Civil Code and the law on joint-stock societies as being outside its competence. In the end, the norms concerning the

12 Decision of the Arbitrazh court of Hanty-Mansiiskii Autonomous District of 9 April 2002, No. A-75-1484-172002 (unpublished).
13 Decrees of the Presidium of the Supreme Arbitrazh Court of 29 October 2002, No. 7414/02 and No. 7444/02, upon the suits of the firm 'Kadet-Establishment' (unpublished). Contrary to the usual practice, the decrees were not published in the 'Herald' of the Court. Possibly, the judicial authorities were reluctant to attach precedential significance to these important decisions.
14 Ruling of the Civil Division of the Supreme Court of 27 December 2002, No. 69-B02-24 (unpublished).
15 See Art 25(3) of the FLJSS, as amended by the Federal Law of 7 August 2001, No. 120-ФЗ (RCCL, pp. 234–235).
16 Article 143 of the Civil Code (CCRF, p. 67).

obligatory purchase-sale of stocks were not found unconstitutional whereas the question of their compatibility with the Code was left unresolved.[17]

At the same time the Constitutional Court 'has uncovered the constitutional legal sense' of the norms relative to consolidation of stocks by trying to strike a balance between contradictory interests within joint-stock societies each of which could find support in the present legal regulation. In Court's view, when making a decision concerning the consolidation of stocks it was necessary to observe 'due legal procedures', including the 'criterion of the common good of the joint-stock society', and to involve an independent auditor to determine the market value of stocks as is required for cases when the stocks are bought out at the demand of stockholders (Art 75). In this way the Court met the claims of the applicants that the price of the fractional stocks was, in fact, determined by the society's council of directors and did not reach the market value. In the view of the Court, to ensure the compliance with these requirements, one needs an effective (that is, not formal) judicial control.[18] So the matter rests at present.

There were a number of other controversial points of law that called for judicial intervention. For instance, an important addition introduced into Art 7 of the FLJSS provides for the defence against violations of the preferential right to purchase stocks of a closed joint-stock society. Any stockholder of the society and/or the society itself have the right to demand in a judicial proceeding the transfer to them of the rights and duties of the purchaser in a purchase-sale contract concluded with a third person.[19] This mode of judicial defence has previously been used in accordance with the explanations of the plenums based on analogy of law [*lex*] with Art 250(3) of the Civil Code regulating the sale of participatory share in the right of common ownership.[20]

In furtherance of Art 34(2) of the FLJSS (old version) it was provided that 'the paying up of stocks and other securities of a society may be effectuated by money, securities, other things or property rights, or *other rights having monetary value*' (emphasis added).[21] The meaning of 'other rights' was elaborated by the plenums. They decreed that as a contribution to the property of an economic partnership (or society) one may give property rights or other rights having monetary value. Therefore, an object of intellectual property, a patent, an object of author's right (including computer programs and the like) or know-how cannot be contributed. But the right of use of such an object being transferred to the society in accordance with a license agreement registered in a legislatively established procedure may be regarded as such a contribution, for it has determinable value.[22]

---

17 Decree of the Constitutional Court of 24 February 2004, No. 3-П, concerning certain provisions of Arts 74 and 77 of the Federal Law 'On Joint-Stock Societies', *HCC*, no. 2 (2004), p. 39.

18 Ibid., pp. 41–42.

19 *RCCL*, p. 222.

20 Point 7, Decree of the plenums of the Supreme Court and the SAC of 2 April 1997, No. 4/8, *HSAC*, no. 6 (1997), pp. 11–18.

21 *RCL*, p. 317.

22 Point 17, Decree of the Plenum of the Supreme Court and the Plenum of the SAC of 1 July 1996, No. 6/8, *HSAC*, no. 9 (1996), pp. 5–19.

Management in a joint-stock society

There are three permanent elements of management structure of a joint-stock society: the general meeting of stockholders, the council of directors (or supervisory council) and the executive organ. All of them have been touched upon by judicial glosses purported to delimit their competences. It is noted that there is a divergence between the Civil Code and the FLJSS as to how they define the competence of the management bodies of a society with respect to certain issues.[23] One is the issue of the changes in the charter capital of the society which by law consists of the par value of its stocks acquired by the stockholders.

On the one hand, there is a set of provisions defining the competence of the general meeting of stockholders. Article 100(1) of the Code says: 'A joint-stock society shall have the right by decision of the general meeting of stockholders to increase the charter capital by means of increasing the par value of the stocks or the issuance of additional stocks.'[24] Furthermore, Art 103(1) reads that to the *exclusive* competence of the general meeting of stockholders shall be relegated, among others, the questions of 'change of the charter of the society, including change of the amount of its charter capital'.[25] As for the FLJSS, its Art 48([1] and [2]) (in its original version) also relegated to the exclusive competence of the general meeting, among others, the making of changes in and additions to the charter of a society, the increase of the charter capital by means of increasing the par value of the stocks or the placement of additional stocks, the reduction of the charter capital by reducing the par value of the stocks, the acquisition by the society of part of the stocks, and the like.[26]

On the other hand, in clear contradiction to it, Art 12(1) of the same version stipulates that decisions to increase charter capital by means of increasing the par value of stocks or the placement of additional stocks may be adopted by the council of directors (otherwise called 'supervisory council'), 'if in accordance with a decision of the general meeting of stockholders or charter of the society the right to adopt such decision belongs to the last'.[27] Article 65, para 2(6) confirms that these questions may indeed be relegated to the *exclusive* competence of the council of directors.[28]

This question was once considered by the Supreme Court.[29] The Federal Securities Commission, by way of point 8.1 of the 'Standards of Issue of Stocks',

---

23 Shapkina, Новое в российском акционерном законодательстве [The New in Russian Joint-Stock Society Legislation], p. 9.
24 *CCRF*, p. 47.
25 Ibid., p. 48.
26 *RCL*, p. 328.
27 Ibid., p. 300.
28 Ibid., p. 347.
29 Decision of the Supreme Court of 8 December 1998 concerning the suit of the closed joint-stock society 'Zernotsentr' on deeming to be invalid Point 8.1 of the 'Standards of Issue of Stocks When Founding Joint-Stock Societies, Additional Stocks, Bonds and Prospects of Issue Thereof' (unpublished).

decreed that a decision concerning the placement of stocks can be adopted by the general meeting only. The plaintiff urged that this was a violation of the rights of stockholders. During the hearing, the representatives of the Commission objected by saying that point 8.1 was in conformity with the requirements of the Civil Code, Arts 100(1) and 103(1). The latter article prohibits the transfer of questions falling within the exclusive competence of the general meeting of stockholders to the resolution of the executive organs of a society.[30] Consequently, in the opinion of the respondent, the norms of Arts 12(1), 27(2), 48(2), and 65(6) of the FLJSS contradicted the Civil Code, to which the norms of civil law contained in other laws should conform. Moreover, the Commission believed that point 8.1 of the Standards was not only conformant to the Code, but enhanced the protection of small stockholders as well. But the Supreme Court disagreed with the arguments of the respondent. It pointed out that the Code prohibits granting such questions to the *executive* organs, but the council of directors (or supervisory council) is not one of them. Therefore, a charter of a joint-stock society or the decision of the general meeting of stockholders can make such an exemption from the exclusive competence of the general meeting in favour of the council.

The problem is, however, that it is not clear what the point of making a competence 'exclusive' would be, if exemptions were possible. In other words, the Civil Code is self-contradictory: when describing a competence as an 'exclusive' one, it adds at the same time that these questions may not be transferred to the executive organ, thereby making one think that they could be granted to anyone else. In such a case the word 'exclusive' might be eliminated without any detriment to the meaning of the provision. But there is a presumption that the legislator's use of words cannot be purposeless. This presumption, however, also causes a difficulty because, if the word 'exclusive' is not superfluous, then, on the contrary, the phrase 'may not be transferred' in the same article is redundant. It is hard to say what the intention of the legislator was (the Court, obviously, did not try to ascertain it) and whether there was a clear intention at all. The Court took the path which seemed to be easier: of two supposedly superfluous provisions, the one seemingly less significant was sacrificed. However, Art 100 of the Code does not allow for an increase of the charter capital other than by a decision of the general meeting. Moreover, the wording of FLJSS is also inconsistent, as its Art 64 provides, quite in conformity with the view of the Federal Commission, that the council should 'effectuate general direction over the activity of the society, except for deciding of questions relegated by the present Federal Law to the exclusive competence of the general meeting of stockholders'.[31]

In fact, the amendments of 7 August 2001 failed to eliminate all contradictions with the Civil Code and within the FLJSS itself. Indeed, Art 12 of the Law was not essentially amended so as to finally deprive the council of directors of any part

30 *CCRF*, p. 49.
31 *RCL*, p. 346.

in the decision concerning the increase of charter capital.[32] However, regarding the right to increase only the *par value* of stocks a change did occur: from now on such decision can be adopted only by the general meeting.[33] Moreover, Art 48(2) now reads that 'questions relegated to the competence of the general meeting of stockholders may not be transferred for decision to the council of directors... except for questions provided for by the present Federal Law'. Besides, the word 'exclusive' has been removed from Art 65(1) defining the competence of the council of directors.[34] Apparently, the legislator understood that this word is confusing in the given context, and abandoned it.

It may be said that in this dispute the Supreme Court construed the competence of the general meeting of stockholders narrowly. It follows from the decision that matters relegated to its exclusive competence could be transferred to the council of directors, since the Civil Code does not directly prohibit this. What is not prohibited is permitted – consequently, the Civil Code tacitly allows such a transfer. But, if this interpretation is correct, the question may be raised as to whether Art 48(2) in the old version of the FLJSS was in conformity with the Code. The said article explicitly forbade the council of directors to solve the questions assigned to the competence of the general meeting, except for those relative to an increase of the charter capital. But why may only these questions be transferred? In fact, the interpretation of the Civil Code by the Supreme Court suggests that *any* questions could be transferred in this manner. If so, it means that the FLJSS has inadmissibly restricted the freedom of the joint-stock societies granted by the Code to distribute the competence among their organs. Or, on the contrary, the interpretation given by the Court was too liberal.

It should be remarked that prior to the adoption of the FLJSS the Presidium of the Supreme Arbitrazh Court was inclined to assume that the powers of the general meeting could not be transferred to anyone else. And this view was normally justified by reference to Art 103 of the Civil Code. The Presidium used to interpret it in the sense that the law did not provide for the possibility of transfer of the powers of the general meeting to the council of directors.[35] An analogous position was taken by the Presidium in other cases with reference to Art 6(3) of the Model Charter of a Joint-Stock Society of the Open Type.[36]

---

32 *RCCL*, pp. 225–226.
33 Cf. para 1(6) of Art 48 and para 2(6) of Art 65 of the 1995 version with paras 1(6) and 2(5) of the same articles, as amended (*RCL*, pp. 328, 347; *RCCL*, p. 272).
34 *RCCL*, p. 272.
35 Decree of the Presidium of the SAC of 14 November 1995, No. 6472/95, in the case of joint-stock society 'Firma Kurganoblsnab', *HSAC*, no. 2 (1996), pp. 96–97.
36 The model charter was confirmed by presidential edict of 1 July 1992, No. 721. See the Decree of the Presidium of the SAC of 20 May 1997, No. 5260/96, in the case of limited partnership 'Electrokabel' (*HSAC*, no. 8 (1997), pp. 58–59), the Decree of 17 September 1996, No. 66/96 in the case of joint-stock society of open type 'Tokam' (*HSAC*, no. 1 (1997), pp. 80–82), and the Decree of 31 March 1998, No. 142/98 in the case of the firm 'Link' (*HSAC*, no. 6 (1998), pp. 59–60).

But later the attitude of the Presidium changed, as followed from the decree of 21 May 2000, which all the same eluded the question of conflict between the provisions of the Civil Code and the FLJSS.[37] Thus, the provisions of the latter law were given preference, although indirectly.

The question is, basically, whether there is a conflict of statutory provisions and, if there is, how it should be approached. The general principle, of course, is that everything that is not prohibited is permitted, but the method of the legislator was clearly prohibitive, as the word 'exclusive' intended to stress. Shapkina believes that the divergence between the FLJSS and the Civil Code in this part is beyond any doubt, and it can be eliminated by dispensing with the relevant provision of the Code.[38] To put it differently, this rule does not bear the liberal interpretation, which the Supreme Court tried to impose.

Perhaps, in order to bring more light into this maze of poorly adjusted provisions it should be reminded that under the Civil Code the creation of the council of directors, unlike an executive organ, is not required for every society. It is mandatory only in the societies with the number of stockholders more than 50.[39] It is the general meeting and the executive organ which are the permanent elements of the management structure, and it is natural that the relations between them were the chief target of the Code's regulation while the council and its competence were not. But, unfortunately, more clarity is to be desired as regards the executive organ too. The question is whether the formation of a 'one-man executive organ' (i.e. the appointment of director-general) is mandatory (as seems to follow from Art 69(1) of the FLJSS) or simply voluntary (that appears to be the position of the Civil Code – Art 103[3]), in which case a collegial executive organ (board or directorate) would suffice.[40] Although the FLJSS is both *lex posterior* and *specialis*, the rule concerning the superiority of the Code gives difficulty again. Therefore, the structure of management may be legally vulnerable when there is no director-general.

In one case the question was raised as to how broadly the provision of Art 65 of the FLJSS should be understood, according to which the decision concerning the *participation* of the society in other organisations is within the exclusive competence of the council of directors.[41] In that case an open joint-stock society sold its contributory stocks in the charter capital of a bank, the transaction having

---

37 Decree of 21 May 2000, No. 1539/99, on the open joint-stock society 'AK Transneft' (*HSAC*, no. 6 (2000), pp. 60–61).

38 Shapkina, Новое в российском акционерном законодательстве [The New in Russian Joint-Stock Society Legislation], pp. 9, 36.

39 Article 103(2), *CCRF*, p. 49. By the way, FLJSS is somewhat different on this point: the council is required if the number of the stockholders possessing *voting* stocks is *less* than 50 (see Art 64(1) in both versions). But not all stocks are voting (cf. Art 49), and the societies with exactly 50 stockholders are not rare because it is a ceiling for closed joint-stock societies.

40 *RCL*, p. 352; *CCRF*, p. 49.

41 Decree of the Presidium of the SAC of 23 January 2001, No. 6282/99, in the case of open joint-stock society 'Surgutskii Gazoneftepererabatyvaiushii Zavod', *HSAC*, no. 5 (2001), pp. 36–37.

been concluded by the director-general of the society. This transaction was consecutively deemed by first, appellate and cassational instances to have been done by the director-general in excess of his powers. However, the Presidium of the Supreme Arbitrazh Court upon the protest of the Chief Judge Iakovlev decided that the courts below imposed an unduly broad interpretation on the relevant norm, extending it to cases of secession of a society from other organisations or the reduction of its participation by way of sale of stocks (or contributions) in the charter capital. However, the decree goes on, this norm has a special, exceptional character, and one should proceed from its literal meaning, that is, the necessity of the adoption by the council of directors of a decision on joining an organisation or creating a new organisation. This norm does not presuppose any other meaning or restrictions.

With respect, this is a strange opinion, for in the Russian language the word *uchastie* (participation) may well encompass both the beginning and the end of someone's taking part in something. But it is true that the broad (and formally correct) interpretation could cause difficulties for business, especially the securities market. Participation in a joint-stock society is effectuated by means of the purchase-sale of stocks of this society. It is not accidental, therefore, that the new version of the law no longer contains this norm. In making such decision the Supreme Arbitrazh Court was no strict constructionist (although it pretended to be); quite the contrary, the needs of the market were preferred to the letter of the law.[42]

The procedure for voting in the general meeting of stockholders is somewhat complicated by the law of 7 August 2001. Shapkina rightly noted that the 2001 formulation of Art 50(2) of the FLJSS which prohibits external voting (by poll) on a number of questions fails to take into account the real circumstances of the societies with many stockholders, some of whom cannot take part in meetings.[43] Some flaws of the present version of the FLJSS are a legacy of the previous one. Article 49(4) in both versions required the quorum of three-fourth of the votes of stockholders who own voting stocks and take part in the general meeting. In practice the question arose as to how to count the quorum: in one case both stockholders of a society took part in the general meeting convened to confirm the charter of the society.[44] One had 35 per cent of the voting stocks, while the other controlled the remaining 65 per cent. The first left the meeting, and the charter was confirmed in his absence. This decision was contested by the minority stockholder on the grounds of there being no quorum. The other stockholder, on the contrary, invited the court to proceed from the assumption that there was the

42 The interpretation of the Supreme Arbitrazh Court was followed by courts below. See the decree of the Federal Arbitrazh Court for the Moscow Circuit of 29 August 2001, No. КГ-А40/4580-01 (unpublished).

43 Shapkina, Новое в российском акционерном законодательстве [The New in Russian Joint-Stock Society Legislation], p. 74.

44 Decree of the Presidium of the SAC of 8 September 1998, No. 5167/98, in the case of 'Reutovskaia Tkazkaia Fabrika', *HSAC*, no. 12 (1998), pp. 57–58.

quorum need, for he controlled all the voting stocks at the time of voting and the decision was unanimous. Under this interpretation, the 100 per cent required for a quorum would be deemed to be the stocks he owned. The Supreme Arbitrazh Court refused to follow the invitation. It held that a quorum should be based on the whole number of voting stocks registered for participation in the general meeting, but not on the number of those who actually voted.

The question concerning a quorum in meetings of the council of directors is also of interest. Once the Supreme Arbitrazh Court had to check the validity of a decision concerning the increase of the charter capital of a bank which was adopted by three of five members of the council of directors.[45] The other two members had notified the council in writing about the voluntary termination of their powers before time. All the same, the charter of the bank required that (1) a decision shall be adopted by the council of directors unanimously, and (2) the council of directors cannot consist of less than five members. Arbitrazh courts disagreed in their legal assessment of these facts. Was the decision valid or not? The appellate instance and the Procuracy indicated that joint-stock society legislation does not prohibit voluntary termination of powers by a member of the council, and the decision of the general meeting to this effect is not needed. Therefore, the decision was adopted by a legitimate composition of the council and unanimously in accordance with the charter. But the position of the Supreme Arbitrazh Court proved to be different. In accordance with para 1(4) of Art 48 of the FLJSS the determination of the quantitative composition of the council of directors, election of its members and termination of their powers before time is relegated to the exclusive competence of the general meeting of stockholders.[46] Since the general meeting of stockholders of this bank did not decide on the termination of powers of those two directors, there is no reason to believe that their powers were terminated. This decision can be criticised for virtually paralysing the work of the council. Furthermore, it is not clear what to do with the powers of the directors who die. Do they retain their powers until they are discontinued by decision of the general meeting? The law is obviously imperfect and needs to be rectified. A judge of the Supreme Arbitrazh Court comments: 'Indeed, the council of directors (or supervisory council) is an organ which represents the interests of stockholders. The termination before time of the powers of a member of such a council may lead to a violation of the balance of interests of stockholders.'[47] But this balance is surely broken even in the event of death of a director or his inability to participate in the work of the council.

This case deserves a closer attention, for it reveals how a legal problem may lack an indisputable solution. Even if the powers of directors ought to have been

---

45 Decree of the Presidium of the SAC of 23 May 2000, No. 6066/99, in the case of the Company 'Sitek', *HSAC*, no. 8 (2000), pp. 48–49.

46 *RCL*, p. 328.

47 I. Sh. Faizutdinov in Комментарий судебно-арбитражной практики [Commentary on Judicial and Arbitrazh Practice], Vol. 8 (2001), p. 15.

terminated only by the decision of the general meeting, one might still wonder whether the decision would have been the same if at the start there were seven directors or more. In such a case even in the absence of two members the unanimous decision of five directors might be possible, as required by the charter. Curiously, there is a resemblance between this dispute and the issue faced by the Constitutional Court when interpreting the concept of the 'total number of deputies of the State Duma'.[48] The Constitutional Court held that for the purposes of voting in Parliament the total number of the members of State Duma and the Council of the Federation is to be understood as the constitutionally established number (that is, the number of the deputy mandates – 450 and 178, respectively), and not as a real number of members elected to Parliament by the moment of voting. The decision of judges was not unanimous and was criticised in legal writings.[49] In a similar way, the 'constitutionally established' number of bank directors would be the number of seats provided for in the charter (that is, not less than five), but not the real number of the taken seats which might be less than five.

In any event, arbitrazh practice is ambiguous on this point. In the case of the open joint-stock society 'Sakhalin' an arbitrazh circuit court sustained the validity of a large-scale transaction approved by unanimous vote of five members of the council of directors who were present at the meeting, the total number of directors being seven. According to Art 79(1) of the FLJSS in the version in force at the moment of the dispute, 'a decision concerning the conclusion of a large-scale transaction, the subject of which is property whose value comprises from 25 up to 50 per cent of the balance sheet value of the assets of the society...shall be adopted by the council of directors (or supervisory council) unanimously, not taking into account the votes of members of the council...who have withdrawn'.[50] Pavlodskii in his commentary on this case maintains that the decision of the court was wrong.[51] But it must be remarked that it was not contrary to a literal interpretation of Art 79(1), for it was uncertain what should amount to 'withdrawal'.

Transactions of a society

Unlike other institutions of Russian company law, large-scale and interested transactions have no roots in the Russian legal past. They were transplanted into the Russian legal system from common law, above all, the American. But there they are interpreted against the rich background of case law capable of

---

48 Decree of the Constitutional Court of 12 April 1995, No. 2-П, *HCC*, no. 2/3 (1995), pp. 17–31.
49 See dissenting opinions of judges Ebzeev and Gadzhiev (Ibid., p. 27 ff) and a comment by E. A. Luk'ianova in her article Конституция в судебном переплете [The Constitution in a Judicial Cover], *Законодательство* [Legislation], no. 12 (2002).
50 *RCL*, p. 364.
51 E. A. Pavlodskii in Комментарий судебно-арбитражной практики [Commentary on Judicial and Arbitrazh Practice], Vol. 8 (2001), p. 20.

guiding courts as to under which circumstances a particular transaction should be recognised unfair. Such an aid was not available for Russian judges, and therefore the implementation of these concepts became a difficult task for courts. Since fairness is a circumstantial notion whose varied overtones are difficult to comprehend by way of formal rules, it should not be surprising that many issues remained unresolved.

For some time arbitrazh practice was uncertain as to whether a credit contract amounts to a large-scale transaction. There is a case in which the Presidium of the Supreme Arbitrazh Court refused to consider a credit contract as a large-scale transaction.[52] It held that pursuant to Art 819 of the Civil Code[53] a credit contract is the granting by a bank or other credit organisation of monetary means to the borrower on condition of its being paid and returned at a certain date. At the same time, the determination of the value of property which is the subject of a large-scale transaction should be made in accordance with the rules of Art 77 of the FLJSS, that is, should involve the determination of the market value of the property acquired or alienated. The conclusion by the parties of a credit contract does not presuppose the determination of the price of the property acquired, because under such a contract monetary means are transferred, and a credit cannot *per se* be considered as an acquisition or alienation of property by the borrower. Consequently, this kind of transaction is not covered by Arts 78–79 of the FLJSS. Such arguments were also given in the protest in a later case.[54] However, this time the Presidium of the Supreme Arbitrazh Court did not follow its previous reasoning. On the contrary, the regime of large-scale transactions was extended to transactions under a credit contract. Faizutdinov thinks this to be correct,[55] and it was expressly confirmed by the amendments of 7 August 2001. This case is indicative of the fact that the Supreme Arbitrazh Court does not consider itself to be strictly bound by its previous decisions and its policy may change from time to time. This, of course, makes it difficult for courts below to pursue a particular line without running the risk of reversal.

What is the procedure for the conclusion of large-scale transactions? Once the Cassation Division of the Supreme Court held illegal certain provisions of the 'Standards of the Issue of Stocks' established by the Federal Securities Commission.[56] The problem was that the procedure for the conclusion of such

52 Decree of the Presidium of the SAC of 15 July 1999, No. 2384/99, in the case of joint-stock society 'Ost-Invest', *HSAC*, no. 10 (1999), pp. 59–60. See also the Ruling of the Presidium of 22 April 2003, No. 2384/99, concerning the refusal to reconsider this decree on the grounds of newly discovered circumstances, *HSAC*, no. 8 (2003), pp. 30–32.

53 *CCRF*, p. 295.

54 As described by Faizutdinov in Комментарий судебно-арбитражной практики [Commentary on Judicial and Arbitrazh Practice], Vol. 7 (2000), pp. 11–15. Unfortunately, Faizutdinov did not provide the exact number and date of the case, which would help to identify it with certainty.

55 Ibid., p. 16.

56 Ruling of Cassation Division of 2 July 2000, No. KAC 00-249, upon the Decision of the Supreme Court of 10 May 2000, No. ГКПИ 00-333 (unpublished).

large-scale transactions as the placement of stocks was not established by the FLJSS. Article 78 provides only that the value of a large-scale transaction connected with the placement of stocks shall be the one involving more than 25 per cent of the stocks previously placed by the society.[57] The Standards resolved the issue by drawing an analogy with the procedure established by Art 79 for large-scale transactions connected with the alienation or acquisition of property. (Under Russian law, the placement of stocks is not an alienation of property, because stockholders do not acquire rights to the company's assets; the company has only obligations to them, such as paying dividends.) So the Standards provided that the decision to make a large-scale transaction connected with the placement of stocks shall be adopted by the council of directors only if these stocks comprise between 25 and 50 per cent of the previously placed stocks. If they comprise more than 50 per cent, such decision shall be adopted by the general meeting of stockholders. But, according to para 1(18) of Art 48 and para 1(17) of Art 65 of the FLJSS, the competence of the general meeting and the council of directors with respect to the conclusion of large-scale transactions was confined to the acquisition or alienation of property. There was no mention of the placement of stocks. The Cassation Division has rejected the argument of the Commission that it was empowered to regulate this issue. With timidity, characteristic of general courts, it held that it was against the law to grant such powers to the general meeting of stockholders, so long it had not been envisaged by the legislation. But the gap in legal regulation was not thus removed. The Supreme Court has effectively blocked the Commission's attempt to fill it, but failed in its turn to indicate which rules are applicable. The new version of the law no longer considers the placement of stocks as a large-scale transaction.[58] But the decision concerning the placement of stocks comprising more than 25 per cent of the common stocks previously placed is relegated to the competence of the general meeting.[59] That is to say, the approach of the Federal Commission was finally approved by the legislator.

The regulation of large-scale and 'interested transactions' under Russian company law is very intricate and difficult in application. Courts made some moderate efforts to improve it wherever possible. For instance, after years of uncertainty it was specified by the legislator that the balance sheet value of the assets of a society (which is instrumental for estimating the scale of a transaction) should be determined according to accounting data for the last report date (Art 78[1]). This rule follows a previous judicial gloss.[60] However, apart from being unduly complex, the corporate law regulations remain unsettled

57 *RCL*, p. 363.
58 Article 79, as amended (*RCCL*, p. 287).
59 Article 39(4), as amended (*RCCL*, p. 247).
60 Point 14, Decree of the Plenum of the Supreme Court and the Plenum of the SAC of 2 April 1997, No. 4/8, 'On Certain Questions of Application of the Federal Law "On Joint-Stock Societies," ' *HSAC*, no. 6 (1997), pp. 11–18.

and changeable, and the rationale of some amendments is not always easy to comprehend. The new version of the FLJSS provides that in the event of a large-scale transaction being simultaneously an 'interested transaction', only the rules concerning the latter shall apply. The abolished procedure under the old version of the FLJSS (Art 83[7]) was exactly the opposite – the (large) scale of a transaction mattered more than an interest in it.[61] On closer examination, it appears that the new procedure makes it easier to conclude a transaction which is both large-scale and 'interested' one than a mere large-scale transaction, because in the former case a simple majority of votes of directors is sufficient (as is normally the case with 'interested' transactions), whereas in the latter case the unanimous vote is required. This is strange because 'interested' transactions can be quite small, and the general requirements for their conclusion are not (and should not be) as tough as for the conclusion of large-scale transactions. Therefore, it appears that by means of subordinating such 'mixed' transactions to the rules applicable to the 'interested' ones the barrier against dubious transactions has been lowered.

Furthermore, in a society where the number of stockholders does not exceed 1,000 an approval of an 'interested' transaction shall be made by the majority of 'disinterested' directors, whereas if the number of stockholders is more than 1,000, the directors should be both disinterested and independent.[62] In other words, in the first instance 'dependent' directors (primarily those who exercise executive functions in the society or their relatives) do qualify for taking part in the decision (Art 83, paras 1–3). The rationale for such indulgence is not clear. As regards the interrelation between large-scale and 'interested' transactions, it is worth noting that the law says nothing as to what the number of 'independent' directors should be for the purposes of approval of an 'interested' transaction. From this one might infer that a 'mixed' transaction (both large-scale and interested) can be approved of by only one 'independent' director provided that all others are not independent. So far no case is known in which the courts have faced such a problem.[63]

Sometimes courts missed the fact that 'interest' of a member of the council of directors may change with time. Therefore, the Presidium of the Supreme Arbitrazh Court once decreed that the 'interestedness' of a director under the FLJSS should be determined by a court with regard to the moment of conclusion of the transaction, but not the moment of registration of the company which is another party to the transaction in question and of which the director was arguably a related person. A commentary calls this 'a kind of a precedent'.[64]

61 *RCL*, p. 369.
62 For definitions of 'independent' and 'disinterested' directors see Arts 79 and 83 of the FLJSS (*RCCL*, pp. 287–288).
63 Shapkina, Новое в российском акционерном законодательстве [The New in Russian Joint-Stock Society Legislation], p. 98.
64 I. Sh. Faizutdinov in Комментарий судебно-арбитражной практики [Commentary on Judicial and Arbitrazh Practice], Vol. 7 (2000), p. 10.

By law 'interested' transactions should be approved by the council of directors or the general meeting *before* conclusion (Art 83[1] of the FLJSS, present version), whereas large-scale transactions do not require this. Shapkina believes, nevertheless, that subsequent approval of an 'interested' transaction is equally admissible, for the invalidation of a transaction which all the parties agreed to conclude does not prevent them from concluding it again and thus can be painful for them, so long as it should entail bilateral restitution.[65] This approach is not, of course, a 'literal' one. Neither is the attitude of the supreme courts to the procedure for conclusion of large-scale transactions. Although this procedure required a decision of the council of directors or general meeting, but not an executive organ, courts significantly relaxed this requirement. The joint decree of the supreme courts of 2 April 1997 makes a reservation that in the event of the conclusion of a large-scale transaction by a director-general or a person empowered by him and in the absence of the necessary decision of the council of directors or the general meeting, it can be deemed by a court to be valid provided that it has been *subsequently* approved by the aforesaid organs.[66] That said, the practice of arbitrazh courts does not recognise the validity of transactions approved *en masse*. In one case the annual general meeting of a society has approved all the transactions previously concluded. An arbitrazh court held, however, that it was necessary to adopt a separate decision for each particular case.[67] A similar norm was subsequently added to the FLJSS (Art 83(6), as amended).[68]

There was a gap in the FLJSS regarding the procedure for approving transaction in a society consisting of one participant. But there is no such gap in the law on limited responsibility societies, which provides that all decisions in such a society shall be made personally and in writing (Art 39 of the Law).[69] The Supreme Arbitrazh Court in the Information Letter of 13 March 2001 has applied *analogia legis* by pointing out that if a joint-stock society has a sole stockholder who possesses 100 per cent of its stocks, then his consent in writing is sufficient for the society in order to conclude a large-scale transaction. This opinion arose from previous arbitrazh practice, as is seen from the accompanying extract of a case, in which the cassation court held that in a society of one participant a decision of this stockholder or any other written expression of his will to conclude a transaction should amount to a decision of the general meeting.[70] The legislation followed the lead of arbitrazh practice by way of amending Art 47(3) of the FLJSS in accordance with it.[71] This approach was

---

65 Shapkina, Новое в российском акционерном законодательстве [The New in Russian Joint-Stock Society Legislation], p. 100.
66 *HSAC*, no. 6 (1997), p. 13.
67 Ibid., p. 101.
68 *RCCL*, p. 293.
69 Ibid., p. 200.
70 The Information Letter of the SAC of 13 March 2001, No. 62, 'A Survey of Practice of Resolving of Disputes Connected With Conclusion by Economic Societies of Large-Scale Transactions and Transactions in Which There Is an Interest', *HSAC*, no. 7 (2001), pp. 71–83.
71 *RCCL*, p. 253.

further elaborated in Art 81(2), which says that the provisions concerning transactions in which there is an interest shall not apply to societies consisting of one stockholder who simultaneously effectuates the functions of the one-man executive organ.[72]

Doctrinal writings have asked what can be taken as subsequent 'express approval' of a transaction concluded by an unempowered person (Art 183, Civil Code).[73] This general norm certainly calls for being elaborated through precedents of interpretation. In one case the Presidium of the Supreme Arbitrazh Court has determined that the fact of payment for a disputed vessel by a purchaser amounts to such approval, the more so that the monetary means received by the seller were used for payment for labour to his employees. The crew of the vessel had been substituted, and the vessel was removed from the balance sheet of the seller.[74] The question which period should apply to cases of express approval has not been settled in arbitrazh practice so far.

A transaction concluded in the course of the 'ordinary economic activity' of a society is not considered to be large-scale. But what is deemed to be 'ordinary economic activity'? The joint decree of the plenums of 2 April 1997 gives by way of example such transactions as raw materials, realisation of finished products and the like, irrespective of the value of the property acquired or alienated by such transaction.[75] In the decree of 15 June 1999 the Presidium of the Supreme Arbitrazh Court held that the credit used by the defendant for the payment of contracts concluded with foreign firms is a case in point, that is, ordinary economic activity.[76]

In the previous version of the law it was not clear whether an unlawful large-scale transaction was void or contested. Whereas a contested transaction can be deemed invalid by virtue of a court decision, a void transaction is invalid irrespective of such decision. For a while courts recognised unlawful large-scale transactions as void.[77] On the other hand, 'interested' transactions violating the rules of FLJSS were deemed to be contestable. However, on 7 August 2001 Art 79 was amended by way of adding para 6, which reads: 'A large-scale

---

72 Ibid., p. 290.

73 Комментарий судебно-арбитражной практики [Commentary on Judicial and Arbitrazh Practice], Vol. 5 (1998), p. 34. The matter was developed in the Information Letter of 23 October 2000, No. 57, 'On Some Questions of Application of Article 183 of the Civil Code of the Russian Federation', HSAC, no. 12 (2000), pp. 63–64.

74 Decree of 27 February 2002, No. 2329/01, in the case of the joint-stock society 'Pallada Pacific', HSAC, no. 6 (2002), pp. 57–59.

75 Point 14, Decree of the Plenum of the Supreme Court and the Plenum of the SAC of 2 April 1997, No. 4/8, 'On Certain Questions of Application of the Federal Law "On Joint-Stock Societies,"' HSAC, no. 6 (1997), pp. 11–18.

76 Decree of the Presidium of the SAC of 15 July 1999, No. 2384/99, in the case of the joint-stock society 'Ost-Invest' cited in the Ruling of the Presidium of the SAC of 22 April 2003, No. 2384/99, HSAC, no. 8 (2003), p. 30.

77 It is observed in point 10, Information Letter of the SAC of 13 March 2001, No. 62, HSAC, no. 7 (2001), pp. 71–83. See also the Decree of the Presidium of the SAC of 23 February 1999, No. 6115/98 in the case of the closed joint-stock society 'Rosinka Odin' (HSAC, no. 6 (1999), pp. 42–43).

transaction concluded in violation of the requirements of the present Article *may be deemed to be invalid upon the suit of the society or a stockholder*' (emphasis added).[78] Thus a large-scale transaction was also made contestable. In fact, it seriously deteriorated the position of a society or stockholder, because the period of limitation for application of the consequences of a void transaction was much longer – 10 years instead of one year only.[79]

It was the point of the first case in which the Constitutional Court has addressed the FLJSS. The Court had to examine the constitutionality of Art 84(1) of the FLJSS in the version of 24 May 1999. The article stipulates that 'a transaction in the conclusion of which there is an interest concluded with a violation of the requirements for a transaction provided for by Art 83 of the present Federal Law may be deemed to be invalid'.[80] The difficulty with this provision was that it failed to specify who could bring an action concerning the invalidation of such transactions.

This case originated in a dispute between several open joint-stock societies. One of them, 'Priargunskoe', sued the societies 'Varieghannefteghaz' and 'Sidanko'. The plaintiff sought deeming to be invalid (void) under Art 166 of the Civil Code and having no legal consequences a contract of purchase-sale of stocks concluded between the respondents. 'Priargunskoe' was a minority stockholder of the seller ('Varieghannefteghaz'), whereas 'Sidanko' (purchaser) owned 20 per cent of the voting stocks of the seller and therefore could be found interested in the conclusion of the contract.

Article 168 of the Civil Code stipulates that 'a transaction not corresponding to the requirements of a law or other legal acts shall be void unless the law establishes that such a transaction is contestable or provides other consequence for the violation'. The Code uses the 'invalidity' of a transaction as a generic term for both 'void' and 'contested' transactions. Paragraph 2(2) of Art 166 says that 'a demand concerning the application of the consequences of the invalidity of a void transaction may be presented by any interested person'.[81] *Priargunskoe* could no doubt qualify as such a person. However, the matter becomes more complex if the transaction is viewed as merely 'contested', for 'a demand to deem a contested transaction to be invalid may be brought by the persons specified in the present Code' (para 2(1) of Art 166). But neither the Civil Code nor the FLJSS as of 24 May 1999 actually specified who such persons with respect to 'interested transactions' were.

The arbitrazh court of first and cassational instances found the transaction to be void. But the Presidium of the Supreme Arbitrazh Court reversed their decisions and remanded the case for new consideration. It pointed out that under Art 84 of the FLJSS the transaction might be deemed to be invalid. In the

---

78 *RCCL*, p. 288.
79 Article 181, Civil Code (*CCRF*, p. 79).
80 *RCL*, p. 369.
81 *CCRF*, pp. 74–75.

view of the Presidium, it warranted the conclusion that the transaction was merely contested, not void.[82] Apparently, subsequent arbitrazh decisions were against 'Priargunskoe', since the laws did not give the right to contest transactions to minority stockholders or anyone else.

That was the main point of the complaint to the Constitutional Court, in which the plaintiff demanded to strike aside Art 84(1) as being inconsistent with Arts 19(1) and (2), 46(1), 34, 35 and 55(3) of the Constitution. The plaintiff described the situation as 'a conflict of norms', which denied him the constitutional right to judicial defence. It led to eight judgments being made at different levels of the arbitrazh system. The vital interest of the plaintiff in deeming the transaction to be void lay perhaps in the fact that the Civil Code provided a significantly longer period for the application of the consequences of a void transaction as compared with a contested one (10 years instead of 1). The transaction was concluded in June 1997, whereas the hearing of the case in the arbitrazh court of first instance took place in January 2000.

So the question before the constitutional tribunal was whether Art 84(1) did deny the right of minority stockholders to bring suits or not. It is important to note that by the time of the constitutional proceeding that article had already been amended (by the Law of 7 August 2001). The legislator had acknowledged the existence of a gap or ambiguity by adding the words 'by action of a society or a stockholder' after the words 'may be deemed to be invalid'.[83]

The Constitutional Court observed that persons having right to demand the invalidation of the transaction in which there is an interest were not defined directly by the FLJSS.[84] But, rather than interpreting the provision in question as containing a gap, the Constitutional Court attempted to treat this situation as 'an uncertainty in understanding' of the legislative norm. By acknowledging the gap the Court would create difficulties for law-application, for there would be no way to provide a remedy. More importantly, this would simply make the provision on invalidation of interested transactions a kind of 'dead letter', because *someone* had to bring a suit in such cases. That is why the Court was reluctant to follow the appellant's invitation to invalidate the provision in question.

In coming to its final conclusion the Constitutional Court implemented both the systemic and purposeful approaches to construing the meaning of the relevant clause. It said that the 'interpretation of norms of a lower level should be effectuated in accordance with the norms of a higher level'.[85] Further, in the absence of *analogia legis*, the rights and obligations of the parties should be determined by the general principles and sense of civil legislation (analogy of *ius*) and the requirements of good faith, reasonableness, and justness (pursuant to Art 6,

---

82 Decree of the Presidium of the SAC of 31 October 2000, No. 3020/00, *HSAC*, no. 1 (2001), p. 55.

83 *RCCL*, p. 293.

84 Decree of 10 April 2003, No. 5-П, concerning Art 84(1) of the Federal Law 'On Joint-Stock Societies' in connection with the petition of the joint-stock society 'Priargunskoe', *HCC*, no. 3 (2003), p. 49.

85 Ibid., p. 51.

Civil Code). The Court reasoning was generally based on an implicit presumption that the legislator could not intend to violate constitutional principles but, rather, tried to implement them in the domain of joint-stock societies law. When enacting Art 84(1), the legislator sought to protect the interests of stockholders, including the minority ones. Therefore, the Court concluded, the norm in question should be interpreted as implying the right of stockholders (including minority) to bring suits concerning 'interested transactions'.[86] By leaving the disputed norm in force and filling the gap by way of creative interpretation, the Court actually completed the job which the legislator did somewhat carelessly.

Reorganisation and liquidation of society

There is yet another discrepancy between the FLJSS and the Civil Code, this time with respect to the liquidation of juridical persons. Article 61(3) of the Civil Code prescribes: 'A demand concerning liquidation of a juridical person...may be presented to a court by a State agency or agency of local self-government to which the right to present such demand has been granted by a law.'[87] However, it may be deduced from Art 35(5–6) of the FLJSS that if the value of net assets proves to be less than the amount of the minimum charter capital, the society must adopt a decision concerning its liquidation. If, contrary to the law, such decision is not adopted, then its *stockholders*, *creditors* and also agencies duly empowered by the State have the right to demand the liquidation of the society in a judicial proceeding. Thus the list of subjects entitled to demand the liquidation is expanded by the federal law in comparison with the Code.

The approach of the FLJSS as against the Code was upheld by the Supreme Arbitrazh Court in early 2002 in the notorious decision on the case *Lukoil-Garant v Moscow Independent Broadcasting Corporation*.[88] The case and its supposed political underpinnings (the corporation was considered to be in opposition to the Kremlin) received wide coverage in the media. The situation was complicated by the fact that by the time of consideration Art 35(6) had been already amended, so that the stockholders no longer enjoyed the right to bring suits concerning liquidation.[89] In other words, judges had to apply the law, which the legislator himself recognised as defective, that is, to exercise what is called 'anticipatory interpretation'.[90] Besides, there was a moral dimension to this

---

86 Decree of 10 April 2003, No. 5-П, concerning Art 84(1) of the Federal Law 'On Joint-Stock Societies' in connection with the petition of the joint-stock society 'Priargunskoe', *HCC*, no. 3 (2003), pp. 52–53.

87 *CCRF*, p. 27.

88 Decree of the Presidium of the SAC of 11 January 2002, No. 32/02, on the suit of non-commercial organisation 'Pension Fund Lukoil-Garant' concerning the liquidation of the closed joint-stock society 'Moscow Independent Broadcasting Corporation', *HSAC*, no. 5 (2002), pp. 65–66.

89 By the Federal Law of 7 August 2001 (*RCCL*, p. 245).

90 This means to interpret a set of legal rules in conformity with subsequent legislative solutions (A. Hartkamp, 'Interplay Between Judges, Legislators, and Academics', in B. S. Markesinis (ed.), *Law-Making, Law-Finding, and Law-Shaping: the Diverse Influences* (1997), p. 90).

decision – in fact, the financial condition of the company being liquidated had significantly improved during the year 2001.

The first and appellate instances allowed the suit, but the cassational court refused to uphold the previous decisions. It referred to Art 61(3) of the Civil Code, which does not permit stockholders to bring such suits, whereas in the case at hand the suit was brought by a stockholder of the society-defendant. However, the Presidium of the Supreme Arbitrazh Court, upon the protest of the deputy Chairman, Eduard Renov, reversed the decision of the cassational court. In the Presidium's judgment, the reference to Art 61(3) of the Civil Code could not serve as the basis for a refusal to allow the suit. It determines only the general grounds and the procedure for liquidation of juridical persons, the decree goes, whereas Art 96(3) of the Civil Code provides that the legal status of a joint-stock society, and also the rights and duties of stockholders, are determined in accordance with the present Code and *the law on joint-stock societies*.[91] Given that this law in the version which was in force at the time of bringing the suit and deciding the case had granted such a right to stockholders, the plaintiff had legal grounds to bring the suit, and its demands should be allowed. It was immediately suspected that extralegal considerations were taken into account by the Presidium: there had been no similar suits before, and the protest against the decision of the cassation instance was extraordinarily prompt (within two work days only).[92] In any event, the case was both morally and legally difficult, and the judgment of the Presidium could be different should it prefer to rely on the principle of superiority of the Civil Code as consolidated by its Art 3(2). The matter was eventually brought to the attention of the Constitutional Court, but it refused to rule on the incompatibility of Art 35(6) with a higher law other than the Constitution. As for the norm of Art 35(5) concerning the liquidation of the society if its pure assets by the end of the second and each consecutive financial year become less than the amount of its charter capital, these provisions were found not to be contrary to the Constitution.[93] No dissenting opinion was filed.

In fact, the decision of the Supreme Arbitrazh Court in the case of the *Moscow Independent Broadcasting Corporation* had no chance to become a leading precedent for the simple reason that the provision in question had been already amended by the legislature. But the consequences of the Presidium decree of 14 January 2003, which represents the next stage of this corporate conflict, may be more enduring.[94] The case was about deeming invalid a decision of the council of directors of the aforementioned broadcasting corporation.

---

91   *CCRF*, p. 45.
92   The decision of the cassation instance was made on 29 December 2001, the amendment came into force on 1 January 2002, the protest was brought by Renov on 4 January 2002, and the Decree of the Presidium was dated 11 January.
93   Decree of 18 July 2003, No. 14-П, *HCC*, no. 5 (2003), pp. 30–43.
94   Decree of the Presidium of the SAC of 14 January 2003, No. 10447/02 in the case *Non-State Organisation 'Pension Fund Lukoil-Garant' v Closed Joint-Stock Society 'Moscow Independent Broadcasting Corporation'*, *HSAC*, no. 4 (2003), p. 70.

The plaintiff was the same, and again the protest against the decision of the cassational court in favour of the defendant was brought by Renov.

This time the dispute disclosed the lack of clarity as to who can perform the duties connected with the liquidation of a society by virtue of a judicial decision. Under Art 61(3) of the Civil Code 'duties relating to the effectuation of the liquidation of a juridical person may be placed by decision of a court...on its founders (participants), or organ empowered to liquidate the juridical person by its constitutive documents'.[95] The cassation instance ruled that the liquidation of the society can be effectuated only by its founders, but the Presidium of the Supreme Arbitrazh Court found this judgment to be in contradiction with the meaning of the provision, which, in its view, makes it possible to place the duty of liquidation of a society not only upon the founders, but also upon its participants, that is, any stockholder. The plaintiff whose intent was to catch control over the liquidation procedure, was stockholder, but not a founder.

The construction imposed by the Supreme Arbitrazh Court upon the provision seems to be erroneous. To my mind, a more feasible interpretation of legislative design would be the following: the duty of liquidation can be placed only on the founders of the society in question, as long as they were among its stockholders at the moment of the liquidation. Otherwise, it would be impossible to exclude the placement of such duties on persons who founded the society, but no longer participated in it. Furthermore, it seems illogical to place them upon any stockholder, however tiny his percentage of stocks might be.

It can be objected, on the other hand, what is the court expected to do if all the founders have already left the society? It may indeed cause a difficulty, but this situation is not common. More importantly, such a hypothetical situation is merely part of a wider problem. Regrettably, the procedure for liquidation is not regulated in sufficient depth by Russian law, as became plain in cases dealing with the liquidation of those societies which existed only on paper.[96] It should be added that if the legislator did want to classify founders and participants separately, the normal way to say that in the given context would be 'its founders, participants, or organ empowered', etc. Furthermore, there is little point to speak of founders as distinct from participants, for they may either be the latter (in which case the duties could be placed upon them) or not be (in which case this provision has no bearing whatsoever upon them). The legislator could simply say 'upon participants' without mentioning founders. In any event, that was a hard case when no ideal solution could be found 'within the four corners of the law', and the decisive considerations were perhaps the extralegal ones.

Finally, it was up to the supreme courts to fill the gap relating to the liquidation procedure. The FLJSS says nothing as to how a court should proceed if the founders of a juridical person evade the duty to liquidate it. An answer was

---

95 *CCRF*, p. 27.
96 Shapkina and Faizutdinov in Комментарий судебно-арбитражной практики [Commentary on Judicial and Arbitrazh Practice], Vol. 6 (1999), p. 16.

provided by point 24 of the joint decree of the Supreme Court and the Supreme Arbitrazh Court of 1 July 1996. It reads that the court should appoint a liquidator charged with such duty. In so doing, the court should apply the relevant provisions of bankruptcy legislation by way of *analogia legis* as provided by Art 61 of the Civil Code. In instances when the founders are natural persons, the practices of courts vary. Sometimes respective duties were placed on them, whereas in other cases it was deemed to be impossible. Judges Shapkina and Faizutdinov sustain the last view.[97] They say that this is against the law, for arbitrazh courts cannot settle questions of rights and duties of natural persons (Art 24, 1995 Arbitrazh Procedure Code). However, the disputes themselves fall into their jurisdiction, irrespective of who were the founders.

In one case the question was addressed as to whether the invalidity of a constitutive contract of a juridical person may affect its legal capacity, including the right to conclude transactions.[98] The Supreme Arbitrazh Court came to the opinion that the juridical person did have legal capacity and the right to participate in the transaction because under Art 49(3) of the Civil Code the legal capacity of a juridical person terminates at the moment of the completion of its liquidation.[99] That was the moment of making an entry to this effect into the uniform State register. Since in the file of the case there was no evidence about this, then the company enjoyed legal capacity. A commentary believes such decision to be correct, despite being somewhat formal.[100] The decision follows an information letter of the Presidium of the Supreme Arbitrazh Court, which admits that transactions of a society whose registration was deemed invalid are not necessarily void.[101]

In the course of operation of the FLJSS it has been revealed that reorganisation (particularly in the form of division) of a society can be used as a means to evade payment of its debts. In such cases the division balance sheet usually shows an unequal distribution of assets between the newly created societies. The law did not offer a way to prevent such fraudulent behaviour. Courts have two choices – either to prohibit the reorganisation by virtue of Art 10(1) of the Civil Code (abuse of right), or, alternatively, to place the duty of payment of debts of the former society upon the newly created juridical persons. Besides, it was proposed to introduce a norm concerning a proportionate distribution of the assets of the reorganised society and its debts.[102] A new explanation of the Plenum of the Supreme Arbitrazh Court suggests to apply the

97 Ibid., p. 15.

98 Decree of the Presidium of the SAC of 16 May 2000, No. 6759/99, in the case of the closed joint-stock society 'NPO ZiP', *HSAC*, no. 8 (2000), pp. 44–45.

99 *CCRF*, p. 20.

100 See E. V. Onoprienko in Комментарий судебно-арбитражной практики [Commentary on Judicial and Arbitrazh Practice], Vol. 7 (2000), p. 10.

101 Information Letter of the Presidium of the SAC of 9 June 2000, No. 54, 'On Transactions of a Juridical Person Whose Registration Has Been Deemed to be Invalid', *HSAC*, no. 7 (2000), p. 70.

102 Shapkina, Новое в российском акционерном законодательстве [The New in Russian Joint-Stock Society Legislation], p. 109.

analogy on the basis of Art 60(3) of the Civil Code, which says that 'if the division balance sheet does not make it possible to determine the legal successor of the reorganised juridical person, the juridical persons that newly arose shall bear joint and several responsibility for the obligations of the reorganised juridical person to its creditors'.[103] It is expected that courts will apply this rule even when it is clear from the dividing balance sheet that there is a violation of the principle of a just distribution of assets and obligations of the reorganised society between its legal successors which may lead to an obvious infringement of the creditors' interests.[104] But sometimes economic expediency may urge an unequal division of assests. It is difficult to regulate the details of this complex matter by legislation. Perhaps, it would be better to allow courts to elaborate a more flexible approach based on new precedents.

The results of this survey of judicial contribution to the area of joint-stock societies are somewhat mixed. Perhaps the only particular trend which, with some reservations, can be ascribed to Russian highest courts is holding minority stockholders in disgrace. This course is evident in the decisions of the Constitutional Court and the Supreme Arbitrazh Court concerning fractional stocks as well as in the Supreme Court ruling on the powers of the general meeting of stockholders which have been effectively reduced to the benefit of the council of directors. The said trend of highest courts need not to be accounted by anything except the desire to improve the efficiency of management which in practice often means to give it more power at the stockholders' expense. On the other hand, the Supreme Arbitrazh Court which is the principal actor in the field certainly does not demonstrate any bias towards particular social groups in its decisions, which can be explained (at least partially) by the largely 'technical' character of entrepreneurial law. Socially, minority stockholders can be very different figures, such as an ordinary citizen or a wealthy corporation. Also, the practice of the Supreme Arbitrazh Court is relatively consistent, mainly because the Court itself is more centralised and manageable. In many cases when faced with a number of alternatives available it chose the one which was purported to facilitate business transactions. By and large, it displayed the empiricist and hard-headed style of judging that Ronald Dworkin has labelled as a 'Chicago' legal pragmatism.[105] At the same time, as we have seen, this Court was sometimes suspected (not without reasons) of being prone to external pressures and the failure to be impartial in those (relatively few) cases where the interests of the State and various political groups were involved.

---

103 *CCRF*, p. 26.

104 Point 22, Decree of the Plenum of the Supreme Arbitrazh Court of 18 November 2003, No. 19, *HSAC*, no. 1 (2004), p. 23.

105 R. Dworkin, 'The Arduous Virtue of Fidelity', p. 1265.

Conclusion

The Russian legal system is currently in search for its identity. It ceased to belong to the family of socialist law, but has not fully returned to its civil law roots. Apart from unavoidable difficulties caused by the necessity to choose the future, the transitional nature of the system has advantages, too. It is more open for experimenting and testing which otherwise would be seriously impeded or unaffordable. Unlike long-established legal systems, it is less fettered by traditions which would be impossible to betray without losing its own identity. The proliferation of judicial review of legislation is just one example of such bold experimenting. This kind of judicial activity was virtually non-existent some 15 or 18 years ago, but now it is developed to the extent which may come as surprise to an outsider.

Largely, Russian legislation in force is very young. New laws were massively adopted during the post-Soviet period, and that is why the abundance of uncertainties and gaps is one of the principal reasons which call for judicial law-creation. But even so it is not correct to say that more detailed legislation would make judge-made law unnecessary. It is perhaps a common perception that English statutory law is more detailed than the law on the continent, and legislative acts are more carefully drafted. All the same, the importance of precedents is not diminished by the improvement of legislative techniques, for precedents turned to be a valuable aid to statutory interpretation. In fact, 'precedentiality' is a quality which is integral to the judicial function, and the only question is how it manifests itself. Judicial decisions always constitute a chain. Those scholars and judges across continental jurisdictions who deny that quality simply overlook the chain; they see only links instead.

What the general public most dislikes in courts is 'arbitrariness', which particularly manifests itself in the lack of consistency. But, paradoxically, any attempts to suppress judicial law-making would hardly rectify the situation. Quite the opposite, the disregard for precedents often makes decisions unpredictable. The less previous decisions are taken into account, the easier it might be for an individual judge to be 'arbitrary'. Of course, so long as the number of published decisions is kept small, it might seem that everything goes fine. But, due to the burgeoning of information technologies the number of available court rulings has grown up tremendously over the last decade, and it may well be expected to grow still more. This makes the dissatisfaction with unequal application of the same norms much stronger than in the past. Contrary to those who fear 'arbitrariness' of judicial creativity, a whimsical interpretation of law is not the easiest way for an unfair judge to arrive to the decision he wants. In Russian courts, given the lack of verbatim transcripts of hearings and judges' formalistic approach to evidence, injustice can be more conveniently done through factual findings, that is, by way of arbitrary selection and interpretation of facts.[1]

On the other hand, each country should work out its own approach to judicial creativity. If the decisions of the Supreme Court and the Supreme Arbitrazh Court were given the status of precedents, it may diminish the intellectual freedom of judges. Given the dependence of lower rank judges in Russia upon the chiefs of higher courts in terms of career and promotion, it may make them unduly constrained. In this case, the task of a lower court will be confined to finding a solution which would correspond to the views of senior judges as neatly as possible and thus secure the court against reversal of the decision on appeal. Therefore, there is no need to make precedents binding through legislation. What is required is granting to judges the right to refer to precedents as (one of) the grounds of their decisions. This practice is already paving the way, primarily in arbitrazh courts. Additionally, the case law of the European Court of Human Rights is, in fact, binding for Russian courts, since the Russian Federation is a signatory to the European Convention. The practice of open citation may also change the style of judicial opinions by making them more deliberative and reflective of real complexities of the cases at hand. The Supreme Court might take the lead and encourage this practice by making references to its previous judgments. It goes without saying that the decisions referred to must be published or at least be accessible in searchable databases, and judges need competent law clerks and an easy access to such databases to be able to take account of relevant case law.

It is common for studies of judicial activism to classify court policies as 'conservative', or 'liberal', or 'progressive', and the like. Does it make sense to apply these categories to Russian higher courts? I think it does, although with some reservations. For instance, in joint-stock society disputes the main purpose for arbitrazh courts was simply to make the system more effective by eliminating inconsistencies and filling gaps. In doing so, they were neither 'conservative' nor 'progressive'. This is not to say that there were no mistakes, simply that they were not reflective of a certain social policy. It should be noted that commercial (or entrepreneurial) law is less 'political', less abundant in mandatory and richer in optional rules. It proceeds from equality of participants of economic activity. This is not the case with respect to labour law. If stockholders and management do not constitute distinct social groups or 'classes' in traditional sense,

---

1 A plenty of examples can be found in Hendley, *Trying to Make Law Matter*, pp. 77 ff.

the socio-political implications of labour law are much stronger. For a variety of reasons, the employee and employer have been at all times viewed not merely as parties to a labour contract but rather as two different classes of society having special interests. Soviet labour legislation (and, to a significantly lesser degree, law-enforcement practices) in the twilight of the USSR ostensibly favoured workers against the administration of enterprises. Given that most judges in Russia were trained in Soviet years, it is no wonder that they have automatically extended this approach to labour disputes in the period of transition to a market economy. The 'conservative' approach of general courts was partially corrected by the Constitutional Court jurisprudence: a number of characteristically Soviet labour law provisions were struck down by the Court. But its liberalism was also quite moderate and should not be exaggerated.

A peculiarity of Russian Constitutional Court jurisprudence is that the decisions of this tribunal are binding upon legislatures. Whereas general and arbitrazh courts are able to make law only interstitially and along the lines already drawn by the legislators, here the legislator himself is bound by the legal position of the Constitutional Court. Unsurprisingly, this court is the most activist judicial agency in the Russian Federation. It is better equipped for being a law-maker. It may refer to general legal principles (justness, equality and the like) to substantiate its decisions. In terms of legal force, its judgments are virtually equal to constitutional provisions. The Court is gradually expanding its competence. The number of cases in which it found matters of 'constitutional significance' has been increasingly growing over the last years. It is also of importance that the judges of the Court have a distinct background. They are not members of a career judiciary. Mostly, they are appointed from the ranks of academic lawyers. It is legitimately expected, therefore, that they should be more susceptible to doctrinal debates than ordinary judges commonly are. And they are more independent-minded, unlike the latter who are accustomed to obey their superiors.

The second place on the scale should be given to the Supreme Arbitrazh Court. The structure of arbitrazh courts is more compact and manageable, and it is almost universally recognised that on the average arbitrazh judges possess better legal skills than judges of general courts. In matters of judicial practice and deciding cases, the Supreme Arbitrazh Court is always represented by a single judicial body, that is, by its Presidium. Certainly, its interpretations may change, but the changes seem to be made consciously. By contrast, the Supreme Court of the Russian Federation lacks such integrity, despite the existence of the Plenum (or full bench) of the Court. Sometimes it operates not as a single body, but as an aggregate of superior judicial instances of general jurisdiction. In particular, the policy of the Civil Division with respect to a certain question may fluctuate, perhaps depending on the attitude of various judicial benches within the Division. As we have seen, some judges might assume jurisdiction over particular types of cases, while others were reluctant to do so. For the purposes of an institutional comparison, not the entire Court, but solely its Presidium could be presented as an equivalent to the US Supreme Court or the Appellate Committee of the House of Lords.

In the Russian legal system only those hard and controversial cases may have a good chance to be duly resolved and in that way become precedents or give rise to new guidelines, which come to the attention of a court of last resort by way of supervision. The supervisory procedure is more orderly in the system of arbitrazh courts. There is only one supervisory court instance in the arbitrazh system as against three levels of supervision in the system of general courts. The Supreme Arbitrazh court made considerable efforts to reduce its caseload, which is necessary in order to be more active in developing the law. At present, the period during which a decision could be appealed against by way of supervision is only three months after the decision comes into legal force.[2] Moreover, the Arbitrazh Procedure Code requires that all other judicial remedies should have been exhausted (Art 393[3]), while the other code does not make such provision.

At the same time, the Supreme Court has retained and even further developed certain procedures which have important implications for judicial law-creation. A small group of superior judges of the Supreme Court (the Chairman and his deputies) and top officials of the General Procuracy retained the right to make supervisory 'submissions'(formerly called 'protests') for the purposes of ensuring 'the unity of judicial practice'. Particularly the right of top judges to bring to the Presidium a submission against any decision of any court allows them to choose freely the cases they think important and thus consciously help their fellow colleagues to create precedents.[3] But, due to the multitude of the supervisory instances the system, in fact, allows competing submissions, which make the outcome of the case still more uncertain.[4] In the more compact system of arbitrazh courts the analogous procedures were abolished by the 2002 Code.[5] Apparently, both branches of judiciary are seeking to promote the powers of courts to develop law and work out uniform models of interpretation. But they are doing it in different ways: whereas arbitrazh system makes emphasis upon the reduction of the caseload of the highest court and comprehensive publication of all court decisions as a medium-term target, the system of ordinary courts relies upon the discretion and wisdom of top judges. The results of these experimentations are not clear yet. In any event, these ways are not incompatible, and there is every reason to believe that some essentials of one system (if not the details) can be emulated in due course by the other.

---

2 In civil procedure there is a one-year period.
3 Article 389 of the present Civil Procedure Code; see also Art 377.
4 For example, in the case *Marta Nirenberg v the Government of the RF* there were conflicting protests on the part of a Deputy Procurator-General and a Deputy Chairman of the Supreme Court. See the Decree of the Presidium of the Supreme Court of 14 March 2001, No. 31пв-01пр (*BSC*, no. 6 (2003), pp. 7–8).
5 The Procurator-General and his deputies are still entitled to bring 'submissions' (former 'protests') under Art 42 of the Arbitrazh Procedure Code.

The discrepancies between the two branches of the judiciary may also cause a problem. A partial remedy is found in the issuance of joint decrees of the plenums of both supreme courts. Regulations governing their joint meetings were adopted in 1999.[6] However, the holding of a joint session entirely depends on the initiative of chief judges. If they disagree on the proper interpretation of certain provisions, there is little chance that a meeting on the matter in dispute will ever take place. Therefore, there should be other forms capable of ensuring the congruence of the policies of both courts in matters legal. The Constitutional Court, which is above them in matters of constitutional interpretation, can eliminate some inconsistencies, as has been seen from the case concerning good-faith acquisition of property. But its capacity to consider cases is limited because of time-pressure and the general requirement that the questions submitted to its attention should have a 'constitutional significance'. Although some observers opine that the number of questions regarded by the Court as having such significance is increasing, not all matters involving divergent interpretations may claim it. Therefore, the suggestion to create a single 'supercourt' for the whole country in the Anglo-American fashion above those three might seem reasonable.[7] This way could have been chosen in the early 1990s, but now the moment for such massive reconstruction seems to have elapsed. The judicial system is among the most conservative elements of the State, and it is unlikely that such a court would come into existence in the near future.[8] Additionally, it is not quite clear what the principal duties of such a court would be as distinguished from those immediately below. The model of a single court of last resort does not require the separate existence of the Supreme Court and the Supreme Arbitrazh Court.

Not long ago there were proposals to amalgamate the general and arbitrazh courts. This idea also seems doubtful, for the arbitrazh system has succeeded in developing its own institutions and rules, and it should be difficult to blend the two together without damaging them. I think that such radical changes are not needed at all. A practical solution can be found in regular joint sessions of both courts (one or two times per year), which would not depend on the good will of their leadership. Such sessions would be specifically devoted to the questions

6 Regulations of Joint Sessions of the Plenum of the Supreme Court of the RF and the Plenum of the Supreme Arbitrazh Court of the RF (confirmed by the Decree of the Supreme Court and the SAC of 7 June 1999, No. 36/6), in Комментарий судебно-арбитражной практики [Commentary of Judicial Arbitrazh Practice], Vol. 6 (1999), pp. 203–209.

7 W. Burnham, I. V. Reshetnikova and V. V. Iarkov, Судебная реформа: проблемы гражданской юрисдикции [Judicial Reform: Problems of Civil Jurisdiction] (1996), pp. 24–25. Cf. A. M. Grebentsov, Развитие хозяйственной юрисдикции в России [The Development of Economic Jurisdiction in Russia] (2002), pp. 242–246. Among other proponents of the idea are the Deputy Chairman of the Supreme Court M. Zhuikov and judge of the Constitutional Court G. Zhilin, to name only two.

8 It is particularly unlikely in view of the rigidity of the present Constitution. In fact, it has never been amended, and it is increasingly felt that the political elite fears to touch any of its provisions, for it may arouse an uncontrolled movement for constitutional reforms.

of consistency and congruence between two branches of the judiciary. They could be preceded by a meeting of senior judges of both courts, who are usually supervising judicial practice of lower courts in a particular region. These preliminary meeting could form a model agenda for the subsequent full session of the Supreme Court and the Supreme Arbitrazh Court. In any event, this agenda should not restrict the right of other judges of the courts to make additional proposals for consideration.

The caseload of the Supreme Court and the Supreme Arbitrazh Court should be further reduced to allow judges to give more time for the consideration of cases. It appears to me that the publication of dissenting opinions of judges should be allowed with respect to the presidiums of the Supreme Court and the Supreme Arbitrazh Court. Their decisions are not subject to reversal, and they cannot be used by the losing party to substantiate its demands at subsequent proceedings, for there are none (except for extraordinary instance of bringing the case before the Constitutional Court on the grounds of unconstitutionality of the rules applied). At the same time, the opinions of the most experienced judges would enrich Russian jurisprudence, give a further lease of life to scholarly debates and could also be of help to legislators when rectifying flaws in legislative acts. The importance of dissenting opinions is stressed by the fresh version of the Regulations of arbitrazh courts (Art 44), stipulating that judges taking part in the consideration of a case at any level must familiarise themselves with the dissenting opinions of other judges in the case. This court-made rule is intended to enhance the uniformity of judicial practice and help judges of higher courts to come to their own conclusions. But not the parties, it should be added, for the content of dissenting opinions is still unduly held secret from them.

There are other issues that equally call for reform. The syllogistic and 'non-problematic' style of judicial writing must be reformed so as to make it more reflective of the factual circumstances of the case and the arguments of parties. Verbatim transcripts of court hearings must be introduced and the existing obstacles which effectively prevent the general public from attending the hearings in violation of provisions of the Constitution and of procedural codes must be removed. Nowadays, an overwhelming majority of cases are heard almost in private. As a result, the controlling function of general public and press with respect to courts is very weak. These practices should not be tolerated, if Russian judicial authorities do want to overcome the gap between the law in books and 'living law'.

When comparing the opinions of Russian and common law courts, one cannot escape the impression that while the latter are inclined to engage in hair-splitting analysis and sometimes try to distinguish what seems hardly distinguishable, the former, on the contrary, frequently ignore the details which might seem to be important and needing more attention. On many occasions they tend to typify and simplify the fact to the detriment of the real complexities of cases. What is called a 'great judge' in American legal culture is a phenomenon completely unknown in Russia. This fact has little to do with the deficit of intellectual abilities or training, but is reflective of the inferior status of judicial service compared with the legislature and the executive, the lack of a tradition of judicial independence and individuality (including the absence of open dissents) and the way judges routinely justify their decisions. There are some signs of change in long-established attitudes, but it is still uncertain how far they might go.

Bibliography

In the Russian language

Abushenko, D. B., Судебное усмотрение в гражданском и арбитражном процессе [Judicial Discretion in Civil and Arbitrazh Procedure] (Moscow: Norma, 2002)

Alekseev, S. S., Теория права [Theory of Law] (Moscow: BEK, 1994)

Barak, A., Судейское усмотрение [Judge's Discretion] (Moscow: Norma, 1999)

Bertgold, V. (comp.), Устав гражданского судопроизводства [Statute on Civil Procedure] (Moscow: Pravo, 1915)

Bogdanovskaia, I. Iu., Прецедентное право [Law of Precedent] (Moscow: Nauka, 1993)

Borisova E., Обжалование не вступивших в законную силу судебных решений в гражданском процессе [An Appeal against Judicial Decisions Not Entered into Legal Force in the Civil Proceeding], *Российская юстиция* [Russian Justice], no. 3 (2003)

Braginskii, M. M., Договор подряда и подобные ему договоры [The Contract of Independent Work and the Contracts Similar to It] (Moscow: Statut, 1999)

Bratus, S. N. (ed.), Судебная практика в советской правовой системе [Judicial Practice in the Soviet Legal System] (Moscow: Iuridicheskaia literatura, 1975)

Burkov, A. L., Борьба за власть между Конституционным Судом РФ и Верховным Судом РФ: пострадают ли права человека? [Struggle for Power Between the Constitutional Court of the RF and the Supreme Court of the RF: Will Human Rights Suffer?], *Российский судья* [Russian Judge], no. 11 (2002)

Burnham, W., Reshetnikova, I. V., and Iarkov, V. V. Судебная реформа: проблемы гражданской юрисдикции [Judicial Reform: Problems of Civil Jurisdiction] (Ekaterinburg: The University of Arts and Humanities Publishing House, 1996)

Cherdantsev, A. F., Толкование права и договора [Interpretation of Law and of a Contract] (Moscow: Iuniti-Dana, 2003)

Cherdantsev, A. F., Толкование советского права [Interpretation of Soviet Law] (Moscow: Iuridicheskaia literatura, 1979)

Комментарий судебно-арбитражной практики [Commentary on Judicial and Arbitrazh Practice], Vol. 1–8 (Moscow: Iuridicheskaia literatura, 1994–2001)

Комментарий судебной практики [Commentary on Judicial Practice], Vol. 1–8 (Moscow: Iuridicheskaia literatura, 1994–2001)

Конституционное совещание. Стенограммы. Материалы. Документы. 29 апреля – 10 ноября 1993 г. [The Constitutional Conference. Verbatim Transcripts. Materials. Documents. 29 April–10 November 1993], Vol. 1–21 (Moscow: Iuridicheskaia Literatura, 1995–1996)

Demchenko, G. V., Прецедентное право [The Law of Precedent] (Warsaw: Tip. Varshavskago ucheb. okruga, 1903)

Ebzeev, B. S., Конституционный Суд Российской Федерации–судебный орган конституционного контроля [Constitutional Court of the Russian Federation – Judicial Agency of Constitutional Review], *Herald of the Constitutional Court of the Russian Federation*, no. 2/3 (1995)

Ebzeev, B. S., Lazarev, L. V., and Vitruk, N. V., Федеральный конституционный закон «О Конституционном Суде Российской Федерации»: Комментарий [Federal Constitutional Law on the Constitutional Court of the Russian Federation: A Commentary] (Moscow: Iuridicheskaia literatura, 1996)

Erdelevskii, A. M., Компенсация морального вреда [Contributory Compensation of Moral Harm] (Moscow: Юристь, 1997)

Fedotov, A., Возможно ли применение contra legem в демократическом правовом государстве [Is Application of *Contra Legem* Possible in a Democratic Rule-of-Law State?], *Журнал Российского Права* [Journal of Russian Law], no. 8 (2002)

Grebentsov, A. M., Развитие хозяйственной юрисдикции в России [The Development of Economic Jurisdiction in Russia] (Moscow: Норма [Norm], 2002)

Iarkov, V. V. (ed.), Гражданское судопроизводство. Особенности рассмотрения отдельных категорий дел [Civil Proceeding. Peculiarities of Consideration of Individual Categories of Cases] (Moscow: Iurist, 2001)

Ioffe, O. S., Советское гражданское право [Soviet Civil Law] (Moscow: Iuridicheskaia literatura, 1967)

Судебная практика как источник права [Judicial Practice as a Source of Law] (Moscow: Institute of State and Law of Russian Academy of Sciences, 1997)

Судебная практика как источник права [Judicial Practice as a Source of Law] (Moscow: Iurist, 2000)

Судебная практика в российской правовой системе [Judicial Practice in the Russian Legal System] (Saint-Petersburg: Saint-Petersburg State University, Law Faculty, 2003)

Karabel'nikov, B. R., Трудовые отношения в акционерных обществах [Labour Relations in Joint-Stock Societies] (Moscow: Statut, 2001)

Kiselev, I. Ia., Сравнительное и международное трудовое право [Comparative and International Labour Law] (Moscow: Delo, 1999)

Kliuchevskii, V. O., Боярская Дума Древней Руси [Boyars' Duma of the Ancient Russia] (Moscow: 1902)

Kozak D. N. and Mizulina E. B. (eds.), Комментарий к Уголовно-процессуальному кодексу Российской Федерации [A Commentary on the Criminal Procedure Code of the Russian Federation] (Moscow: Iurist, 2002).

Kryshtanovskaia O., Анатомия российской элиты [An Anatomy of Russian Elite] (Moscow: Zakharov, 2005)

Lazarevskii, N. I., Судебная и административная практика как источник права [Judicial and Administrative Practice as a Source of Law], *Вестник гражданского права* [Herald of Civil Law], no. 1 (1916)

Lebedev, V. M., Судебная власть в современной России [Judicial Power in Modern Russia] (Saint-Petersburg: Lan, 2001)

Luk'ianova, E. A., Конституция в судебном переплете [The Constitution in a Judicial Cover], *Законодательство* [Legislation], no. 12 (2002)

Madiarova, A. V., Разъяснения Верховного Суда Российской Федерации в механизме уголовно-правового регулирования [Explanations of the Supreme Court of the

Russian Federation in the Mechanism of Criminal Law Regulation] (Saint-Petersburg: Iuridicheskii Tsentr Press, 2002)

Marchenko, M. N., Сравнительное правоведение. Общая часть [Comparative Law. General Part] (Moscow: Zertsalo, 2001)

Medushevskii, A. N., История русской социологии [History of Russian Sociology] (Moscow: Vyshaia Shkola, 1993)

Meier, D. I., Русское гражданское право [Russian Civil Law] (Moscow: Statut, 2001; 1st edn. – 1861–1862)

Mikhailovskii, I. V., Наказание как фактор культуры [Punishment as a Factor of Culture] (Moscow: Kushnerev, 1905)

Mitiukov, M. A. Судебный конституционный надзор 1924–1933 гг. [Judicial Constitutional Control in 1924–1933] (Moscow: Formula Prava, 2005)

Muromtsev, S. A., Суд и закон в гражданском праве [The Court and the Law [Lex] in Civil Law], Юридический вестник [Legal Herald], no. 11 (1880)

Muromtsev, S. A., Определение и основное разделение права [A Definition and Basic Division of Law] (Moscow: Mamontov's Printing House, 1879)

Muromtsev, S. A., Право и справедлвость [Law and Justness], Судебный Вестник [Judicial Herald], no. 2 (1892)

Novitskii, I. B., Источники советского гражданского права [Sources of Soviet Civil Law] (Moscow: State Publishing House of Juridical Literature, 1959)

Orlovskii, Iu. P. (ed.), Комментарий к Трудовому Кодексу РФ [Commentary on the Labour Code of the Russian Federation] (Moscow: Infra-M, 2002)

Petrov, K. V., «Прецедент» в средневековом русском праве (XVI–XVII вв.) ['Precedent' in the Medieval Russian Law (XVI–XVII centuries)], in Государство и право [State and Law], no. 4 (2005)

Pokrovskii, I. A., Основные проблемы гражданского права [Basic Problems of Civil Law] (Moscow: Statut, 1998; 1st edn. – 1916)

Polonskii, B. Ia., Экономическое правосудие: единство правоприменения [The Economic Justice: the Unity of Law-Application], Законодательство [Legislation], no. 5 (2003)

Radchenko, V. I. (ed.), Комментарий к Уголовно-процессуальному кодексу Российской Федерации (постатейный) [A Clause-by-Clause Commentary on the Criminal Procedure Code of the Russian Federation] (Moscow: Iustitsinform, 2004)

Radchenko, V. I. (ed.), Комментарий к Уголовно-процессуальному кодексу РСФСР [A Commentary on the RSFSR Criminal Procedure Code] (Moscow: Iurait-M, 2001)

Российское законодательство X–XX веков [Russian Legislation of the 10–20th centuries], Vol. 1–9 (Moscow: Iuridicheskaia literatura, 1984–94)

Saidov, A. Kh., Сравнительное правоведение [Comparative Law] (Moscow: Iurist, 2000)

Savitskii, V. M. (ed.), Судебный контроль и права человека [Judicial Review and Human Rights] (Moscow: Prava cheloveka, 1996)

Shapkina, G. S., Новое в российском акционерном законодательстве. Изменения и дополнения Федерального закона «Об акционерных обществах» [The New in Russian Joint-Stock Society Legislation. Changes and Additions to the Federal Law 'On Joint-Stock Societies'] (Moscow: TsDI, 2002)

Shershenevich, G. F., Общая теория права [General Theory of Law] (Riga, 1924)

Shershenevich, G. F., О чувстве законности [On the Feeling of Legality] (Kazan: Printing House of the Kazan Imperial University, 1897)

Solomon, P. H., Состояние судебной системы в современной Росии [State of Judicial System in Contemporary Russia], Конституционное право: восточноевропейское обозрение [East European Constitutional Review], no. 2 (1999)

Tagantsev, N. S., Русское угловное право (Общая часть) [Russian Criminal Law (General Part)], Part 1 (Saint-Petersburg: Gos. Tip., 1902)

Tikhomirov, Iu. A. (comp.), Судебная власть в России. Роль судебной практики [Judicial Power in Russia: The Role of Judicial Practice] (Moscow: Higher School of Economics, 2002)

Tiutriumov, I. M. (comp.), Устав гражданского судопроизводства [The Statute of Civil Proceedings] (Saint-Petersburg: Zakonovedenie, 1912)

Tuzov, D. O., Конституционный суд о защите добросовестного приобретателя [The Constitutional Court about the Protection of the Good-Faith Acquirer], Эаконодательство [Legislation], no. 10 (2003)

Vas'kovskii, E. V., Правотворческая деятельность новых судов в сфере процесса и права гражданского [The Law-Creating Activity of New Courts in the Sphere of the Civil Law and Procedure], in Судебные уставы за 50 лет [Court Statutes over 50 Years], Vol. II (Petrograd: Senate's Printing House, 1914)

Vas'kovskii, E. V., Руководство к толкованию и применению законов [Manual for Interpretation and Application of Laws] (Moscow: Gorodets, 1997; 1st edn. – 1902)

Vengerov, A. B., Теория государства и права [Theory of State and Law], Part 2 (Moscow: Iurist, 1997)

Vil'nianskii, S. I., Значение судебной практики в гражданском праве [Significance of Judicial Practice in Civil Law], in Ученые труды Всесоюзного института юридических наук [Scientific Reports of All-Union Institute of Legal Sciences], Vol. IX (Moscow: 1947)

Zagainova, S. K., Судебный прецедент: проблемы правоприменения [Judicial Precedent: Problems of Law-Application] (Moscow: Norma, 2002)

Zhilin, G. A. (ed.), Комментарий к Гражданскому процессуальному кодексу Российской Федерации (постатейный) [Clause-by-Clause Commentary on the Civil Procedure Code of the Russian Federation] (2nd edn., Moscow: TK Velbi, 2004)

Zhuikov, V. M., Возмещение морального вреда [Compensation of Moral Harm], *Bulletin of the Supreme Court of the Russian Federation*, no. 11 (1994)

Zimnenko, B., Международное право в судебной практике России [International Law in the Russian Court Practice], *Российская юстиция* [Russian Justice], no. 9 (2003)

Zor'kin, V. D., Муромцев [Muromtsev] (Moscow: Iuridicheskaia literatura, 1980)

In the English language

Alder, J., 'Dissents in Courts of Last Resort: Tragic Choices?', *Oxford Journal of Legal Studies*, Vol. 20 (2000) 221

All England Law Reports: Annual Review (London: Butterworths, 1982–)

Armstrong, G. M., *The Soviet Law of Property: The Right to Control Property and the Construction of Communism* (The Hague; Boston: M. Nijhoff Publishers, 1983)

Baade, H. W., 'Stare Decisis in Civil Law Countries: The Last Bastion', in Birks, P. and Pretto, A. (eds.), *Themes in Comparative Law. In Honour of Bernard Rudden* (Oxford: Oxford University Press, 2000)

Barak, A., *Judicial Discretion* (New Haven: Yale University Press, 1989)

Barry, D. D., Butler, W. E., and Ginzburg, G. (eds.), *Contemporary Soviet Law* (The Hague: Martinus Nijhoff, 1974)

Barry D. D., Feldbrugge, F. J. M., and Lasok, D. (eds.), *Codification in the Communist World* (Leiden: A. W. Sijthoff, 1975)

Bennion, F. A. R., *Statute Law* (London: Oyez, 1980)

Bennion, F. A. R., *Statutory Interpretation: A Code* (2nd edn., London: Butterworths, 1992)

Bix, B., *Jurisprudence: Theory and Context* (London: Sweet & Maxwell, 1996)

Bix, B., *Law, Language, and Legal Determinacy* (Oxford: Clarendon Press, 1993)

Bork, R., *The Tempting of America: The Political Seduction of the Law* (London: Sinclair-Stevenson, 1991)

Braun, J. I., 'Eighth Circuit Decision Intensifies Debate over Publication and Citation of Appellate Opinions', *Judicature*, Vol. 84 (2000) 90

Brugger, W., 'Legal Interpretation, Schools of Jurisprudence, and Anthropology: Some Remarks from a German Point of View', *American Journal of Comparative Law*, Vol. 42 (1994) 395

Bulow, O., 'Statutory Law and the Judicial Function', *American Journal of Legal History*, no. 39 (January 1995) 71

Butler, W. E. (ed. and transl.), *Civil Code of the Russian Federation* (Oxford: Oxford University Press, 2003)

Butler, W. E., 'Judicial Precedent as a Source of Russian Law', in Nafziger, J. A. R. and Symeonides, S. C. (eds.), *Law and Justice in a Multistate World. Essays in Honour of Arthur T. von Mehren* (New York: Transnational Publishers, Inc., 2002)

Butler, W. E., 'Necessary Defence, Judge-Made Law, and Soviet Man', in Butler, W. E., Maggs, P. B., and Quigley, J. B., Jr (eds.), *Law After Revolution* (New York: Oceana Publications, 1988)

Butler, W. E. (ed. and transl.), *Russian Civil Legislation* (Simmonds & Hill Publishing Ltd; Published by Kluwer Law International: The Hague – London – Boston, 1999)

Butler, W. E. (ed. and transl.), *Russian Company and Commercial Legislation* (Oxford, New York: Oxford University Press, 2003)

Butler, W. E., *Russian Law* (2nd edn., Oxford, New York: Oxford University Press, 2003)

Butler, W. E., *Soviet Law* (London: Butterworth, 1st edn., 1983; 2nd edn., 1988)

Butler, W. E. (ed. and transl.), *The Tax Code of the Russian Federation* (London: Simmonds & Hill, 1999)

Butler, W. E. and Gashi-Butler, M. E. (eds. and transls.), *Russian Company Law. Basic Legislation* (3rd edn., Published by Kluwer Law International and Simmonds & Hill Publishing Ltd: The Hague – London – Boston, 2000)

Butler, W. E. and Henderson, J. E. (comp. and eds.), *Russian Legal Texts* (London: Simmonds & Hill Publishing Ltd, 1998)

Caenegem, R. C., van., *An Historical Introduction to Private Law* (Cambridge: Cambridge University Press, 1994)

Caenegem, R. C., van., *Judges, Legislators, and Professors: Chapters in European Legal History* (Cambridge: Cambridge University Press, 1987)

Card, R., Cross, R., and Jones, Ph. A., *Criminal Law* (12th edn., London: Butterworths, 1992)

Cardozo, B., *The Nature of the Judicial Process* (New Haven: Yale University Press, 1921)

Cohen, M. (ed.), *Ronald Dworkin and Contemporary Jurisprudence* (London: Duckworth, 1984)

Cross, R., *Statutory Interpretation* (3rd edn., London: Butterworths, 1995)

Cullinane, S. S., 'Can the Constitutional Court of the Russian Federation Lead the Way to the Creation of a True Democratic Society in the New Russia in the 21st Century?', *Touro Law Review*, Vol. 17 (Winter, 2001) 397

Danilenko, G. M. and Burnham, W., *Law and Legal System of the Russian Federation* (Yonkers, NY: Juris Publishing, 1999)

David, R. and Brierley, J. E. C., *Major Legal Systems in the World Today: An Introduction to the Comparative Study of Law* (3rd edn., London: Stevens, 1985)

Denning, A. T., *The Discipline of Law* (London, Boston: Butterworths, 1979)

Devlin, P., *The Judge* (Oxford, New York: Oxford University Press, 1979)

Dougherty, V. M., 'Absurdity and the Limits of Literalism: Defining the Absurd Result Principle in Statutory Interpretation', *American University Law Review* (Fall, 1994) 134

Dworkin, R., 'The Arduous Virtue of Fidelity: Originalism, Scalia, Tribe, and Nerve', *Fordham Law Review*, Vol. 65 (1997) 1249

Dworkin, R., 'The Judge's New Role: Should Judge's Personal Convictions Count?', *Journal of International Criminal Justice*, Vol. 1 (2003) 1

Dworkin, R., *Law's Empire* (Cambridge, MA: Belknap Press, 1986)

Dworkin, R., *A Matter of Principle* (Cambridge, MA: Harvard University Press, 1985)

Dworkin, R., 'Response to Overseas Commentators', *International Journal of Constitutional Law*, no. 1 (October 2003) 651

Dworkin, R., *Taking Rights Seriously* (London: Duckworth, 1978)

Edmund-Davies, H. E., 'Judicial Activism', *Current Legal Problems*, no. 28 (1975) 1

Eskridge, W. N. and Frickey, P. P., 'Law as Equilibrium', *Harvard Law Review*, Vol. 108 (1994) 28

Feldbrugge, F. J. M., 'Epilogue: Reflections on a civil law for Russia', in G. Ginsburgs, D. D. Barry, and W. B. Simons (eds.), *The Revival of Private Law in Central and Eastern Europe. Essays in Honour of F. J. M. Feldbrugge* (The Hague: M. Nijhoff, 1996)

Feldbrugge, F. J. M., *Russian Law: The End of the Soviet System and the Role of Law* (Dordrecht: M. Nijhoff, 1993)

Gonzales, C. E., 'Reinterpreting Statutory Interpretation', *North Carolina Law Review*, Vol. 74 (1996) 585

Goodhart, A. L., *Essays in Jurisprudence and the Common Law* (Cambridge, England: The University Press, 1931)

Griffith, J. A. G., *The Politics of the Judiciary* (5th edn., London: Fontana Press, 1997)

Hailsham of St. Marylebone, Q. H., *Hamlin Revisited: The British Legal System Today* (London: Stevens, 1983)

Hale, M., *History of Pleas of the Crown*, vol. 1 (London: Sollom Emlyn, 1736)

Halverson, K., 'Resolving Economic Disputes in Russia's Market Economy', *Michigan Journal of International Law*, Vol. 18 (Fall, 1996) 59

Hart, H. L. A., *The Concept of Law* (1st edn. – Oxford, 1961; 2nd edn., with a Postscript, edited by P. A. Bulloch and J. Raz, Oxford: Clarendon Press, 1994)

Hayek, F. A., *Law, Legislation and Liberty: A New Statement of the Liberal Principles of Justice and Political Economy* (Vol. 1–3, London: Routledge and Kegan Paul, 1973–1979; One-volume edn., London: Routledge and Kegan Paul, 1982)

Hazard, J. N., 'Is Russian Case Law Becoming Significant as a Source of Law?', *Parker School Journal of East European Law*, Vol. 1, no. 1 (1994) 23

Hazard, J. N., 'Russian Judicial Precedent Revisited', *Parker School Journal of East European Law*, Vol. 1, no. 4 (1994) 471

Hazard, J. N., *Settling Disputes in Soviet Society. The Formative Years of Legal Institutions* (Columbia University Press, 1960)

Hazard, J. N., 'Understanding Soviet Law without the Cases', *Soviet Studies*, Vol. VII, no. 2 (1955) 121

Hendley, K., 'Growing Pains: Balancing Justice and Efficiency in the Russian Economic Courts', *Temple International and Comparative Law Journal* (Fall, 1998) 301

Hendley, K., 'Remaking an Institution: The Transition in Russia from State Arbitrazh to Arbitrazh Courts', *American Journal of Comparative Law*, 46 (Winter, 1998) 93

Hendley, K., *Trying to Make Law Matter: Legal Reform and Labour Law in the Soviet Union* (Ann Arbor: University of Michigan Press, 1996)

Herget, J. E. and Wallace, S., 'The German Free Law Movement as the Source of American Legal Realism', *Virginia Law Review*, Vol. 73 (March 1987) 399

Holdsworth, W. S., *Some Lessons from Our Legal History* (London, New York: Macmillan Co., 1928)

Holland, K. M. (ed.), *Judicial Activism in Comparative Perspective* (Houndmills: MacMillan, 1991)

Ioffe, O. S. and Maggs, P. B., *Soviet Law in Theory and Practice* (London, New York: Oceana Publications, 1983)

Jacob, H., Blankenburg, E., Kritzer, H. M., and Provine, D. M., *Courts, Law, and Politics in Comparative Perspective* (New Haven and London: Yale University Press, 1996)

Jaffe, L. L., *English and American Judges as Lawmakers* (Oxford: Clarendon, 1969)

Kelsen, H., *The General Theory of Norms* (Oxford: Clarendon Press, 1990)

Kiselev, I. Ia., 'En Route to a Civilised Labour Market in Russia: On the Adoption of the Labour Code of the Russian Federation', *Sudebnik*, Vol. 7, no. 1 (March 2002) 9

Korkunov, N. M., *General Theory of Law* (Boston: Boston Book Co., 1909)

Krug, P., 'Assessing Legislative Restrictions in Constitutional Rights: The Russian Constitutional Court and Article 55(3)', *Oklahoma Law Review*, Vol. 56 (2003) 677

Krug, P., 'Departure from the Centralized Model: The Russian Supreme Court and Constitutional Control of Legislation', *Virginia Journal of International Law*, Vol. 37 (Spring, 1997) 725

Krug, P., 'The Russian Federation Supreme Court and Constitutional Practice in the Courts of General Jurisdiction: Recent Developments', *Review of Central and East European Law*, no. 2 (2000) 129

Kuechtle, J. C., 'Isn't Every Case Political? Political Questions on the Russian, German, and American High Courts', *Review of Central and East European Law*, no. 2 (2000) 107

Leoni, B., *Freedom and the Law* (3rd edn., Indianapolis: Liberty Fund, 1991)

Livshits, R. Z., 'Judicial Practice as a Source of Law in Russia', *Sudebnik*, Vol. II, no. 3 (1997) 625

Lyons, D., 'Justification and Judicial Responsibility', *California Law Review*, Vol. 72 (1984) 178

MacCallum, G. C., Jr, 'Legislative Intent', in Summers, R. (ed.), *Essays in Legal Philosophy* (Oxford: Blackwell, 1968)

MacCormick, D. N. and Summers, R. S. (eds.), *Interpreting Precedents: A Comparative Study* (Aldershot: Dartmouth, 1997)

MacCormick, D. N. and Summers, R. S. (eds.), *Interpreting Statutes: A Comparative Study* (Aldershot: Dartmouth, 1991)

MacWhinney, E., *Supreme Courts and Judicial Law-Making: Constitutional Tribunals and Constitutional Review* (Dordrecht, Boston: M. Nijhoff; Hingham, MA, USA, 1986)

Maggs, P. B., 'Constitutional Commercial Cases in the Courts', at [http://home.law.uiuc.edu/~pmaggs/concom.htm]

Maggs, P. B., 'The Russian Constitutional Court's Decisions on Residence Permits and Housing', *Parker School Journal of East European Law*, Vol. 2, no. 4/5 (1995) 561

Maggs, P. B., 'The Russian Courts and the Russian Constitution', *Indiana International & Comparative Law Review*, Vol. 8 (1997) 99

Manchester, C., Salter, D., and Moodie, P., *Exploring the Law: The Dynamics of Precedent and Statutory Interpretation* (2nd edn., London: Sweet & Maxwell, 2000)

Manning, J. F., 'The Absurdity Doctrine', *Harvard Law Review*, 116 (June 2003) 2387

Markesinis, B. S. (ed.), *Law-Making, Law-Finding, and Law-Shaping: The Diverse Influences* (Oxford: Oxford University Press, 1997)

Marmor, A., *Interpretation and Legal Theory* (Oxford: Oxford University Press, 1992)

Marmor, A. (ed.), *Law and Interpretation: Essays in Legal Philosophy* (Oxford: Clarendon Press, 1995)

Martineau, R. J., *Appellate Justice in England and the United States: A Comparative Analysis* (Buffalo, NY: W. S. Hein, 1990)

Merryman, J. H., *The Loneliness of the Comparative Lawyer: And Other Essays in Foreign and Comparative law* (The Hague: Kluwer Law International, 1999)

Merryman, J. H., Clark D. S., and Haley J. O. (eds.), *The Civil Law Tradition: Europe, Latin America, and East Asia* (Charlottesville, VA: Michie Co., 1994)

Nanping Liu, *Judicial Interpretation in China. Opinions of the Supreme People's Court* (Hong Kong: Sweet & Maxwell Asia, 1997)

Paterson, A., *The Law Lords* (London: Macmillan, 1982)

Pether, P., 'Inequitable Injunctions: The Scandal of Private Judging in the U.S. Courts', *Stanford Law Review*, Vol. 56, no. 6 (2004) 1435

Pizzorusso, A. (ed.), *Law in the Making: A Comparative Survey* (Berlin: Springer-Verlag, 1988)

Posner, R. A., *Law and Legal Theory in Europe and America* (Oxford: Clarendon Press, 1996)

Price, P. J., 'Precedent and Judicial Power after the Founding', *Boston College Law Review*, Vol. 42 (2001) 81

Quigley, J., 'The Presumption of Innocence in the Russian Constitution', *Parker School Journal of East European Law*, Vol. 1, no. 3 (1994) 329

Raz, J., *The Authority of Law: Essays on Law and Morality* (Oxford: Clarendon Press; New York: Oxford University Press, 1979)

Raz, J., 'Dworkin: A New Link in the Chain', *California Law Review*, Vol. 74 (1986) 1103

Raz, J., *Ethics in the Public Domain: Essays in the Morality of Law and Politics* (Oxford: Clarendon Press, 1994)

Raz, J., 'Why Interpret?', *Ratio Juris*, Vol. 9, no. 4 (1996) 349

Rosenkranz, N. Q., 'Federal Rules of Statutory Interpretation', *Harvard Law Review*, Vol. 115 (2002) 2085

Rudden, B., 'Courts and Codes in England, France, and Soviet Russia', *Tulane Law Review*, Vol. 48 (1974) 1110

Rudden, B., 'The Role of the Courts and Judicial Style under the Soviet Civil Codes', in *Codification in the Communist World* (Leiden: A. W. Sijthoff, 1975)

Scalia, A., *A Matter of Interpretation: Federal Courts and the Law* (Princeton: Princeton University Press, 1997)

Schlink, B., 'Hercules in Germany?', *International Journal of Constitutional Law*, Vol. 1 (October 2003) 610

Shapiro, M., *Courts. A Comparative and Political Analysis* (Chicago: University of Chicago Press, 1981)

Sharlet, R., 'Russian Chief Justice as Judicial Politician', *East European Constitutional Review*, Vol. 2, no. 2 (Spring, 1993) 32

Sharlet, R., 'The Russian Constitutional Court: The First Term', *Post-Soviet Affairs*, Vol. 9, no. 1 (1993) 1

Shestakova, N., 'Transactions under the Russian Civil Code: Invalidity and the Protection of Rights', *Review of Central and East European Law*, no. 5/6 (1998) 429

Simpson, A. W. B., *Leading Cases in the Common Law* (Oxford: Clarendon Press, 1995)

Smith, J. C., 'The Sad Fate of the Theft Act 1968', in Swadling, W. and Jones, G. (eds.), *The Search for Principle: Essays in Honour of the Lord Goff of Chieveley* (Oxford: Oxford University Press, 1999)

Smith, J. C. and Hogan, B., *Criminal Law* (7th edn., London: Butterworth, 1992)

Solomon, P. H. (ed.), *Reforming Justice in Russia, 1864–1996: Power, Culture, and the Limits of Legal Order* (Armonk, NY: M. E. Sharpe, 1997)

Solomon, P. H., *Soviet Criminal Justice under Stalin* (Cambridge: Cambridge University Press, 1996)

Solomon, P. H., 'USSR Supreme Court: History, Role, and Future Prospects', *The American Journal of Comparative Law*, Vol. 38 (1990) 127

Strongman, J. A., 'Unpublished Opinions, Precedent, and the Fifth Amendment: Why Denying Unpublished Opinions Precedential Value is Unconstitutional', *Kansas Law Review*, Vol. 50 (November 2001) 195

Sturgess, G. and Chubb, P. (eds.), *Judging the World: Law and Politics in the World's Leading Courts* (Sydney, NSW: Butterworths, 1988)

Trochev, A., 'Implementing Russian Constitutional Court Decisions', *East European Constitutional Review*, Vol. 11, no.1/2 (Winter–Spring, 2002) 95

Vereshchagin, A. N., 'Dissents in Russian Courts', in Erpyleva, N. Iu., Gashi-Butler, M. E., and Henderson, J. E. (eds.), *Forging a Common Legal Destiny: Liber Amicorum in Honour of W.E. Butler* (London: Wildy, Simmonds & Hill, 2005)

Volcansec, M. L. (ed.), *Judicial Politics and Policy-Making in Western Europe* (London: Frank Cass & CO.LTD, 1992)

Wagner, W. G., *Marriage, Property and Law in Late Imperial Russia* (Oxford: Clarendon Press, 1994)

Waldman, J. and Holland, K., *The Political Role of Law Courts in Modern Democracies* (New York: St. Martin's Press, 1988)

Waldron, J., 'Legislators' Intentions and Unintentional Legislation', in Marmor, A. (ed.), *Law and Interpretation* (Oxford: Clarendon Press, 1995)

Waldron, J., 'Vagueness in Law and Language', *California Law Review*, vol. 82 (May 1994) 539

Ward, R. W., *Walker & Walker's English Legal System* (8th edn., London: Butterworths, 1998)

Zander, M., *The Law-Making Process* (4th edn., London: Butterworths, 1994)

Zweigert, K. and Kotz, H., *Introduction to Comparative Law* (2nd rev. edn., Oxford: Clarendon Press, 1992)

Index